BUENAS NOCHES, AMERICAN CULTURE

D1712847

BUENAS NOCHES

AMERICAN CULTURE

LATINA/O AESTHETICS OF NIGHT

María DeGuzmán

INDIANA UNIVERSITY PRESS
Bloomington and Indianapolis

This book is a publication of

Indiana University Press
601 North Morton Street
Bloomington, Indiana 47404-3797 USA

iupress.indiana.edu

Telephone orders   800-842-6796
Fax orders   812-855-7931

∞ The paper used in this publication meets
the minimum requirements of the American
National Standard for Information Sciences—
Permanence of Paper for Printed Library Mate-
rials, ANSI Z39.48-1992.

Manufactured in the United States of America

LIBRARY OF CONGRESS
CATALOGING-IN-PUBLICATION DATA

DeGuzmán, María.
  Buenas noches, American culture : Latina/o
aesthetics of night / María DeGuzmán.
    p.   cm.
  Includes bibliographical references and index.
  ISBN 978-0-253-00179-5 (cloth : alk. paper) —
  ISBN 978-0-253-00189-4 (pbk. : alk. paper) —
  ISBN 978-0-253-00190-0 (electronic book)
  1. American literature—Hispanic American
authors—History and criticism. 2. Night in lit-
erature. 3. Central American literature—History
and criticism. 4. South American literature—
History and criticism. 5. Night in art. I. Title.
  PS153.H56D44 2012
  810.9'868073—dc23

                              2012002234

      1 2 3 4 5   17 16 15 14 13 12

FOR MY STUDENTS

CONTENTS

PREFACE

A word on the organization of *Buenas Noches, American Culture: Latina/o Aesthetics of Night.* This study concentrates on Latina/o literature and some film and photography from the 1940s to the present, focusing chiefly on Latina/o cultural production during the last three decades. Though the study flows more or less chronologically within its individual parts, it also follows a spatial logic that arcs and spirals across the United States and between the Americas, exploring the groupings within and the sheer variety of "Latina/o" culture(s) as well as historical and contemporary connections among identities and locations. Chapter 1, on Chicana/o cultural production, is mostly situated in California and the Southwestern borderlands. Chapter 2, on continental U.S.-based Puerto Rican and Cuban American poets, concerns itself with the Hispanic Caribbean in relation to New York, New England, and the Midwest. Via the writings it examines, chapter 3 journeys to Central America, Guatemala, and Panama but also to New York, Los Angeles, and the Washington, DC, area as well as to Nicaragua and El Salvador. Chapter 4, on the transcultural night work of U.S.-based South American writers and one photographer, moves among the United States, South America, Spain, and Eastern Europe. Some segments of the arcs and spirals may be familiar to readers, and others surprising, disorienting, or vertiginous. Such were the mappings that unfolded before those tenuous instruments, my eyes, as they contemplated tropes of night in Latina/o cultural production.[1] As for temporality, within the framework of the contemporary period this book shuttles back and forth not only between postmodernism and modernism but, via the works themselves and sometimes in the blink of an eye, between a pre-Columbian era and the twenty-third century (2280 AD, to be precise). Simultaneously, this study takes its time. The introduction shades into its subject matter through various deepening degrees to arrive at Latina/o aesthetics of night. Such is the fluidity of time—movements made simultaneously at very different speeds—under the auspices of night.

ACKNOWLEDGMENTS

For insightful remarks, conversations, and many other kinds of intellectual exchange over the years that helped me to see more keenly into the dark of this book's subject matter during its conception, research, and composition, I would like to thank Arturo and Frederick Aldama, Frances Aparicio, Rane Ramón Arroyo, Stuart Bernstein, W. Fitzhugh Brundage, Bernadette Calafell, Brooke Church, Lucha Corpi, María Cotera, Elyse Crystall, Elizabeth and Luis de Guzmán, Samuel R. Delaney, Theresa Delgadillo, Arturo Escobar, Rebecka Rutledge Fisher, María Alicia Garza, Tanya González, Nan Goodman, Kirsten Silva Gruesz, Minrose Gwin, Laura Halperin, Carlos Jiménez Cahua, Randall Kenan, Sherryl Kleinman, Michael P. Kramer, Alice Kuzniar, Larry La Fountain-Stokes, Antonio López, Debbie López, Ashley Lucas, Rita Martin, Claudia Milian, Amelia María de la Luz Montes, Achy Obejas, Brenda Palo, Richard Pérez, Cecile Pineda, Della Pollock, John Ribó, Jonathan Risner, Ralph Rodriguez, Mariana Romo-Carmona, Ruth Salvaggio, María Sánchez, Betsy Sandlin, Alberto Sandoval-Sánchez, Alan Shapiro, Glenn Sheldon, James Smalls, Patricia Juliana Smith, Margaret Diane Stetz, Xavier F. Totti, Luz María Umpierre, Antonio Viego, Linda Wagner-Martin, and Sue Wells. I would also like to thank Indiana University Press, notably Janet Rabinowitch, Jane Kathleen Behnken, Sarah Wyatt Swanson, Raina Nadine Polivka, Angela Burton, Marvin Keenan, and Kira Bennett as well as the anonymous readers of this manuscript for their thoughtful comments, their helpful suggestions, and their belief in this project. Many thanks to Denise Carlson for her careful indexing. I am grateful to The Institute for the Arts and Humanities as well as to the Department of English and Comparative Literature at the University of North Carolina at Chapel Hill for making research leave possible. My deep gratitude goes to my parents, Brooke Church, and my cat "Cuchi" for their presence.

BUENAS NOCHES, AMERICAN CULTURE

CRITICALLY INHABITING THE NIGHT

Buenas Noches, Readers

Tropes of night in U.S. Latina/o arts take up the stigma of darkness as a condition to be inhabited ethno-racially and philosophically despite claims that the fate of U.S. Latina/os is to conform to an Anglo-American hegemony. Evocations of night might seem to be a way of making oneself palatable to a dominant Anglo culture through romanticization as people for whom the night is one long *fiesta*. However, exoticism within this rhetoric of night transgresses policed borders: a language of night and "vision-illuminated darkness" emerges to disturb people's sleep.[1] The escapism that is often associated with night—particularly in the idea of night as *fiesta* or respite from the day—is channeled to wake the comfortable sleep of dreamers, challenging the habits of readers and viewers.

Illustrative of this aesthetico-political practice is the mention of night in Cuban American author Cristina García's 2007 novel *A Handbook to Luck*.[2] Under cover of night, the character Marta Claros flees the civil war in El Salvador and her abusive husband, who works on the firing squad killing rebels for the U.S.-backed military government:

> Marta had never seen a sky this dark. There was no moon, and the stars seemed to hide in the black folds of midnight. The silence was so complete that Marta feared life itself had withdrawn from these parts. At any moment she might cross the border from one world to the next, imperceptibly, like death.
>
> The coyote said that a night like this was good cover, that the *yanquis'* fiercest lights couldn't penetrate it.[3]

The dark night presents an escape route for Marta, a birth canal from El Salvador across Guatemala and into the United States where she must begin life all over again. She must survive the illegality of her status despite the forces ranged against her. García deploys night in connection with the experiences of Marta Claros, who is always journeying, like Lena Grove in Faulkner's novel *Light in August*, originally titled *Dark House*. The relationship between darkness and light (and light as birth) is extensive and complex in both novels. García's novel mobilizes whatever escapist romance might be associated with night to portray the precarious passage into the United States of those dehumanized under the label "illegals." The darkest period of night is represented as the paradoxical medium of baptismal birth and survival for so many twentieth-century and recent immigrants from the Other America south and southeast of the United States, who become "Latina/os" with all the chaotic disorientations that attend the category that is not one category.[4] Tropes of night are equally important to Latina/os who have been living for centuries within what became the geographical boundaries of the United States of America and yet, time and time again, have been rendered foreigners in their native land or, at best, second-class citizens. Tropes of night express and construct the multiple dimensions of being *los otros americanos*.

To convey the range of meanings of the Spanish phrase "*buenas noches*," English must furnish at least two phrases: "good evening" and "good night." "*Buenas noches*" serves a dual function in the Spanish language. It does likewise in my study, signifying hello and good-bye, arrival and departure, recognition and transformation, beginnings and endings, and beginnings. *Buenas Noches, American Culture: Latina/o Aesthetics of Night* takes as its subject Latina/o novels, short stories, poetry, essays, nonfictions, photo-fictions, photographs, and films that evoke night. These night works suggest that the presence of Latina/os forms the dark underside and projecting shadow of "American" culture, constituting both its end and its beginning and calling to mind the Other America that was there before America as the United States, that remains alongside it, and that represents its culturally transforming present and future. Night as the Other America is a major overarching trope that is concerned with the power of the supposedly formless to give form to experience and with the relations among aesthetics, identity, identification, and history. "Trope," from the Greek meaning "turn," is a pattern of speech or writing that stands out from the ordinary flow of thought precisely because it turns away from the merely literal.[5] Latina/o figurations of night have constituted an aesthetics of self-representation as well as a form of resistance to compulsory state-sanctioned definitions of Latina/o identities and conditions for exclusion from or inclusion in the body politic of the United States. Tropes of night are composed of multiple literary, visual, and critical devices that express and shape relations among Latina/os and non-Latina/os in the Americas as well as among Latina/o groups in terms of power, cultural identity, and socio-temporal maps of affiliation.

Despite the cultural work performed by tropes of night in Latina/o cultural production, no other scholarly study exists on this topic. By "cultural production" I mean everything that a group of people produce as users, transmitters, and transformers of sign, symbol, and image systems that they inhabit and that inhabit them. My book focuses mainly on literary production, but it also engages with some film and photography. The topic of an aesthetics of night in Latina/o cultural production has been occluded on account of the familiarity and universality of "night" in the linguistic division of the period of the earth's rotation on its axis into the categories "night" and "day," "*noche*" y "*día.*" Night as a trope, especially in relation to historically politicized areas of study such as ethnic studies, critical race studies, and postcolonial studies, constitutes "the overlooked," by which I mean that which is unseen because it is taken for granted as both an experiential and conceptual category. The overlooked is taken for granted and assumed to be a universal, thus engendering analytical passivity or paralysis. This book focuses active attention on Latina/o aesthetics of night.

The Night of Latina/o Cultural Producers

Latina/o cultural producers employ rich, expansive, and protean tropes of night to great effect, an effect hitherto overlooked in critical and theoretical studies of Latina/o literature and culture more generally. In Latina/o literature, for example, nocturnal references compose a very persistent means of conveying the sense of being the Other Americans spreading, like *la noche,* in both directions, into the past and into the future of the Americas and of the United States as part of those Americas. If these claims concerning a Latina/o rhetoric of night are reminiscent of Hitchcock or film noir, that is because, among other things, they are. Consider, for instance, Alfred Hitchcock's film *Vertigo* (1958). Madeleine, the principal mystery woman, has a historical alter ego or possessing spirit named Carlotta Valdes—a Latina name that is part of "the things that [really] spell San Francisco." Throughout the film, both Madeleine and her alter ego Carlotta Valdes are associated with night and shadows. The Anglo male protagonist, a noir anti-hero, falls prey to the pull of these shadows when Madeleine plunges into the dark waters of San Francisco Bay. He rescues her only to lose himself, as male noir protagonists usually do, under the hypnosis or "spell" of their beautiful and deadly *femmes fatales.*

Tropes of night may be plumbed to articulate relations of Latina/o literature and visual culture to the Anglo-American canon, to African American literature and visual culture, and to the work of Latin American writers and artists. The book focuses mainly on contemporary Latina/o literature, visual production, and literature concerned with visual production from the 1940s to the present—and not just that of Chicana/o writers/visual artists, the obvious choice given that a large portion of the current-day United States was once Mexico.[6] I examine Latina/o literary and visual production in its cultural variety and differences and yet also in its relative constancy with regard to the invocation of night as figure and discourse for the inversion and re-orientation of cultural norms and expectations, for speaking of an Other America.

As phrases such as the "Other America" and "*Nuestra* [Our] *América*" suggest, I set this contemporary Latina/o literature and visual production in relation to keynote elements from essays and poems written by certain Latin American intellectuals and writers from the mid nineteenth century onwards, such as Simón Bolívar, José Martí, José Enrique Rodó, Arturo Uslar Pietri, César Vallejo, Adolfo Bioy Casares, Octavio Paz, Julia de Burgos, Jorge Luis Borges, Roberto Fernández Retamar, Reinaldo Arenas, Fernando Ortiz Fernández, Nelly Richard, and Aníbal Quijano. One of the implications of such a framing is the recovery and creation of a transnational, transcultural intellectual and cultural tradition that includes Latin American and U.S. Latina/o writers/artists and a re-visitation of the distinctions often made between them and among U.S. Latina/o ethnic groups.

I situate the work of contemporary Latina/o writers and artists in relation to essays and fictional works by Latin Americans and U.S. Latinos from the nineteenth century onward, particularly those that address concepts of the Other America, what Cuban writer Alejo Carpentier termed "*lo real maravilloso*," and epistemologies that challenge some of the assumptions of rational liberal humanism born of the Enlightenment's sometimes totalitarian radiance that passes for reason, clarity, and even "democracy."[7] The focus on the 1940s to the present, however, has much to do with the history of civil rights; the demands on the part of Latina/os of different ethno-national backgrounds for recognition by the majoritarian non-Latina/o culture; and the ongoing realities of discrimination, marginalization, and invisibility despite the demographic preponderance of Latina/os in certain areas of the United States and the long historical legacy of Latina/o presence in the United States and across its contested borders.

This study consists of this introduction, four chapters, and a conclusion. Within that span, I attempt to do justice to the variety and heterogeneity of the populations and cultural productions designated as Latina/o. "Latina/o" is an umbrella term for people of Latin American and Iberian heritage living in the United States. The term tries to do the impossible: classify people from more than twenty countries and with many different spatio-temporal and geopoliti-cal relations to the United States, the Americas, and various kinds of transna-tional and transcultural situations. Studies such as Suzanne Oboler's *Ethnic Labels, Latino Lives* (1995) and Marta Caminero-Santangelo's *On Latinidad: U.S. Latino Literature and the Construction of Ethnicity* (2007) problematize the term "Latina/o."[8] For example, are Latin American immigrants who iden-tify primarily with their country of origin or a particular district or province of that country Latina/os? Are the Hispanos of New Mexico or the Californios of California Latina/os? Are Latina/os really only those "Hispanics" who have adopted a transcultural, transnational identity within the United States—those who recognize a particular origin or identification and yet do not cling to it so closely that they refuse identification with other Latina/o groups?

I employ the term "Latina/o" advisedly, distinguishing among groups according to ethnic and ethno-racial identification but also according to other factors—generation, gender, sexuality, class, and regional and local affiliation. I move from Chicana/o literature and cultural production to mostly Puerto Rican and Cuban works (these being derived from the three traditional groups of Latina/os in the United States). From there I concentrate on work by Cen-tral Americans (Guatemalans, for instance). Then, in chapter four, I examine works by Chileans, Colombians, and Peruvians in the United States as well as by Latinas/o from the traditional three main U.S. Latina/o groups (Mexican Americans, Puerto Ricans, and Cubans) whose texts and visual images mark-edly transculturate, transnationalize, border-cross, and even transvest cultur-ally. I analyze these transculturations in terms of the kinds of re-definitions of nation, citizenship, personhood, inclusion, exclusion, and collectivity I argue they are putting forth under the guise of night.

Latina/o Studies and the Relevance of Aesthetics

Art acquires its specificity by separating itself from what it developed out of . . . There is no *aesthetic refraction* without something being refracted; no imagination without something being imagined . . . Aesthetic identity seeks to aid the non-identical [which I also understand to mean the non-mimetic function], which in reality is repressed by reality's compulsion to identity . . . Artworks are *afterimages of empirical life* insofar as they help the latter to what is denied them outside their own sphere [emphasis mine].[9]

German-born, U.S.-naturalized philosopher, sociologist, composer, musi-cologist, and member of the Frankfurt School Theodor Adorno (1903–1969) posited that art or cultural production is different from that which is merely empirical or socially reflective. In his *Aesthetic Theory*, Adorno speaks of the function and movement of art in terms of visual refraction—a change in the direction of a wave (of light or sound, for instance) due to a change in speed when it passes from one medium to another and the concomitant change in appearance of an illuminated object. The emphasis is on transformation, not on reflection or even on imprint, as with the notion of an afterimage. At the same time, Adorno places art in a dialectic with social forces. Though it is not merely reflective of the social, art is dependent on social forces even as it constitutes a refracted articulation of those forces:

> The aesthetic force of production is the same as that of productive labor and has the same teleology; and what may be called aesthetic relations of production— all that in which the productive force is embedded and in which it is active—are sedimentations or imprintings of social relations of production. Art's double character as both autonomous and *fait social* is incessantly reproduced on the level of its autonomy. (5)

Buenas Noches, American Culture: Latina/o Aesthetics of Night examines the refractions of the social that constitute art or cultural production while simultaneously attending to art's double character. Art's double character as both reflecting and transforming social relations of production leads me to suggest that art functions not only as an afterimage but also as a pre-image, an image that necessarily precedes and mediates social change and transformation.

Within more ethnically bounded fields such as Chicana/o, Puerto Rican, or Cuban American studies that preceded the larger rubric of Latina/o studies, much scholarship has been produced to redress the potential reductionism of art to its reflective aspects.[10] The increasingly multi-ethnic, transnational field of Latina/o literary and cultural studies is also yielding work that concerns itself with aesthetics, philosophy, and affect. The intersection between philosophy and affect has gained the attention of particular Latina/o scholars. Take, for instance, Jorge J. E. Gracia's *Hispanic/Latino Identity: A Philosophical Perspective* (2000) or José Esteban Muñoz's interest in affect and phenomenology in the productions/performances of Latina/o identities. See, for example, Muñoz's 1999 study *Disidentifications: Queers of Color and the Performance of Politics* and his 2000 essay "Feeling Brown: Ethnicity and Affect."[11] Wisely, most of these scholars have emphasized that questions of aesthetics, philosophy, and affect are social and political. For example, in the chapters concerning Latina/o identities of the 2005 *Visible Identities: Race, Gender, and the Self*, feminist philosopher and ethnic studies scholar Linda Martín Alcoff deftly keeps phenomenologi-cal/philosophical/affect studies approaches from becoming separated from socially grounded questions about Latina/o identities and identity formation. Hers is a realist post-positivist approach that, as with Paula Moya's, Michael R. Haimes-García's, and Satya P. Mohanty's contributions to the study of minority experience and cultural production, has allowed for a judicious and hard-won balancing act between empirical and conceptual approaches and between, in the case of my concerns here, sociological and philosophical/aesthetic ques-tions without capitulating to reductionism, determinism, or deconstructive nominalism in any of these spheres of inquiry.

My book foregrounds Latina/o cultural production in relation to philosophy and aesthetics and to the politics informed by and fashioned from their mutual imbrications. Following Paget Henry's caveat in *Caliban's Reason: Introducing Afro-Caribbean Philosophy* that philosophy must entail more than "an affirma-tion of the autonomy of a thinking subject," my book is concerned with aes-thetics and philosophy marked by historical and contemporary sociological forces.[12] I am interested in the aesthetic and philosophical dimensions of the works I investigate to the extent that they are doing conceptual work—produc-ing paradigms of and for collective psychosocial cultural re-orientations and dis-orientations. I consider how, in their figurations of night, Latina/o literary and visual productions suggest new modes of American cultural identity.

I realize that when invoking the term "aesthetics," one must acknowledge the pitfalls of what may seem, on the surface, to be a turning away from pressing issues related to human rights, citizenry, education, health, legal representation, and job opportunities. George Yúdice, citing the concerns of John Beverley, reminds and warns readers of the existence of a "neo-Arielism" in the appro-priation of the legacy of Latin American intellectuals by the U.S. academy in an essay titled "Rethinking Area and Ethnic Studies in the Context of Economic and Political Restructuring."[13] By neo-Arielism he means a latter-day version of "Arielism," based on Uruguayan essayist José Enrique Rodó's *Ariel* (originally published in 1900) that called for Latin American intellectuals to "eschew the allure of U.S. instrumental culture and instead model their politics on a quasi-Kantian disinterested aesthetics" (98). Between the idealist mode of criticism of the neo-Arielist Rodó (with its distaste for the everyday world of socioeconomic and political struggle) and a sociologically and politically engaged mode of inter-pretation as suggested by Cuban intellectual Roberto Fernández Retamar, this study leans heavily toward the insights of the latter's *Caliban* with regard to the implicit political nature of all cultural production, though it attempts to redress the masculinist bias of this contest between Ariel and Caliban.[14]

Talk of aesthetics can seem precious in the face of urgent practical concerns. Nevertheless, I speak of aesthetics because a politics and a praxis depends heavily on aesthetics, if by "aesthetics" one understands the ways or manners in which things present themselves or are presented, the material shapes that concepts and passions take. Style is part of aesthetics. Style is often misunderstood in writing as a question of sentence structure and diction when, in fact, it also manifests itself in choice of subject matter, key tropes, point of view or angle, stance, and myriad other factors. All these factors combine to create and sustain an entire environment of effects which readers or viewers are invited to inhabit.

The term "aesthetic" derives from the Greek word "*aesthesis*," meaning sensation (as opposed to thought, denotated by "*noesis*"). With the exception of philosophers such as Giambattista Vico and Immanuel Kant (*The Critique of Judgment*) in the mid to late eighteenth century, the likes of Søren Kierkegaard and Friedrich Wilhelm Nietzsche in the mid to late nineteenth century, and people such as Benedetto Croce, Theodor Adorno, Walter Benjamin, and the Frankfurt School in the early to mid twentieth century, a majority of philosophers have regarded aesthetics as a philosophy of beauty, and beauty in relation to its effects on the senses. The senses in Western philosophical traditions tend to be subordinated to thought, idea, or concept. Thus, the treatment of aesthetics as primarily concerned with sensations meant that it too was subordinated to what were deemed more serious concerns—theology or statecraft, for example. With Croce, Adorno, and Antonio Gramsci, for instance, and later with art scholars influenced by Gestalt psychology such as Rudolf Arnheim, Marxist phenomenologists such as Maurice Merleau-Ponty, and a host of postmodern thinkers as well as feminist philosophers, aesthetics has been increasingly understood as a central element of philosophy, ideology, and praxis, not merely a minor branch of philosophy. Furthermore, Marxist theory and psychoanalysis, while antagonistic in many aspects, both have as their best aim a liberating re-organization of material and psychic investments, whether collective or individual. Their confluence in post-structuralist theory underscores aesthetics as demonstration and catalyst of human motivation and behavior in relation to cultural values and vice versa. Aesthetics is as much about patterns of value as is ethics.

Major Trends in Twentieth-Century Uses of Night

In the twentieth century alone, the century by which we persist in defining contemporary modernity although we are well into the twenty-first century, tropes of night took on major importance in works that have since been classified as expressionist or existentialist or both and that were reworking, among other cultural influences and affinities, texts of the "dark side of the Enlightenment" and, more specifically, texts of German Romanticism. Here I am thinking of texts of German Romanticism such as *Hymns to the Night* (1800) by Georg Philipp Friedrich Freiherr von Hardenberg, otherwise known as Novalis; the poem "The Night" (1805) by Friedrich Hölderlin; *Views from the Nightside of Natural Science* (1808) by G. H. Schubert; *Faust, Part I* (1808) and *Faust, Part II* (1832) by Johann Wolfgang von Goethe; and *Nachtstücke* or *The Night Pieces* (1816–17), tales by E. T. A. Hoffman. Night figured prominently in much Romantic composition, textual and musical. Consider Frédéric Chopin's twenty-one nocturnes, for instance. But so strong was the preoccupation with night and everything associated with it in German Romanticism, and so effective was the dissemination of this preoccupation, that the Scottish author Catherine Crowe of the highly influential collection of ghost stories *The Night Side of Nature* (1848)—the title was taken from a German term for the darkest part of the night—introduced into the English language a German term for a ghost that went bump in the night: *poltergeist.*[15]

To return to the twentieth century and the expressionist and existentialist cultural productions to which I was referring earlier, Francophone literature contains significant examples of uses of night, among them the expressionist naysayer Louis-Ferdinand Céline's *Journey to the End of the Night* (1932), throughout which night figures, and many of the Algerian/Africa-born Albert Camus's existential works, especially *The Plague* (1947) and *Exile and the Kingdom* (1957). The deployment of night in both these works by Camus is particularly relevant to my present investigation. Their uses of night are connected with colonial situations, colonial malaise, and the stirrings of a growing decolonial consciousness against the oppressions of colonial rule. Both take place in French-occupied North Africa. *The Plague* is specifically located in Oran. During French rule in North Africa, Oran was a prefecture in the Oran *département*. Similarly, *Exile and the Kingdom* unfolds in the cities and deserts of French-controlled North Africa. One may assume that its stories are set in the city of Oran and its environs, but the stories do not always specify. Though the setting of the story "The Growing Stone" is Brazil, the effect is similar to those of the stories set in Oran. Readers find a society pervaded by colonialism and also overcome by the very people it has tried to subjugate and control. The colonial French are shown to have become exiles, not masters, in a land that is too much for them: "Yonder, in Europe, there was shame and wrath. Here [whether North Africa or Brazil], exile or solitude...."[16] Both the failure of colonial ventures and the revolt against their structures are represented in terms of night. *The Plague* represents the plague as "thick darkness"[17] and extensively parallels a dark, muggy heat (30) with a "queer kind of fever, which is causing much alarm" (28). The novel is replete with many descriptions of various kinds of night-related darkness. It concludes with fireworks soaring over Oran's harbor at night (271) to celebrate the supposed end of the plague that the novel reminds readers will return.

Figurations of night in *The Plague* are complex. Night is something to be both feared and yet also half-desired inasmuch as it overwhelms the colonial machine of the day, the machine of commerce and numerous kinds of enslavement. "The Adulterous Woman," a story from *Exile and the Kingdom* published three years into the Algerian War of Independence (1954–1962) from France, depicts an active desire for night and all that the trope entails. The woman of a married heterosexual couple on a business venture to French-controlled Arabic Africa—North Africa, most likely Algeria, though the location is unspecified beyond the presence of "a uniform of the French regiments of the Sahara"[18] and "French officers in charge of native affairs" (371)—escapes, late at night, from the hotel room where she has been staying with her husband. Feeling utterly stifled, she temporarily leaves her slumbering husband to step "out into the night" (377). The story's title, "The Adulterous Woman," would suggest that the wife has escaped to have an affair with some person. But the French woman flees the stuffy hotel room and her husband's heavy, slumberous breathing to embrace not another person but, instead, the desert night. An eroticized encounter with the night encapsulates the discovery of a relation between the French woman desirous for liberation from the constraints of her life and the night world of the North African desert that defies the colonial, patriarchal order of commerce and French rule partly represented by her husband. The story powerfully articulates night as that which exceeds the patriarchal colonial order, that which cannot be contained by it, that which challenges the very foundations of that social order and the subjectivities within and under it. The story is written from the wife's perspective. However, the effect of the story is not so much to have readers side with her as to have readers confront an alternate dimension, something both human—the Arab "nightwatchman" (377) she passes on the way to her encounter with the night—and inhuman, the night as it is portrayed. The implied relationship between the ethnicity and culture of the night watchman and the desert night toward which Janine, the French woman, runs is fleeting yet significant. It serves to remind readers that Janine is moving not merely toward nature but toward the alterity of another culture's nature, toward the nature of the colonized culture—a nature that reveals none other than the limits of the colonial structure.

Night in "The Adulterous Woman" is not simply nature. It is alterity in many forms blended together: Janine's difference from her husband, the Arabic culture's difference from French culture (whether of the metropole or the colony), and the difference of what is not human from what is human. *Exile and the*

Kingdom by Camus—who was born in Mondovi, Algeria, in 1913 and who lived in Algeria during all his formative years (he moved to France in 1940)—was published in France three years into the Algerian War of Independence that raged in and around Oran. These facts propel me even further toward a reading of "night" in these stories within the context of a colonial/decolonial struggle. What has since been classified as European "existentialist" literature used night to address both historically situated and transhistorical philosophical and political issues. A number of the Latina/o cultural producers whose work I examine demonstrate a critical and finely honed familiarity with European Romantic, expressionist, existentialist, and phenomenological traditions and have integrated and transmuted them to their own ends.

Tropes of night have a long, convoluted history in the Americas; they were partially carried over from Europe but intensified by the colonial project of the Americas that entailed fraught encounters with difference and alterity. Despite socioeconomic, political, and religious differences among colonizing Old World nations and empires (Spanish, Portuguese, French, Dutch, and British), the colonizing powers tended toward a Manichaean dualism in which European and "white" or light were equated with the civilization and the good, whereas non-Europeans (Indians, Africans, and a host of others) were equated with darkness, night, savagery, or evil. Thus, a Gothic mode runs throughout literature of the Americas, especially in Anglo-American cultural production, with its more Protestant-based, binary divisions between heaven and hell, good and evil, and light and dark. The Gothic mode that signaled the dark side of the Enlightenment and that inflected the cultural production of early British Romantics (Horace Walpole and Ann Radcliffe, for example), German Romantics, and the "dark Romantics" of Anglo-American literature, such as Edgar Allan Poe, Nathaniel Hawthorne, and Herman Melville, generally represented night negatively and fearfully. Night was associated with tragic love, madness, loss of personal and communal identity, invisibility, nightmares, apocalypse, the void, knowledge and experience beyond the pale of social sanction, the frightening blurring or erasing of boundaries, and border-crossing into darkness.

The Anglo-American tradition of fearful and confusing night continues across the twentieth century with novels such as Thomas Wolfe's *Look Homeward Angel* (1929), F. Scott Fitzgerald's *Tender is the Night* (1934), Djuna Barnes's *Nightwood* (1936), William Styron's *Lie Down in Darkness* (1951) and the much later memoir *Darkness Visible: A Memoir of Madness* (1990), Richard Bausch's *Good Evening Mr. and Mrs. America, and All the Ships at Sea* (1996) and *In the Night Season* (1998), and Patrick Stettner's 2006 thriller film *The Night Listener,* which was based on Armistead Maupin's 2000 novel of the same name and featured a screenplay by Armistead Maupin, Terry Anderson, and Patrick

Stettner. Much of this Anglo Teutonic Gothicism about night feeds into both text-based and film-based noir. This flow of Gothic sensibility about night into noir productions of many kinds is significant because it has served to disseminate stereotyped ways of seeing and not seeing the existence of anyone deemed to be African American, Hispanic or Latina/o, Asian, marginal, foreign, or alien. A partial exception to this trend in Anglo-American cinema is Richard Kelly's 2004 cult status film *Donnie Darko,* in which the night, darkness, shadows, and noirish alienation are gnostically valorized for the inconvenient truths they bring, however fearful, and in which marginalized characters, white and Asian (though not Latina/o or African American), are shown to be more receptive and trustworthy than those who attempt to complacently inhabit the dominant, authoritarian, conformist, manipulated, middle-class, largely white suburban U.S. culture.[19]

The Gothic coding of the subaltern and alien through tropes of night takes more self-conscious, reflective twists in fiction by Jewish American writers, most notably Paul Auster in novels such as *Moon Palace* (1989), *Oracle Night* (2003), and *Man in the Dark* (2008). The very title of *Oracle Night* announces an extensive engagement with night. This engagement is, by and large, very Gothic. It is replete with the dead, the sick, and dying; with mysterious and uncanny accidents that take place at night, including crimson nosebleeds[20] and the near death of a character called Nick Bowen from a gargoyle head dislodged from "the façade of an apartment building" (25); with paper ghosts in the form of photographs (39) and telephone directories (91–93) of people no longer living or exterminated; with villains such as Jacob and victims such as Grace; with time travel (120–26) and preoccupations with psychic gifts and, at the very least, disturbing dreams and premonitions (65); with urban zones of "horror and devastation" (70), not just cosmopolitan cornucopias; with truth as "a swamp of uncertainty" (81); with episodes of crypt-like solitary confinement (105); with anxieties about sexual reproduction typical of Gothic novels such as Mary Shelley's *Frankenstein;* with "dumbfounding shifts of mood . . . enigmatic utterances . . . disappearance" (212); with personal and collective catastrophe; and with Poe-like phraseology such as "a man so sensitive to the vibrations around him that he knew what was going to happen before the events themselves took place" (223).

As with the Anglo Gothic fiction of night, Auster's *Oracle Night* evinces an obsession with non-white Others in relation to identity-challenging experiences, as demonstrated by the episodes involving Mr. Chang, the Chinese owner of a stationery store called The Paper Palace that becomes a big American dream flop (141); an African American World War II veteran Edward M.

Johnson (aka Ed Victory) (102, 68), a supposed member of the American unit that "liberated" Dachau (92); Martine (151), a Haitian sex worker in a sex club at the back of a garment sweatshop in Flushing, New York; and, finally, Régine Dumas (157), a black woman from Martinique. *Oracle Night* conscripts non-whites into a pattern of unsettling events that befall the central male protagonist Sidney Orr, shaking him out of his complacencies. The non-white characters are not directly associated with night as in the Anglo Gothic stories. Rather, they are part of a larger narrative frame in *Oracle Night* that involves all the characters at multiple levels of smaller narrative frames, a storytelling architecture that attests to the metafictional nature of Auster's novel.

With regard to night as a spatio-temporality, Auster's novel, unlike many Anglo-American works about night, does manage to rehistoricize the fear associated with night. In *Oracle Night,* night, like a photograph and the 1937/1938 Warsaw telephone book full of the names of the dead (many of them exterminated by the Nazis), is a time machine. Night is a time machine that takes readers back into a confrontation with some of the "darkest truths" (47) of history—the Holocaust, for example. The novel's darkest thought is articulated by a twenty-year-old pale, emaciated (198) drug addict who dyes his hair black and wears a "long dark overcoat" (232) and thick leather boots (236), melding concentration camp victim with Nazi with punk and suggesting "some futuristic undertaker" (232). He articulates not only the absence but also the irrelevance of God or any kind of divine intelligence (198). His cynical despair sounds one of the more devastating notes of *Oracle Night.* The general tenor of the novel, with its attempt to navigate radical uncertainty and both experience and salvage "Grace" (the person, the state of being) from the nightmarish maelstrom of events, reminds readers that informing Auster's 2003 novel *Oracle Night* is Jewish concentration camp survivor Elie Wiesel's account of his time in the camps, which is titled *Night* in English and was originally published in France in 1958 as *La Nuit.* Wiesel writes,

> NEVER SHALL I FORGET that night, the first night in camp, that turned my life into one long night seven times sealed.
> . . .
> Never shall I forget those things, even were I condemned to live as long as God Himself.
> Never.[21]

In Wiesel's book, night becomes the "Kingdom of Night," of which all concentration camps and the Nazi project of extermination were a part—a space-time characterized by the absence of God and humanity. Though the "Kingdom of Night" is a concept and phrase that sounds fairy-tale-like, Elie Wiesel's work rehistoricizes Gothic tropes, making them point toward history and not away from it. So do Paul Auster's novels *Oracle Night* and *Man in the Dark* (2008) and other Jewish and Jewish American cultural productions. *Man in the Dark* involves an aging book critic who lives in a paradoxically "real" fantasy world during war, assassination plots, and the televised beheading of his granddaughter's friend in Iraq. Norman Mailer's 1968 apocalyptic novel *The Armies of the Night: History as a Novel, The Novel as History* deals in detailed social commentary about the October 1967 anti–Vietnam War rally in Washington, DC, among other historical events.

This historicizing tendency is also strongly evident in the cultural production of African Americans. Some of the most nuanced explorations of the possibilities of night as a form of cultural critique and deep-structure revision exist in African American literary production. Take, for instance, Langston Hughes's over forty-year (1920s–1960s) output of night poems that constitute some of his most striking examples of cultural critique and call for social action. Among those poems, I would count "Negro" with its opening lines "I am a Negro: / Black as the night is black, / Black like the depths of my Africa"[22] as well as "Summer Night" (59), "Harlem Night Club" (90), "Lenox Avenue: Midnight" (92), "Black Seed" with its "World-wide dusk / Of dear dark faces" (130), "Moonlight in Valencia: Civil War" (306), and "Night Song" (330–31). After the mid 1960s, consider Clarence Major's *All-Night Visitors* (1969); the formidable *Night Studies* (1979) by Cyrus Colter; Toni Morrison's *Playing in the Dark* (1992) and *Jazz* (1992); a more marginal work such as Walter Dean Myers's *Somewhere in the Darkness* (1992); the philosophically night-steeped, discourse-revising, deliberately scandalous black male homosexual underground classic by Samuel Delany titled *The Mad Man* (1994) with its hundred-page fifth part titled "The Mirrors of Night";[23] or the poems, published in the United States, of Afro-Caribbean St. Lucian writer Kendel Hippolyte. I would point in particular to Hippolyte's collection of poems titled *Night Vision* (2005), in which "night vision" is the ability to see transhistorically through history, to remember the history of slavery in the Old and New Worlds and yet also to be able to see beyond that history—to see "your self in the illumination that discovers you / only in darkness."[24] Inspiring, complementing, and often intertwining with African American literary production on night is African American musical production—particularly in the song lyrics to the blues (see those of Muddy Waters or Howlin' Wolf, for example), jazz, soul, funk, and disco. Multivalenced references to evening, nighttime, midnight, and darkness are scattered everywhere in these musical traditions. These references do not simply mark the time of day or night or describe a nocturnal environment or landscape. They are shorthand to the singer's affect (melancholy, rebelliousness, anger, sorrow, and so forth) and, frequently, to the racialized, socioeconomic position of the singer and that of his or her community.

Methodology for Looking at Night in Latina/o Cultural Production

Methodologically, this project, located within Latina/o studies, brings to bear historical analysis, philosophy, psychoanalysis and depth psychology, postcolonial theory, semiotics, aesthetics, critical race studies, and gender/sexuality studies to the study of relevant texts, artifacts, and performances. I also read primary texts as theoretical contributions in themselves that prompt a reformulation of existing paradigms of identity and identification in the Americas. As part of that reformulation, this study takes a comparatist approach to Latina/o literary and cultural production. It stresses the necessarily comparatist nature of Latina/o studies. It acknowledges the historically and culturally shaping force of certain ethno-national, ethno-regional identities (Chicana/o, Caribbean, Central American, and South American). At the same time, it considers these various kinds of cultural production in relation to one another. My comparatist approach also entails contextualization of Latina/o cultural production in relation to European and Euro-American/Anglo-American cultural production along with the cultural production of African Americans whose work was and continues to be especially important to Chicana/o cultural producers and to U.S.-based Caribbean Latina/os with respect to intersecting histories and struggles. My invocation of European and Euro-American philosophy and texts underscores the fact that Latina/o cultures in the Americas are simultaneously the inheritors, users, and transformers of other cultural traditions that are both part of their cultures and alien to them. Latina/o cultures show a much more informed awareness about these other cultural traditions than they have received credit for by readers and critics with more bounded, closed-system models of culture and difference.

This study negotiates what is particular and unique about the use of tropes of night within various groups and groupings of Latina/o culture while at the same time acknowledging that this investigation necessitates a continual awareness of the transcultural and transhistorical aspects of the topic. When I write "in the Americas," I do not mean to imply that tropes of night belong solely to cultural production of the Americas. References to night can be found transculturally and transhistorically employed for a wide range of purposes and effects.

"Night" is a topic belonging to "world literature." It crosses borders along with the people and cultures employing those tropes, as with the case of the Renaissance and early modern conquistadors, missionaries, and colonizers from Spain who brought their Baroque poetry to the New World, where it mixed with the nocturnal imagery of Mesoamerican cosmologies. Night as a topic and tropes of night are *transfronterizos,* border-crossers.

My book draws out the implications of this night work for the theorization of Latina/o studies in relation to comparative ethnic studies and transnational Americas studies and, conversely, the import of Latina/o studies for these areas of investigation. It traces the extent to which Latina/o literary and visual productions suggest new models of American cultural identity. Latina/o aesthetics of night deconstruct scenarios of assimilation into an *inframundo* (a Spanish term for an Aztec concept positing a world lying "within, amidst, and still beyond this world" or social order) that resists not only conformity to specifically Anglo-American models of ethnic and cultural identity but also to expected melting pot assimilation, including assimilation into a neoliberal socioeconomic order.[25] Night is figured as a kind of vast assimilatory space-time, a place where borders are transgressed and are disrupted, where borders bleed or melt into one another depending on the circumstances and situations involved. Whatever the case, the figuration of night—or lack thereof, to the extent that night trumps defined figures—recalls that assimilation does not have one meaning but several, some of them quite opposed to one another. Assimilation as a function of tropes of night negates the historically hegemonic notion of assimilation as conformity to one Anglo-American culture.

Assimilation under the sign of night, to echo public intellectual and cultural critic Susan Sontag's evocative phrase for melancholy "under the sign of Saturn," entails a far more multi-layered exchange between various minority or sub-cultural groups that singly, and certainly when counted together, are no longer in the minority.[26] Although *Buenas Noches* could be subsumed under studies of a melancholic rejection and reformulation of the social order, I emphasize that much Latina/o cultural production entails a more activist collectivization of melancholy that does not come to full expression in a practice of individual alienation or flaneur-like solitude. Instead, the sensibility in these Latina/o works is better described by the words of the African American male protagonist hero in Cuban and Lithuanian American George A. Romero's 1968 horror film *Night of the Living Dead* to the white Anglo female protagonist, whose brother has been killed and devoured by cannibalistic (white) zombies as the day turns into night: "We got to get out of here. We got to get where there are some other people [not the zombie people] . . . I know you are afraid. I'm afraid, too . . . but we have to work together. You have to help me."

CHAPTER ONE

DREADED NON-IDENTITIES OF NIGHT: NIGHT AND SHADOWS IN CHICANA/O CULTURAL PRODUCTION

> How do you make the invisible visible? You take it away.
> —Lila Rodriguez in *A Day Without a Mexican*

The Nighttime of a Day without a Mexican

Of the more than fifty million Latina/os currently within the continental borders of the United States, Mexican Americans have had a long borderlands history—defined by military battles and treaties in the name of U.S. national expansion, by laws, and by daily discriminatory practices—of being treated as the other Americans, *los otros americanos.* They became aliens in their own land with the 1848 Treaty of Guadalupe Hidalgo that officially concluded the Mexican-American War and in the years subsequent to that treaty, which involved an Anglo landgrab of previously Mexican areas. In 1971, Chicano attorney, writer, and political activist Oscar "Zeta" Acosta pointedly summed up the situation:

> The American government took our country away from us in 1848, when the government of Mexico sold us out. They sold not only the land, but they basically sold us as slaves in the sense that our labor and our land was [*sic*] being expropriated. The governments never gave us a choice about whether to be American citizens. *One night* we were Mexican and the next day we were American. This historical relationship is the most important part of the present day relationships, but it's totally ignored or unknown or rejected by the Anglo society. [emphasis mine][1]

As Chicano critic Raymund A. Paredes observed over a quarter of a century ago, "According to Guadalupe Hidalgo and succeeding documents, Spanish and

Mexican land grants were to be honored by the American government, but after the war, Mexican Americans were systematically stripped of their property."[2] They were not only dispossessed of their property; they were (and still are) systematically discriminated against in terms of education, employment, the law, health services, and many other areas of daily experience. This systematic discrimination is described in great detail and without apology in Julián Segura Camacho's 2005 manifesto *The Chicano Treatise*.[3] Traces of this alienation can be found everywhere in Mexican American and explicitly politicized Chicana/o cultural production, from early- to mid-nineteenth-century *corridos* (or narrative ballads that serve as a musical form of news) to the latest comic strips. Those traces are composed of a proliferating network of signs that denote or connote socioeconomic and psychosocial marginalization, erasure, and invisibility, ranging from masks to utter darkness. Night is the ur-sign, the penumbral trope, for this repressive Othering. Night is also a response to the Othering that challenges it with a dissolution of the terms and conditions of containment and subordination encapsulated by the concept of "illegal alien."

Contemporary Mexican visual artist and political cartoonist Sergio Arau's 2004 mockumentary *A Day Without a Mexican* (co-written with Sergio Guerrero and Yareli Arizmendi) demonstrates the extent to which Mexicans in the United States have been turned into aliens, non-citizens, and hardly residents in the United States generally and in land once Mexican (such as California) specifically. In response to the alienation, "illegalization," and dehumanization of Mexicans and Mexican Americans, the film depicts the massive disappearance of Mexican and other workers from the United States one dark, foggy night and examines how U.S. society would be helpless without the presence of the Mexicans and other Others whose labor thoroughly supports it. The film renders meaningless nativist claims of insider status in contrast to the supposed alien status of Mexicans, dissolving these claims in the nightmarish reality of having no more Mexican and Latin American labor on the highways, in the kitchens, in the factories, in the vineyards, or anywhere else in the infrastructure of Gringolandia. The dominant metaphor for this suspension of business as usual is a dense wall of fog that arises one night and surrounds California, cutting it off from telephone, internet, and radio communications and thus "isolating the population from the rest of the world," as one reporter observes during one of the film's news reports. Inside the state, more and more people with "Hispanic background" (largely Mexicans but also Guatemalans, Hondurans, and Salvadorans) disappear, bringing the system to a halt and making California feel like a ghost town. The film deploys California, the fifth-largest economy in the world, to displace the functioning of the United States. It implicitly argues for the centrality of Hispanics, who made up a third of the population of California in 2004, to the very existence of California and the United States by literalizing the logical conclusions of the disappearance of Mexicans and other Hispanics: widespread panic and malfunction of the U.S. socioeconomic system. An intense curtain of fog that begins one night and disastrously raptures a Hispanic reporter, Joe Velasquez Diaz of the "Buenos Diaz Report" (a homophonous play on the phrase "*buenos días*," meaning "good day"), hangs around the edges of the film's action as a reminder of the crippling obfuscation of an isolationist, anti-immigrant ideology and its laws and policies. The dense pink fog becomes like the toxic event in Don DeLillo's 1985 novel *White Noise*. The confusion brought on by the fog is symptomatic of the confusion of values in a culture that wants cheap labor but refuses to be responsible for the source of that labor, human beings, in any way other than punitively. The film's association of the fog with a selective bomb that searches out the L-factor ("the Latino factor") and destroys targeted people without a trace is remindful of the concept and development of the neutron bomb, circa 1958, that was designed to destroy tissue but minimize damage to property. Black-humor spoofs of this horrific concept and invention are numerous, among them Kurt Vonnegut's novel *Deadeye Dick* (1982) featuring Midland City, Ohio, a town depopulated when a neutron bomb detonates on a freeway. Not so funny is the parallel between this imagined night and fog disappearance of Latina/os in *A Day Without a Mexican* and an actual 1941 Night and Fog Decree issued by the Nazis. Sociologist Avery F. Gordon writes about this decree, which pertained to Germany's western occupied territories, in her 1997 book *Ghostly Matters: Haunting and the Sociological Imagination*, which illuminates the relationships among ghosts, historical trauma, and the persistent drive to face and address social injustice (a legacy of slavery, racism, state-sponsored terrorism, etc.):

> The Night and Fog Decree "ordered that, with the exception of those cases where guilt could be established beyond a doubt, everyone arrested for suspicion of 'endangering German security' was to be transferred [secretly] to Germany under 'cover of night.'" . . . Secret arrest, transportation under cover of darkness, the refusal to give information "'as to [the prisoners'] whereabouts or their fate,'" and the belief that "deterring" resistance could be best accomplished by people vanishing "without leaving a trace" are the elements that prefigure the system of repression known as disappearance.[4]

Gordon mentions this 1941 Night and Fog Decree in her chapter on the practice and effect of disappearance in Argentina during the military government's so-called Dirty War of 1976–1983 and on the political resistance of the Mothers of the Plaza de Mayo, who refused to let the disappeared be forgotten and swept out of sight. She observes that disappearance is not unique to Argentina but is "a worldwide phenomenon that may have a history antedating this name" (72). The night and fog and the disappearance of California's Latina/os in *A Day Without a Mexican* seem to take their cue from landmark disappearances in the history of the twentieth century, including those that occurred during the Nazi regime in Germany and those of an estimated thirty thousand people during the Dirty War in Argentina. *A Day Without a Mexican* implicates the United States of America in the same totalitarian tactics, and yet the film enacts disappearance to make the invisible blatantly visible. The film takes as a given the invisibility of Latina/os in California and particularly the invisibility (to the dominant culture) of Latina/o labor. It seeks to re-appropriate disappearance as a technique of state-sponsored terrorism and political repression, using this disappearance instead to materialize what is painfully missing: a socio-political, economic, and ethical acknowledgment of the existence of Latina/os in the United States and of their vital contributions to U.S. economy and society. In this regard, the film's tactics resonate with Gordon's analysis of the function of spectrality and ghosts in her study *Ghostly Matters*. She writes at the beginning of chapter 3 of her book on the *desaparecidos,* those who disappeared "under the auspices of state-sponsored terror in Argentina" (63):

> I have also emphasized that the ghost is primarily a symptom of what is missing
> . . . Finally, I have suggested that the ghost is alive, so to speak. We are in rela-
> tion to it and it has designs on us such that we must reckon with it graciously,
> attempting to offer it a hospitable memory *out of a concern for justice.* (63–64)

The disappearance of Latina/os in this film aims to compel the recognition, the ethical acknowledgment, of their crucial existence. That it should have to mimic state-sponsored terrorism to do so signals the depth of the socio-political disconnection in the United States at the beginning of the twenty-first century.

The 2004 film *A Day Without a Mexican* exposes the dependence of the United States on Latina/o labor. While it does not seem to do so centrally through the trope of night, it does through a related one: an obscuring veil of fog. It also does so through the idea of the inversion of the ordinary daytime order of things—hence, a day without a Mexican. Though at first glance, night does not seem like the main trope, many of the film's newscasts take place at night. These newscasts document Immigration and Naturalization Service (INS) *migra* raids on people crossing the border at night, house fires occasioned by votive candles burning unattended, nighttime candlelight vigils for the disappeared Latina/os, an improvised tribal nocturnal slam-dance for the disappeared, the waxing of the full moon, and the rotting of unpicked fruit in the warm California night. In the wake of the disappearance, the film portrays the growth of conspiracy theories that associate undocumented workers with aliens from outer space, reinforcing the association of Mexicans with the enigmas of the night sky. In its own way, *A Day Without a Mexican* deploys the trope of night and some of its related associations, including fog, a common element of horror and noir films. This film deploys these tropes in a mock-epic way, parodying contemporary TV shows trading in the scary and the strange, such as *The X-Files*.

For all its ironic levity, the film does pose a serious philosophical question through the lips of its one surviving supposed Latina, anchorwoman Lila Rodriguez, who turns out to be Armenian, Eastern European, by birth and not Mexican. Yet her biological heritage matters to her less than her cultural heritage and ethnic identification growing up. She was raised Mexican; she has suffered the discrimination and tokenism experienced by U.S.-based Mexicans. After finding out that she is Armenian by "blood," she counters: "Love is thicker than blood. My heart is Mexican." In a nighttime newscast seen as if on a black-and-white TV, she asks: "How do you make the invisible visible? You take it away. And I think that is why they left. So, tonight, at—what time is it?—at 7:09 PM I am going to cross into the fog hoping that, on the other side, there is an answer. I am doing this of my own free will, totally conscious of the risk involved." Then this Lila Rodriguez, at great risk to herself since INS border patrol agents have shown up pointing guns at her, proceeds to try to scale the wall between the United States and Mexico, a wall "twelve feet high" made of "recycled Gulf War landing plates." The scene is both nerve-racking and ridiculous, as is much real-time TV, but the purpose of this film's massive disappearing act has been succinctly articulated nonetheless: How do you make the invisible visible? You take it away.

Introduction to Night and Shadows in Chicana/o Cultural Production

This double negative space that involves making visible the invisible through a vanishing trick worthy of a thousand David Copperfields opens onto the heart of this chapter's subject matter, Dreaded Non-Identities of Night: Night and Shadows in Chicana/o Cultural Production. Chicana/o cultural production is replete with images of night, shadows, masks, and veils, all discernible signs of the invisible and that which both eludes and has been denied ready identity and identification. As Chicana/o cultural production is a hybrid mixture of the

production of many other cultures—Mexican, Native, Spanish, and Anglo—
it contains within it traces of the histories of these motifs in those cultures,
traces transmuted by the concerns of Chicana/o history and culture. Masks, for
instance, have long been considered a salient part of Mexican culture. Octavio
Paz famously insisted that masks and labyrinths constitute an essential part of
Mexican identity. Such arguments that seek to explain a "core" aspect of any
given culture are essentializing in the ways that they reify culture through the
assumption of certain ahistoricized patterns. They do not do justice to the plasticity of culture as a matrix of shifting identities and identifications over time.
Thus, I would point out that transhistorical, transcultural elements such as
night, shadows, masks, and veils carry a particular historical and cultural charge
at a particular time in the history of any given culture, where culture is understood not as a closed circuit but as permeated by other cultures.

The use of images of and references to shadow and night has a long trajec-
tory in Mexican poetics reaching back to colonial times. Some of its extensive
historical roots are the poetry of Spanish mystics and heretics, such as St. John
of the Cross (1542–1591) with his treatise on "The Dark Night of the Soul" and
his famous poem "En una noche oscura" or "During a Dark Night." The predominance of night and shadows might be attributable, in part, to the confluence of
Spanish baroque aesthetics; Mesoamerican, especially Aztec, mythologies with
their goddesses and gods of the night and darkness; and the experience of class-
caste stratification in colonial and neocolonial Mexican society.[5] Chicana/os,
politicized Mexican Americans, have inherited confluences of Spanish and
Mesoamerican cultures. Or, if they have not inherited these cultures, they have,
as in the case of cultural producers, such as Ana Castillo (see the "Introduction"
to her Massacre of the Dreamers, 7–9), actively worked on acquiring, through
research and study, knowledge of the complex strands of culture that fall under
the rubric "Indo-Hispanic." Scholars debate whether the term "Chicana/o"
should be applied to cultural production prior to the emergence of Chicana/o
pride and the Chicana/o civil rights movement in the 1950s. However one
chooses to apply the designation, one thing is certain. Shadows and night have
been as pivotal to Mexican articulations of identity as masks have been. In fact,
it is not especially difficult to find all three elements—shadows, night, and
partly invisible social identities—occurring together, as in the nocturnal poetry
of the homosexual Mexican poet Xavier Villaurrutia (1903–1950).[6] Mexican
articulations of shadow and night received new life and historical granularity
with the emergence of a Chicana/o consciousness—a double consciousness
of in-between-ness, of not being either fully Mexican or fully American to the
extent that "American" was and still is arrogated by Anglos to themselves.

From the late sixteenth century into the seventeenth century, "the dark night of the soul" that was featured in the meditative practices and writings of the sixteenth-century Spanish mystics St. John of the Cross and Santa Teresa de Ávila crystallized, focused, and projected a thick plaited filament of Catholic Reformationist Baroque sensibility. Though not always orthodox by any means, this sensibility represented a threat to the authority and control of the Catholic Church. The sensibility involved, among other contradictory characteristics, a critical involution away from the worldly entanglements of empire, religious and secular—including the institution of the Catholic Church and the exploration, genocide, conquest, and colonization of the New World and other areas of the globe. It was a sensibility that sometimes clashed with the conformist authority of the Inquisition on account of its heretical mysticism, which was sometimes akin to the dissenting night rhetoric of witchcraft.[7] If this trope of "the dark night of the soul" begins to show up in U.S. Latina/o writing of the post-war and contemporary period, this is not because Latina/os have a culturally over-determined connection on account of some vague *Hispanidad* shared with the Spanish mystics of the sixteenth century. Rather, it would seem that a more conscious historical and cultural recovery project is under way among Latina/o cultural workers. A trope of Catholic Reformationist Baroque sensibility gets re-coded as part of a contemporary critique of colonization, neocolonialism, and a discourse of civil and human rights confined within a hyper-capitalist mode that systematically exploits certain segments of the population for the benefit of other segments. The uses of night in Chicana/o cultural production are not limited to this particular manifestation of a historical cultural recovery project. On the contrary, the notable role played by night and shadows has its sources in numerous cultures, including various Mesoamerican ones that feed into Mexican American and Chicana/o cultural production. Furthermore, instances of the uses of night resonate with specific historical moments or movements.

Américo Paredes and Gloria Anzaldúa: Collectors and Practitioners of Night

Consciously contributing to Chicana/o civil rights and a cultural self-awareness movement, Américo Paredes and Gloria Anzaldúa were both collectors and practitioners of the uses of night and related tropes of darkness in Mexican American and, specifically, Chicana/o cultures. As ethnographers and creative writers, they gathered and distilled the political, socioeconomic, and cultural alienation of U.S.-based Mexicans in their writings. The alienation of Mexicans in the United States is documented and illustrated in Anzaldúa's well-known collection of essays and poems *Borderlands/La Frontera: The New Mestiza* (1987) and in Chicano scholar and writer Américo Paredes's vast academic output on the folklore of "Greater Mexico" as well as in his fiction, such as the collection of short stories titled *The Hammon and the Beans and Other Stories* (1994), and in his novels *George Washington Gómez: A Mexicotexan Novel* (1990) and *The Shadow* (1998).[8] These fictional pieces simultaneously reference night, shadows, illness, wounds, and borders/barriers. The image of the border as *una herida abierta,* an open wound, has been discussed and analyzed in both Anzaldúa's and Paredes's texts. Other concepts, such as night and shadows, have not received much critical attention though they feature throughout Anzaldúa's and Paredes's work. Perhaps they have been overlooked as being part of the "atmosphere" of a piece and not crucial to its ideological methodology. Critics have spent some concerted effort on the importance of the Jungian notions of the Shadow and the collective unconscious for understanding many of Anzaldúa's writings. However, night and shadows have thus far received sparse attention, a fact that becomes more significant when one considers that both Paredes's and Anzaldúa's texts function as repositories of tropes and figures especially potent in Chicana/o culture and as repositories of a Chicana/o image repertoire. Anzaldúa and Paredes are not the first Chicana/os to have made night and shadows such a central part of their projects combining aesthetics, philosophy, and socio-cultural politics. However, I focus closely on these two creative writers and scholars because of their respective monumental contributions to the preservation and dissemination of the cultural forms of and realizations about the relationship between power and knowledge in the U.S.–Mexico borderlands and their memorably concentrated and extensive arrangements of night.

José David Saldívar observes that Paredes, a scholar of ethnic studies who fundamentally re-oriented "American" cultural studies, was "by far one of the most commanding figures in proto-Chicano/a studies . . . crossing the border-patrolled boundaries between discourses and cultures alike."[9] At the beginning of the chapter "Américo Paredes and Decolonization" from *Border Matters* (1997), Saldívar sums up Paredes's contribution to Mexican American and proto-Chicano/a culture thus:

> No contemporary figures of the proto-Chicano/a movement generation have so extensive an oeuvre to their credit. In a working career of over forty years, Paredes has pursued his intellectual, creative, and critical concerns across a range that includes almost every majority and minority cultural form: ethnographies of the people of "Greater Mexico," literary criticism, analysis of *décimas* and

corridos, collections of folktales, semantic inquiry, poetry, film scripts, the short story, and the novel. (37)

Clearly, this section of my chapter "Dreaded Non-Identities of Night: Night and Shadows in Chicana/o Cultural Production" cannot do justice to the range and variety of Paredes's work. Thus, I have selected examples of two of the genres that José David Saldívar mentions—the short story and two novels. I provide a concrete, but condensed analysis of each example with regard to the deployment of tropes of night, including shadows to the extent that shadows take on the larger-than-life immensity of night. I encourage scholars and general readers to use these three abbreviated but nevertheless detailed analyses as guides to further research on the uses of night in Paredes's voluminous work.

The short story "The Hammon and the Beans" (written around 1939, set in the 1920s, and published in a collection by the same name in 1994) and the novel *George Washington Gómez: A Mexicotexan Novel* (1990) starkly associate night and shadows with a kind of psycho-socio-somatic illness, *susto,* and feelings of guilty complicity with the ongoing U.S. occupation and dominance of formerly Mexican territory that was appropriated in the Mexican-American War. The short story concerns life for Mexican Americans at the militarized little city of Jonesville-on-the-Grande, a fictionalized Brownsville, Texas— once a Mexican town and subsequently, after the Mexican-American War and the coming of the railroad in the early twentieth century, an Anglo-dominant one. The story focuses on one family and, in particular, on a young girl named Chonita whom the soldiers from the U.S. fort tease when she shows up hungry at their mess hall, looking for something to eat. Chonita dies of an unnamed illness, which may be "[p]neumonia, flu, malnutrition, worms, the evil eye."[10] The incidents of the story are told from the point of view of a young Mexican American boy of a slightly higher class than the poor, working-class Chonita. He contemplates Chonita's marginalization as a poor Mexican child and then as a dead one. Lying in the dark, recovering from a fever or illness himself, he experiences these sensations and thoughts:

> I lay there for a long time while behind my darkened eyelids Emiliano Zapata's cavalry charged down to the broad Santee, where there were grave men with hoary hairs. I was still awake at eleven when the cold voice of the bugle went gliding in and out of the dark like something that couldn't find its way back to wherever it had been. I thought of Chonita in heaven, and I saw her in her torn and dirty dress, with a pair of bright wings attached, flying round and round like a butterfly shouting, "Give me the hammon and the beans!" (253)

Ramón Saldívar points out that the boy "begins to confuse and transpose the heroes of the American Revolution (Marion the Fox) and those of the Mexican Revolution (Villa, Zapata)" (*The Borderlands of Culture*, 297). The boy's ability to understand his own condition as a subject of internal colonization has been compromised by confusion and transposition that index the socio-political and cultural alienation from which he suffers along with Chonita. Night and darkness are closely associated with illness (of body and mind), grief, and displacement—"something that couldn't find its way back to wherever it had been" (253). Night and darkness underscore the young Mexican American boy's sense of futility and even complicity in not being able to rescue Chonita. He has insomnia, often a symptom of an uneasy conscience or malaise more generally. Though he cries and feels better, the cathartic last line of the short story—"But cry I did, and I felt much better after that" (253)—has a hollow, deadpan ring to it. About the story's ending, Ramón Saldívar observes the deliberate way in which Paredes is reworking the beginning of Mark Twain's *Adventures of Huckleberry Finn*, where Huck Finn "feels the mournful loneliness of subjectivity" (298). I would add to Ramón Saldívar's elaboration of this comparison that, like Twain, Paredes was showing the twisted workings of colonial domination and ideology upon impressionable minds. Huck Finn feels bad about not betraying his friend Jim, an African American runaway slave, to the slave hunters, and the young Mexican American boy of Paredes's story feels "better" after he cries for Chonita when in fact he ought to feel worse because Chonita is irremediably dead.

Night and shadows lend form to a force field of negative affect that results from being "the occupied," to quote the title of Rodolfo Acuña's *Occupied America: A History of Chicanos*, published multiple times since the early 1970s. Night is also when the young boy becomes aware, however confusingly, of his grief at the unjust and disappointing status of most Mexicans living in U.S. territory after the Mexican-American War. The reference to a vision of Emiliano Zapata's cavalry behind the narrator's darkened eyelids underscores how far from the heroic ideals of the Mexican Revolution—redistribution of land and wealth that would redress the socioeconomic privations of the peasant class—the 1920s were for Mexican Americans in south Texas.

The 1930s, when jobs were scarce during the Great Depression and Mexican Americans had to compete with Anglos, were not better than the 1920s, as is amply shown in *George Washington Gómez*, the novel Paredes started in 1936, finished in 1940, and published fifty years later in 1990. Rolando Hinojosa, Chicano writer and professor of creative writing, describes this novel thus: "a first draft of a work set against the Great Depression, the onset of World War II in Europe, and set also against the over 100-year-old conflict of cultures in the Lower Rio Grande Valley of Texas, not far from where the Rio Grande empties into the Gulf."[11] The novel, a historical fiction, follows a Mexicotexan family in the south Texas Rio Grande Valley and the life of a young boy named Guálinto/George Washington Gómez. The novel details through *corrido*-like tragic episodes the kinds of pressures his community, his family, and he encounter as Mexican Americans trying to preserve their "property, culture, and identity in the face of Anglo-American migration to and growing dominance over the Rio Grande Valley" (back book cover). The result is a detailed depiction of the conflictual socioeconomic and ethno-racial stratifications of south Texas, which have implications way beyond a specific region. An omniscient narrator editorializes, ". . . a Border Mexican knew there was no brotherhood of men,"[12] and "It was the lot of the Mexicotexan that the Anglosaxon should use him as a tool for the Mexican's undoing" (42). Cultural conflict in the Lower Rio Grande border zone is, as José David Saldívar points out, quoting Paredes himself (from *Folklore and Culture on the Texas-Mexican Border*), "many-layered" (*Border Matters*, 41).

In the visceral representation of this treacherously hierarchical and humiliating state of affairs, and as part of an effort to transmit some of the recurring images of Mexican and Mexican American "structures of feeling," to borrow Raymond Williams's phrase, Paredes carefully creates some significant moments of night and shadows. Shadows are a tangible sign of guilt, of an unhappy double consciousness, or a self torn apart by a minefield of allegiances and betrayals of a border zone such as Texas, especially south Texas. Shadows function as ghosts (91) in a material economy of exploitation of the poor by the wealthier and a psychic economy of guilt and resentment for participating in one's own oppression and the oppression of one's people. The key representation of night appears in part II, chapter 4, through the eyes of young Guálinto Gómez. He has been fed stories about coyotes and wolf men howling at the full moon as well as about the Mexican and Mexican American folktale figure of *La Llorona*, the Weeping Woman, who, near any body of water, cries nightly and searches for children she herself drowned to spare them from a life of poverty.[13] Night in the "vast jungle of banana trees choking" (50) the backyard of Guálinto's boyhood home is a time of terrors and fears pooled from actual incidences of violence in the "Golden Delta of the Rio Grande" (52):

> But night changed the world. With darkness the banana grove and the trees beyond it became a haunted wood where lurked demons, skeletons and white-robed women with long long hair. The city's stormy politics had thrown up a vomit of murders and gun battles. . . . Here, there, everywhere were memories

of the unhallowed dead. They haunted the night. They made the darkness terrible. (50)

In all of Paredes's work, night appears as a time of uneasiness and dread, a time of hauntings and unsettling premonitions that refuse to fade in the assimilationist light of the American dream. Night is a time of hallucinatory reckoning with a history of oppression, injustice, and guilt-ridden complicity in a system of segregation, discrimination, and exploitation. This is especially true for Guálinto, who, as José David Saldívar describes, "acculturates through stages" (*Border Matters*, 44) and, I would add, assimilates to the degree possible for a Mexican American in the 1940s. Saldívar's description of this process (whether termed "acculturation" or "assimilation") follows:

> [A]t the novel's end Paredes's protagonist graduates from high school; attends the University of Texas; marries a white ethnographer, Ellen Dell (whose father was once a Ranger); legally changes his name to George G. Gómez; and becomes a "spy" for the U.S. Army during World War II. Claiming that he is a lawyer for a multinational plant that is expanding in the global borderlands, he returns to South Texas as a first lieutenant in counterintelligence whose new job is "border security." (44)

But however much Guálinto, or rather "George," acculturates or assimilates, he has, as José David Saldívar points out, recurring dreams of defeating the army of the United States with his own "well-trained army that included Irishmen and escaped American Negro slaves" (282). This dream echoes that of the 1915 revolutionary manifesto "Plan de San Diego" of Mexican Americans in south Texas endeavoring to create a Spanish-speaking Republic of the Southwest. As Ramón Saldívar explains, "That manifesto called for a union of Texas Mexicans with American Indians, African Americans, and Asian Americans to fight social and political injustice" (152). Out of the darkness behind closed eyes, Guálinto's boyhood fantasies of being a Mexican hero against successive encroachments of the United States reshape themselves and will not let him be. The shadow of his former self springs from his nocturnal dreams and pursues him, a dark Mexican alter ego of the "yellow hair" and "gold coins" (282) assimilationist he has become, who wants to get "the Mexican out of himself" (283).

Night and shadows also shape Paredes's novel *The Shadow*, first written in the 1950s and revised and published in 1998. In this novel, set in post-revolutionary Mexico, the shadow materializes the susto (or haunting fright) that mestizo Antonio Cuitla, a once-fierce revolutionary who helped to overthrow Mexico's ruling elite, feels on account of his compromised status as overseer of the Indian peasants and of the Afro Mexican man Del Toro, in whose murder he participates indirectly. The shadow is Cuitla's guilt, a volatile reminder of the Afro Mexican he rubbed out for presenting a challenge to Cuitla's authority and his sense of identity. The shadow is also the part of himself that Cuitla fears and will not accept; it is whatever does not square with his desired identification with the Euro-Mexican and the rationality he has been taught to associate with the European in contrast to what he views as the superstitions of the Indians and the Africans.

Shadows multiply in *The Shadow.* Though the very opening line of the novel begins in the "glaring quietness" of "noon"[14] with Cuitla's fear of "a shadow on the road, in the middle of the day" (11), by the second chapter the shadow has morphed into a "black shapeless mass" (12) inside Cuitla's eyes or head, an anti-figural figuration that signals the degree to which he is psychologically troubled and self-divided, fighting his own darkness, which he fears as much as that of Del Toro or of the supposed irrationality of the peasants he oversees, whom he considers animals and savages. After the murder of his former revolutionary companion Del Toro and beginning with the funeral vigil for Del Toro (70), the shadow as black shapeless mass merges with night. Halfway through the book, day turns into night, and much of the action takes place at night. The predominance of night conveys the darkening of Cuitla's consciousness with unresolved guilt and fear over his participation in Del Toro's murder and Cuitla's inability to own up in any real sense to his own kinship with what he associates with darkness—that is, with the native, the African, and with forces beyond his limited control: "He was lost, frightened and trembling in the dark . . . And into the darkness came his name, looking for him, and when his name found him he heard it . . ." (76).

This novel presages Anzaldúa's use of the shadow and darkness to signal ethno-racial coordinates and also introduces a historically based conflict precipitating an existential crisis. Paredes's novel does not lengthen the shadow to include gender and sexuality in the way that Anzaldúa's essays and poetry do, however. Or if it does include gender and sexuality, then the main concern is with the relation of masculinity to power and the fear that Cuitla has of being unmanned by the ghost of Del Toro, whose superior strength he feared in life. The narrative reiterates familiar lines of association in Western culture of the black man with prowess and telluric strength unmatched by the slaveholders or overseers, who are cast, by this logic, as more effete.

Overall, night in Paredes's work functions not only as a chronological temporality but also as a state of mind and, furthermore, as a condition with its own uncanny agency. Both night and shadows behave almost as characters, with agency of their own. Herein lies one of the salient similarities between Paredes's versions of night and shadows and Anzaldúa's. Night is a living condition. It has ontological as well as epistemological dimensions. To experience night and shadows is to come face-to-face with a dreaded non-identity, a space-time where the basic moorings of one's identity (defined in relation to what one has been taught to believe and/or what one has convinced oneself about oneself and others) have become unmoored, when the scripts of the daytime existence have been suspended. This living condition can be liberatory or can be the precondition for some kind of emancipation, but it is not without fear and dread—a vertiginous sense of not being where and what one thought one was. That shadows are deployed in the novel along with descriptions of night emphasizes the fact that these nighttimes are part and parcel of an imagined relation to a social and existential self.

Both Paredes's and Anzaldúa's writings are populated with this combination of night and shadows. In 1997, art historian Victor I. Stoichita published *A Short History of the Shadow*. He claimed that the birth of painting coincided with "the first time the human shadow was circumscribed by lines" and that "it is of unquestionable significance that the birth of Western artistic representation was 'in the negative.'"[15] When painting first emerged, it was part of the absence/presence theme (absence of the body; presence of its projection). Painting may have begun with this limned shadow, with this absent presence. Some scholars have argued that photography began this way, too, if one recalls the experimental attempts of William Henry Fox Talbot to "secure the shadow" of people and objects.[16] Whatever the case, it would seem that those people designated as non-Western or questionably Western have most thoroughly understood the relation of aesthetics, ontology, and epistemology in terms of shadows. Such an understanding has derived from cultural and political marginalization.

One of the chief differences between Paredes's and Anzaldúa's representations of night and shadows is that Anzaldúa delved into depth psychology explorations of the Shadow, with a capital "S," and of night as a space-time for vital confrontations with that Shadow. Being "torn between ways" on the border spells pain, disorientation, and dread in both Paredes's and Anzaldúa's texts. However, Anzaldúa's writing puts itself in a different relation to the border zone experience of being "torn between ways" as a Mexican American and a Chicana, among other identities. Anzaldúa's project labors to transvalue what is a negatively described condition in Paredes's works for the purpose of creating a new consciousness, *la conciencia de la mestiza*.

"Darkness, my night": The Philosophical Challenge
of Gloria Anzaldúa's Aesthetics of the Shadow[17]

Let us take a closer look at the representation of "the negative" and the dialectic of absence/presence and projection through absence in the aesthetics and politics of Anzaldúa's "*nepantilism*," an Aztec term meaning "torn between ways." This nepantilism involves a tactical embrace of insecurity, uncertainty, and the indeterminate (or what I call a dreaded non-identity of the night) in the essays and poems of *Borderlands/La Frontera* (1987). Anzaldúa's concept of nepantilism combines a topography of displacement with the lived experience of colonization, persecution, subordination, self-imposed limitations or internalized colonization, and past and present resistance in the Americas and in the Mexico-Texan borderlands (*Borderlands*, 43).[18] I would like to take a closer look at nepantilism in terms of the Shadow and darkness, for together these elements compose the difficult *conocimiento* which Anzaldúa writes of and describes in stages in a piece titled "now let us shift . . . the path of conocimiento . . . inner work, public acts" published more than a decade after the 1987 collection.

To explain the consciousness of resistance, *Borderlands/La Frontera* (1987) calls on theories about the collective unconscious of the Swiss psychiatrist and philosopher Carl Jung (1875–1961). Jung is widely discussed by depth psychologists, among them James Hillman, with whose archetypal psychology Anzaldúa was familiar.[19] To describe a consciousness that subverts or does not countenance the subject/object and mind/body dualities of so-called Western culture and its frightened rationalism, she invokes Jung's concept of the Shadow self (*Borderlands*, 59). The Shadow self comprises the unacceptable aspects of ourselves, the unsocialized, supposedly animal-divine ones that rebel against man-made rules and categories. According to Anzaldúa via Jung, this Shadow self is connected to the unrepressed drives and instincts. It thinks and feels through the body and the sensual world as much as through the intellect. As Shadow self is a shadowy concept, she concretizes it with images drawn from Jung's and her own understandings of Mesoamerican lore: snakes, serpents, the dark earth, the *Llorona* wailing for her lost children in the night, night dreams, sexuality and latent sexual forces, the glossy black surface of obsidian mirrors, the darkness of night, and the association of night and darkness with the maternal, as in the womb of night, mother night.

Anzaldúa focuses on "this first darkness" (*Borderlands*, 71) as she substitutes it for what she implies has become a Western and ethnocentric (as in "white") equivalence of light with goodness and dark with evil. She elaborates her associational constellation: "Shadow," "shadow," the "shadow-beast," "dark," "*diosa de la noche,*" and "creature of darkness." The insistence on Shadow/shadow and "darkness, my night" out of which the new mestiza is born functions to tinge nepantilism's tactical embrace of insecurity, uncertainty, and the indeterminate with color. This color, while containing within it the traces of certain ethno-racial coordinates (as in "darkskinned people," Anzaldúa's phrase in *Border-lands*, 71), is not confined to them or to bodily phenotype. Anzaldúa honors "darkskinned people" (71) and yet moves beyond physical traits in her journey to transform the mind, the imagination, the spirit, and, with them, social reality. All people may opt to be included in darkness rather than stake an investment in whiteness and light, the hegemonically valued side of the dark/light binary.

Darkness of many sorts becomes the standard we are invited to transvalue positively. This transvaluation entails the hard work of transforming conscious-ness and action by embracing the terms of abjection—hence the emphasis on the negative, the unacceptable, that which oppressive structures (imposed and internalized) have taught us not to accept. "Darkness, my night" encompasses numerous other factors besides ethno-racial ones. Some of those factors per-tain to gender ("maternal" night) and sexuality. Anzaldúa mentions "*loquería*" (*Borderlands*, 41). This term connotes not only craziness or madness but also an altered consciousness in a dialectical relationship with libidinal choices besides heteronormative ones. The term "queer" covers not only the homosexual but also the absurd, crazy, atypical, deviant, exceptional, extraordinary, preternatu-ral, strange, and uncanny.

The qualities of absence and negativity accompanying and attributed to "darkness, my night" are the parts of nepantilism that are not colored in an ethno-racial manner and that are not socially categorizable even as the breaking of conventional categories. These qualities are more philosophically ontologi-cal or existential than specifically phenotypic and social. Thus, "darkness, my night" connotes a gamut of conditions, from the ethno-racial to the marginal to the existentially alienated—in fact, from the recognizably identitarian (as in darkskinned people or people of color) to the seemingly anti-identitarian, those states of dreaded non-identity. By states of dreaded non-identity I mean situations and states of mind or feeling where known languages and codes fail to adequately convey the experience one is having, where conceptual and linguis-tic categories are revealed to be insufficient. Anzaldúa, in the tradition of many mystics, saw, in such often-terrifying states, a potential for the actual re-making of consciousness and for growth toward social change.

Anzaldúa's deployments of the shadow and of night are capacious and even contradictory. These aspects lie at the crux of Anzaldúa's nepantilism. Shadow and night are well suited in their particularities and in their generalities to signify both visibility (darkskinned people) and invisibility (an absorption into the night of people, identity markers, and territorial boundaries). *Borderlands/La Frontera* deploys shadow and night to argue for particularity (the particular struggle of politicized Chicanas, for instance) and universalism at the same time. This double movement plays the particular against the universal to spotlight difference and the hierarchical power dynamics of societies in which darkskinned people are subordinated and considered lesser in every way. And yet, at the same time, her work universalizes the particular. She turns shadow and night into the touchstones of sensibility, ethics, and a coalitional politics of the marginalized and the oppressed. Anzaldúa's shadow darkness presents a decolonizing challenge to some of the most fundamental assumptions within the binaries "dark/light" and "absence/presence" in dominant Western epistemology. I say "dominant" because Western epistemology does have its heretics. The shadow darkness is decolonizing in the way that it frees darkness from the reservation of shame to which it has been confined and brings forth a way for us to identify with what has been historically devalued and persecuted.

Anzaldúa borrows Jung's concept of the Shadow with a capital "S" to address the unacceptable and/or unsocialized aspects of ourselves. In doing so, she grants the Shadow more than ground. She converts it into a space of (in)habitation, a place where we are invited to dwell. The Shadow, while signaling some aspect of the corporealized or embodied personality, refers not merely to an alter ego but to another world—*un otro mundo,* something akin to the *inframundo.* This formless form entails the fearful and fearlessly passionate act of living at the crossroads, on the border. It means confronting our fears, our insecurities, our defensiveness, and our vulnerabilities. It also means recognizing in ourselves and the Other what exceeds social categories and ingrained ways of thinking, feeling, and acting, particularly when what exceeds has been negatively valued or stigmatized. It entails a terrifying openness to possibility and the willingness to act on possibility against the socioeconomic, historical, and psychological odds, most of which spell injustice and harm to the many for the sake of the few who manage to acquire privilege and security in their social system.

The Dark Night of the Body-Mind-Spirit

Anzaldúa's concepts of *nepantla* and *la facultad* lend themselves to an understanding of her work in relation to a recuperation of melancholia for the cause of self-transformation and political change. This recuperation needs to be understood in the context of the rise of mental depression worldwide over the last decade and a concurrent interest in the humanities, social sciences, and medical sciences in studying "depression." Art historian and cultural studies scholar Christine Ross observes, "[a]ccording to the National Institute of Mental Health, major depression is the leading cause of disability worldwide."[20] She adds that "melancholia is the main notional ancestor of depression" and that "the melancholy tradition" is "a disappearing aesthetic strategy in an era when melancholia has been absorbed by the category of depression" (xxvii). Ross's study makes a strong case for refusing this "foundational debasement of the melancholy attachment to loss" (200). The book validates much of contemporary art for being "still attached to the creativity traditionally associated with melancholic insight" (200).

Anzaldúa's work can be understood in terms of melancholic insight related to "deep depression" (a phrase she uses in "now let us shift")[21] or melancholia not containable by a clinical definition. Nepantla—which Anzaldúa defined in "now let us shift" as the difficult "overlapping space between different perceptions and belief systems" (541)—involves being torn from security, comfort, and complacency. It implies a willingness to confront darkness and declare oneself its creature. Confronting darkness means confronting loss and, moreover, the possibility of profound loss. Christine Ross notes that depression results not only from loss but from anticipated loss: "the depressed numbs himself in relation to an anticipated loss" (3). That numbing expresses itself in art as an aesthetics of disengagement—for instance, in contemporary performance art, standing or sitting impassively and not looking at spectators. Anzaldúa's work manifests an aesthetics of engagement rather than detachment or disengagement. Her melancholia or constellation of Shadow, darkness, shadows, and night does not proceed from or result in numbing. Instead, she calls for and embodies "excruciating aliveness." Her "black sun of melancholy" (to borrow French Romantic and occultist Gérard de Nerval's image) shines full of passionate intensity. Fiery warmth radiates from the dark night of the soul. Bulgarian-French linguist, semiotician, psychoanalyst, and literary critic Julia Kristeva characterizes Nerval and his black sun of melancholy as a poet who finds a way to overcome the wretchedness of being deprived of paradise (in Anzaldúa's case, one might read this as being deprived of a borderlands of justice and genuine harmony between all its peoples and cultures). Similarly, Anzaldúa finds a way, through her writing, her activism, and her writing as activism, to control "both aspects of deprivation—the darkness of disconsolation and the 'kiss of the queen'" or the kiss of that highly sought-after goddess, mother, mistress, lover, apotheosis of an ideal that has been betrayed by history:[22]

The "black sun" . . . again takes up the semantic field of "saturnine," but pulls it inside out, like a glove: darkness flashes as a solar light, which nevertheless remains dazzling with black invisibility. (147)

And so it is with Anzaldúa's "black sun of melancholy," but in the specific context of her massive project of creating a heroic, queer, Chicana identity in and of the expanding borderlands not only of south Texas but of the United States of America and of the Americas more generally.

Night and Shadows for Other Chicana/o Writers post Paredes and Anzaldúa

Anzaldúa and Paredes were not the first or only Chicana/os to make night and shadows a central part of their projects combining aesthetics, philosophy, and socio-cultural politics. Rather, their works, and especially Anzaldúa's texts, synthesize many of the strands of night that appear elsewhere in Chicana/o cultural production. *Borderlands/La Frontera* had such a big impact in this regard that traces of its distilling contribution (particularly to the exploration of night and darkness) can be found in many other works. For example, Ana Castillo, in her 1994 *Massacre of the Dreamers: Essays on Xicanisma,* sums up Anzaldúa's contribution thus:

> *Borderlands* requires close reading in order to appreciate its schema of ciphering and deciphering, its interweaving of a journey of self-understanding and the challenges of the writing process itself. "This book, then, speaks of my existence," Anzaldúa declares in her preface and for her readers, *Borderlands* is a blood curdling scream in the night.[23]

Significantly, the image with which Castillo chooses to encapsulate her evaluation of Anzaldúa's *Borderlands* is a scream in the night that affects one's very life blood. The force of Chicana/o uses of night seems to have converged in *Borderlands* and also streamed out of it in highly potent form for the purposes of later cultural workers. The distinct contribution of *Borderlands* to the deployment of night is its synthesis of tropes of night in a concentrating, versus diffusive, way. In Anzaldúa's work, night very intricately exhibits the intersections between non-normative libidinal choices and energy, unconscious forces, the socially and psychosocially marginalized and unrecognized, and both a historical and transhistorical sense of displacement. Ana Castillo understood the impact of Anzaldúa's formulations of night and herself supplied more representations of night along Anzaldúan lines. For example, her 1990 novel *Sapogonia* heavily emphasizes dreaming, nighttime as a time of altered consciousness, and women as avatars of Coatlicue. Coatlicue is the Aztec goddess who gave birth to the nocturnal bodies of the moon and the stars as well as the sun and war; she is associated with a skirt of writhing snakes, the womb of life, and the devouring earth of the grave.[24] *So Far from God* (1993), another novel, begins at "twelve midnight" with the howling of animals and the death of a young child.[25] It dwells on the entities and forces of the night, such as susto, *malogra,* and La Llorona. In Anzaldúan fashion, *So Far from God* transvalues La Llorona from a Lilith-like monster to a long-suffering heroine (160–161). The novel at various times references "moist dark earth" associated with Coatlicue (211). Castillo's 1996 collection of short stories entitled *Loverboys* sustains this exploration of night with its allusions to the Mexican *Noche Triste*[26] (of the slaughter between the Spaniards and the Aztecs in early July of 1520), to nightmares about home-less children and women murdered in cemeteries (103), and to the nocturnal coalitional rituals on St. John's Eve (June 23) between three women of color in Chicago's Grant Park (211). The novel *Peel My Love Like an Onion* (1999) begins with an apostrophe to Tezcatlipoca, an Aztec god of night and darkness, fol-lowed by the line "I remember him dark."[27] The narrator and main protagonist, flamenco dancer Carmen la Coja, confesses dramatically, "I had spent all my adult life living for the night" (4).

Aspects of Anzaldúa's carefully encompassing project can be found in earlier and other later Chicana/o writers. For example, John Rechy, in his novels *City of Night* (1963) and *The Coming of Night* (1999), explores non-heteronormative sexuality through shadows and night. As scholar and critic Juan Bruce-Novoa observes, "the protagonist [of *City of Night*] thrusts the dark world of Night into the light of Day, evoking values linked to the opposing imagery of each."[28] Rechy did so in 1963, twenty-four years before Anzaldúa's *Borderlands/La Frontera* was published. Night is not only ambiguous ethno-racial identity in *City of Night;* it is also queerness, the gay, male, generally anonymous sex trade in America's dark cities, full of both secrecy and disclosure.[29] Night is also the compendium of nights that compose the narrator's odyssey counterclockwise around the United States, from El Paso to New York, Chicago, the West Coast, New Orleans, and El Paso again. And night is what that compendium implies not only about the narrator's experience but, furthermore, about the collective experiences of the denizens of the United States. In this respect, *City of Night* can be read as an extensive cultural critique of the alienating commodification of human relations in a money-work system where "value" is measured in monetary and material terms, where market value dictates, and where everything is on the market:

Later I would think of America as one vast City of Night stretching gaudily from Times Square to Hollywood Boulevard ... America at night fusing its darkcities into the unmistakable shape of loneliness ... along the streets of America strung like a cheap necklace from 42nd Street to Market Street, San Francisco.[30]

The cheap necklace suggests that Americans live by a logic of replaceability and disposability, though the dominant, daytime culture does not care to openly admit it. Rechy uses the night and an underground, gay male subculture of the pre-Stonewall early 1960s to comment on and expose this logic by describing furtive, anonymous sex, often in exchange for money. This subculture forms a parallel economy to the main capitalist economy, though in sections of *City of Night* (1963), as in most of the later novel *The Coming of the Night* (1999), the relentless cruising and pickup scene within gay male subcultures presents a challenge of excess to the money-work system; cruising becomes an end unto itself, a profitless motive defying the profit motive.

In *The Coming of the Night,* shadows represent gay men waiting in parks for sexual encounters, and night is the time for cruising: "He would not come until deepest night, and then he would be the hottest. . . ."[31] The novel moves from morning to afternoon in ever-wilder encounters. Night represents the breaking down of all boundaries, the merging of the shadows that are the men waiting their turn at the orgy. The orgy culminates, however, in a specter of crucifixion, a harbinger of the plague as well as of apocalypse, as if the novel were crushing together the advent of AIDS in the mid to late 1980s and a fantasy of the Second Coming of an accepting Christ blessing this persecuted gay male world. Writing about Rechy's *City of Night* (1963), Bruce-Novoa observes:

> John Rechy's search has never been for an Augustinian City of God, but more in the line of that of his own patron saint, St. John, and in this case, "of the Cross," the Spanish medieval mystic and author of *The Dark Night of the Soul*—referenced in Rechy's text itself ... Rechy's discovery at the end of his pilgrimage is that of the mystic: if God is to appear it will be in his body here on earth. (23)

Taken as whole, I contend that John Rechy's oeuvre is a prime example of Chicana/o revisionist uses of Catholic Reformationist Baroque sensibility—of the dark night of the soul, and, with Rechy, of the body in relation to the soul and the revolt of this body-soul against the empty materialism of normative culture that does not offer sufficient sustenance.

What is missing from Rechy's formulation of night, as with so much Chicano writing from the 1940s through the mid 1980s, is a feminist consciousness.

Also lacking is a specific program to overturn the metaphysics of dark/light, evil/good mapped onto ethno-racial coordinates in Western philosophy and perception and perhaps even in cultures that might not be considered Western. Migration, colonization, diaspora, neocolonization, and globalization have made it difficult to say with any accuracy where cultures begin or end or what is Western and what is not, even if one can discern certain patterns.

Chicano poets such as Jimmy Santiago Baca and Juan Felipe Herrera, who wrote in the early to mid 1990s with an awareness of the massive contributions of Chicana feminists to the discourses on civil rights and feminism (or, more especially, womanism, including Third World womanism) of the 1980s, code shadows and night along more seemingly gynocentric lines. Night is the great womb of creative chaos. Night is what births the authors as poets. In Baca's poetry, one finds phrases such as "working in the dark,"[32] "burning ember floating in darkness," (11), "vision-illuminated darkness" (20), "search in the darkness for a light" (25), "while the rest of the world took photographs / in the day / I was taking photographs in the dark, / seeing the hidden, / capturing the soul in its darkness" (145), "while the eye looks on the page, the image slides past, there is peripheral cognition on another level, awareness of shadow, the image works in darkness not in light" (146), and "like a bulbflash in nighttime photography . . . caught in a flash of the spirit, groping in the darkness" (147). Night encircles him at all times, the walls of a limitless dark womb. Within this context, he sparks, a man who allies himself with British Romantic poets such as Wordsworth whom he read in jail and thus converts the vulnerability and receptivity culturally associated with the feminine into that of the sensitive male, counterbalancing his macho rage against the system that landed him in jail in the first place.

Juan Felipe Herrera's collection of poetry *Night Train to Tuxtla* (1994) comes closer to Anzaldúa's vision of shadows and night. Though as with Jimmy Santiago Baca, Herrera manifests a tendency to cling to the sparks, which in this case are imagined to fly up from a plunging train engine in the pitch-black night, the gendering, sexualization, and ethno-racializing of night harmonizes with Anzaldúa's aesthetics. For Herrera, night conjures the bisexual blues singer Janis Joplin (1943–1970) with "Roman candles stuck inside her left arm,"[33] a reference to her death from a heroin overdose; the "night-wire" (13) sounds of Carlos Santana's Afro Caribbean Mexican American guitar work; darkroom development of latent images on photographic negatives; memories of late-night reunions with his comrades in the Chicano civil rights movement (22–23); the supposedly "suicided" Chicano activist and criminal lawyer Oscar "Zeta" Acosta (author of *The Autobiography of a Brown Buffalo*, 1972), his decomposed body "blocked out in black" (30); the black torches of the hair of Indians at an Indio and Chicano meeting in Taos, New Mexico (36); rage, desire, and lonesome dreams (47); the terrible darkness of gunpoint cover-ups of the U.S. military's involvement with drugs, arms, and prostitution in Central America (51–54); the Indian rebels hidden in the midnight recesses of the Lacandón rain forest in Chiapas, Mexico (64); the "blue-black nightsticks" of the cops who beat Rodney King and turned him into the "Black Christ of Los Angeles" (79) with "the brown crown of thorns" (82); the absent presence of the souls on the Day of the Dead (131) and of La Llorona (132); and the Mexican migrant workers "inside train cars" remindful of those boxcars of the Holocaust (140). Finally, the night is all these concatenated fragments forming *The Night Train to Tuxtla*, reminding readers that, as Anzaldúa would put it, the Americas and the border zone compose one big, dark, gaping wound and that a sense of night is wedded, inextricably, to loss and the call to address that loss. Juan Felipe Herrera's poetry harmonizes with the philosophical challenge of Anzaldúa's aesthetics of the shadow and night, with the notable exception of his version of the civil rights movement among Chicanos. In Herrera's work, this movement is entirely androcentric and is not particularly queer, save for a few scattered references to "drag" (39) and to performers who might be construed as queer.

Closely associated with Jimmy Santiago Baca's and Juan Felipe Herrera's sensibilities—yet also traversing the path of Anzaldúa's radical confrontation with night and darkness as a space-time of soul-challenging sorrow and dread or a big, dark, gaping wound—is Andrés Montoya's 1999 collection of poems titled *the iceworker sings and other poems*. A poem marked by the year 1981 begins: "the night always scared you / ever since they shot efraín in the face / leaving him to bleed to death on the long dirt road."[34] The poems repeatedly refer to night and the graveyard shift, both as an assigned time of physical labor and as a time of spiritual travail, to lament the exploitation and murder of Chicana/o, Mexican, and Indian working-class people in and around Fresno, California: "I'm just chicano, an Indian / who sees life swallowed up in a dream [more like a nightmare] and wants to explode" (44). Night is represented as the time of "sad anger / hanging around like the dark clouds / of madness . . ." (48). The word "madness" indicates more than anger; it signifies "despair" (62). "Fresno night" is the last poem of the collection. Here another aspect of the night beckons to the Baroque "dark night of the soul" in a manner reminiscent of jazz, funeral blues, and gospel: "a jazz trumpet finds the lips of someone unsuspecting and the stars / find huge caves / of light to hide in" (78). The poet associates the call of the jazz trumpet—night being the quintessential time of jazz—with a glimmering drop of hope proceeding from the blood of Christ. This is contrasted with the night that, earlier in the collection of poems, was referred to as "the dying city of progress" (62): "let your [Christ's] blood bathe me and not night's nasty / glare . . ." (78). The spark of hope in the dark night of the soul is, in this case, a specifically Christian one. The jazz trumpet also resonates with the image of the trumpets or trombones of the Last Judgment and the Resurrection promised by the Risen Christ. To this extent, Andrés Montoya's *the iceworker sings and other poems* stands out on its own for identifying hope with one particular person, figure, and concept, that of Christianity's crucified God in human form: "i [*sic*] am determined to know nothing / but Christ and him crucified" (79). The poems never once mention any other gods or goddesses, though they do invoke Mexican historical heroes (heroes especially for *indígenas*), such as "zapata or cuauhtemoc" (55) and Aztlán, more than once in a kind of Chicano (emphasis on the "o") civil rights warrior cry: "and where, raza, are our heroes? / the heroes of aztlán?" (15). Nevertheless, despite their declaration of allegiance to Christ and a Christian cosmology, they do speak a language of night and darkness remindful of Anzaldúa's passionate, intimate relation with night, darkness, shadows, and deep depression. The emphasis in Montoya's poetry on the crucified Christ rather than the risen one is telling; it brings his project much closer to the Anzaldúan exploration of the border as an ever-open, deep, dark *herida*, or wound.

Like Anzaldúa, Montoya speaks a language of darkness, a language similar to that of yet another Chicano poet, Ray Gonzalez, with his "new, black language" in *Turtle Pictures* (2000).[35] With this "new, black language" derived from a metaphoric jalapeño, a rather Anzaldúan alchemical appeal to the spiritual effects of the fruits of the earth, "[t]he passion of speech becomes the stem at the end of the bite when the black fire is the orange moment in the heart and stomach . . ." (69). With this "new, black language" (which I posit is not so new, for there is a long, multi-stranded tradition of it), Gonzalez speaks of the night when "Cortez burned Mexico City" (3), following his shadow (24), a "black beaded rosary" (29), black butterflies and black widow spiders (41), the brown "Virgen de Guadalupe" (47), "howling coyotes" in the night (47), black lakes of water (80), "the black figure of the old woman" pushing a grocery cart across the street (96), "[d]eep shadow despite confession" (98), an "illegal" showing up on his doorstep "one night, in the bitter cold of January" (117), and "moths" (145), those butterflies of the night. The major difference between Montoya and Gonzalez is that the former anchors his melancholy in the figure of the Man of Sorrows whereas Gonzalez's new black language traverses many different cultural spheres and deliberately draws in an intricate skein of references to cultural production in the United States, from that of Beat poets such as Allen Ginsberg (6) to the music of Carlos Santana (55).

If Emerson found his poet in Whitman, Anzaldúa might find her poet of shadow and night—if she had to pick among Chicano poets—in Francisco X. Alarcón, who was born in Los Angeles in 1954, grew up in Guadalajara, Mexico, and is the author of at least ten volumes of poetry, most notably, for my purposes, *From the Other Side of Night / Del otro lado de la noche* (2002). Here one finds, once again, a Baroque mysticism of the night (the volume begins by quoting *Noche oscura* by St. John of the Cross); an identification of queer lovers of Aztlán with shadows who know their "country has yet to be built";[36] an invocation of a god humbled by those in pain physically and socio-politically (7–10); the emphasis on Western culture's association of dark skin with the night and vice versa (10–11); an ongoing homage paid to his grandmother and later to the mother goddess Tonantzin and to Tlazoltéotl, *Madre de la Noche* [Mother of the Night] (190); a sustained critique of *machismo* (35); the association of Chicano/as and Latino/as with the "*entrañas*" (the insides, the guts) of America's body (52); and poems combining English, Spanish, and Nahuatl as well as poems written fully in Spanish and fully in English, obscuring the question of which are original and which translation, giving equal weight to both languages, and creating an in-between space out of the other side of night. Alarcón's poetry brings together, as if reflected in the obsidian mirror of Anzaldúa's gaze, marginality, political commitment, multivalent queer love, indigenism, and feminism.

Among Chicana poets, Demetria Martínez's night talk in her 1997 collection of poems, *Breathing Between the Lines,* stands out as an Anzaldúan project to transform the night into a mode of addressing loss and also finding that which exceeds the routine and authoritarian "lines" of the day. In the section called "Code Talkers" of a poem titled "Night," night becomes the time for those physically separated by time and space to communicate, but they do so in a language of revelation and animals, not an ordinary, day-charted, technologically conveyed and monitored human language: "no one can understand / us except those who speak / in tongues and the language of birds."[37] The lovers, one assumes, "boil the roots of telephone cords torn / from the black soils of sleep" (7). Demetria Martínez's "night talk" unfolds in the context of the discourse of romance, an eroticized relationship between one party and another. However, this "romance" develops along the lines of Doris Sommer's *Foundational Fictions: The National Romances of Latin America,* which demonstrates that narratives about attraction, romance, and love are vehicles or containers for fierce debates and struggles over national, regional, and local identities and trajectories.[38] In a later section of Martínez's collection entitled "First Words," the poem "Wanted" (after Allen Ginsberg, 1988) appears between a poem entitled "Imperialism" and another called "Sonogram." "Wanted" begins with the Chicana Latina poet's apostrophe to America, which is cast in the role of a rejecting spouse: "America our marriage is coming apart / I've done everything right got my degree / Now you tell me my English won't do / America I'm not good enough for you?" (37). The poem goes on to detail what is destroying the marriage: America's domestic and foreign-policy violence and its persecution of immigrants and thinkers who do not agree with the policies of the White House and the Pentagon. The last part of the poem concludes with stunning lines such as: "America I don't want progress I want redemption / . . . / America I'm your dark side embrace me and be saved" (38). The rhythms are hypnotically insistent, like those of Allen Ginsberg, but Martínez's words speak particularly to the condition of *los otros americanos*.

The idea of Latina/os—or, more specifically, Mexicans and Mexican Americans—as forming America's dark side has a history as long as the historical reality of more than one America, which one might say was true from the very first moment the term "America" was applied to the continent over five hundred years ago. Native Americans were seen and treated as the dark Other, as wild savages, by the Europeans. So were African slaves brought to the Americas. So were Euro-Americans by each other in the complex history of whiteness and off-whiteness. This Othering was and still is of special relevance with regard to Mexicans, Mexican Americans, and the United States. As practically the entire Southwest was Mexico until 1848 and "Mexicans" compose over two-thirds of the Latina/o population that is the largest "minority" group now, Mexicans and Mexican Americans have a particular historical and contemporary relationship to this long-standing notion of America's dark side. Demetria Martínez demonstrates her awareness of this relationship. She deploys it in a very Anzaldúan manner, suggesting a project for U.S. culture: "embrace me and be saved" (38). She does not mince words. The cultural work that must be done is not destructive second- or third-class citizen assimilation or hostile rejection but an open-armed acknowledgment of the fact that Mexicans and Latina/os more broadly are Americans. The reference to the "dark side" could be read in terms of phenotype. But it also resonates with the notion of the depth psychology work that must be undertaken, the introspection that has to happen in the national psyche, for such an embrace to be anything but fleeting or commodifying.

The Beat Nights of Chicana/o Writers

The implied dedication of Martínez's poem "Wanted" to Allen Ginsberg (with the words "after Allen Ginsberg, 1988") is a significant detail with respect to Latina/os and representations of night. In fact, Chicano writer Ray Gonzalez in

Turtle Pictures (2000) also makes direct reference to Beat writers such as Allen Ginsberg (6) and Kenneth Rexroth (7). He does so again in his 2009 collection of poems, *Cool Auditor:* "Beginning with Two Lines from Kenneth Rexroth."[39] These references constitute more than isolated instances. The Beat rejection of the values and procedures of military-industrial capitalism and post–World War II conformity occurred more or less simultaneously with the Chicana/o civil rights movement in the mid to late 1950s through the 1970s. Martínez's dedication of her poem "Wanted" functions as an acknowledgment of a kinship between the socio-political critique of U.S. society and government by the Beats and by Chicana/o activists. The kinship between the Beats and Chicana/o cultural workers involves both separate and consciously shared histories of representations and uses of the night as protest or transgression against dominant culture's enforcement of the exploitative, capitalist, white supremacist, militarized order of the day, which extends back into the night shift introduced in the nineteenth century with the invention and implementation of electricity. Both Chicana/o cultural workers and Beats participated in and actively fomented a transgressive culture of the night.

As Canadian historian Bryan D. Palmer recounts in his chapter about the Beats, "A Walk on the Wild Side: Bohemia and the Beats" in his 2000 study *Cultures of Darkness: Night Travels in the Histories of Transgression [from Medieval to Modern]*, on the night of October 7, 1955 in an experimental art gallery in the African American section of San Francisco,

> Allen Ginsberg built a rhapsodic outline of the United States as a civilization encased in its own nightmare, constrained and distorted by a coercive and ultimately destructive materialism and its many mechanizations which had overtaken what remained of American individualism.[40]

One might add, more nightmarishly, that effective solidarity and collective action had also been overtaken. Ginsberg had delivered an oral performance of "Howl." And, as Palmer observes, "[i]t was unmistakably dark and focused emphatically on the night, which was obviously where the angry young men of the 1950s felt they had some room to roam, space to create, and possibility to live" (371). Night provided physical and psychic space-time both for disaffected, generally "white" male Beats and also for ethno-racially and socioeconomically marginalized groups—i.e., African Americans and Latina/os—to ponder their predicament, to engage in all manner of "night studies," to quote African American writer Cyrus Colter. If night did not provide this space literally, a significant number of cultural workers from these groups turned night into a trope to signify critique of and transgression against, as Palmer puts it, "the political economy and cultural philistinism of mainstream America" (371). The difference between Chicana/o thinker-activists and the non-Latina/o Beats, the celebrated and vilified angry white men (and some women, too), was and has been the hitching by the former of bohemian "down-and-outness" to struggles to actually change oppressive laws—the Chicano lawyer Oscar "Zeta" Acosta being a case in point. However, the connection between bohemian rejection of the order of the day and socio-political change was not and has not always been such a direct one. In general, Chicana/o cultural producers could not afford, as their white counterparts might, to be what Norman Podhoretz called "Know-Nothing Bohemians," part of his hostile harangue against the Beats (Palmer 372).

Also important to recognize is that who and what have been understood as Beat has been limited by the usual prejudices in favor of "white" men. "White" women Beat writers have had difficulty garnering attention. It took entire studies, such as Brenda Knight's *Women of the Beat Generation: The Writers, Artists, and Muses at the Heart of a Revolution* (1996), to somewhat rectify this situation. So it may come as no surprise that few Chicana/o writers are discussed as "Beat." In John Rechy's and Oscar "Zeta" Acosta's work, one sees very clearly the confluence of their thought with that of the Beats in terms of their uses of night, Mexico, and Mexico in relation to night. This should remind us that there were indeed Chicana/o Beat writers, though they are not often critically flagged as such. Beats such as Jack Kerouac, Allen Ginsberg, Neal Cassady, Ruth Weiss, Diane Di Prima, Brenda Frazer, Joan Vollmer Adams, and William Burroughs were obsessed with Mexico and Mexican culture, both in Mexico and in the U.S. Southwest, as an alternative (often dark, edgy, life-giving, and death-dealing) to what they considered bland, bourgeois, diurnal, suburban Anglo culture that atrophied the senses. They romanticized Mexican cultures with their own brand of dark primitivism, wanting, as Ginsberg put it, to disappear "into the volcanoes of Mexico leaving nothing behind but / the shadow of dungarees and the lava and ash of poetry scattered in / fireplace Chicago."[41] The Beat version of Mexico characterized countercultural representations of Mexico in the late 1950s, the 1960s, and the early to mid 1970s.[42] One can find strong traces and continuations of Beat ideas about and images of Mexico in the lyrics and poems of Dionysian singer and rock idol Jim Morrison, with his images of Mexicans as killers on the run in the dark and Tijuana as "the anus of night." The latter image appears in the second stanza of Jim Morrison's poem "The Dark American Sunset."[43]

What might be seen as fairly stereotypical capitulations to such primitivizations also function as alternative modes of knowledge, symbol-making, and anti-narration; the seeming capitulations work as deliberate plumbings of the seemingly non-linear, irrational, and atemporal (embracing past and future in a glance) to deliver backhanded blows against the European and Gringo colonizer/conqueror, the electro-chemical and media-controlled malaise of military-industrial Anglo-America, and Western rationalist notions of linear, sequential history, progress, time, and space.[44] Chicano Beat writers seem to have been well aware of non-Mexican Beat fascination with Mexico and to have employed it for their own self-representational purposes, often choosing to explore and riff off the more ominous or "nightmarish" representations of Mexico and Mexican culture purveyed by other Beat writers.

New Mexican Chicano writer Leo Romero's long short story "Pito" in the collection *Rita & Los Angeles* (1995) takes on Beat signifiers of "Mexico" and "Mexican" very much within the context of representations of night. Though the story makes only a single reference to Mexico, one of the central characters, Pito, is modeled on an actual Mexican dwarf, Cha Cha, whom Diane Arbus photographed in the early 1970s.[45] Romero's story concerns the relationship between two men, the male narrator and a male dwarf who might be viewed as a separate person or as an alter ego. The dwarf functions as both. These two characters live an isolated existence in a large unnamed city. The location could be Los Angeles, San Francisco, New York, or somewhere else. The narrator and the dwarf have a co-dependent relationship based on the fact that misery likes company. Both of them are single, seem to be out of work (no job is ever mentioned, and the narrator complains about hardly ever having money, 47), and lonely. They temporarily band together to invite women over to Pito's apartment, presumably to seduce them, but the women generally find the dwarf repulsive and leave. Being without financial means and unsuccessful in their pursuit of live women, the narrator and the dwarf fall back on their own devices: fantasy as mimetic desire in which what one man wants becomes an object of contagious obsession for the other.

The story itself is written within the mode of the fantastic as described by Tzvetan Todorov, a Bulgarian critic in the Russian formalist tradition, in his study of what he called a "literary genre." The fantastic operates in such a way that one cannot decide between a supernatural or a mundane explanation for phenomena.[46] When Pito dreams that Diane Arbus visits him nightly—mostly Diane and sometimes James Dean, the two armed with cameras to photograph him—the narrator becomes absorbed with these dreams and himself begins dreaming, adding the ghostly presence of Jack Kerouac to the mix. Not only in typical fantastic fashion but also in specifically Beat fashion, the line between the real and the imagined blurs and dissolves. The twenty-four sections of the story become increasingly nightmarish, and much of the action (imagined or not) unfolds at night. Pito, whose position vis-à-vis the ghost of Arbus wielding a camera is similar to that of Cha Cha, whom the living Arbus actually photographed, is repeatedly visited by dead icons of U.S. culture: Diane Arbus, James Dean, and Jack Kerouac. These are not just any icons; they are well-known countercultural ones who subverted their own success and the attainment of the American dream. Not only are they dead, but all of them expressed what one might well interpret as a strong (even if unconscious) death wish—James Dean by speeding in his cars, Arbus by slitting her wrists in a bathtub and thus committing suicide, and Kerouac by fatally abusing alcohol and speed. The icons are what neither Pito nor the narrator is or can be. And yet they share an uncanny cultural kinship—a certain legacy of failed romance and violence between the "American" (the U.S.-ian) and the Mexican. Pito and the narrator, like these suicidal icons, carry a stigma of failure (according to the happy, materialist credo of the American dream), and they all have connections to Mexico and/or to *Latinidad* in one form or another: Arbus with the dwarf, Dean with Mexican bullfighting, and Kerouac with travels and writings such as *On the Road* (1957) and *Mexico City Blues* (1959).[47] All three icons led rather non-conformist lives, rebelling against a heteronormative, suburban existence in which a white picket fence and property count as freedom and happiness.

Pito and the narrator do not lead a conventional existence at all except for the ordinariness of their poverty and desperation. Their relationship cannot be described by the commonly reassuring word "friendship": it is instead "friendship or whatever you'd call it" (47). It is too filled with mimetic libidinal desire to be comfortably contained under the label of friendship. There is something of the erotic, but Pito and the narrator are not lovers in any clearly defined physical sense. They are deeply connected psychically, yet they are often antagonistic toward one another. Furthermore, Pito's identity as a Mexican—"He's been stuck in this city for twenty years. Born in Mexico, he's never found anything better than this city, this room, an efficiency" (55)—suggests that perhaps the narrator is also Latino. When teaching this text, I have found that readers tend to automatically Latinize the narrator on account of his constant association with the Mexican dwarf and also on account of the author's ethnicity. So, in effect, the story offers readers two Latino men and their Beat fantasy life as well as their Beat existence. By "Beat" I mean not only "unconventional" but the street slang meaning of the word, the state of being all washed up without hope of better times. The story pushes the stereotypes of lazy Mexicans or Latinos who are social and economic failures or dropouts.

The story itself immerses readers in a Beat world, but it does so via Latinos, Mexicans, as much as by references to three Beat icons. Immersing readers in this world is part of its own transgressive aesthetics. The transgression makes use of night, nighttime, nightmares, and descriptions of night such as "Pito's talking all night . . . And all night long I hear car tires driving through the wet streets . . . and it's like a musical accompaniment to his talking" (55). One of the things that Pito says, laughing a "chilling laugh," is "We're all dead men some night" (69). This statement resonates in ever-widening circles like a stone thrown into a pool of dark water. "Dead" can mean physically dead, but also socially dead—as in people who are so marginalized that they are treated and live as if they do not exist or have only a ghostly existence. One of the transgressive tactics of Romero's story is the use of a Beat repertoire—of down-and-out people, dharma bums, and Mexicans as exotic Others—to draw readers into this night world of socio-economic, ethno-racial, and psychological alienation where they begin to experience (vicariously, anyway) the anger, pain, depression, humiliation, shame, and discomfort of being poor, marginalized, and exploited as well as seduced by a dominant culture (dominant relative to themselves, that is). Dead Beat or Beat-like icons Diane Arbus, James Dean, and Jack Kerouac live off of Pito and the narrator. The dead cannibalize the living—or, more to the point, the living dead, the socially marginalized. Countercultural Arbus exploits Pito for her photo projects. The story suggests that eventually, in dreams, she exploits the narrator's psychic and physical pain when Pito, crazed by too many dreams of Arbus and by too much wine, tries to kill him with a long, flashing switchblade knife: "That night [the narrator] dreamt of Diane. . . . She placed a hand on my bleeding wound that was flowing like a river. I couldn't believe how deep the wound was" (70). The narrator yells at Diane that she must get out of his wound, that the wound is his, not hers (70). So marginalized is he—without a job, property, or person to care for him—that all he has left is his pain, his symbolic castration, to defend as rightfully his and no one else's. For all the mention of pain, however, desire or the desirous wish to feel something rather than nothing pervades the story and partially explains the two living protagonists' participation in what amounts to a séance with the dead.[48] As the narrator states in the concluding line of the story, "Even with such intense pain, I was at peace" (71).

The transfer of alienation and pain as emotion that tinges one's perception, much as looking through smoked glass does, is one of the story's aims. Indeed, the story draws readers in through its twenty-four sections of carefully sparse narration, description, and dialogue. The story builds in intensity and tension toward its violent and, quite literally, haunting conclusion. The effect of reading each of the twenty-four sections is similar to that of looking at an Arbus photo—one wants to look away from the grotesque mixture of beauty and deformity, but one cannot. The insistence on nighttime and nightmares in a bare, working-class setting—Pito's grimy efficiency in a dying city—also recalls photographer Weegee's (Usher Fellig's) nocturnal photography of crimes and accidents in

New York City in the late 1930s and the 1940s. Arbus's work is informed by Wee-gee's gruesome night photos, many of which he attributed to his clairvoyant gift for being at the scene of a crime in the nick of time. These night photos are luridly illuminated by the flash bulb "introduced by General Electric in 1930."[49] Leo Romero's story picks up on these affinities and associations.[50]

The story's net effect is to deploy these countercultural icons and Beat con-tent and style to re-appropriate the alienated pain of the marginalized for the marginalized—for those immigrants such as Pito. The story, written by New Mexican Chicano author Leo Romero, also re-appropriates non-Hispanic Beat uses of Mexico, Mexicans, and Latinidad more generally to underscore the way in which neither the U.S. dominant culture nor the dominant culture's counter-culture has sufficiently examined its relationship to ethno-racial and socioeco-nomic peripheralization. Confrontation means stepping into the Other's shoes, and this is what Pito hypnotizes readers into doing by recognizing themselves in the Other's failed fantasies of acceptance, reciprocity, and the pursuit of happiness.

That the story concludes with a scene of Sartrean no-exit, more or less hori-zontal violence between the narrator and Pito, illuminates a central aspect of Chicana/o cultural workers' uses of night: the noirish tendency to link night with the remembrance of a particular crime or a history of conflict, crime, and injustice. I attribute this tendency to a desire to remind readers that night is not so much about respite as it is about confronting the past and everything that has led up to the present and is informing the future. This tendency to concatenate night with the contemplation of a history of crimes and injustices, including the systematic disenfranchisement of Mexican Americans within U.S. territory from the Mexican-American War onward, works to offset any escapist con-sumptions of the idea of night. Furthermore, the pattern could be interpreted as indicative of an attempt to address and redirect dominant culture's association of Mexicans with criminality, implicating dominant culture in the very crimi-nality being projected onto the scapegoated, marginalized Other.

In fact, Romero's story underscores the failures of dominant culture through a focus on countercultural icons with name recognition within that dominant culture. For all its oneirism, or dream-like quality, it is historically based and aware, another attribute that characterizes most Chicana/o deployments of night. This historical awareness can be detected, above all, in its handling of the figure of James Dean, the quintessential countercultural "white" icon of the 1950s, the rebel without a cause transformed into a photographic specter con-jured by a Chicano writer and cultural worker. The portrayal of Arbus as a pho-tographer, whether experimental or exploitative or both, comes as no surprise.

But the presentation of James Dean as another photographer armed with a camera in the story "Pito" may indeed surprise readers and critics on account of the almost recherché historical mimetism at work.

The fact that James Dean himself was, in actuality, the object of the camera's gaze, moving and still, is evident from his three feature films and the hundreds of photos that exist of him by well-known professional photographers. A much less known fact is that James Dean himself counted the study of photography as one of his passions along with bullfighting, modern dance, poetry writing, and car racing. The 2005 Michael J. Sheridan film *James Dean Forever Young* on James Dean's rise to fame makes enough of this photographic passion to dedicate a section to it titled, in the DVD version of the film, "Photos." Given his penchant for befriending photographers such as Roy Schatt, Sanford Roth, and Phil Stern and the fact that he studied photographic techniques with Roy Schatt and took his own pictures with a 16-millimeter Rolex camera that he carried with him on film sets, it would seem that photography—and being a photographer himself—was more important to him than his other *aficiones* and was surpassed in importance, along with car racing, only by acting.

When Leo Romero casts James Dean as a photographer, or at least a man with a camera along with Diane Arbus, visiting Pito in his dreams at night, Romero is showing that he has done his research. He has carefully chosen the elements of his story, including which American icons to bring into the night-vision optics of his tale. Such knowledge may encourage readers to linger on and scrutinize the sometimes riddle-like pictures which Romero offers us—for they are simultaneously loaded with the obvious and the obscure, with what is plain to see and with the shadowy side of all that reveals itself.

Cameras are not only about being everywhere at once but also, as Susan Sontag reminds her readers, about a will to conquer and dominate:

> Like a car, a camera is sold as a predatory weapon—one that's as automated as possible, ready to spring. . . . Like guns and cars, cameras are fantasy-machines whose use is addictive. . . . The camera/gun does not kill . . . [s]till, there is something predatory in the act of taking a picture. To photograph people is to violate them, by seeing them as they never see themselves, by having knowledge of them they can never have; it turns people into objects that can be symbolically possessed. Just as the camera is a sublimation of the gun, to photograph someone is a sublimated murder—a soft murder. . . .[51]

Romero's story suggests that the narrator and his friend the dwarf are being softly murdered by the American idols with whom they are obsessed, however supposedly countercultural or rebellious Arbus, Dean, and Kerouac may have been. After all, the countercultural exists in definitional relation to hegemonic culture and is imprinted with and often contained by it.

Leo Romero's story "Pito" taps into darker undercurrents in dreams both of and about American idols. One of the broader streams of those undercurrents is what the idol and idolization, along with photography (a mechanism for these immortalizations), conceal—death of various kinds, meaning failure as well: failed masculinity, failed ethnic subjecthood, failed existence. For the Latina/o characters in this story, death exists in various forms: "social . . . representational . . . literal," to borrow an insightful triadic phrase from Lázaro Lima's 2007 book *The Latino Body: Crisis Identities in American Literary and Cultural Memory*.[52] Any number of critics—including Susan Sontag, Roland Barthes, Christian Metz, Eduardo Cadava, and Jay Prosser—have pointed out the complicity of photography in death, loss, and disappearance.[53] Though photography may seem to immortalize, every photograph also marks the passing, the evanescence, of its object. To the extent that the photograph comes to substitute for the living, breathing, and dying object (human or otherwise), it partakes of a dynamic of usurping double, that which denies the actual condition of the other's existence. As such, photographs and photography can be seen as exploitative. The story "Pito" certainly presents photography this way. Both Diane Arbus and James Dean usurp Pito's and the narrator's existence—though, complexly, the point of convergence between these idols and Pito and the narrator is that they, too, are dead, even killed—vis-à-vis the privileged living of dominant culture. Leo Romero's story employs the nocturnal haunting of the Latino characters by paradoxically countercultural icons from the dominant culture with strong death drives—for whom the American dream was neither enough nor a dream (but rather a nightmare)—to reveal the psychic and material eclipse of its Latino characters from full inclusion as citizens and persons in the U.S. body politic.

I use the term "eclipse" deliberately. "Eclipse," from Latin derived from Greek meaning "to fail or suffer," referring to the partial or total obscuration of one celestial body by another, is generally an astronomical term. The dark, nocturnal optics of Romero's story could be read in astronomical terms, though this understanding is not immediately obvious. The story contains not only human existential implications but also cosmological ones. Both those existential and cosmological implications feed into its cultural critique of the alienated and eclipsed position of Latina/os, and Mexican Americans in particular, within U.S. society. The relationship between the narrator and Pito the dwarf, triangulated as it is by ghostly dead people deemed celebrities or "stars" in "an old and dying city" (55), is suggestive of the apocalyptically explosive relationship between two kinds of astronomical stars dying in close proximity to one another: a white dwarf and a red giant. The astronomical parable in Leo Romero's story "Pito" could be read as both paying homage to and rivaling the cosmic "howl" of pain and protest in a Beat work such as Allen Ginsberg's *Howl*.[54]

From Beat Nights to Noir

Not all invocations of night are necessarily noirish (that is, part of a mysterious crime story with an ambiguous resolution that typically entails a deepening shadow chase),[55] but among Chicana/o writers, the handling of the trope of night is often associated with some kind of crime. I turn to the use of night in Chicana/o noir detective literature as a response to the complicated history of U.S./Mexico encounters and as a counter-response to the images of Mexicans and Mexican Americans in U.S. noir films such as Elia Kazan's *Panic in the Streets* (1950), Orson Welles's *Touch of Evil* (1958), and Alfred Hitchcock's *Vertigo* (1958). Chicana/o appropriations or re-appropriations of noir are a crucial part of the Anzaldúan project of regarding night as the signifier of wounding and loss and the call to confront these dark conditions and transform them into a deep-structure engagement with histories of both socioeconomic and ethnoracial oppression and psychic repression. Any number of Chicana/o writers and filmmakers have gravitated to the noir detective mode, as demonstrated by studies such as Ralph E. Rodriguez's *Brown Gumshoes: Detective Fiction and the Search for Chicana/o Identity* (2005) and Susan Baker Sotelo's *Chicano Detective Fiction* (2005). Among the writers, one finds the usual suspects, covered in both these studies: Rudolfo Anaya, Rolando Hinojosa, Lucha Corpi, Manuel Ramos, and Michael Nava. However, many other Chicana/o cultural workers have been drawn to aspects of noir detective fiction—for instance, Oscar "Zeta" Acosta, Sergio Troncoso, Alicia Gaspar de Alba, Cecile Pineda, Margarita Cota-Cardenas, Emma Pérez, and Manuel Muñoz as well as transnational Mexican writer Paco Ignacio Taibo II (whose works have been translated into English), performance artist Harry Gamboa Jr., and filmmaker Lourdes Portillo in films such as *The Devil Never Sleeps* (1994) and *Señorita Extraviada* (2001). The draw to noir detective fiction also entails a draw to its visual codes, among which night and shadows predominate. Though "noir" (black) is by no means the same as "*nuit*" (night), and detective stories might not necessarily be especially noir, the stories of detection that constitute these fictions, performances, and films foreground night, shadows, and darkness in ways that plunge readers and viewers into epistemological uncertainty and ambiguity while simultaneously exploring the ontological obscurity and occlusion of being *los otros america-nos,* the other americans. That is, the texts, performances, and films deploy a double tactic: they employ mimesis of dominant noir detective conventions of night, shadows, and a preoccupation with socio-economically and ethno-racially exoticized or marginalized others. However, they also transvalue the chains of association evident in dominant narratives, where Mexicans, African Americans, Asians, homosexuals, and women are aligned with forces of evil or troubling moral ambiguity. In *Noir Anxiety* (2003), Kelly Oliver and Benigno Trigo argue persuasively that the style, plots, and mood of classic film noir are the products of "condensations and displacements of symptoms of concrete anxieties over race, sex, maternity, and national origin that threaten the very possibility of identity by undermining its boundaries."[56] I would add that often in classic film noir, these concrete anxieties are hardly even encoded by conden-sations and displacements. They are out in the open; Mexicans and Mexican Americans are blatantly villainized as threats to the Anglo-American patriar-chal hegemony. Eric Lott states succinctly, "Film noir is replete with characters of color who populate and signify the shadows of white American life in the 1940s."[57] Chicana/o writers and filmmakers have shown and continue to show an awareness of both the blatant and subtle manifestations of these anxieties about boundaries and identities.

This does not mean that Chicana/o noir detective stories effect a simple transvaluation of what was deemed bad into something good or heroic. The transvaluation is more challenging. Though it does provide a counter-discourse in and against stereotypes about Mexican Americans, many of these works entail an uncanny journey through the dreaded non-identities of night rather than around them. For this reason I use the term "transvaluation" instead of "re-valuation." The cultural productions I examine in this chapter take audiences through and across the darkness into the dreaded non-identities of night. Such is most certainly the case with Chicana writer Lucha Corpi's detective novels, which recast noir's visual tropes of night and their related phenotyping of night and shadows in the inevitable association of certain characters as people of the night. In addition to the U.S. typecasting of Mexican Americans and Latina/os as "people of the night," the classic Hollywood movie production system often confined Latina/o actors to non-prime-time use of studio resources, which meant nighttime use only of studios. After-dinner film shooting generally entailed a strong tendency to be cast in "night" genre films such as detective stories and vampire films.[58]

Mexicans and Mexican Americans have figured prominently as types of crim-inals, victimizers, and generalized evildoers in Anglo-American film noir culture.

One need only think of films such as Edwin L. Marin's Anglo-audience-aimed *Nocturne* (1946), Fritz Lang's *The Secret Beyond the Door* (1948), John Farrow's *Where Danger Lives* (1950), Phil Karlson's *Kansas City Confidential* (1952), Orson Welles's *A Touch of Evil* (1958), Alfred Hitchcock's *Vertigo* (1958), or neo-noirs such as Ridley Scott's *Blade Runner* (1982), Curtis Hanson's *L.A. Confidential* (1997) based on a James Ellroy novel, and David Lynch's *Mulholland Drive* (2001), the latter featuring, among other "Mexican" elements, the mysterious nightclub *Silencio*.[59]

In *A Touch of Evil*, the Mexican characters are associated explicitly with the visual pattern of shadows and night more than any of the other characters. Early in the film, a young Mexican man approaches an Anglo protagonist with a message. He is figured doubly—as himself in black and as a menacing shadow against a gleaming white column. In a subsequent shot, he is cast into darkness while the Anglo woman's face remains in the light.[60] Even the upper-middle-class dandy Mr. Vargas (played by Charlton Heston) appears tinged by his own shadow and the words "Welcome Stranger," which associate him with an alien nationality. He is not a proper native either of Mexico or of the United States. Not only his last name, Vargas, but also the shadow and the words (and perhaps his mustache) signify his Otherness, though his all-American accent would allow him to pass as an "American."

Similarly, in Hitchcock's *Vertigo*, the alter ego of the Anglo Madeleine Elster is the supposedly possessing spirit of Carlotta Valdes, a haunting personality with a Latina-sounding name, part of "the things that [really] spell San Francisco." A gravestone indicates that the woman by that name lived for twenty-six years in the mid-nineteenth century, from December 3, 1831, to March 5, 1857. Her midlife coincides with the Mexican-American War of 1846–1848, in which a large chunk of formerly Mexican territory became one-third of the United States. References to empire building and conquest subtly abound in the film—from the time line signage on a sectioned redwood tree trunk to the neon sign of the Empire Hotel at night. Madeleine/Judy/Carlotta's face appears subliminally superimposed on that imperial sign. The takeovers are psychological as well in this psychological thriller noir. The Anglo Johnny becomes obsessed with Elster's wife and finds himself tailing her and her alter egos Carlotta Valdes, the upper-class Mexican, and Judy Barton, I would argue, the lower-class Anglo Mexican. Judy's skin is darkened. She, like Carlotta, is associated with *flores*, not *canto*, and with darkness. There are shots of Judy at night in the Empire Hotel, her face lit up by the green neon sign, and ones of her dressed in brown with a white flower crying in Johnny's apartment at night—and, of course, drawing him deeper into a vertiginous plot, as the femme fatale is supposed to do with the hero. Johnny's attempted takeovers of Madeleine/Judy/Carlotta are framed by a lowering night sky in the Spanish mission-style bell tower. In *Vertigo*, all things Spanish and Mexican are figured in terms of darkness: shadows, night, the return of the dead, and death itself. Though seemingly conquered and a part of the past, they threaten to take over the Anglo hero's mind and destabilize any identity or consciousness—hence the dark rising and falling motion of vertigo.

These associations of darkness, shadows, and night continue in neo-noirs such as *Blade Runner* (1982) and *Mulholland Drive* (2001). In *Blade Runner*, Gaff, a hunter of replicants, is played by Edward James Olmos. Gaff appears as a kind of Sinofied Mexican, a Latin Asian of a Los Angeles of the future. He first shows up plaguing the Anglo hero Rick Deckard at a sushi bar. He is framed in darkness and is dressed like a hybrid between an undercover agent, a *chulo*, and a pimp. The last time we see him, he is also framed in darkness and appears more like a shadow than a fully defined person. His final words to Deckard contain a veiled threat and a note of ironic sorrow: "I guess you're through, huh?" referring to Deckard's manhunt of the replicants.

David Lynch's *Mulholland Drive* plays up the association of Mexicans, Mexico, and the Spanish language itself with darkness, night, shadows, and loss. Soon after the film opens, viewers are introduced to the dark-haired femme fatale Rita riding in a jet-black limousine at night. Her name and her looks are deliberately calculated to cast her as a Rita Hayworth double, as can be seen in a later scene with a poster of Rita Hayworth (whose birth name was Margarita Carmen Cansino) reflected in a cosmetic mirror. Rita Hayworth played the femme fatale more than once, most notably in a remake of *Blood and Sand*. Hayworth was the daughter of a Spanish flamenco dancer father and a "chorus girl" mother of Irish and English heritage. When she was cast as a femme fatale and an alluring sex symbol, part of her image added to the pre-existing Hispanics-in-Hollywood stereotype of the hot-blooded, beguiling, and ultimately dangerous Latina. Though Hayworth was not Mexican herself, her association with Los Angeles and the Hollywood stereotype predisposed audiences to view her as such when she appeared in her brunette phase. Here, the brunette Rita of *Mulholland Drive* is shown exerting her femme fatale fascination on the Anglo would-be starlet Betty. The dark fascination is not confined to phenotypic features. Even when Rita's hair is dyed blonde and she appears Anglo, the language she speaks in her dreams at night in the dark anchors her in *hispanidad* and more specifically *mejicanidad*: "*Silencio . . . silencio. No hay banda. No hay orquesta.*" "Banda" means not only a band but moreover a type of *norteño* or Northern Mexican music heavily dependent on brass instruments such as the trombone. A trombone, an instrument mythically associated with the realm of the dead or the underworld, features in the Club Silencio, where a devilish-looking MC announces in Spanish, "*Señoras y señores, el Club Silencio.*" The culminating act in the dark nightclub clinches the references to Mexican American culture: the Texan-born Roy Orbison's 1961 ballad of lost love, "Crying," is rendered in Spanish by "*La Llorona de los Angeles . . . Rebecca del Río.*" Most of the references to Mexican American culture in *Mulholland Drive* are connected specifically with a plunge into night, grief, and loss.

As in Hitchcock's *Vertigo,* Mexico and Mexican American culture constitute the fundamental political unconscious of the film. The statement "*No hay banda*" resonates with absence and lack, but it carries a special valence with regard to the presence of Mexicans and Mexican Americans in Los Angeles. Scholar of black studies and sociology George Lipsitz, in the chapter "Banda: The Hidden History of Greater Mexico" of his 2007 study *Footsteps in the Dark,* argues that banda music became very popular in Los Angeles beginning in the early 1990s, that its rise and existence signal a "recombinant Mexican identity inside the United States," and that it was and is an expression from recent Mexican immigrants effectively indicating that they are in the United States and are not going away.[61] In *Mulholland Drive,* the repeated "*no hay banda*" functions as the trace of both the presence and the shadowy, nocturnal occlusion in the film itself of Mexican and Mexican American people and cultures.

As suggested in Susan Baker Sotelo's recently published book, *Chicano Detective Fiction: A Critical Study of Five Novelists* (Rudolfo Anaya, Rolando Hinojosa, Lucha Corpi, Manuel Ramos, and Michael Nava), Chicana/os have a long history of literary intervention in the conventions of the detective novel. I would argue that they have an equally long history of counter-discourse interventions in and against the stereotypes about Mexican Americans in relation specifically to film noir and its dreaded non-identities of the night. By "dreaded non-identities of night" I mean those identities that provoke or inspire anxiety, fear, and even loathing in viewers on account of a constellation of qualities attributed to a character or personage—qualities such as darkness in physical, phenotypic, or ethical senses; ambiguity; slipperiness; and shape-shifting that has a temporal as well as spatial dimension often associated, quite literally, with nighttime. Dread arises out of an encounter with negatively defined identity—a fearful darkness without fixed shape or borders. For instance, one might view John Rechy's great American novel *City of Night* (1963) in light of this interventionist project. Furthermore, one might extend such an argument back to a work such as Américo Paredes's *The Shadow* (1950s/1998) or Oscar "Zeta" Acosta's *Autobiography of a Brown Buffalo* (1972), or forward to Margarita Cota-Cardenas's *Puppet* (1985, 2000), Cecile Pineda's *Face* (1985, republished in 2003), or Emma Pérez's *Gulf Dreams* (1996).

Visualizing the Noir of Night in Lucha Corpi's Detective Novels

Poet, novelist, children's book author, and teacher Lucha Corpi deploys and re-arranges some central tropes of Anglo-American noir in her Gloria Damasco series, that is, in the novels *Eulogy for a Brown Angel* (1992), *Cactus Blood* (1995), *Black Widow's Wardrobe* (1999), and *Death at Solstice* (2009). Additionally, I consider *Crimson Moon* (2004), the first of the Brown Angel mystery series. These novels engage tropes of visualization with the awareness and self-consciousness of an urban photographer, like the supposedly clairvoyant Weegee with his *Naked City* (1945) photos. This section elaborates the convergence of the visual and the literary, arguing that such a convergence is already implicit in these novels by Corpi. I explore this convergence as cultural intervention.

Her novels represent a very careful and continuous melding of fact and fiction, of history and storytelling, and of storytelling with a visual repertoire purveyed through verbal description that is acutely aware of film and photography, particularly Anglo or more generally dominant U.S. visual representations of Mexicans, Mexican Americans, and the idea of Mexico. Part of the fascination of Corpi's work resides in the way in which it alludes to and incorporates Mexican history, U.S.-Mexico relations, Mexican American history, and the struggles of the Chicana/o Movement. Readers will find references to the National Chicano Moratorium and riot (August 29, 1970) in *Eulogy for a Brown Angel*; to the United Farm Workers 1973 strike and grape boycott in *Cactus Blood*; and to the early-sixteenth-century conquest of Mexico and the exploitative relationship of the Spanish conqueror Hernán Cortés with Malintzin (Doña Marina, la Malinche) in *Black Widow's Wardrobe*. In *Death at Solstice*, readers will find rather extensive allusions to the history of racial discrimination during and since the California gold rush of the 1840s; to the lasting importance for Chicana/o culture of the history and legends surrounding the controversial figure of Joaquín Murrieta and other California-based Mexican outlaws; to corruption among law enforcement officials involved in human trafficking and neo-slavery of undocumented workers; and to the rape, mutilation, and murder of hundreds of young women in the border town of Cuidad Juárez. As *Death at Solstice* unfolds, it offers a pointed critique of the racial profiling affecting Latina/os and other people of color in the wake of September 11, 2001, and since the re-enactment of the Patriot Act. *Crimson Moon* alludes to the 1968–1970 Federal Bureau of Investigation (FBI) infiltrations of the student movements at Berkeley, to the Chicano youth movement and "Crusade for Justice and Corky Gonzalez's activities in Denver,"[62] and to Oakland, "home to people of countries from every continent" (xi), around the year 2000. In *Brown Gumshoes: Detective Fiction and the Search for Chicana/o Identity*, scholar Ralph Rodriguez claims that via "her Gloria Damasco series,

Lucha Corpi investigates the various historical shifts and constructions of Chicanidad since the Chicana/o Movement (roughly 1965–1975) even more systematically than her Chicano counterparts in the detective genre."[63] He goes on to argue that "[w]ith each novel, Corpi, a feminist writer steeped in the Chicana/o activism of the 1960s and 1970s, struggles more and more with the often monolithic construction of Chicana/o cultural identity associated with the Chicana/o Movement" (55).

I concur with this assessment but would like to change the angle of analysis by highlighting the ways in which Corpi passes tropes of Anglo-American noir as they apply to the representation of Mexicans and Mexican Americans through her particular renditions of night, darkness, and what Gloria Anzaldúa elaborated as the spatio-temporal nepantla of darkness. Corpi manipulates the noir of night and the night of noir to counteract and confound U.S. dominant cultural representations of Mexicans and Mexican Americans at the very same time that she struggles with any monolithic construction of Chicana/o cultural identity. In all the Gloria Damasco novels and in *Crimson Moon*, Corpi shows the ways in which Mexican American communities and also Mexican society are divided within themselves—particularly along class, gender, and ethno-racial lines. For instance, the novels show Chicana/os with widely varying class allegiances, from the poor Chicana/os of East Los Angeles to those living in wealthy parts of San Francisco and L.A. or those living transnational lives with lines of global capital (in all forms, some of it illegal contraband) running among the United States, Mexico, Brazil, and Europe. *Black Widow's Wardrobe* contains references to the disapproval and contempt felt by some upper-class and upper-middle-class Mexican Americans toward politicized Chicana/os. [64] All the novels investigate oppressive codes of masculinity among Chicanos/as of all classes. *Black Widow's Wardrobe* is unsparing in its investigation of domestic violence, particularly of husbands against wives and children and of men against women but even of sons against their mothers. The Chicano Movement was troubled by machismo. Corpi, as a Chicana feminist, indicts oppressive patriarchal aspects of Mexican and Mexican American history from Cortés and Malintzin up to the turn of the second millennium in *Black Widow's Wardrobe*. In all her novels, women suffer the effects of male violence and poor choices and are also, sometimes, complicit in their own degradation. This complicity is especially evident in the fourth book of the Damasco series, *Death at Solstice*, where a woman turns out to be the killer and the violently jealous mistress of a violent man, Sal Gallardo, who abuses his wife. She does not cover up problems such as these for fear of making Chicanos look bad in the eyes of the dominant culture.

But Corpi balances the exposure of these problems with an appropriation to her own ends of the noir of night and the night of noir in relation to Mexicans and Mexican Americans. Those purposes begin in *Eulogy for a Brown Angel,* which announces the Chicana detective Gloria Damasco's "dark gift," which is very much remindful of Gloria Anzaldúa's *"la facultad,"* of clairvoyance that defies the rationality and positivism to which Western culture clings. Even Gloria must get used to her dark gift—"[a]t age twenty-three I had first confronted this other self, this psychic being."[65] But she does accept it and even identifies it with aspects of Chicana/o culture, such as her Catholic childhood spent both tempting the devil and saying "Hail Mary's" for good measure (*Eulogy* 50) or the prominent role given to La Llorona, who wails in the dark for her lost children and those who are missing, murdered, or otherwise dead. *Eulogy for a Brown Angel* commences the association of Gloria's clairvoyance with darkness. She sees best in the dark, not in the light. And that darkness is proudly Chicanaized. Hence, I argue, the pointed reference to an oil painting by Chicano artist Malaquías Montoya titled "Los perros de medianoche" (the dogs of midnight) (*Eulogy* 156). It is as if Corpi were saying, "This thing of darkness is mine" to play off of Shakespeare's *The Tempest.*

Cactus Blood, the next novel after *Eulogy,* continues this reclamation of darkness beginning with the section titled "Foreshadows," gradually unfolding a mystery about women murdered in the valleys of California (cactus blood)—"'Into the darkness,' the woman in my dream was saying . . . 'always, always, always'"[66]— and culminating in the description of a Bay Area earthquake that leaves San Francisco and Oakland in darkness with only fires and stars "punctuating the canvas of night" (249).

Death at Solstice develops the association of night with Gloria Damasco's "dark gift[s]" of telepathy, pre-cognition, and empathy.[67] The novel reinforces this association by having the visions themselves be about events that happen under "the proverbial mantle of night" (2008), including during a 2005 Solar-Lunar Midsummer Celebration sponsored by "Plenitude: A Monterey Peninsula Witches Coven" (208). New Age neo-pagan alternate spiritual practices (208–217) and the nocturnal rituals of white supremacist UFO-seeking stargazers (168–173) are montaged. They are also juxtaposed with Gloria's dark gifts; numerous references to the Mexican and Mexican American veneration of the dark Virgen de Guadalupe; and a Chicana woman's nighttime impersonation, on a dark horse and dressed in black (228), of the Mexican American outlaw hero Joaquín Murrieta (104–108), Robin Hood of El Dorado (106), whom many Mexican Americans consider an avenger of Mexicans dispossessed of their lands and lives by Anglo-Americans who moved into the Southwest and California. The montage of what many readers might consider "irrational" elements—neo-paganism, white supremacist UFO-ology, Mexican Catholicism,

and belief in the continued intercession, even if only via a deliberate performance, of a figure such as Joaquín Murrieta—underscores the shaping impact
of belief systems on the production of social reality and the consequent unfolding of history. At the same time that *Death at Solstice* engages in this montage,
it also operates by an implicit juxtaposition of the elements it montages. The
nocturnal and dark aspects of Mexican American culture are revealed to be
mostly aligned with concerns for social justice as well as with an open acknowledgment, rather than denial, of the power of "Death" (239) over human lives.
The ultimate darkness of death is deployed not so much for vicarious thrills
(though most noir stories lend themselves to that effect) as for a reminder of
social responsibility in the face of mortality and the brevity of earthly lives.

Finally, *Crimson Moon*—the first book of the Brown Angel mystery series
because it introduces another detective, Dora Saldaña, in addition to Gloria
Damasco, who only makes a cameo appearance—reveals its very deliberate
cognizance of visual and textual tropologies and their reworking with the sentences: "A scene worthy of a cheap spy novel or movie. She [Ramona Serna]
could come up with a better scenario than that one" (X). The novel gradually
converts the image of a crimson moon in a night sky, a blood-tinged moon,
"silent conspirator in human affairs since the beginning of time" and also "witness" (XIII) into a kind of depth psychology investigation of the effects, political and psychological, of FBI and Central Intelligence Agency (CIA) misdeeds
during the beginnings of the Chicano Civil Rights Movement and the student
revolts of the late 1960s and early 1970s. These events that occurred thirty years
before have live-wire connections to social movements for social justice in the
present, such as the Zapatista one in Chiapas, Mexico. Thus, Corpi anchors the
moon that sails the night skies and descriptions of night and darkness to particular histories and to the ongoing struggles of Mexicans and Mexican Americans in the Americas. The last image of *Crimson Moon,* again coded in terms of
the noir of night, suggests the struggles are far from over: "One day, she [Dora]
prayed, her new friend and partner [Justin Escobar, whose first name sounds
like "justice"] would stop waking up in the dead of night, his heart pounding in
his chest like a caged bird yearning for unbound flight" (177).

Indeed, the struggles are far from over, which brings me to the last section of
this chapter. Mexican Americans still battle many stereotypes and much socioeconomic and legal discrimination, particularly those who are recent arrivals.
In fact, any continuing civil rights movement based on the identity categories
"Mexican American" and "Chicana/o" (politicized Mexican American) must
take into account that many new immigrants are not seen and also do not see
themselves as "Mexican Americans." They are *americanos* but transnationals

who, when asked where they come from, will, unless under some kind of duress, point to their town, city, or rural locale in Mexico—Guanajuato, for example. To complicate the picture even further, other immigrants from Latin America—particularly Central America—are mis-recognized as Mexicans by the dominant culture. This is an observation that Sergio Arau's 2004 film *Day Without a Mexican* underscores. In fact, the title alludes to the confusion, as "a Mexican" stands in for any and all immigrants coming from south of the U.S. border.

Furthermore, before "Mexican American" and "Chicana/o" and even "Mexican" were being challenged by the complex realities of immigration at the end of the twentieth and the beginning of the twenty-first century, *Chicanidad*, or the Chicano civil rights movement, was challenged in the 1970s, 1980s, and 1990s by feminism; by gay and lesbian and later LGBTQ political activism for representation and equal treatment; by regional differences in experience of identity (New Mexico versus Texas versus California); by class issues; and by an awareness of more or less connection with and understanding of indigenous issues, such as the desire for tribal or nation status recognition, the actual restoration of expropriated lands (an appeal to a mythical Aztlán being insufficient), and so forth.

The question of what constitutes a non-identity of night is, of course, more complicated than the first-order dynamic between a dominant, visible, and, for the most part, well-represented "Anglo" culture and peripheralized Mexican and Mexican American culture within the United States. All the issues just mentioned that have to do with geopolitical variations, gender, sexuality, and class (as dramatized in the Corpi novels, for instance) complicate what it means to be Mexican American and, specifically, politicized Mexican American or Chicana/o. The dreaded non-identities of night exist at many levels within Chicana/o communities as well as between them and the dominant culture.

A relatively recent Chicana/o cultural production to copiously foreground night in its descriptions, structure, title, and cover art (which is a painting by Patssi Valdez of a bed with a young woman in it floating on a nighttime ocean illuminated by a full moon) is Carla Trujillo's 2003 novel *What Night Brings*. This novel transposes the noir detective story to another genre—young adult literature—and thus expands the range and kind of Chicana/o night work. This specific transposition involves an intimate domestication of noir fear and terror as it concerns a dysfunctional family scenario of an abusive father, a battered mother and children, and the eventual exposé of the father's double life. The actual mode of the novel is not noir but comedy, as the protagonists with whom the readers are supposed to have the most sympathy (a young girl named María Cruz and her sister Corin) not only survive their trials of terror but thrive. Night emerges not so much as a time of terror (though it is that, too, when the father returns home each evening) as a time of surprising transformations associated with another kind of darkness—that of the interior of a small photographic camera, which I refer to, speaking of another ingenious confrontation with loss and its metamorphosis into social change, as the (de)phallicized chamber of gender and sexual transformation.

Though the novel is not illustrated with or accompanied by any actual photographs, the convergence of representations of night with that of cameras and photography as the quintessentially modern/contemporary tool of representation indicates the extent to which this novel, in its unassuming way as young adult fiction, breaks new ground with regard to Chicana/o cultural productions and dreaded non-identities of night. The novel shows an awareness of the primacy of visual representation in this day and age. Moreover, it takes on the camera as part of a phallic economy of technology and knowledge historically employed, among other purposes, to document and often manipulate colonized or subjugated people. In this novel, the subjugated people—or, more precisely, those subjugated by the marginalized (the children of two Chicana/o working-class parents)—appropriate the prime instrument of representation in the contemporary period, the camera (the basis for all other kinds of visual imaging), and use it to work toward some kind of survival from and transmutation of the nightmare into a night that brings possibility. I demonstrate how in the following section.

Toys for "Boys": The (De)Phallicized Chamber of Gender and Sexual Transformation in Carla Trujillo's *What Night Brings* (2003)

Chicana writer and scholar Carla Trujillo is probably best known as editor of two volumes of essays that have greatly contributed to queer and feminist Chicana studies: *Chicana Lesbians: The Girls Our Mothers Warned Us About* (1991) and *Living Chicana Theory* (1998). In 2003, Curbstone Press, Inc., based in Willimantic, Connecticut, and self-described as dedicated to "literature that reflects a commitment to social change" and that "seeks out the highest aesthetic expression of the dedication to human rights and intercultural understanding," published Trujillo's first novel, titled *What Night Brings*. Trujillo's story, set in San Lorenzo, California, and in Gallup, New Mexico, concerns a young, working-class, part Chicana, part Native American Catholic girl named Marcía Cruz and her sister Corin in 1967 (with Vietnam and the civil war in Nigeria raging, two events to which readers find periodic allusions). The girls live with an abusive father and a mother who will not leave him or truly question his patriarchal rule until they frame him by taking photos of him cheating on their mother with another woman, a gringa named Wanda Pickett. In this way, the young girls visually and graphically attempt to counter their mother's enslaving patriarchal *imago*. The mother's patriarchal imago is her image of their father as someone who, despite his repeated actions of beating up his children and abandoning the home for extended periods of time, should be forgiven and revered because he is the father, the man of the house, the family's supposed protector, and her husband and lover, who cannot really be doing the cheating of which she suspects him.

The narrative is not exactly utopian; it is guarded with regard to the effect of Marci's and Corin's intervention in the symbolic order that structures the relations of the immediate family members to one another. The iconoclasm that Marci and Corin practice on their mother's imagination concerning (or illusory relation to) their father does not manage to psychologically or materially liberate her. The mother never leaves the father; she continues to live in some degree of denial, privileging her husband's well-being over her children's. However, the mother no longer insists that she, the father, and the children all live in the same house together once the children run away from home to take up residence in another state (New Mexico) with their switchblade-carrying, Lucky Strike–smoking paternal grandmother Flor, who is fully cognizant and vehemently disapproving of her son's drinking, womanizing, and acts of domestic violence.

The novel is deceptively accessible, perhaps even transparent, like its pared-down title *What Night Brings*. The title conveys romance and mystery, expectation and dread. What does night bring? It brings nightmares (both imagined and real, the latter in the form of nightly violence when the father gets home from work and acts out his frustrations on his family). The night also brings desires that exceed the constraints of the oppressive, dysfunctional family scenario and that morph into wish-fulfillment rescue fantasies symptomizing Marci's development into a gender non-conformist who prays to God to "change her into a boy" and who later describes herself as a consciously queer girl who "likes girls."[68] As Marci, the narrator, tells her readers:

> When night comes, that's when everything is best. Right before I go to sleep, I turn into Supergirl. . . . I'd make a better Superman [than Superman] because I'm stronger and smarter. They ought to put *me* on that show. . . . Every night I dreamed I saved beautiful girls. Usually, a mean man was hurting the girl. I'd beat the man up, then carry her away. She would be so happy I saved her, she'd want to marry me. I'd say yes and the dream would end with me kissing her neck. (5–6)

The tale is deceptively simple inasmuch as it is basically a coming-of-age novel told from the perspective of a queer little girl who has two fundamental wishes:

first, that her "dad disappear" (1), and second, that she be turned into a boy so that she can have girls (10). Over the course of the narrative, the first wish remains the same; it only comes true to the extent that Marci and her sister expose her dad and then disown him by going to live with their supportive and unconventional paternal grandmother. The second wish undergoes a mutation as Marci slowly realizes that she will not be changed into a boy and yet that another girl may be attracted to her and have a physical relationship with her nonetheless.

The novel mixes various kinds of popular genres: it is part Hardy Boys tale, part *Bastard Out of Carolina* (1992), part history from below or herstory of two young mixed-heritage girls, and part roman noir turned comedy *bildungsroman* (involving the evolution of Marci and her sister from dependents on unreliable parents locked in a life-threateningly violent heteronormative patriarchal power structure to active agents who expose the dysfunction of their nuclear family and escape from it). It does so in a direct, easy-to-read style written from the point of view of a young girl under the age of twelve. The greatest difficulty it presents might be, for readers unfamiliar with two languages, the occasional code-switching from English into a vernacular Chicana/o Spanish or its use of Spanglish and the technique of sometimes lapsing in and out of a dream sequence with no warning. Still, *What Night Brings* can be and has been classified as young adult fiction.

Despite its apparent formal and stylistic simplicity, the novel is conceptually sophisticated. It takes Lacanian theory about the relation to power, namely to the phallus, and rewrites it. Lacanian theory, originally elaborated by French psychoanalyst Jacques Lacan, was itself patriarchal in its ideology at the very same time that it provided conceptual tools by which to analyze the patriarchalism of rule by the father. The idea and theory of the phallus (elaborated in the 1950s) is one of the most controversial aspects of Lacanian theory on account of its complicity in the very dynamics it seeks to describe. According to Lacanian theory, the phallus should be distinguished from the biological penis; it refers to the imaginary and symbolic value accorded to the penis in the course of the subject's interpellation into language and the social order. The phallus in this sense is linked with the owner of a penis but is not synonymous with the fleshly penis. The phallus is a symbolic penis, a kind of transcendent signifier of authority, power, and strength, that may migrate from an actual father to another kind of authority figure who is not necessarily biologically male. However, to the extent that Lacanian theory treats the phallus as the symbol of sexual difference in that there is no corresponding female symbol or signifier—both male and female subjects are constituted as male and female with reference to it—such a theory (or this element of it) shows itself to be invested in male dominance.

Lacanian theory might have revolved around the absence or presence of a symbolic clitoris or vagina, for instance, but it does not. Furthermore, consider Lacan's concept of the imago, which makes its appearance in some of his earliest work only to be subsumed later into the concept of the imaginary. In a 1938 essay on the family, Lacan attributes the malaise of modern society to the declining importance of the paternal imago.

This novel—*What Night Brings*—does not traffic in the maintenance of the paternal imago. It strongly suggests that the paternal imago is to be questioned and dismantled. Whether it completely banishes it is another matter. I would argue that it reconstructs it and transfers it onto unlikely subjects, or rather subjects who have been disqualified according to a patriarchal, heteronormative script. That is, the novel transfers the paternal imago onto a gay uncle (Tommy), who is married but in love with a priest and having a closeted relationship with this priest until he divorces his wife. This gay uncle, the abusive father's brother, gives Marci and Corin some of the care of which their biological father deprives them. In other words, the gay uncle serves as a surrogate and symbolic father, a bearer of the phallus, in this case in place of the penis that is partly responsible for their being in the world. On the one hand, the logic of the phallus is upheld (it is a symbolic penis, anyway). On the other hand, the novel attempts to dephallicize this symbolic phallus by making the bearer or carrier of the role of the father a homosexual man, a "little *jotito*," as the abusive biological father mockingly calls him. Traditional Chicano ideology or Chicanismo did not countenance gay men. It regarded homosexuality as a betrayal of its cause, as an *agringado* or gringo-ish effeminacy not worthy of the Chicano warrior.

Trujillo's novel, like the work produced by much Chicana feminism and certainly by Chicana queer feminism, has no patience with the authoritarian, homophobic patriarchalism of Chicanismo. The novel further questions the Lacanian phallus and paternal imago by comically referring to the penis as a birdy every time it references one and also by putting typical phallic toys for boys—such as switchblades (95, 98), cigarettes used in gestures of authority (93), daddy's or the "master's tools" to quote Audre Lorde (102), daydreams and nightdreams of being heroic, karate moves, a rifle, and, finally, a camera—in the hands of rebellious grannies and girls who refuse to submit any longer to male violence and patriarchal rule. The irony is that they themselves wield the gestures and tools that have been utilized in perpetuating this problematic masculinity.

I argue that *What Night Brings* is written with a keen awareness of this irony and the need to transform these toys for boys into tools to dismantle the master's house, dephallicizing these tools not by denying their power but by wresting that power away from male dominance and using them to build another kind of social order, not a matriarchy (though there are touches of that *matriarcado* in the figure of the switchblade-carrying, chain-smoking *abuela*) but something else—a "revolution of little girls," to borrow the title of Blanche McCrary Boyd's 1992 novel. Significantly, Trujillo's novel effects this transformation under the cover of night, that time that undermines and engulfs daylight's social order.

Night is the time of subversive metamorphosis during which Marci dreams of being a girl transformed into a boy to attract girls. Out of a camera—a little chamber, dark as night—emerges the means for the transformation of the family power dynamics. Trujillo carefully selects a particular kind of camera for the girls to use in exposing their father's cheating on their mother with Wanda Pickett. Marci tells her readers:

> After supper, we called up Uncle Tommy [the gay uncle] and asked him if we could borrow his camera. He didn't even care. He said he got it used, but that it took good pictures. He even said he'd drop it by, but we told him no, that we'd pick it up after school the next day. So, the next day we got to Uncle Tommy's house, he gave us the camera. It was a Brownie. He showed us how to put the film in it. (194)

Marci and Corin obtain the camera from their *jotito* uncle, not from their father or some impersonal male-space camera store. Although a camera is typically regarded as a toy for boys—seldom are girls or women depicted brandishing one—the narrative selectively associates the camera with a gay man, delivering a blow to the heteronormative, patriarchal script about who the proper possessor of the phallus is. Moreover, it is important to note the type of camera involved: a Brownie. Several versions of the Brownie camera, which was manufactured by Eastman Kodak in 1900 and priced inexpensively enough to put photography within the reaches of the working class, were in circulation from the late 1950s into the mid 1960s. In fact, one version was called the Brownie Chiquita Camera. This camera was basically a small, brown, user-friendly plastic box with no protruding lens. It was advertised in Spanish as "*camara pequeña . . . fotos grandes*" or "small camera . . . big photos." It did not have a large, impressive lens, but it did take large 127-millimeter photos, with ten or twelve frames to a roll. The image resolution obtained from this type of camera was not high. It generally yielded low-contrast images with the trademark Brownie blur. Trujillo's novel contains a reference to this blurring of the images. Marci complains:

The camera wasn't very good, and when I took the pictures, I didn't think I was that far away, but I guess I was, because the ones of Eddie [her dad] and Wanda looked more like gray, blurry squirrels. (214)

Nevertheless, the photos are good enough; they do the job of providing proof for those people who know Eddie and Wanda in the flesh and recognize them in the photos (214). *What Night Brings* offers this camera as the phallic and yet also de-phallicized vehicle for re-making old masculinities and making new ones, if by new ones one understands that the masculine/feminine binary has been mostly deconstructed and that the revolution of little girls is also about the right to live beyond existing gender paradigms and their usual distribution of power. One can see why the Brownie (the name of which is remindful of the girl-power equivalent of the "male" Cub scouts) becomes the focal point of this conversion. Its shape, combined with its large-format film, confounds the notion that small can't mean big. Translate this correction into gendered, biological terms and one gets the message. The inscription of the Brownie camera into the novel's narrative presents a playful as well as serious challenge to a phallic economy of technology and knowledge. Though often humorous in tone (in the way the story is told), the use of the camera, this particular toy for boys, entails the use of an object generally considered phallic against the paternal image. If the girls' mother continually forgives the father his bad behavior and if he justifies his authority by invoking the ultimate phallocentric signifier, God—as in, if you rebel against your father, "God's gonna punish you" (152)— then nothing could be more loaded than to cross phallus (camera) with imago (the images it produces). *What Night Brings* conscripts this crossing or meeting of phallus and imago to counteract the image of paternal authority the father wants to protect and project to get others to do his bidding because they have uncritically internalized his image.

The last fifth of the novel takes up this small-big tool of visual representation and self-representation and wields it to advance a Chicana, lesbian, feminist version of queer social transformation that appropriates various stances of masculinity for its own purposes—including that of a primary "toy for boys," the camera, as optical phallus penetrating into the ontological enigmas that uphold patriarchal power structures. *What Night Brings* as narrative space is its own kind of chamber, or *camara*, and it takes up the camera to effect both an ontological and epistemological break from a patriarchal social order. Not content with mere critique—with identifying the problem (which it does by representing an abuse cycle that repeats over and over), the novel dramatizes intimate revolutionary action that overthrows the existing relations of production and transforms the material conditions of Marci's and Corin's existence.

The novel turns the stuff of noir and gothic *corrido* into comedy—as in *All's Well that Ends Well.* This transformation could be deemed a weakness inasmuch as it reads more like a fairy tale with a big bad ogre of a father, a rather uselessly complicit mother figure, and a fairy-tale grandmother in the shape of a rebellious, chain-smoking, switchblade-carrying paternal grandmother. The novel, while not entirely utopian, is like a fairy tale, and one wonders if night has lost some of its powers of "dreaded non-identity" in this approach. The novel seems a far cry from Américo Paredes's memorably searing stories from the 1930s through the 1960s. Nor does it have the intensity of Anzaldúa's "darkness, my night." Its sensibility is, curiously, closer to Sergio Arau's joking yet dead serious *A Day Without a Mexican* (2004). Self-effacing humor characterizes both that film and the novel *What Night Brings.* And yet this self-effacement—their vanishing acts (humor becomes a kind of mask behind which to hide and speak)— operates in the service of its opposite, for the purpose of underscoring marginalized and invisible existences. What does the dreaded non-identity time of night bring? It brings to the center of attention those who have been moved to the peripheries of both the dominant and the marginalized social orders (as with Carla Trujillo's novel).

Self-effacing humor becomes one more means by which to accomplish this night work I have been analyzing. Is it an effective tactic? Both Arau's film and Carla Trujillo's novel have done reasonably well. This first novel was blurbed by well-known writers, Latina and non-Latina alike, such as Sandra Cisneros, Dorothy Allison, and Margaret Randall. The relative success of both cultural productions raises a question worthy of consideration (though it is outside the scope of this present study): Does the significant increase of the number of Latina/os in the United States widen the range of effective tactics by which to approach deadly serious issues such as the exploitation of workers and domestic violence? Is there, despite the ongoing struggles for and ever-present challenges to equality, justice, and basic human rights, a growing confidence that there are many roads (including humor) through the dark night of the soul and body for *los otros americanos,* Mexican Americans who are struggling to change the U.S. "American culture," struggling for another kind of "*buenas noches*" than goodnight and good riddance (*hasta la vista,* baby)?

I have considered a wide range of cultural productions, including Américo Paredes's 1950s short novel *The Shadow* and 1963 short story "The Hammon and the Beans," the 1987 poetry and essays of night, shadows, and nepantla in Gloria Anzaldúa's work, poetry and short stories written in the latter half of the 1990s by Chicana/o writers, more than a decade's worth of noir detective fiction by Lucha Corpi, early twenty-first-century young adult fiction, and late 1990s films such as *A Day Without a Mexican* that look ahead to the twenty-first century of transmigrational transnationalism and examine how it continues to challenge and change notions of "American culture" and the U.S. body politic. Clearly, night plays a politicized, transformational role across a very wide range of genres, both textual and visual. And when I say "visual" I mean not only the film *A Day Without a Mexican,* which is just one of many films I could analyze, but also the texts that engage with visual media, such as Lucha Corpi's noir detective novels, Carla Trujillo's *What Night Brings,* and Leo Romero's short story "Pito." While these works do not literally combine the visual with the verbal—i.e., none of these texts incorporates actual photos—they engage with legacies and regimes of the visual, as I have shown. This particular kind of engagement is significant in the context of their sustained deployments of tropes of night and the associated constellation of shadows and darkness—of, in a word, obscurity and invisibility.

At first glance, it might seem contradictory that texts primarily concerned with the invisible and the not-seen should be so engaged with photography and film, media that are dependent on light and about making things visible. But this is where it is crucial to remember Lila Rodriguez's rhetorical question in the film *A Day Without a Mexican:* How do you make the invisible visible? You take it away. Thus, these texts informed by visual media make visible the invisible by immersing themselves in various shades of night, darkness, and shadows—by exploring those dreaded non-identities of night.

CHAPTER TWO

QUEER "TROPICS" OF NIGHT AND THE *CARIBE* OF "AMERICAN" (POST) MODERNISM

We define nations tonight.

—Rane Arroyo, "Nights Without Dawns" for James Baldwin,
from *The Portable Famine*

I turn from night among Chicana/o cultural producers to an investigation of its uses among contemporary queer poets of Hispanic Caribbean descent who are living in the United States and are at least half Anglographic. What I mean by "Anglographic" is writing in English, hence "graphic" and not merely "Anglophone." Why queer Anglographic poets of Caribbean descent? Why their deployments of tropes of night? What does an investigation of this cross section of variables—queer, Anglographic, poets, Caribbean descent, living in the United States—entail? A starting point for addressing these questions is the work on queer, transnational Caribbean and U.S. identity formations initiated in the mid to late 1990s. Scholars such as Manuel Guzmán have written about sexiles, "those who have had to leave their nation of origin on account of their sexual orientation.[1] Arnaldo Cruz-Malavé,[2] Rubén Ríos Ávila,[3] Frances Negrón-Muntaner,[4] José Quiroga,[5] and Cruz-Malavé and Martin F. Manalansan[6] have grappled with homosexuality and Caribbean displacements as forms of double sexual and geopolitical exile that intersect with each other in a history of colonialism. Lawrence La Fountain-Stokes synthesizes a great deal of this scholarship and contributes highly original and detailed readings of his own in his book *Queer Ricans: Cultures and Sexualities in the Diaspora* (2009).[7]

The social structures and identity formations of the Caribbean islands have been shaped not only by colonialism but also by coloniality. Following the work of Peruvian historical social scientist Aníbal Quijano, coloniality is what continues to structure epistemology and ontology in the wake of colonialism, even after colonialism may be said to be officially over, as in post-independence societies.[8] According to Quijano, the social orders of the Americas are not only marked but thoroughly structured by coloniality—ethno-racial distinctions and hierarchies being one of its characteristic features. A colonial policing of sexuality and of gender roles marks the social orders of the Americas. This policing varies from region to region according to received ideas from sundry parts of Europe and historical interactions with those from native populations and populations forcibly brought to the Americas, such as African slaves. Nevertheless, the social orders of the Americas share many similar features of dominance and subordination despite these variations.

The Caribbean islands—and, with regard to Latina/o identity formations, those of the Hispanic Caribbean, such as Puerto Rico, Cuba, and the Dominican Republic—have been New World crucibles of coloniality, places of hybridity both as the ultimate technique of colonialism (Robert Young's thesis)[9] and that which exceeds, perhaps even escapes, the colonial order (Homi Bhabha's thesis).[10] They have been places of oppressive typecasting, branding, violent plantation-system punishment of any difference perceived to challenge a racialized, patriarchal class stratification. They have also been places of that which resists, disorders, and reconfigures the slavery-and-indentured-servant-based status quo of the colonial order. The Caribbean islands, plantation-system experiments of the most thorough kind, are crucibles within the larger crucible of the Americas.

However, Caribbean-ness and queerness (which is not to be confined to the mere identification of the writer) are only two of the intersecting factors I will be exploring in this chapter. The poetry I examine here is mostly written in English. If it code-switches into Spanish, it does so relatively briefly, with the English language predominating, at least on the surface of things. I argue, however, that these texts often inhabit English to establish a relationship between inside and outside, dominant and subaltern, familiar and alien, marking English with Spanish and sometimes indigenous Caribbean or African concepts, phrasing, and rhythms. In terms of coloniality, the language most ostensibly represented is that of the colonizer of the colonizer—the Anglo colonizers of the Hispanics who colonized the Amerindians and the Africans. The majority of Anglographic texts I examine by their very nature raise the question of whether it is possible to write resistantly in English, the language of the colonizer of the colonizers. If so, how and to what effects? What is generated by writing in English despite the obvious cultural limitations of writing in the hegemonic language, limitations of which the growing possibility of a genuinely bilingual future reminds readers?[11]

How does the Anglographic work of poets such as Luz María Umpierre, Miguel Algarín, Rafael Campo, and the late Rane Ramón Arroyo signify in ways that challenge a possessive investment in what might be termed the white man's language (English), to extend George Lipsitz's concept of "the possessive investment in whiteness" to language usage and choice?[12] As Barbara Christian inquired of critical theory, which is sometimes bent on giddily deconstructing the "identities" even of those populations trying to reclaim identity that they have never gotten to express without fear of major reprisal, how does writing in English become other than another tool of a "neocolonial ideology of power"?[13] And why is writing poetry of particular relevance to this endeavor of challenging a possessive investment in the white man's English language through appropriation, hybridization, and manipulation of that very language?

I chose poetry as the vehicle for making my argument about what Caribbean Latina/o writers are doing with tropes of night, conveyed largely through the English language, in relation to their position as U.S.-based writers of Puerto Rican and Cuban heritage and to their uses of the Caribbean(s) of American modernism. As this chapter considers many variables at once, it is important not to take poetry for granted as one of the variables. Caribbean Latina/o writers obviously write using many different genres: novels, plays, short stories, essays, and so forth. Some of the writers I examine in this chapter, such as Rane Arroyo, have written in other genres. But this chapter focuses on poetry and tropes of night. Poetry is language intensified to an incantatory degree designed to transform how readers experience meaning and perceive the relationship between things. The poetry I am about to examine is designed to re-orient readers: to transmit a different sense of orientation with regard to the main preoccupations of these poets and the larger questions posed by this chapter. Poetry is a mode of expression and transmission that condenses, in both space and time, a great many semiotic traces of the imagined relations to historical, cultural, and personal experiences and impressions. Poetry is the artful and mysterious, conscious and unconscious, compression and crystallization of these traces.

Poetry has a public and political life in Latin America that it does not seem to have in the United States. The uses of José Martí's or Pablo Neruda's poetry across Latin America, including the Caribbean, are prime examples. But I would venture to claim that even in a more prosaic society such as that of the United States, poetry casts its influence (on the page, spoken, and sung). The four poets whose work I have chosen to examine are well aware of poetry's magical and at times prophetic force. They work at the crossroads of several cultures of the Americas in crafting the socially transformative possibilities of poetry through a dis-orientation and re-orientation of their readers' and listeners' imagined relations to the people, places, histories, and events with which their poetry concerns itself.

Poets such as Luz María Umpierre, Miguel Algarín, Rafael Campo, and Rane Arroyo were not all born on Caribbean islands. If they were, it is not clear that they left—if they did indeed leave—on account of their sexual orientation. So, if the term "sexiles" applies to them, it does so in both multi-national and transnational dispersed contexts. Few places in the Americas are truly welcoming of sexual and affectional differences. The works of these poets demonstrate an awareness of the long history of suppression and ill treatment of queer people on the islands; as Emilio Bejel points out, the "specter of homosexuality has always haunted" the discourses of those islands.[14] The works also attest to a keen sense of the colonial and neocolonial treatment of the populations of Puerto Rico, Cuba, and the Dominican Republic by the United States itself.

In other words, the sexile condition of these poets is one of layered dispersals, refracted dislocations, that do not follow linear trajectories with simple correlations or correspondences. Their sexile condition is not the result of something as straightforward as exile from one's home country on account of one's sexual orientation, particularly as the concept of home is already contested for any number of reasons. For instance, what does it mean to be a person of Caribbean descent based in the United States or to be a United Statesian (as is the case of Rane Arroyo) who was displaced from a Caribbean place of origin or even a place of origin within the United States that is typically tropicalized or Caribbeanized? What does it mean to conceive of oneself or even of a community as being so unmoored that the term "origin" is too dispersed and refracted to be relevant according to any of the conventional narratives? Origin cannot be narrativized or ordered according to predictable, anticipated patterns. New York City is commonly accepted as a neighborhood of San Juan, Puerto Rico, and vice versa—certainly since 1948 with *Operación Manos a la Obra* (Operation Bootstrap) that resulted in the mass influx of Puerto Ricans from the island to the the city of New York as well as to other East Coast cities such as Philadelphia. What happens to people of Puerto Rican descent born in Chicago or based in some part of the country other than a main Latina/o metropolis, such as New York, Los Angeles, Miami, or Chicago?

The poetry of the writers I have mentioned manifests complex flows of issues, associations, desires, and ideologies that express themselves in what I identify as a significant and critically under-explored pattern, a pattern that I signaled in the second half of this chapter's title, "the *Caribe* of 'American' (Post) Modernism." With this title I am indicating that the dislocations and dispersals, as represented in literary form, of these first- and second-generation queer *Caribeños* based in the United States and writing at least half in English are involved in several related cultural interventions not obvious from a consideration of the phenomena of sexual and geopolitical exile, displacement, or marginalization. I contend that the work of these poets reflects these kinds of exiles, but it also creates new and powerful maps or experiential space-times of cultural production that revisit some of the idealist philosophy and codes of Anglo-American modernism and rework these codes while extending modernism's challenges to nineteenth-century realism and realist mimetic codes. Contemplating the material of this chapter in light of the ground covered in José Quiroga's chapter "The Mask of the Letter" on circumlocution, circuitousness, and queer modernist texts in his book *Tropics of Desire: Interventions from Queer Latino America,* I suggest that the poets I examine are extending into the contemporary period a queer modernist legacy of networked U.S. and Latin American modernisms. For example, Quiroga writes of queer Cuban modernists such as José Rodríguez Feo meeting with Wallace Stevens and T. S. Eliot, and queer American modernists such as Hart Crane meeting with Cuban modernists (39–41). While the poets I examine are inserting themselves into these legacies of contact and circulation among queer writers from the United States and the Caribbean, their poetry is critiquing and reworking some of the tropes and codes of U.S. Anglo-American modernism regarding the Caribbean and national and transnational Caribbean identities.

This chapter examines the particular Caribbean Latina/o uses of concerns central to the work of Wallace Stevens and Hart Crane, among other Anglo-American modernist figures, while simultaneously considering why these uses and re-workings occur in relation to a persistent figuration of night, nighttime, and night beings and to an echoing and extension of the thematic concerns and techniques of Harlem Renaissance poetry (in other words, not just "white" modernism) and of African American cultural production more broadly. The chapter is dedicated to outlining and elaborating the connections among the ingredients signaled in the title: *Caribe* or Caribbean, queerness, modernism, postmodernism, and especially the tropics of night, a fluid, dark sea in which all these other particles are suspended, emitting effects upon one another.

A Caribbeanized "Tropics" of Night

Though this is a multi-variable chapter, I would like to reiterate that the focus of this chapter is on the uses of night among contemporary queer Anglographic poets of Hispanic Caribbean descent living in the United States. However, I claim that night in this poetry cannot be adequately understood apart from the conscription gestured to in the second half of this chapter's title: ". . . the *Caribe* of 'American' (Post) Modernism." The work of these poets puts itself in dialogue with the work of modernist American poets such as William Carlos Williams, Wallace Stevens, Hart Crane, and others via not only a trope but a tropics of Caribbeanized and Caribbeanizing night. This night attempts to effect particular kinds of dis-orientations and re-orientations of U.S. dominant culture and its imagined relations to the Others within its sphere and to the rest of the Americas, particularly the Caribbean Americas. Indeed, what we find in this poetry by Umpierre, Algarín, Campo, and Arroyo is a tropics of night, "tropics" being a term that amasses the intersection between the term "the tropics," which entails matters of geo-cultural-political location and dislocation, and the term "trope," which means a rhetorical figure of speech that involves a play on words or the use of a word in a way other than what is considered its literal or ordinary form. The phrase "tropics of night" is itself a trope indicating the entanglement of place, space-time, the received ideas and approaches embedded in a rhetoric, and the deliberate artistry or intervention that characterize the calculated turn as in the previous chapter but with a new set of cultural coordinates, toward night.

The title "Queer 'Tropics' of Night and the *Caribe* of 'American' (Post) Modernism," constructed as two parts of an equation separated by an "and" that acts as a concatenator of factors and as an equals sign in which what is done to one half of the equation affects the values of the other half, advances the argument that a queer tropics of night places the Caribbean, the United States, modernism, and postmodernism in relation to one another. The title points to the way in which the construction of a particular and even peculiar space-time (night) is harnessed to the manifestation of an important linkage between modernism and postmodernism—hence (post) modernism—that must be understood with respect to the Caribbean as it relates to the United States and vice versa. Turns are dependent on turns. This "tropism" or expressivity that is not tied down to the conventions of realism or to instrumental "imperatives and systems of social classification" and "strict designation"—to borrow phrases from Kevin Bell's 2007 book *Ashes Taken for Fire: Aesthetic Modernism and the Critique of Identity*— is, as Bell argues, a hallmark of modernism, or of plural U.S., Latin American, and European modernisms.[15] It is also characteristic of much postmodernist literary, visual, and theoretical cultural production, as attested to by both the analysis and the very modes of expression of deconstructionists and the poststructuralists. However, my purpose here is not to perpetuate generalizations about modernism or postmodernism. Rather, I wish to suggest a continuity of some features of modernist aesthetics in the work of contemporary—and hence post-modernist, as in "after modernism"—Caribbean Latina/o poets including Rane Ramón Arroyo. The latter has been described as a truly "postmodern" poet who employs allusive pastiche, self-referential wordplay, and the kind of effect for effect's sake associated with both "aesthetic modernism" and postmodernist discourses and modes of expression. Furthermore, understanding the queer tropics of night in the work of these poets entails an awareness of the elements of the second half of this current chapter's title: the *Caribe* of "American" (post) modernism. I call attention to the ways in which the work of these Caribbean Latina/o poets resonates with and transmutes some of the preoccupations of certain U.S., Latin American, and Spanish modernist poets. Moreover, this chapter pursues how these works engage with the modernist hallmark of "expressivity" that Kevin Bell describes at the end of the introduction to his book *Ashes Taken for Fire: Aesthetic Modernism and the Critique of Identity:*

> This inherent relationality between the visible and the invisible, which is sounded and silenced at the very moment of speech, unfolds within an agonistic scenography that literary modernism stages and restages incessantly as a the-atre of paradox that its texts theorize and dismantle relentlessly as the supremely ecstatic and shattering moment of narcissism and sacrifice, of sovereignty and enslavement, of self-actualization and self-relinquishing . . . a scene in which questions of style, impression, and sensation materialize in such a way as to demonstrate that the stakes of the political are never separable from the modes of their expression, and that, therefore, nothing about expressivity can be said to be in any way nonpolitical. (33)

My exploration of this (post) modernist articulation of the inherent relational-ity between the visible and the invisible, sound and silence, being and noth-ingness differs from Kevin Bell's in that I do not find the work of Caribbean Latina/o poets to be as skittish about "any project of identity formation, how-ever liberationist any such formation may be conceived" as Bell finds British and American modernism (3). The role that Bell assigns to "blackness" and the "dark night" of entropy (Bell quoting J. Hillis Miller) associated with "lan-guage's incapacity to secure the truth of its own propositions" (3) and "mod-ernism's imagining of subjectivity as an endless interstitiality rather than any project of identity formation" (3) on account of language's emanation from the void plays differently in the texts on which I focus. In the works by Umpierre, Algarín, Campo, and Arroyo, queer tropics of night, while they give "the lie to imperatives and systems of social classification," do not cede that "all strategies of definition and naming" are "nothing more than discursive instruments of naked power and narcissism," to quote Bell (4). As I shall demonstrate, tropics of night in the poems of Umpierre, Algarín, Campo, and Arroyo disorient and disfigure, but they also re-orient and re-figure. These processes involve defining, naming, and identity formation that are not necessarily antithetical to complexity, ambiguity, and loss. For instance, these poets create a status-enhancing intertextuality between their work and that of U.S modernists (Anglo and African American) and of other modernist poets beyond U.S. borders—such as Spanish poet Federico García Lorca (*Sonetos del amor oscuro* or *Sonnets of Dark Love*) for Rafael Campo or Puerto Rican poet Julia de Burgos for Luz María Umpierre. However, the poets steep their relationship to these modernists in an often melancholy discourse of night, which is sometimes borrowed from the modernist poets themselves—as Campo borrows "*amor oscuro*" (dark love) from Lorca, for example.

What does it mean to steep a relationship to modernist antecedents in queer tropics of night? In some cases, these contemporary Latina/o poets are pulling night references out of modernist works already characterized by such references, as in, for example, Hart Crane's 1933 epic poem "The Bridge" in which "telegraphic night," shadows, darkness, "blackened tides," "nightly sessions," and the bridge itself as a giant "index of night" feature prominently.[16] In other cases, these Latina/o poets would seem to take modernist concerns—for instance, the investment in Kantian idealism for the revitalization of subjectivity evident in Wallace Stevens's work with his "palm at the end of the mind"— and nocturnalize them, subject them to a queer, *caribeño*, Latinized logic of night. By "queer logic" I mean one that questions and bends the ethno-racial, sexual, and geo-cultural-political orders of things. Night stories would seem to do that anyway, so adding the term "queer" creates an exponential bending of the status quo, the exponential refraction of coloniality. Again, individual readings demonstrate how this works. But, on the whole, the effect is powerfully transformative of objects and subjects in place, space, and time and of the space-times themselves, inhabiting one space-time with another. To reference Betsy A. Sandlin's insightful article "'Poetry Always Demands All My Ghosts': The Haunted and Haunting Poetry of Rane Arroyo," a queer tropics of night haunts one space-time with another, not just imbuing the contemporary moment or the postmodern moment with modernist moments, authors, or texts but haunting modernist idealism (proclaiming the autonomy of the thinking subject and the primacy of subjective experience) with the historical pressures, the embodied knowledge—Avery F. Gordon calls this "sensuous knowledge" (60)—of colonialism, neocolonialism, and exile.

Sandlin's article hinges on the application of Jacques Derrida's discussion of "hauntology" in his *Specters of Marx: The State of the Debt, the Work of Mourning, and the New International* (translation published by Routledge, 1994) to *Chicago-riqueño*, or Puerto Rican, Chicago-born Rane Arroyo's conjuring of ghosts. Sandlin writes,

> Arroyo works within and through discourses of hauntology in his poetry, and ghosts serve as identificatory metaphors in his personal, cultural, and metaliterary meditations. Arroyo's cadre of ghosts include famous figures like William Carlos Williams, Reinaldo Arenas, Emily Dickinson, and Juan Ponce de León, as well as more personal specters. Ghosts and a broader concept of ghostliness, both of which are omnipresent in Arroyo's poetry, serve as metaphors for identifications that spectrally float between, around, and through socially constructed categories such as race, ethnicity, nationality, and sexuality. While metaphorical ghostliness can prove painful, confusing, or unsettling, spectrality—the state of being a specter/ghost—at times allows the poetic subject to adapt to his situation, to make his own choices regarding identity, and to question social restriction and immobilization.[17]

Spectrality or hauntology—the state and contemplation of being neither alive nor dead, of confounding borders and boundaries—does have the effect of questioning social restriction and immobilization, of getting around and beyond gatekeepers. But even more than "allow[ing] the poetic subject to adapt to his situation," hauntology in the form of a queer tropics of night adapts what is being called up to its own purposes. Not only does the poetry proceed on the basis of specters, it also provides an atmosphere, an environment, for them. This is a nighttime that transforms them as much as it conjures them. Arroyo conjures William Carlos Williams, Hart Crane, and Wallace Stevens along with James Baldwin, Motown divas, and more contemporary divas who draw on the legacy themes and techniques of Motown divas of the 1970s. When we discover that a "singing shark" is calling them forth, or devouring all of them, as he wends his way through the Americas on a diasporic Puerto Rican dark jet-stream tide of bittersweet lyricism, then we know that something other than "adaptation" or self-canonization—as the poet includes himself among the names—is unfurling.

What is expressed in the nocturnalizations of these Anglographic queer Caribbean Latina/o poets is a kind of "archive fever" such as the one Derrida discusses, citing Freud, in his mid-1990s work by that title: that which is driven to destroy the archive, the canon, the erected and memorialized status quo.[18]

The specters or ghosts are mischievous poltergeists, sometimes destructive, even perhaps "malevolent" from the perspective of those who would rather remain the masters. They are revenants, a point that the last third of Sandlin's article dwells on at some length. They are bent on revenge: revenge on the colonial order and, even more importantly, on coloniality itself inasmuch as they can alter its consignations, repetitions, and monuments. And yet, I hasten to add, their *ars poetica* is not content with being mere destroyers of an archive—of the canon, for instance, that is limited and owned by an investment in whiteness or the accumulation and capital of Euro-centricity or other dominant cultural mode. No, the specters or ghosts conjured within a queer tropics of night are heralds, harbingers, of a re-negotiated relation between the past and the present. This new relation creates particular cultural re-orientations and the possibility of alternate kinds of historical memory, of transhistorical vision, as we shall see: it forms an alternative archive rather than destroying history, memory, and the traces that encode these and carry them into the future.

I contend that more than archive destroyers, or ghosts who take revenge on the Anglo-American canon, modernist or otherwise, and on various aspects of the lingering colonial order, they are archive devourers. Sandlin's discussion of the revenant—that which returns, that which refuses to die (173)—evokes another image often associated with both Caribbean and Brazilian culture: that of the cannibal, that of *anthropophagie*. If these queer tropics of night partake of specters and revenants, then I have observed that these specters or ghosts—if and when they engage in archive trouble—devour or incorporate the archive rather than destroy it. Their "adaptation" is a form of incorporation. Caliban, that "thing of darkness," proclaims Prospero his by eating him, as Old Testament prophets and mystics ate bitter scrolls so that they would then "speak."

But there is yet another crucial aspect of the hauntology of the work of poets such as Umpierre, Algarín, Campo, and Arroyo. If it is commonly understood that night tales, stories, and fragments (whether narrative or not) belong to the broad genre of the ghost story—for instance, Paul Auster's 2003 novel *Oracle Night* has been labeled "a postmodern ghost story"—then by the phrase "queer tropics of night" I wish to indicate a fundamental inversion of figure and ground with respect to what is privileged. The conventional use of figure and ground privileges the figure above the ground. The ground exists to display the figure. Specters are not quite figures; they are chimerical ones. And yet specters usually appear as a translucency or transparency against a dark background or, sometimes, as dark shadows themselves. In many instances of the poetry by Umpierre, Algarín, Campo, and Arroyo, the specters appear as a dark, enveloping space-time or atmosphere. They are not confined to discrete appearances. For example, there may be so many of them that they become an "obscure" medium through which or to whom the poet speaks, as with Arroyo. Rafael Campo's poem "Night Inexpressible" was written in memory of Audre Lorde, who was born in New York to parents of West Indian (Caribbean) heritage and who died in 1994. Lorde is imagined as a "[d]ark wind through trees . . . In a gust, a vast, black woman embraces me."[19] The young Cuban American poet welcomes this embrace, this incorporation into the dark wind of Lorde, who appears not as a figure but as an encompassing mothering night. However culturally loaded this image or anti-image may be, it illustrates the primary dynamic between figure and ground I am emphasizing.

"Night" is a trope that is often anti-figural. It cannot be contained by figuration. It exceeds it. Instead, it devours or incorporates figuration. Thus, as a form of hauntology, night—and a queer tropics of night—reverses power dynamics between the living and the dead, the dominant and the marginal, the center and the periphery, the visible and the invisible. A significant portion of the poetry calls up particular ghosts or specters with historical names. However, the poetry I am examining manifests another layer or dimension of hauntology. It haunts it readers with its tropics of night. Specters, though individually important, are even more significant as part of a dark current or wind that engulfs and transports readers into a different space-time and horizon of values, not only into deconstructed categories of race, ethnicity, nationality, sexuality, class, and rhetorical affiliation but into a project that reconstructs these variables by refracting them through dislocation, diaspora, exile, and transculturation.

According to Avery Gordon's argument about the function(s) of spectrality, one of the motives for this reconstruction of values is a concern for justice. The deconstruction of categories of race, ethnicity, nationality, sexuality, and class and their re-presentation through the affective communication of dislocation, diaspora, exile, and transculturation entail a politics of greater attention to both difference and coalition building among the sub-alternized. Doubly exiled sex-iles are frequently attempting to work transversally across minority discourses about ethno-racial and sexual exclusion or discrimination. The geopolitical dislocation from the Caribbean into the cities and towns of the United States brings an extra dimension to this transversal project of speaking across subalternizations. Such dislocation brings the crucible of colonialism and coloniality into the mix with notable results not limited to the poets whose works are discussed in this chapter.

The deconstruction and refraction of race, nationality, sexuality, and class through dislocation, diaspora, exile, and transculturation via tropes of night gathers its energy not only from a concern with justice but, furthermore, from an urgent engagement with loss that is both collective and personal, both historical and contemporary. The work of all four poets—Luz María Umpierre, Miguel Algarín, Rafael Campo, and Rane Ramón Arroyo—is heavily marked by loss. Of course, one can observe this about a great deal of poetry and art, following Friedrich Hölderlin's claim that art is mourning. What may seem, at first glance, a general observation is two-fold and specific. First, in these poets' work loss is often encoded through tropes of night; and second, the details of the encoding push the sense of loss or "melancholia"—following Freud's 1917 essay "Mourning and Melancholia," which distinguishes between "mourning" (grief work that eventually gives up the lost object) and "melancholia" (that refuses to give up the lost object)—into a generative space-time that restructures consciousness, social formations, and territorializations connected to ethno-racial, national, sexual, and class coordinates.[20]

The work of these poets engages loss with an understanding of the subversive and liberating forces entailed in that loss, forces to which they attempt to give an anti-figural figuration through tropes of night. In the poetry of this chapter, tropes of night are as much a part of a "politics of loss"—to quote from the title of Latina/o scholar Antonio Viego's 2007 book *Dead Subjects: Toward a Politics of Loss in Latino Studies*—as they are of a concern for justice.[21] This concern for justice and a politics of loss are, in this poetry, in a dialectical relation with one another. Antonio Viego's book suggests nothing short of the idea that a Lacanian dismantling of an identitarian ego psychology (53)—designed to shore up a strong ego with definite identity boundaries and markers—constitutes a liberating, antiracist loss. In Foucauldian terms, this deconstruction and critically willed "loss" of ego psychology and its identitarianism means that a given social order has not succeeded entirely in imposing its identity and "diversity management" (46) strategies on the person or persons in question. Viego's work celebrates the "incalculable" Latina/o subject associated with loss. Loss here is understood in terms both of an acknowledgment of the split in the subject occasioned by the entry into language (the "me" is not the "I") and of rebellion against language and categories. Thus, Viego, drawing from Lacan, theorizes loss as, paradoxically, a counterforce to the disciplining loss imposed by language and the managerial "biopower"—reproduction and control of biological life (11)—effected through its categories and labels and the social practices based on these categories. Viego argues that the radical aspect of the umbrella term "Latino" is that it does not yield coherent and cohesive racializations. He compares the ambiguity of the label or term "Latino" to the way in which the notion of queerness works:

Throughout this project, I attempt to read for the overlaps whenever possible between the critical operations performed by *Latino* and *queer* with respect to ethnicity, race, sexuality, and sexual difference. Just as *queer* attempts to disturb binary categories like homosexuality/heterosexuality, female/male, masculinity/femininity, *Latino* similarly, due to its general inconclusivity with respect to remarking on categories of race and ethnicity, disturbs the logic by which ethnicity/race can be posed as a binary pair. In short, *Latino* queers ethnicity and race.[21]

I understand the loss that Viego theorizes as being figured anti-figurally through tropes of night. These tropes of night often function in terms of what Viego describes when he writes of a Lacanian, antiracist critique of ego psychology and its identitarian categories that compose social hierarchies and make possible diversity management. Sometimes, as we shall see, tropes of night are part of claiming, not eschewing, a particular identity. The blurring of boundaries is not always antithetical to the claiming of a particular identity, as I already intimated in my discussion of Kevin Bell's book on aesthetic modernism, *Ashes Taken for Fire.* However, claiming an identity in the works that I will be analyzing generally entails the acceptance of impurity, mixture, and whatever challenges triumphalist complacencies about space, time, and place in relation to identity as well as whatever challenges assimilationist imperatives, on the one hand, and easy ethno-nationalist ones, on the other.

As for loss and how it is depicted through and by tropes of night, I take guiding insight from the 2003 collection of essays titled *Loss,* edited by David L. Eng and David Kazanjian with an afterword by Judith Butler. This collection of essays offers apprehensions and representations of loss that simultaneously depathologize and re-politicize melancholia, a key aim of my own project on Latina/o aesthetics of night. Instead of viewing melancholia as mere lack and impoverishment of the individual or of a particular collectivity, this book of essays demonstrates the many ways in which confrontation with loss produces (without apology) social formations, aesthetics, politics, and assorted negotiations of survival and endurance. Unfortunately, not a single essay is dedicated to Latina/o cultural production in the United States. Nevertheless, two essays function as nearest corollaries: Vilashini Cooppan's "Mourning Becomes Kitsch: The Aesthetics of Loss in Severo Sarduy's *Cobra*" on an "alternative aesthetics of lost space" in the Paris-based Cuban writer's experimental novel,[22] and "A Dialogue on Racial Melancholia" by David L. Eng and Sinhee Han that argues, following José Esteban Muñoz's claim, that for people of color, as for queers, "melancholia is not a pathology but an integral part of daily existence and survival" (363). Overall, the volume *Loss* explores and demonstrates a conceptual phrase from Juliana Schiesari's study *The Gendering of Melancholia: Feminism, Psychoanalysis, and the Symbolics of Loss in Renaissance Literature*— "habitus of cultural empowerment" in relation to melancholia.[23] This, I suggest, is one significant lens through which to view tropes of night in the cultural productions I myself explore in this chapter.

The Immanence of Night in Luz María Umpierre-Herrera's *The Margarita Poems* (1987)[24]

Puerto Rico–born U.S.-based writer Luz María Umpierre-Herrera's *The Margarita Poems* (1987) written in the mid 1980s and published by Third Woman Press (located, at the time, in Bloomington, Indiana, and later in Berkeley, California) constitutes a slim but very powerful collection of nine poems marked by melancholic loss and the quest for social justice—and by night. In prefatory remarks titled "In Cycles," Umpierre emphasizes, in no uncertain terms, that these poems were "written between 1985 and 1986 with a sense of loss and urgency":

> The loss centered itself on the fact that some women whom I love more than my Self were no longer in my life. The urgency was dual. . . . What I needed to verbalize is the fact that I am, among many other things, a Lesbian. Second, I wanted to communicate in some viable form with some One who came to represent all women to me.[25]

This and succeeding passages of "In Cycles" clarify that the poet writes as part of an effort to make herself visible as a lesbian rather than to capitulate to the silencing invisibility or the fear of socio-political reprisals for not conforming to normative expressions of gender and sexuality. I say gender as well as sexuality because readers are given the definite impression in the preface and in the third of the nine poems, "No Hatchet Job," that, both on the island of Puerto Rico and within the continental United States, the woman writer is expected to conform to the heterosexist patriarchal system. If she does not, she is considered to be an "unruly woman" (21) fit to be nothing short of eliminated. The same prefatory remarks also reveal that Umpierre writes because she refuses to let go of her grief over her affective losses: "I wanted to communicate in some viable form with some One who came to represent all women to me" (1). Instead, she turns the loss that she refuses to relinquish into the nine poems that follow her introduction and the commentaries on her work by Julia Alvarez (at the

University of Illinois at the time), Carlos Rodríguez (at Seton Hall University), and Roger Platizky (at the Pennsylvania State University).

Recalling and anticipating criticism and incomprehension of her bold, openly lesbian poetry, she draws inspiration from other bold women of letters, particularly Chicana writers such as Cherríe Moraga and African American women such as Audre Lorde and Cheryl Clarke. She is inspired by an assortment of other women writers. Some are her contemporaries, such as Jewish American women Marge Piercy and Adrienne Rich, and still others are from a previous generation, such as Sylvia Plath, or are writers that preceded Plath, such as Virginia Woolf and Julia de Burgos (1914–1953). Julia de Burgos, the Puerto Rican poet, civil rights activist, champion of Puerto Rican independence from the United States, and promoter of African/Afro Caribbean writers, is perhaps the most important muse, model, and inspiration for Umpierre. De Burgos is also Umpierre's bridge to techniques and themes of the modernist periods in Latin America, the Caribbean, and the United States. I say "periods" because "modernist" does not mean quite the same thing in Latin American literary and cultural studies as it does in U.S. literary and cultural studies. By "modernist," I mean works that bear influences of and have affinities with the works of Pablo Neruda, Gabriela Mistral, Rafael Alberti, Clara Lair, and Luis Llorens Torres via the writings of and influences upon Julia de Burgos herself.[26] Among other signs of indebtedness, Umpierre takes the name "Julia" as a vehicle for the projection of her own errant Puerto Rican exile persona who addresses herself to "Margarita" like a medieval troubadour addressing the Lady. Umpierre's poems construct "Margarita" as a female muse locked in the tower (at one point in San Juan, Puerto Rico's Morro citadel) and the underwater tomb of patriarchal, colonial ideology. The Julia persona seeks to liberate this Margarita muse, whose name plays on the concepts of *mar* (ocean) and *garita* (garrison). The poems make this conceptual play explicit on numerous occasions. The basic archetypal movement of the nine poems is that of a quest. This quest melds the modernist mythic odyssey or penchant for exile with the medieval mystical desire to liberate the Lady from the tower and a contemporary, feminist postmodernist project to deconstruct and reconstruct the very logic of patriarchal language. Latina/o Studies scholar Lázaro Lima argues in "'Una Isla Amazónica Libre': Luz María Umpierre and the Critique of Transnational Boricua Subjectivity" that *The Margarita Poems* engage in "the critical practice she [Umpierre] terms homocriticism."[27] I would like to point out that Umpierre herself coined this term in the early 1980s as a theory of reading, and explains its function, among other places, in an essay titled "Lesbian Tantalizing in Carmen Lugo Filippi's 'Milagros, Calle Mercurio.'"[28] Homocriticism can be understood as the undoing of "compulsory heteronationalism and the near absence of lesbian and gay agents in Puerto Rican literary history," in this case, according to Lima, by forming a dialogue with and correcting the "compulsory heteronationalism" of Puerto Rican nationalist author and educator Antonio S. Pedreira's 1934 work *Insularismo* (130–140). Pedreira's *Insularismo* is dedicated to the meaning of being Puerto Rican and cultural survival of that identity in the wake of U.S. invasion and cultural dominance of the island. Lima states, "The critique [of Pedreira's *Insularismo*] posits personal *herstory* as an antidote to the erasure of the Boricua lesbian body from the discourses of cultural participation and national belonging" (134). According to Lima, *The Margarita Poems* are in dialogue with Pedreira's *Insularismo* as its "implicit subtext" (131). I, however, wish to emphasize that Umpierre's poems take on a much larger and older battle against the history of machismo and compulsory heterosexuality in Puerto Rico and the Americas (including the United States) more generally. I would add that the poems do not only posit a personal herstory; they do so by harnessing elements of modernist mythic odysseys as well as a modernist deep-structure play with language to promote Umpierre's specific liberationist purposes.

Of the nine *Margarita Poems*, four are almost completely in English, three are completely in Spanish, and two are composed of an extended mixture of English and Spanish. The last poem—"The Mar/Garita Poem"—flows from English to Spanish (mixed with a third language, Jeringonza) and ends in Spanish. Lázaro Lima writes that this collection of poems "alternates effortlessly between the diasporic English and the island Spanish," a technique that allows Umpierre "to defamiliarize the assumed monological logic of national languages and borders" (139). For a poet such as Umpierre, writing in English is not synonymous with linguistic ethnocentrism or linguistic exclusivity. English is not viewed in terms of purity but, instead, as a mixture of Anglo-Saxon, Germanic, and Latinate strains. Spanish could be considered part of the Latin heritage of English. Furthermore, as U.S.-based Dominican writer Julia Alvarez observes in her essay "Freeing La Musa," which is included before the actual poems,

> If the first task was finding the muse, then for those of us who are Latina writers, whether we write in English or en *español* or in a mixture *de los dos,* there's a second task: to mine deeper, to find *la raíz de la musa,* so that whether we write in English or in Spanish, we do not lose the Spanish voices, the cadences, the rhythms, in translation. (5)

It is possible to write in English without translating from Spanish and yet still write in such a way that this English is part of an open rather than closed cultural system—to write in English remembering that English owes a tremendous debt to Latin—among other languages, that English is a pidgin language, after all, hybrid, not pure. Umpierre reminds her readers of this hybridity of English with every turn of phrase and with the poetic persona of "Julia," a Latin name English speakers employ without blinking an eye. Despite the fact that approximately half of the poetry of *The Margarita Poems* is written in Spanish, I have still included Umpierre within the category of "Anglographic" writers because she does indeed write in English, inhabiting more than two languages at once. In her preface, Umpierre claims that she writes *"for* a place between New Jersey and Massachusetts; in other words, Margarita. And it [Umpierre's book of poetry] is addressed *to* another place between New Jersey and Kansas called Julia. I have to add that it is also *from* Puerto Rico" (2). About the movement in the enunciation of the poems, Latina/o Studies scholar Lázaro Lima writes,

> The prepositions for, to, and from point to the difficulty of situating a movable subject of enunciation—the poetic voice of *The Margarita Poems* is at once in Puerto Rico, the U.S. heartland, and the eastern seaboard. (131)

Building on Lima's observation, I argue that this invocation of multiple places—New Jersey, Massachusetts, Kansas, Puerto Rico, and the unnamed places between the named ones—creates a map of relations that conveys subjectivity transculturating, like English and Spanish and, in the last poem, a third language—"Jeringonza" (34), between various subject and object positions. I say both subject and object positions because the poems involve both an I and an Other, Julia and Margarita, and the exploration of the Other within the self and vice versa toward the goal of their mutual liberation from the oppressions of a gendered and jingoistic coloniality—a patriarchal, heteronormative, ethnocentric coloniality—whether Puerto Rican or United Statesian or both.

Roger Platizky's essay focuses on the techniques by which Umpierre attempts to produce this liberation of both Julia and Margarita from the *garita* (prison house or fortress of patriarchal coloniality) of "Mar/Garita." He speaks of the poetry's awakening "dystonic imagery of pleasure and pain," "semiotic incantations," "representations of lesbian love and female sexuality," "revisionist treatment, from a modern, feminist, and lesbian perspective, of traditional love sonnets and quest poems inspired by beatific women," "[d]etranscendentalized . . . orgasmic celebrations of the female body and its potential to nurture, arouse, or torment," its invocation of "insanity . . . as a

liberating force (both socially and existentially)," and, finally, its "ritual of linguistic and physical communion" that "takes place underwater through the
immanence of Julia and the unconditional love of the narrator" (12–15). Like
the other essays by Julia Alvarez and Carlos Rodríguez, his is only a few pages
long. Many of the insights could be developed further. I am especially interested in two of them—one signaled in the phrase "semiotic incantations" (12)
and the other in the emphasis on the poems' investment in immanence and
the general movement from transcendence to immanence; from rationality
to madness; from the sky, air, and light to that which lies darkly submerged
and must be freed. I see the "semiotic incantations" and the movement down-
ward and inward as related. Though none of the writers whose essays preface Umpierre's *Margarita Poems* mentions Julia Kristeva's notion of the *chora*
from, among other parts of her scholarship, "Noms de Lieu" (translated "Place
Names"), the semiotic chora—a pre-symbolic space (in the Lacanian sense)
of sounds, utterances, gestures, rhythms, touch, and mother-child-like bodily
interdependence—drives this poetry, providing its powerful subcutaneous
pulse of rebellion against patriarchal, colonial structures.[29] The semiotic chora
is a function of the aesthetics of immanence and vice versa in Umpierre's *The
Margarita Poems*.

The first Furthermore, I propose that this chora-like aesthetics of immanence—of
a physical drive from within that defies the structure of a patriarchal, colonial
social order and its oppressions—manifests itself very significantly in the nocturnal images. These images or references appear among the many images of sun,
light, sunlight on the ocean, "yellow" margaritas (16) or "glorious" daisies (16),
"yellow leaves" (17), "brilliant" daisies (17), "rosie colored lips" (18), "lady laza-
rus" rising from the tomb (18), "yellow full moon" (23), "colores" (28), "limones"
(28), "líquido rojo" (29), "líneas amarillas" (30), "rojo" (30), "luz medianera que
alumbre el camino" (32), "fuego de la pasión" (35), "ojos amarillos" (38), "luz y
mar" (38), "falda de colores" (38), and "libertad y luz" (39). The predominant
references in *The Margarita Poems* are to light and sunny colors, such as yellow
and red. And yet folded within these many references to light, like shadows
within and under the petals of a flower, is some potent magic of night.

The first of these references to night occurs in the fourth of the nine poems,
"The Statue," which creates, as it unfolds, the center of this book of poems. The
poem laments the betrayal in the United States of the rebellious promise of the
1960s against the military-industrial complex. In fifty-four lines, the poem chronicles the historical and cultural co-option from the 1960s to 1985 of the "flower
child" from symbol of an alternate society organized around the arts of peace to
an empty marketing device for a production machine of militarized capitalism.

The poem also offers a trenchant critique of the perpetuation of a superficial commodified counterculture: "Flower child / twirling around a yellow full moon / ... / Flowered blazer from Saks on her back / ... / At the core of her fabric and emblems: / economics, gastronomics, the computer" (23). The poem does not end there. It chronicles a progressively hideous transformation—the complicity of the flower child, hippie turned yuppie, in the rigged games of the stock market, apartheid, and neo-slavery. Again, the poem deploys night to speak of this hideous transformation: "Flower child, slave making ant / in a midnight assembly of forgeries, / transferential concoction: / love to hate / peace to war" (23). The final third of the poem associates the transformed flower child with a bitter and ironic depiction of the Statue of Liberty as a "theatrical forgery" standing on the Hudson garishly lit at night: "Fully neonized, / fully galvanized, / fully modernized, / face lifted fully" (24). The poet finishes the poem by calling this transformed flower child and presumably the Statue of Liberty herself "glory hole of the nation"—an image that manages to transform the night itself into a sexualized and frighteningly nihilistic black hole. The last line is simultaneously a curse on, critique of, and lament for the flower child turned *vendida* (to echo Cherríe Moraga's phrase "long line of vendidas"[30] with which Umpierre was surely familiar when she wrote these poems). The date of the poem—somewhere between 1985 and 1986—adds weight to its bitterly ironic and dark purport given that 1986 marked the centennial of the Statue of Liberty's 1886 dedication by France to the people of the United States as a symbol of freedom and democracy. The mid 1980s also marked the middle of the presidency of Ronald Reagan (1981–1989), a presidency whose value system stood in decided opposition to the cherished values of the 1960s and early 1970s.

It may come as a surprise, given the often positive valorization of night in the cultural production I am examining, that night should appear so negatively, so devastatingly, in *The Margarita Poems*. However, another way to look at this seeming negativity of night is as an essential ingredient of the *brebaje*, (32) or witch's potion, against the patriarchal, colonial order that suppresses any other kind of expression or life. The yellow moon and the hideous nocturnal transformation of the flower child into a prostituted icon of capitalism and neo-slavery is as necessary to the alchemical transmutation that the poet seeks in her liberation of Margarita as the *nigredo* phase of rot and putrefaction is to the alchemical creation of the healing philosopher's stone or as the quest for the sun's life-giving *rubedo*, that yellow-red that runs like lifeblood itself through *The Margarita Poems*.

That night is a very important, though seemingly minor, ingredient of these poems is confirmed once again in the eighth poem of the sequence,

"Ceremonia Secreta" ("Secret Ceremony"). Here readers learn that the narrator/poet searches everywhere at night for her missing lover and that she rejects other lovers who approach her, for none but Margarita will do. Eventually, a witch approaches the speaker to help her conjure back her missing lover and the person she seeks to free from being buried alive. Not only the witch but the night and the night's moon, who is of feminine gender ("*la luna*"), will aid her in her quest: "La luna, que es siempre mujer, / ayudará esta noche / permitiendo sacar de aquel Castillo / la eme que suena en los corridos de aquel, otro país" (32). Here both the darkness and, in alchemical terms, the *albedo* of darkness—the silvery light of the moon—will collaborate to rescue the "*eme*" or "M" of Margarita, initiating the liberatory mission. This liberatory mission involves rescuing the allegorical damsel from the capitalized Castle, *Castillo*, of the patriarchal, colonial order.

The ninth and final poem—"The Mar/Garita Poem"—does not contain any direct images of night. However, the poem goes underwater into a subterranean realm akin to night before it concludes with its images of air, light, swallows flying, and the liberty of the island at last joined with the much desired *mar*, sea, and also "Margarita" freed of the *garita*, or garrison. Though the poem offers no direct images of night, it does contain a very telling line: "nightwatching for years to see her [the Muse's] words emerge" (34). This line occurs in the midst of other lines: "Observant of the Muse's burial of her language, / nightwatching for years to see her words emerge / to dismember the patriarch, / to destroy the colonizer's tools" (34). The poet's powers of observation, vigilance, and testimony are equated not with watching in general but with nightwatching in particular. This nightwatching is associated with bringing to the surface the new language—the new language that in its visceral syntax and sense-breaking manifestation suggests the pre-symbolic chora of which Kristeva writes, except that the model is not so much mother-and-child (the poem "Madre" notwithstanding) as between woman and woman. Moreover, the emergence of a new language is posited as an essential part of the liberation of the island. The island, though nameless, is also characterized by El Morro castle, lending it a specific place identity—that of San Juan, Puerto Rico—within what might have remained a universal or mythic abstraction. The island could be any island. It is both an abstraction and a specificity, like other abstractions in Umpierre's poetry. Some of these specificities, however, are encoded in such a way that, staying within the purview of the poems' verses, it would be impossible to say who exactly "Margarita" is. But this is not so with the island. The island is both any island historically subjected to the designs of patriarchal empire and also Puerto Rico. The nightwatching, with its martial, Amazon-like connotations of taking on the night watch while at war, is connected with the liberation or independence project of the island of Puerto Rico. Exactly what the independence might mean in practical political terms the poems do not indicate. But they most definitely conscript night as part of a trenchant critique of the American way, including its co-opted counterculture, and a strong push toward the decolonization of the island. The poems move toward an almost Edenic pre-colonial vision of Puerto Rico with only the swallows flying, the air, the ocean, and the island's shores. What differentiates this vision from an Edenic one is that it is lesbian, cast in terms of the long-sought (re)union of Julia and Margarita freed from her *garita*. Of course, such a vision, within still-patriarchal societies, can easily be dismissed as utopian and impossible.

The seeming impossibility of this alternative world—this utopia or no-place—is in fact part and parcel of its queer immanence. It is the immanence of lesbian, feminist, postcolonial, and more generally resistant rebellion against the patriarchal, colonial order. Night and nightwatching both accompany and compose this resistance, which is multi-variable in terms of gender, sexuality, and geopolitical location. Conceptually, I link impossibility and immanence together because immanence is usually in contradiction with itself. For instance, when one speaks of the immanence or in-dwelling of divinity within nature and the human, one is often in the ambiguous position of emphasizing a latent quality or presence—something not readily visible but believed to pervade everything despite evidence to the contrary. Arguments about transcendence of divinity never bear the same burden of evidence, by the very definition of the concept of transcendence. If something or someone is transcendent, then it is outside and beyond this world, this troubled realm in which we live. And so, by virtue of its separation from the known order, it can be posited as existing even if it is not known at all. But immanence cannot get away with this aloofness. On some level it must show itself as existing within a realm that contradicts at every turn its sought-after qualities. "The Kingdom of God is within you," and yet this "you" is tethered to this world that is not the kingdom of God but must be transformed, bit by bit, by the pulse and the resistance that dwells within. Such is the enormity and the difficulty of the task undertaken by *The Margarita Poems* in their desire to witness to the possibility of decolonization in a colonized world, in the oldest colony in the Western hemisphere, Puerto Rico, and in the midst of the Reaganomic empire of the (post) modern world of the United States in the 1980s.

And yet these poems are nothing if not persistent in their belief in and adherence to a nightly aesthetics and politics of immanence, suffering in body and soul, the very transformation the poet desires to keep alive within the hegemonic order structured to repress and control this resistant lesbian, feminist, pro-independence existence. *The Margarita Poems* adapt the modernist quest motif and structure—exemplified, for instance, in a work such as James Joyce's *Ulysses* or Hart Crane's *The Bridge*—to a queer, Caribbean, decolonial project to free women and the poet's beloved island of Puerto Rico from the internalized oppressions of a patriarchal empire. Part of the power of Umpierre's collection is its relative brevity; it accomplishes much in little time and space via a condensed economy of images and tropes, among them those of the night. Ten years after the publication of *The Margarita Poems* (1987), a striking use of night that applies Umpierre's "immanence of night" to the Lower East Side of New York City and to the heart of the Nuyorican aesthetico-political project of social and artistic transformation can be found in Miguel Algarín's collection of poetry *Love is Hard Work: Memorias de Loisaida* (1997).

Miguel Algarín's "Nuyorican Angels" of Night and the Critique of Enwhitened Idealism[31]

Miguel Algarín's 1997 collection of poetry *Love is Hard Work: Memorias de Loisaida* is grounded in experiences of living on the Lower East Side of New York City, but its modes of representation and cultural critique are far-reaching. The collection is divided into four parts: "Nuyorican Angels," "Shared Love (Bio/Ethics in the Age of Plagues)," "August in Loisaida," and "Nuyorican Kaddish." The poems celebrate life in New York City's Lower East Side but also confront, more diasporically and globally, life and death situations including the deadly effects of racism and ethnic hatred.[32] A physical immediacy characterizes the poems. Yet they are also engaged with Western philosophy and metaphysics— with what I am calling "enwhitened idealism." I say "enwhitened" rather than "enlightened" to indicate the ways in which philosophical idealism and its precursor metaphysics have been used to justify, however subtly, institutionalized racism by trafficking in ideals that are given conceptual body through the privileging of light, whiteness, and transparency. Algarín's "Nuyorican Angels" does not eschew idealism; rather, the poems re-appropriate a central idealist and metaphysical trope of angels and angelic bodies as figures, among other things, for "live-wire ideas" visiting or intersecting with human bodies. However, the poems underscore the physicality, rather than any conventional ethereality, of angels and, moreover, present them in relation to a specific temporality, nighttime, as nocturnal bodies.

Miguel Algarín, Puerto Rico–born, continental U.S.–based Nuyorican poet, critic, editor, playwright, theater producer, screenwriter, Shakespearean scholar, and founder of the Nuyorican Poets Café on the Lower East Side of New York

City, has over nine collections of poems to his credit. He has fostered the spoken and written word for over three decades, on his own and in collaboration
with others—for instance, with the late Miguel Piñero. Repeatedly, his poetry
and performances have been described as visceral, direct, energetic, and alive.
The very titles of his books—*Love is Hard Work, Action, Aloud: Voices of the
Nuyorican Poets Café, Times Now,* and *Body Bee Calling,* among others—emphasize physical presence. Physicality as art and vice versa bespeak a personal pref-
erence and also a larger cultural or intercultural one that is Puerto Rican and
Afro Latino or, most specifically, Afro Latino Puerto Rican. In *From Bomba to
Hip-Hop: Puerto Rican Culture and Latino Identity* (2000), Juan Flores reminds
readers that Puerto Ricans in the United States have long suffered on the bottom rung, socioeconomically, of Hispanics or Latinos/as, and they have been
represented as such, too. Flores observes,

> I attribute this special, and especially unfavorable, position and representation
> of Puerto Ricans to the colonial relation between the United States and their
> country of origin. Unlike the other Latino groups, the Puerto Rican diaspora
> hails from a nation that has languished in a dependent and tightly controlled
> political status for its entire history, a condition that has persisted throughout
> the twentieth century.[33]

Affirmations of the body, of physicality, of spatio-temporal three-dimensional
existence, and of the here and now must be understood in the context of ongoing
colonialism, neocolonialism, marginalization, and discrimination. They must be
understood in terms of the larger cultural under-valuation of Puerto Rican, Afro
Puerto Rican, and, even more specifically, *Nuyorican* existence. Nuyoricans are
Puerto Ricans who either were born in New York City or who primarily identify with that location and secondarily with the island in their lived experiences
as Puerto Ricans. One might say that Nuyoricans operate under the additional
burden of being Puerto Rican but not properly so—being seen by other Puerto
Ricans as even more colonized than the islanders. Within the rubric of primitivism, African Americans, Latina/os, and Afro Latino Nuyoricans have been
viewed as more physical and, by implication, more savage or mentally and culturally un-evolved than their Euro-American "white" counterparts, though class
may play a complicating role. Such a framing of African Americans, Latina/os,
and particularly Afro Latina/os results in their being reduced to their bodies and
physical actions. At the same time, these cultures have celebrated bodies, physicality, and earthly existence in ways that Euro-American, and particularly Anglo-
American, culture does not habitually endorse.

These are generalizations, of course, that have historically been implicated in stereotyping. However, bodily existence is usually a more contested and central conceptual and empirical category for socially marginalized people whose history is intimately involved with the facts of colonialism and neocolonialism than for those who have had the luxury of occupying more unmarked, transcendent, or privileged positions, socioeconomically and geopolitically. Thus, the work of Afro Latino Nuyorican writer Miguel Algarín features embodiment and insists on an aesthetics and ethics of the body. Many manifestations of the body appear in his poems and particularly in the "Nuyorican Angels" sequence from *Love is Hard Work*. Readers can find muscular bodies, bodies in a state of physical decay or collapse, the bodies of dancers, dead bodies lying in coffins, olive-skinned, brown, black, and white bodies, obese bodies, female, male, and androgynous bodies, HIV-positive bodies, the bodies of victims and killers, the bruise-covered body of Rodney King, neo-Nazi bodies, famished Somalian bodies, and the bodies of U.S. marines. Bodies are described, body parts are invoked, and bodily experiences are conveyed in vivid, visceral terms.

So, what does it mean to invoke the body? Algarín's poem sequence privileges bodies but complicates their very matter. "Nuyorican Angel of Despair," the last poem of Algarín's "Nuyorican Angels" sequence from *Love is Hard Work,* ends with the images of famine in Africa, of hungry African bodies, and of military invasion by U.S. Marines. The body in question is not one, but multiple; it is both white and black simultaneously, encompassing the marines conscripted into the service of a white imperialism, crawling on their bellies, and the hungry Africans pierced by bullets of military intervention and consumed by lack of sustenance. The poetic voice claims at the beginning of this last poem that "liberty weighs 'round my neck" and "ropes tie my mind to Somalia" (50). This is not the bounded, reified body of wholeness and health; it is a body of thought bound in slave-like service to the remote viewing of "the U.S. Somalian / relief operation [that] yields the best / Channel 7 Eyewitness Nightline News / foreign occupation television special" (50). It is a body that witnesses what dis-integrates it, what demolishes it—"the news crumpled internal space" (22)—and experiences an inside-out, an outside-in. If "relief" is a cover for foreign "occupation," then this body-mind resists that occupation by acknowledging that it has already been occupied by other bodies, cultures, and agendas that the speaking subject cannot ethically deny as a Puerto Rican, a Nuyorican, an Afro Latino, and an HIV-positive bisexual man living in the United States of America, which, like other imperial powers, has long held out the promise of freedom for some at the expense of slavery and occupation for others.

In these poems, a body is not unitary, not only because multiple bodies are invoked but precisely because it is a body—material and physical—and thus undergoing mortal disintegration. It is a body that sometimes lives through its implosion, "resuscitation started / after inner body building collapsed" (22). This resuscitation in the midst of occupation, brutal imperialism, social and environmental devastation, and "the age of plagues" (53) is given bodily forms in the images conveyed by the poems of "Nuyorican angels" entering "the temple of live bodies" and "kicking the mind apart" (21) but also healing "human pain" (36). The descriptions of the angels suggest that physical phenomena are mental phenomena and vice versa and are thus inseparable from cultural constructions. One of the central premises of Algarín's poems is the inseparability of bodies from ideas, ideas from emotions, or ideas and emotions from bodies. A recognition of such imbrications does not result in the usual privileging of the mind over the body in the manner of Western idealism or even of concept foregrounded a priori to sensation and sensibility, the corporeal and empirical, as one finds in, for example, the German philosopher Immanuel Kant's *Critique of Pure Reason* (1781), a form of modified idealism. The further modification of this modified idealism is of great importance to Miguel Algarín's poetry and his expressivity more generally.

Kant (1724–1804) was not a metaphysician like Plato. In fact, of Plato, Kant wrote,

> Plato left the world of sense, as opposing so many hindrances to our understanding, and ventured beyond on the wings of his ideas into the empty space of pure understanding. He did not perceive that he was making no progress by these endeavours, because he had no resistance as a fulcrum on which to rest or apply his powers, in order to cause the understanding to advance. It is indeed a very common fate of human reason first of all to finish its speculative edifice as soon as possible, and then only to inquire whether the foundation be sure.[34]

For Kant, the realm of unearthly forms was not more important than the substance of this world. In fact, most of his critiques reacted against what he considered to be empty transcendental metaphysics. Kant insisted that knowledge depended on the application of concepts to what lies within (not beyond) the bounds of physical sensation. One can appreciate the appeal of Kant's writings to Algarín, who finds inspiration in this philosopher's modified idealism just as Anglo-American modernist poet Wallace Stevens did for his poetry of "not ideas about the thing / but the thing itself,"[35] of "an invisible element of that place / Made visible" through the poet's perception/art (52), of "Things as they are / . . . changed upon the blue guitar" (165) of the poet's imagination, and of "that Spaniard [who] . . . rescued the rose / From nature, each time he saw it, making it / As he saw it, exist in his own especial eye" (316).

I mention Wallace Stevens's Kantianism because Stevens is the poet about whose aesthetics Algarín began his doctoral work before shifting his focus to the poetry of the Chilean Pablo Neruda. Judging from many of the preoccupations and techniques of Algarín's poetry, this interest in Stevens was not a casual or momentary one. The initial commitment to something as time-consuming as a doctoral dissertation suggests more of a link. Although Algarín's doctoral work shifted to Pablo Neruda's poetry, an ongoing connection to Wallace Stevens's poetry can be traced to the two poets' mutual interest in Kant's modified idealism.

The manifest contents of Algarín's poetry, however, contain an implicit critique of Kant's creation of hierarchies among the faculties (concept over sensation, for instance) and of the tendency, typical of the Enlightenment age, to associate knowledge with light and ignorance with darkness. One can find instances in Kant's rhetoric of ignorance being equated with darkness, as in, for example, the 1781 Preface to *Critique of Pure Reason:* "[t]hus reason becomes involved in darkness and contradiction, from which, no doubt, it may conclude that errors must be lurking somewhere" (*Basic Writings of Kant,* 3). Kevin Bell in his book *Ashes Taken for Fire* explicitly reminds readers of the interrelation between this treatment of darkness and blackness and that which is simultaneously philosophically nullifying and racially stigmatizing:

> Black, as a universalist figuration of void itself, is therefore niggered long before it is attached to its anthropomorphic nonsubject, Kant's "Negro," Hegel's "African," the animalistic non-I, the rank, subhuman of Kant's "Observations on the Feelings of the Beautiful and the Sublime," from his *Critique of Judgment,* and Hegel's *Philosophy of History.* Black, in other words, is radical nothingness long before it finds its radically (sub)human "referent"—. (30)

Regardless of whether black is or is not radical nothingness before it comes to settle on the sub- or de-humanized figure of African descent,[36] my point is that Kant's equation of ignorance with darkness is informed by a racializing discourse about epistemology and ontology. Algarín's poetry demonstrates an awareness of the racialization of Kantian discourse about knowledge and challenges such stigmatizing racializations. Algarín's poetry addresses widespread feelings of historical exclusion and discrimination shared by people of African heritage and others associated, particularly in the Western imaginary, with "darkness"/"blackness," as U.S.-based Dominican scholar Silvio Torres-Saillant eloquently articulates in regard to much of Western discourse:

> As a person who embodied the problem of blackness that had for so long triggered the antipathy of Western discourse, I [Torres-Saillant] at one point realized that the so-called great books did not for the most part speak amicably when addressing me. Some in effect were scandalous in their degree of bad manners. I came upon passages galore containing rabid hostility in the words of Immanuel Kant, David Hume.[37]

Similar Kantian tendencies are detectable in Wallace Steven's poetry that evinces a distrustful ambivalence toward darkness and night. Take any of the following verses as examples: "I saw how the night came, / Came striding like the color of the heavy hemlocks / I felt afraid" from "Domination of Black" (9); "This gloom is the darkness of the sea" from "The Man with the Blue Guitar" (179); "The little owl flew through the night / As if the people in the air / Were frightened and he frightened them" from "On the Adequacy of Landscape" (243); "After the final no there comes a yes / And on that yes the future world depends. / No was the night. Yes is this present sun" from "The Well Dressed Man With a Beard" (247); and "The night / Makes everything grotesque. Is it because / Night is the nature of man's interior world? / Is lunar Habana the Cuba of the self?" from "A Word with José Rodríguez-Feo" (333). Though darkness and night appear in any number of Stevens's poems, indicating their relevance to his neo-Romantic modernist aesthetic, they are often coded to convey doubt and negation, not belief (as with Algarín). However, some lines might have served as inspiration for the Nuyorican poet's conjuring of his angelic nocturnal bodies, his angels "of reality" (Stevens 496): "He was as tall as a tree in the middle of / That night. The substance of his body seemed / Both substance and non-substance, luminous flesh" from "Chocorua to Its Neighbor" (297); "It is to the hero of midnight that we pray" from "An Ordinary Evening in New Haven" (466); and "I am the archangel of evening and praise" from "One of the Inhabitants of the West" (504).

The "Nuyorican Angels" section of Algarín's *Love is Hard Work* begins with a proem that purveys what seems like a familiar idealist formula of Western philosophy. However, it ends elsewhere:

> [A]ngels are human interactions with the incorporeal world. Sometimes it seems as if the angel is an object outside the body that is transforming internal time and space into a metaphysical thunderstorm. However, more often it is

the possession of the body by biological changes in pulse rate, blood pressure, and oxygen levels that can make you levitate internally . . . angels are sometimes people, objects, or simply live-wire ideas. (19)

Throughout the poems that follow this proem, "live-wire" ideas are visually and viscerally materialized, not dematerialized. The ideas are like flesh, living or "live-wire," not only in the sense that they are absorbed by the eyes but also in the sense that they are spoken by the breath, which is dependent on a pulse quickened by angels that are powerful felt ideas or ideal passions.

In hermetic treatises and popular lore, angels involve concepts of a metaphysical realm. Postulates about this realm partake of idealism, not only in the common sense of that word as meaning utopian or perfectionist but also in the philosophical sense of privileging the contents of the mind over reality. Idealism posits the dependence of reality on the contents of the mind. Idealism generally insists that there is no access to reality apart from the mind and thus what is in our minds matters a great deal; what is there is or will become what we know as reality. Hence, idealism can be viewed as a theory of mental perception. Algarín's angels can be interpreted as an exploratory personification of idealism as a philosophical stance. Angels are messengers; messages frame experience just as perceptions do. The emphasis is on the perception of the thing and not necessarily on the thing itself. When an angel speaks, reality is transformed in some way. One cannot see it as one did before. Such an emphasis on the perception or vision of a thing can be heady because it runs the risk of dematerializing the material world into ideas about that world.

The angels of "Nuyorican Angels," however, are grounded at every turn in the grain and grit of a material world, including its homoerotics. While the poems privilege the role of ideas and visions in determining whatever is regarded as reality, that reality tests all ideas about it. Idealism in both the common and specifically philosophical sense is tested. Normative reality, including heteronormativity, is shaken. The angels bring balm and tribulation, but Algarín's poems in turn test the angels—the very notion of angels—against the socioeconomic, medical, psychological, interpersonal, juridical, historical, and political circumstances represented in the "Nuyorican Angel" poems. Even when beauty is the issue, this is the case. When I asked Algarín how his "Nuyorican Angel" sequence was negotiating a Western philosophical tradition, he replied as follows:

Nuyorican angels began at a point where I was trying to round my last book out. And it fell into place when all of a sudden all the philosophical issues got crystallized in these conversations and encounters with angels, when it became clear that the spiritual issue was talking to an entity just above being human but not quite in the stellar round table that God conducts. They [angels] began to bring me information about everyday earthly issues and how they edged into the more spiritual moral philosophic dealings that dwelled more in the house of God than in the earthly house.

The Western philosophical metaphysical tradition is simply about the earthly quest for clarity somehow melding into the larger theoretical issues of well-being beyond the earthly everyday confrontations that we live through.

Immanuel Kant's "The Analytic of the Beautiful" [part of *The Critique of Judgment*] was for me one of the great insights into the human mind because he really did try to look at what the beautiful is and he never tried to avoid the blemishes of the beautiful. He tried to look at it. And as a young mind at the time I felt privileged to fall into his quest.

I tried to bring the intellectual playground he [Kant] was inhabiting in writing "The Analytic of the Beautiful" to a tar and concrete sidewalk slide. His was very abstract; mine was grounded in the Lower East Side—combustible flesh and abstract thought brought into an actual living moment.[38]

Even the beautiful, a concept that is most readily accepted as transporting a thinker to a metaphysical realm without leaving the physical one, is made to touch ground, to come down from its high perch—to be marked by mortality, imperfection, socioeconomic inequality, and struggle, as the images of the "tar and concrete sidewalk slide" and "combustible flesh" suggest.

Angels, the materializations of an essentially metaphysical category, have particular social manifestations and ramifications in "Nuyorican Angels" that entail the deepening of their already hybrid status as intermediaries between "the house of God" and "the earthly house," to use Algarín's language. Angels, already inherently hybrid forms between the human and the divine, especially to the extent that they appear to resemble humans (though they are usually winged and luminous), are much further hybridized in Algarín's poetry, composed as they are of numerous kinds of darkness and what, in conventional metaphysical terms, usually signifies impurity and the morally suspect—darkness, the socio-politically abjected or racially stigmatized, and night. The angels in Algarín's poems, when given obvious fleshly form, are usually associated, like the poetic persona, not only with some form of masculinity, a patriarchal convention that is not innovative, but with striking and innovative adjectives such as "maroon-colored" (25), "Nubian," "black," "olive," "olive-skinned," "Mayan" (26), "dark-brown fluid" (37), and "schwarze" (48). When I spoke to Algarín about the coloration of both the angel bodies and the bodies visited by angels in this sequence, he explained that these poems were "taking the archaic image of an absolutely transparent whiteness to more useful and applicable darker hues where they have to live with ordinary people . . . angels become more life-like and more useful—you can call them down more easily because you identify with their physical condition and mental being" (Interview).

To borrow from and riff off of Latina/o Studies scholar Theresa Delgadillo's highly insightful 2006 article "Singing 'Angelitos Negros': African Diaspora Meets *Mestizaje* in the Americas" and her analysis of the various interpretations of the ballad "Angelitos Negros" based on Venezuelan poet Andrés Eloy Blanco's poem "Píntame angelitos negros," Algarín's "calling down" of Nuyorican angels of physical darkness and night does not accommodate enwhitening mestizaje.[39] Rather, Algarín's poems meld African diasporic pride in the multiplicity and heterogeneity of black heritage with a Nuyorican celebration of the hybridity of mestizaje to move away from enwhitening models of idealism, including of the Latin American ideal of mestizaje.

In Algarín's poems, the transformation in terms of color is twofold. First, the poems change transparency into color; then, whiteness (a color after all) becomes brown and black, and, furthermore, nocturnal with regard to the temporality of appearance. This first step takes place in "Transparent Nuyorican Angel." The HIV-positive narrator imagines his own death in the third person, not the first. "He" is already disassociated from himself, split into the poet narrator who tells and the "he" who looks at the double of himself lying in the coffin. He contemplates the room's maroon-colored wallboard, its rocking chair, its cut, dried red carnations (a sure symbol of death in Hispanic cultures), and its "rickety coffee table." He sees everything there "except himself" (25). He has become transparent. This is in keeping with the dominant cultural coding of angels as either transparent or white. However, the poem works against this code by replacing the reflection of a "maroon-colored wallboard" for the narrator's image. The color is not casual. Maroon, in Spanish *marrón*, indicates a dark reddish brown, sometimes chestnut. That is actually its third meaning. The first two are a fugitive slave of the West Indies (the Caribbean) and Guiana and the act of being left isolated without hope of ready escape. Thus, the word denotes both a color and a social and ontological status. All of these denotations come into play in the poem when the narrator, Mitch, is alone in his room thinking about his death and what the room will look like without him. He is marooned in the age of war and plagues, diasporas of people and viruses. As an English-alias "Mitch" for Miguel Algarín himself, he is also a maroon—not simply a black man but specifically an Afro Latino from Puerto Rico now on the U.S.

mainland, in New York City, in the Lower East Side. In embodied visible form, the transparent angel is, therefore, maroon, not white or black.

"Nuyorican One Wing Olive-Skinned Angel," directly following "Transparent Nuyorican Angel," develops what was subtly begun with that maroon-colored wallboard and with transparency taking on the color of what one sees through it. This time an angel visits the character Mitch, the now sleeping double of the narrator, who is supposedly not dead, but merely sleeping; he is in his bed, not his coffin yet. The angel is described as follows: "[H]e had a tattoo of a Nubian boy / at the top of his right calf, behind the knee. / His long black hair covered his olive skin. / He began to spin on his right leg" (26). The angel commands Mitch to harvest balms from his body and cure his wounds. Here the browning and queering of angels is complete. The angel is described as olive-skinned and has the provocative tattoo of a "Nubian boy" on his leg. Nubia was the ancient state of northeast Africa, which extended from Khartoum in the Sudan almost to Aswan in Egypt. The olive-skinned angel is marked by Africa, or one might say by blackness, in a complex diasporic sense inclusive of Afro Latinos as much as of Nubians. The tattoo suggests that an olive-skinned African angel is not merely a lesser or secondary version of the fair-skinned, fair-haired angel. Nubia is ancient, and so are its gods, goddesses, and divine beings, which do not derive from Judeo-Christianity. Nubia was converted to Christianity in the sixth century, but it had its own pantheon before that. Another way of looking at it is that some forms of African Christianity are older than Christianity in the New World, the United States included.[40]

In a dialectical mode, the transformations that "Nuyorican Angels" enact on the physical representation of angels have implications for any conceptions of divinity, God, or what in Enlightenment fashion is called "higher law." The poems de-whiten those "[entities] just above being human but not quite in the stellar round table that God conducts," to borrow Algarín's words. In so doing, "Nuyorican Angels" begin to map out a different vision of a supernal world by changing the appearance of the intermediaries, as angels are supposed to be, between that realm and the earth. What does it say about divinity if the intermediaries between God and humans are no longer exclusively transparent or white? In these poems, divinity appears in terms of darkness—physical and temporal—and homoeroticism. The hermeneutic circle continues in a reversal of Ludwig Feuerbach's thesis that religion is composed of the projection of human ideals and aspirations onto an object designated as a God or a divinity. The "Nuyorican Angel" poems testify to an awareness that human ideas about divinity—those projections once externalized and deemed to be external reality—shape perceptions of oneself and others.

An underlying question emerges from the angel praxis of the poems. Can one achieve social justice without modifying or amending notions of higher law and those ideals that serve as templates for personhood or that impinge on value systems within society? The past two decades have seen an incredible emphasis on angels in the arts and in mass culture more generally. For their devotees, angels often replace God as the source of comfort and aid. In terms of theater and performance, what comes to mind most readily is Jewish American queer playwright Tony Kushner's award-winning play in two parts, *Angels in America: A Gay Fantasia on National Themes* (the first part premiered in 1991and the second in 1992). The play was made into a television miniseries by the same name as well as an opera by Peter Eötvös. The popularity of the television show *Touched by an Angel* is also indicative of this angel trend. Notably, on that show, which ran on CBS from September 1994 to April 2003, the main intercessor, the wisest of the angels, is an older black woman (played by Della Reese). At one time the show featured a Latino angel.

When Algarín's poems turn angels Nuyorican, African American—as in "Nuyorican Angel on Maundy Thursday," about the collaboration between dancers Savion Glover and Gregory Hines—Mayan (31), or Japanese (35), they entail a coalitional effort to add other ethno-racial and socio-cultural hues not only to conceptions of divinity but also to ideals of love, hope, collaboration, acceptance, healing, creativity, and spiritual plenitude. Unlike the conventional angels of European traditions or even ancient Judaic and Zoroastrian traditions, they are not represented by a blinding white light or by whiteness.

Brown and black entities appear in the spatial "darkness" of a temporal night. They are also associated with the memory of historic nights such as the Fourth of July, Kristallnacht, and the night of Rodney King's beating. These implode for the poet into reminders of interdependence, not independence. New York, Los Angeles, Berlin, the Sudan, Somalia, and the Caribbean—the latter arguably present in the references to hurricane-like thunderstorms and typhoons as well as the transculturation of Puerto Rico in the "Nuyorican"—are connected through interlinked histories of ethnic conflict and cleansing in the name of progress. Nuyorican angels of night and night's darkness (as both mourning and physical marking) offer a different kind of universal than an abstracted white body. This alternative universal, that hard work of "love," is conveyed through the critique of an enwhitening idealism and of its privileging of immateriality (including the abstraction "the body") and its reification of a potentially fatal purity.

This critique of an enwhitened idealism is effected not merely through an intervention in the coloration of angel bodies and bodies visited by angels but in the very space-time coordinates that map the existential conditions of those angel and human bodies' materializations. What of the recurring temporal or spatial darkness of night and darkened rooms? The poems engage with Kantian formulations of the centrality, the *a priori* status, of both space and time: "Space is a necessary representation *a priori*, forming the very foundation of all external intuitions" (Kant 19) and "In time alone is reality of phenomena possible. All phenomena may vanish, but time itself (as the general condition of their possibility) cannot be done away with" (Kant 25). The poems bring these philosophical pronouncements down to earth. Time becomes a particular time: nighttime, when angels are shown visiting sleepers, as in "Nuyorican One Wing Olive-Skinned Angel." And space in "Nuyorican Angel Hypericin" (37) becomes the darkened room, the room with shades drawn, where HIV-positive Mitch lies shielding himself like a vampire from his Saint-John's-wort-induced sensitivity to sunlight.

Hypericin, one of the major active constituents of Saint-John's-wort, has been used as a folk remedy for hundreds of years, but HIV-positive people began ingesting and taking intravenous treatments of it following 1988 reports that it countered retroviruses. In Algarín's poem, hypericin was supposed to have brought hope to HIV-infected people but is toxic in large quantities. It "entered Mitch / in the form of scalding intra-venous infusions" (37). It "came as a dark brown fluid" in a hypodermic needle—"piercing the skin, entering the vein" (37) and producing "a hot tingling sensation that quickly becomes an unbearable skin melt-down" (38). Hypericin "requires funereal darkness" (38) due to the photosensitivity it causes. In this case, light becomes a destroyer: "Mitch welcomed Hypericin's visits," but he "knew that Hypericin's visits / were a roast of the soul and of the self" (39).

In both "Nuyorican One Winged Olive-Skinned Angel" and "Nuyorican Angel Hypericin," night and darkness, not day and light, bring much-needed balm to their sufferers. When I asked Algarín about the detectable relationship between angels and night/darkness, he replied,

> The angels don't necessarily find light antagonistic but they can work well without it. It is significant to meet an angel at night. Night visitations are not necessarily evil. They can be and are often ways into specific release of the body into a positive, clear, clean space. (Interview)

The poems transvalue night and conventional Judeo-Christian associations of it with evil, chaos, and danger. They do not romanticize night, but they do suggest that night, like the darker hues of bodily coloration, is sacred; it is a locus of creativity, healing, and life as much as is daytime lit up by the white light of the sun, the day star.

The "Nuyorican Angel" poems, however, do not shy away from other valences of night and darkness, destructive ones—as in the night of the soul and the body. The last three poems of the sequence are titled "Nuyorican Angel of Revenge," "Deutsche Nuyorican Angels" (with its internal section "Schwarze Angels"), and "Nuyorican Angel of Despair." The first of these is preoccupied with revenge that manifests itself as horizontal violence of minority against minority in reaction to racism, classism, and other hierarchical structures of oppression and social injustice. The first part of the poem outlines a violent incident near the Nuyorican Poets Café, and the second part expands its focus to encompass the Rodney King nighttime beatings that set off the Los Angeles riots in 1992 and also similar incidents of racial violence pitting minority against minority in the New Jersey and New York area. The second-to-last poem considers the physical violence of revenge and then narrows in on the connections between ethnic and racial violence in the United States and Germany—the Nazi persecution of the Jews, the German persecution of the Turks, U.S. complicity with Germany and vice versa, and the contemporary militarization of some Jewish communities. A cycle of persecution and violence continues as victimized people guard their identities and their lives with automatic rifles, threatening counterviolence. The image that dominates the last section of "Deutsche Nuyorican Angels" is "Schwarze Angels," or black angels. The first verses of that section read:

African-German diaspora,
can there be Turkish pride?
What's happened
to ethnic purity?
It's there,
the Simpsons don't see it,
don't even dream it—(48)

The references range from a Jewish diaspora out of Germany to German colonies in Africa and other parts of Africa as well as immigration from the south and east (from Africa and Turkey) into Northern European countries and a pro-nativist racial and cultural purity backlash in Germany and other places (including the United States) against this immigration.[41] Liberal satire thinly disguised as children's cartoons, alluded to as the TV show *The Simpsons*, does not look squarely into the eyes of a coming race war or ethnic cleansing pogrom symbolized by the "*schwarze*" angels. Here, black is not a liberating color of the African American freedom movement; rather, it reminds readers of the black shirts of the fascists in the 1930s. These black angels are angels of death. Their "purity" is fatal, for it will be in the name of severance, of a resistance to mixing, that revenge, violence, and death will come—possibly on the part of white nativists as well as minorities of color who retrench into separatism for the ostensible sake of self-protection.

The last poem "Nuyorican Angel of Despair" moves from First World countries such as Germany and the United States to one of the poorest nations in Africa: Somalia, historically subject to intervention by Britain, France, Italy, and the United States. In 1980, Somalia granted the United States permission to establish military bases. The U.S. presence was supposed to be a liberating one; it was to act as a redeemer nation in the role of both a peace-keeping and an avenging angel. The poem opens with an image that points to the paradox, fallen (like a fallen angel) into blatant contradiction: "So free that liberty weighs 'round my neck, / so without restraint that ropes tie my mind to Somalia, / so world-wide-bright-eyed gone wild / that Africa is the brilliant white-and-black / of an opaque 1934 Tarzan flick" (50). The U.S. Somalian relief operation yields the best "Channel 7 Eyewitness Nightline News" foreign occupation special. War, a "theater of operations," becomes a form of entertainment more exciting than football. Generals appear on TV running for presidential office. Marines crawl on their bellies up to microphones already awaiting their words. They state the obvious: "Hey, these Africans don't have bullets, / they're just hungry" (51). The poem positions itself as a millennium poem—"December 31, at the End of the Millennium" and spells despair.

What does it mean to end the sequence "Nuyorican Angels" with an angel of despair, the loss of hope, with the conversion of night and darkness, previously associated with creativity and healing, into the blazing bonfire of "Channel 7 Eyewitness *Nightline* News" (emphasis mine)? Or into the *schwarze* angels of revenge, scapegoating, and despair? When I asked Algarín why he ended his "Nuyorican Angels" sequence this way, he replied,

> Aren't they [revenge, scapegoating, and despair] the most prevalent human passions in life? If I have a world of angels and I see that these are the prevalent master feelings, I wanted to handle it. Instead of ending on a pretty note, I ended on a real note. Looking for angelic hues, I found these the most prevalent. (Interview)

Transvaluation of darkness and night does not preclude coming to grips with the historical, political, socioeconomic, and psychological factors that resist transvaluation. "Nuyorican Angels" re-inscribes and sacralizes darker bodily

hues and intervenes in representations of the space-time associated with those
bodies. African Americans have long been dubbed "people of the night," and
Latina/os are often thought of in these terms as well. Thus, how much more
so are Afro Latina/os? However, while offering vindication and balm for the
psychic wounds inflicted by racism, ethnic hatred, and so on, the poems distinguish strongly between balm and panacea. These poems are not wish-fulfilling
cure-alls; they do not offer the poetic quackery of heroic invulnerability or tri-
umphalism over the dangerous light of enwhitened idealism or the violence of
white supremacy. While they valorize darkness, bodily and spatio-temporally,
they also acknowledge the existence of evil variously associated with light and
dark and do not show chromatic favoritism. The poems steer clear of a physical
essentialism even while they turn a celebratory spotlight on Nuyorican angels
of night—the angels of the Lower East Side: Puerto Rican, African American,
Afro Latina/o, maroon, and Mayan, among others. They also evince a Nuyorican—New York Puerto Rican—and queer sensibility that by necessity
acknowledges mixture, not purity of any sort (neither white nor black), as the
source of enlightenment. To that extent, Nuyorican angels of night dwell not in
a reification of one color or hue per se but in their chaotic mixing, in night as the
promise of a creative and life-generating chaos.

Nuyorican angels of night, represented as they are in terms of creative and
life-generating chaos, speak to the issues in *Love is Hard Work,* but they also per-
sonify the mission of the Nuyorican Poets Café, which was founded in 1973 by
Miguel Algarín with the help of co-founders Miguel Piñero, Lucky Cienfuegos,
Richard August, Tato Laviera, and Bittman Rivas. The Nuyorican Poets Café
was the mainstay of the Nuyorican poetry movement and still serves as such
for the neo-Nuyorican arts movement as well as for many other artists-activists,
most often of color though not exclusively so, who practice a radical multicultural (and "culture" here includes factors of gender, sexuality, class, and creed,
not only "race," ethnicity, and nationality),[42] multi-lingual, and multi-media
aesthetics through writing, spoken word performance, theatre, music, and the
visual arts. Although among Nuyorican writers and poets such as Tato Laviera,
Piri Thomas, Victor Hernández Cruz, Sandra María Estevez, Willie Perdomo,
Pedro Pietri, and Carmen Bardeguez-Brown, Algarín is the only one to elaborate such a prolonged and dark-hued figuration of angels—taking on the role
of the modern, Nuyorican Emanuel Swedenborg (who claimed to commune
with angels and other spirits and fascinated Kant himself)—other Nuyorican
cultural producers have invoked angels. Consider, for instance, Martín Espada
with his poetry collection *Imagine the Angels of Bread* (1996). They zealously
have practiced and still practice an aesthetics of radical mixture and impurity

as the source of enlightenment, wisdom, and much-needed social transformation.[43] Algarín's distinctive contribution to this aesthetics of mixture and impurity is to "legendize" (if I may be permitted the neologism) it in a way that encourages readers to partake of the mysteries of communion with presences beyond the self that are brought close to, or that even inhabit or possess, the self. Furthermore, while calling angels down to earth in "more useful and applicable darker hues where they have to live with ordinary people" (Interview), Algarín's poem sequence elevates this "live-wire" lived experience and practice of mixture and impurity into a realm between "the earthly house" and the "house of God" (Interview), the dynamic, multifaceted realm of the Nuyorican angels of night. Night is both ontological condition and conduit passage between the "human" and God's "stellar round table" (Interview). The Nuyorican angels of night poems retain much of the Kantian idealism and sublimity of Wallace Stevens that resulted in concepts such as *The Palm at the End of the Mind*, but Algarín's poems also revise this idealism, the idealism both of Kant himself and of Anglo-American modernist aesthetics, to undo the epistemological, ontological, and social bias, both conscious and unconscious, against night and the darker hues it represents, infusing Kantian idealism with a more relevant and socially inclusive immanence.

From consideration of two continental U.S.-based Puerto Rican poets I move to a Cuban American poet, Rafael Campo, before concluding the chapter with an examination of a Midwestern-based poet of Puerto Rican descent, Rane Arroyo. This move may seem out of step. Why include a Cuban American poet in the middle of three continental U.S.-based Puerto Rican poets? Why not just concentrate on the poets of Puerto Rican heritage? I include the Cuban American poet because this chapter does not simply concern cultural producers of Puerto Rican heritage. Rather, it focuses on the occurrence of a combination of factors indicated by the title, "Queer 'Tropics' of Night and the *Caribe* of 'American' (Post) Modernism." With regard to this combination, Rafael Campo qualifies. His poetry engages in a queer tropics of night in a polyphonic, polyvocal manner that encompasses a (re)visitation of modernist poets and aesthetics, including the poetry of the U.S. modernist poets William Carlos Williams and Wallace Stevens and the Spanish modernist poet and playwright Federico García Lorca in addition to other more contemporary writers and cultural producers, such as Audre Lorde and Reinaldo Arenas. In each case, the turn to modernist poetics signals a certain experimentalism and breaking from realist mimetic modes. However, it is also an attempt to deal with colonial legacies and modernist aesthetics that are steeped in a mythos of finding or making new worlds, including the Americas, and an effort to redefine the relationship between colonizers and the colonized, masters and slaves. Though Campo is a Cuban American, I posit that consideration of his poetry belongs with that of Umpierre, Algarín, and Arroyo as writers who deploy their Caribbean diasporas under the signs and effects of a queer tropics of night, asking their readers to accompany them on complex, transversal journeys of cultural disorientation and transformation.

Passed through by Night: Rafael Campo's Mysticism of Night

As Rafael Campo tells readers on his website, he "was born in 1964 in Dover, New Jersey. A graduate of Amherst College and Harvard Medical School, he currently teaches and practices general internal medicine at Harvard Medical School and Beth Israel Deaconess Medical Center in Boston, where his medical practice serves mostly Latinos, gay/lesbian/bisexual/transgendered people, and people with HIV infection."[44] In many ways, he embodies the assumptions made about Cuban Americans by other Latina/os—that they tend to be of a much higher-class status and educated. Though such is not the case for many Cubans, especially the Mariel refugees of 1980 and visibly Afro Cubans who contended and still contend with socioeconomic disadvantages, the perception of Cubans as more privileged than other Latina/os of the Caribbean does have its basis in sociological realities exemplified by someone such as Rafael Campo. In his five collections of poetry, *The Other Man Was Me: A Voyage to the New World* (1994), *What the Body Told* (1996), *Diva* (1999), *Landscape with Human Figure* (2002), and *The Enemy* (2007) as well as in his memoir, confession, and testimony *The Desire to Heal: A Doctor's Education in Empathy, Identity, and Poetry* (1997), he does not disguise his relatively privileged condition. He grew up in an affluent New Jersey suburb, attended the highly selective, very expensive private liberal arts college of Amherst, the third-oldest college in Massachusetts, and then studied and taught at Harvard Medical School. Furthermore, both his poetry and his memoir reveal that his paternal grandfather was from Santander, Spain, and that in Cuba he owned a sugar plantation and a large number of cattle, which means that his family was landed.[45] Latina/os studies scholar Ricardo L. Ortíz points out that Campo's heritage is not in fact Cuban on his maternal side, but that in all accounts of his background, Campo emphasizes his Cuban heritage:

> Campo's public accounts of his life, in his poetry, his prose work, and in published interviews, all favor the Cuban part of his heritage and not only over the obviously "American" facts of his birth and his upbringing but also over his mother's Italian American heritage, which appears so rarely in those accounts

that even the January 2004 interview states incorrectly that he was born "to Cuban exile parents."[46]

The facts of heritage in relation to the narrativized and poeticized accounts of heritage demonstrate the extent to which ethnicity is a construction of choice and rhetoric. For the purposes of my analysis, I focus on Campo's rhetoric about his Cuban heritage and his Cuban American identity.

In terms of the legacy of his Cuban heritage and its impact on his Cuban American identity, a series of phrases from his memoir, confession, and testimony *The Desire to Heal* provide some telling clues: "the Cuban expatriate community, whose rabid patriotism and reactionary anticommunist anti-Castro right-wing politics repulsed me, but to whom I nonetheless belonged in the most obvious ways" (258). The passage indicates discomfort with the political allegiances of much of his socioeconomic Cuban exile class. Also, as a person who finally recognized his homosexuality and learned to accept himself despite culturally and religiously instilled fear and self-loathing, Campo addresses his conflicted feelings toward the Catholic Church and the fact of being Catholic, however lapsed (42). As a doctor and poet, he identifies with Christ's healing mission at the same time that he is confronted and affronted by the Church's historic persecution of homosexuals and its contemporary official refusal to grant gay Catholics the same respect and support as heterosexual Catholics (42–53). Despite his socioeconomic privilege as a U.S.-born Cuban American of upper-middle-class parents and upper-class grandparents, Campo experiences several kinds of exile—not only the one passed down to him from his Cuban exile father—that he palimpsests together in his memoir and his poetry.

Though he is privileged, unlike the Nuyorican/Puerto Rican poets Algarín and Umpierre, like them he identifies as a Caribbean American sexile. About the officially sanctioned homophobia of the Catholic Church he writes in his memoir: "The direct line to a higher power was thus disconnected for me, and I was banished to live in a house without lights (but with all the other modern conveniences), a frustrated missionary on the dark, unholy outskirts of God's luminous city" (52). According to Campo, queer people rejected by their religions replace churches and temples with nightclubs: "The dark drafty three-level nightclub evoked the cavernous internal space of the cathedral, campy Abba anthems were substituted for solemn hymns, and the priests' satin robes became the sequined dresses of drag queens" (53). The imagery of darkness or night is striking, and, of course, it constitutes part of the tropes of night so central to Campo's work.

Meanwhile, ostracization by the Catholic Church, and by *machista* Cuban as well as larger American culture for being homosexual, for living queerly, is compounded by a sense of U.S.-based ethno-racial stigmatization that Campo felt

growing up and even at various points in his adult life in spite of his socioeconomic and educational privileges. In his 2002 collection of poetry *Landscape
with Human Figure*, a poem titled "American, the Beautiful" contains the lines:
"Saluting it [the American flag?], I half-forgot I was / a fag, a spic, a goddamn
immigrant."[47] His memoir articulates the fear of difference that characterized
the affluent New Jersey suburb in which he was raised and his own reaction of
shame and self-censorship, both bodily and linguistic:

> I mostly grew up in an affluent New Jersey suburb. I was the darkest note in the
> white harmony of classroom after antiseptic classroom—I worried that I made
> discordant sounds when I smiled or played. (104)

The concern about being "the darkest note in the white harmony" and making
"discordant sounds" symptomizes both the racism and the linguistic (English-
only) ethnocentrism of Campo's social environment. One of his reactions is to
more desperately want to fit in, to belong, to this conformist world—a reaction
complicit with the conformity, as Campo more or less confesses: "in spite of
myself I have always wanted to enter the dependable squares of New England"
(106). And enter them he certainly did—in the form of Amherst, Harvard, and
so forth. And yet his memoir, his verse, and his life testify to the fact that he was
not and is not content with being an assimilationist Latino (88) who "listened
to Led Zeppelin and not salsa, who preferred pizza to paella . . . who spoke
English more naturally than Spanish" (88). At one point, he emphasizes, "I desperately want everyone in the world to understand the Spanish I almost never
learned, and I want to master English myself, indisputably. I want to write in the
entirely new language of my own country, the United States of America" (118).

Besides bilingualism, writing in both Spanish and English (which Campo
does), this "entirely new language" involves a subtle hybridization of English
with Spanish. This hybridization, for Campo, entails writing in English but with
Spanish rhythms and sounds—the "Anglographic" writing I alluded to in the
section on Umpierre's poetry, though hers is more bilingual both in its mixture
of English and Spanish poems and in its extensive use of Spanish within poems
that are also written in English. Campo describes the hybridization he envisions
and aspires to practice:

> If I can make English rhyme and sing, if I can be graceful and seamless, maybe I
> can touch the gleaming shell that rests on the beach of my Cuban heritage, the
> conch that when blown has always seemed to me to produce sounds sung in the
> melody of Spanish. (117)

Throughout his memoir, he demonstrates a tremendous wish to overcome what has been culturally construed as divided allegiances between English and Spanish, medicine and poetry, homosexuality and spirituality (particularly his Catholic faith), Cuban and New England Anglo-American culture, Cuba and the United States more generally, and formal poetry (Campo writes metered verse) and expressiveness. His search for a "new language of my own country, the United States of America" actually entails going beyond a declaration of conformist assimilation to one country, the United States, or one culture. This is clear in a statement such as

> Spanish and English were immediately the same, they had the same sounds, they were spoken in the same mouth, and they lived in confluent gyri in my temporal lobe. Being gay was joyfully not to have a country of origin at all, only a place in my heart where a man was extending his arms toward me. (120)

While Campo does crave normalization that partakes of a conformist assimilation—"I wanted my sexuality to be a normal variation, I want to be a good son and a good American" (117)—another impulse to declare himself different and unassimilable vies with conformity. He proclaims, "I see now that I always was the monstrous, pink-mouthed iguana lurking in the closet: I am the truth that I was always afraid to tell" (119).

Additional factors contribute toward a less conformist assimilation of a Latino, specifically Cuban American, sexile into the privileges of life as a well-educated and well-employed doctor in the United States. The subtitle of his memoir points to an "education in empathy, identity, and poetry," and a reading of the memoir, confession, and testimony clarifies that this education did not come painlessly. At the heart of this education—an education in the traditional sense of a bildungsroman, or the maturation of a protagonist from childhood into adulthood—resides a struggle with being branded "a degenerate homosexual" (47) and, later, a gay doctor in the age of HIV infection, when gay men are scapegoated for bringing AIDS to the rest of society. This branding comes from multiple sources—the Catholic Church, Cuban culture, and U.S. mainstream culture. To some degree, the poet internalizes this branding. Campo recounts in frank detail his initial fearful, judgmental, cold, and clinical attitude, as a "new intern on the wards in San Francisco," toward patients, particularly other gay men, with HIV and toward people of color (28). He tells his readers that over time and with much conflicted soul-searching, he came to see his cold, clinical response as inadequate in relation to his patients and self-defeating in relation to himself as a gay man, a doctor, and a Cuban American who was not entirely part of the mainstream Anglo culture. He credits "the bits and shreds" (15) of his inherited Cuban culture with helping him to hold on to conceptions of healing in relation to touch, words, music, magic, and poetry (15) despite his "chilly, fluorescent" (14) indoctrination in medical school and residency. In the face of potential disapproval from his medical school peers, he takes courage from the example of partly Anglo, partly Puerto Rican, New Jersey–born modernist and socialist poet and physician William Carlos Williams (1883–1963), who had a full literary career as a poet and doctor. Campo writes in *The Desire to Heal,*

> I marveled at William Carlos Williams, one of the many temporary heroes of my early adulthood, who through his poetry brought the immediacy of his particular experiences with poor patients into the consciousness of an impersonal, chaotic, and relentlessly industrializing outside American culture; for me, to become a medium for such connections was to perform the real work and drama of healing. (199)

The example of William Carlos Williams spurs Campo to write poetry and to fuse the heightened sensitivity required for poetry with his practice of medicine. He learns that being a doctor means something other than attempting to "conquer the dark inner continent that might remind him [Campo's father, in this case, but also Campo himself] of the lost Cuban homeland to which neither of us could ever return, and whose myriad wounds he [the father] had never been able to heal" (200). If *In the American Grain* (1925), William Carlos Williams's extended meditation on the discovery and colonization of the Americas and what composed "the American grain," insists that the colonizer was changed by the new world and by the colonized, Campo explores what it means to abjure conquest and colonization as a doctor poet and allow himself to be inhabited by "the dark inner continent" that emanates from his own fears and sorrows and from his patients' experiences.

Instead of trying to "conquer the dark inner continent," a line reminiscent of Freud's remark about the dark continent of the unconscious, Campo acknowledges the night(s) passing through him. In his first published book of poems, *The Other Man Was Me: A Voyage to the New World* (1994), the title of the third poem, "Another Poem in English," is another way of acknowledging that "the Other Was [Is] Me." He writes, "Each night extracts, on passing through us, lives / immeasurable."[48] Toward the end of the same poem, he observes, "Night / outlives us all" (16). These verses testify to a power dynamic opposed to that of the conqueror mastering the "dark inner continent" and all that is implied by that phrase. Rather, the physician poet is passed through by night. The image is a Baroque one remindful of the rhetoric of sixteenth-century Spanish mystics such as St. John of the Cross and Santa Teresa de Ávila, whom I mentioned earlier. I suggested that among some current-day Latina/o cultural workers, a conscious historical and cultural recovery project is under way in which a trope of Catholic Reformationist Baroque sensibility gets re-coded as part of a contemporary critique of colonization, neocolonialism, and the violation of civil and human rights. Rafael Campo is one of those Latino cultural workers for whom this is true. Reinforcing the connection between Campo's overall deployment of night and this mystical Baroque sensibility is part 5 of his third collection of poems, *Diva* (1999), in which he translates a sequence of relatively unexamined and homoerotically charged sonnets by the Spanish modernist poet and playwright Federico García Lorca called *Sonetos del amor oscuro* (*Sonnets of Dark [or Obscure] Love*).[49] Lorca's sonnets of dark love were inspired by San Juan de la Cruz's mystical treatise of poetry *La noche oscura del alma / The Dark Night of the Soul* and by the stylistically and thematically experimental work of the Spanish Baroque poet Luis de Góngora (1561–1627).

Translating Lorca's *Sonetos del amor oscuro,* with its numerous images of dark love, conveys to Anglophone readers queer love, both in the sense of same-sex love and the sense of a passion for the ineffable, that which cannot be captured in conventional terms. Moreover, it is yet another vehicle by which to express the night that both inhabits the poet—"my soul's long night eternally devoid of stars" (87)—and pierces or passes through him—"O boundless night with certain boundaries" (88). Campo evinces an aesthetics of active passivity that counters the conquistador's blind aggression toward the "dark continent" (whether internal or external).[50] Instead, darkness and night in Campo's poetry combine to create an active force that embraces him, penetrates him, and passes through him. He as poet physician is passed through by dark love and night. The role reversal of sexuality and gender (in which a male poet is penetrated by night) contributes to a queer tropics of night throughout all five books of his poetry. I do not mean to imply that night is gendered male (it is not, for instance, when it is associated with the ghost of Audre Lorde). What is apparent, however, is that night acts upon the poet as a force that both encompasses and possesses him in gender-bending ways, in ways that exceed conventional expectations and figurations. Night in some of these poets' work radically ungrounds the figure and is a way of talking about that un-grounding.

The un-grounding of night passing through the poet-physician explicitly entails coming to terms with his social, psychological, and physical pain and loss (despite his positions of privilege or the degrees of his assimilation) and cultivating empathy. Empathy, of course, has its ethical dangers, as it can too easily shade into appropriation of the "pain of others," to quote the title of Susan Sontag's 2003 book on the failures of the imagination and empathy.[51] In each of Campo's five collections of poetry, tropes of night function to offset the danger of that condescension—at least it is fair to say that they are conscripted for that purpose. Night, blurring borders and boundaries and dissolving daytime hierarchies, functions rather effectively to question distinctions between self and Other that get in the way of empathy—of feeling (and not merely regarding) the pain of others. In *The Other Man Was Me* (1994), night is associated with namelessness in a poem titled "I Dream I'm Him" (59). "The Distant Moon" in the same collection is about an AIDS patient who has "lost his sight to CMV" (cytomegalovirus) (112). The poem moves from concern about viewing a remote object to a dream about the patient's breath filling the doctor's lungs and to that tactile sensation coming from inside the body and resting on "his lips, my lips" (115). When the distant moon is mentioned again, it appears in a mirror, but the implication is that the mirror registers a tactile trace of the dying patient's last breath (115). The poet physician calls down the distant moon to bridge the distance between himself and the patient. The penultimate poem of this first collection also contains salient images of moonlight, the night, and a similar dissolution of boundaries between self and Other. The poem is titled "Finally," and it concerns the meeting of two lovers, two anonymous men, on "a lesser travelled road" (116). They could be any two male lovers searching for one another. The verses build on a vicarious mixture of anxiety and pleasure at the contemplation of their tryst: "They glowed like ghosts / Of lovers who had died before" (116) and "like finding the moon / From behind a once-obscuring cloud" (117). As with the earlier poem about the patient dying of AIDS, the last part of the poem closes the gap between the poet narrator and the subject matter of his poetical tale—these two male lovers meeting. The concluding line of the poem reads: "Two lovers met. The other man was me that night" (117). This line echoes the title of the book and vice versa with one important addition—the two telling words "that night." Night is the medium for this transference of identity between the anonymous lovers and the poet physician.

Night as the medium for transference continues in the next collection of poems, *What the Body Told* (1996). This book is divided into five parts: 1, Defining Us; 2, *Canciones de la Vida*; 3, For You All Beauty; 4, *Canciones de la Muerte*; and 5, What the Body Told. The poems are heavily focused on the body's pleasures, passions, and sufferings; they examine what the body reveals that spills over the bounds of cultural prejudices and proprieties even as it is marked, bound, and traumatized by them. The first poem, "So In Love," opens in the spirit of a William Carlos Williams poem with the eating of "a fruit that looked delicious, sweet."[52] Following this paradisiacal beginning, the collection moves into literally sublunary—"[b]eneath the moon" (7)—territory filled with passion but also with the pain of homophobia (internalized and external) and knowledge of a world "so full / Of the intent to hate" (13). The second section, *"Canciones de la Vida"* ("Songs of Life") opens with *"Canción de las Mujeres"* ("Song of the Women"), dedicated to Professor Eve Kosofsky Sedgwick, whose classes Campo took at Amherst College. The first section of that poem is titled "Some Uses for the Moon." As in Umpierre's *The Margarita Poems,* the moon is associated with women's magical powers of creation, transmutation, and conjuration/birth/death, the complete life cycle. Campo's poem associates this transformation with transexualism that involves the changing of a man into a princess, a change as much about morphing gender roles as about physical metamorphosis: "The moon provides this starting place for myth, / And as we're wandering the beach, it's sand / On which is made a princess from a man: / The moon is climbing slowly from the mist" (21). Again, night and the night's most visible celestial body are associated with a bridging of seeming oppositions (man/woman, self/Other). This bridging of male-female, masculine-feminine, and even human-nonhuman (with people and the moon) is especially significant in light of the poet physician's self-confessed journey to confront his own internalized homophobia and machismo, or patriarchal codes of masculinity, as well as his self-confessed fear of the physical transformations wrought by mortality and by what homophobia has branded as the "gay disease," AIDS. Later in the collection *What the Body Told,* the poet physician more fully embodies a sex/gender transformation by imagining himself as "The Last Great Empress of the Dark," a palm reader, a sorceress who works with night as a time for visions of things that have happened throughout history, affecting individuals and nations (36). Many of the poems in *What the Body Told* are actually glimpses into the case histories, the lives and deaths, of patients through their wounds and illnesses, the marks upon the palms that represent and connect to the rest of their bodies. The collection ends with some brief but potent mentions of night. The poem "Safe Sex Revisted" ends with the words "Everywhere is night" (121), which suggests that there is no such thing as safety and thus that a phobic reaction is inadequate. The statement "Everywhere is night" metaphorically emphasizes a generalized condition of loss that calls for empathy and care as we all share in the same ultimate fate, mortality, regardless of our diseases or health. Night appears one more time in the last poem titled "What the Body Told": "I've studied medicine until I cried / All night. Through certain books, a truth unfolds" (122). Here "night" measures the amount of work done and time dedicated by the poet physician to learning what the body told. Books can only tell so much. Equally important is Campo's direct experience with patients who teach him, through their lives, suffering, and deaths, to accept himself and to see himself in them and them in him. The enjambment of the phrase "All night" heightens readers' awareness of the night and its relationship to "crying," that physical trace of strong emotions of both sorrow and joy that permeate the boundaries between the inner and outer self—tears flow out of the eyes and down the cheeks of a face—and between the self-contained persona and the expressive one. Again, night is the medium for such transference between inner and outer, person and person. Part of what is transferred is the acceptance of mortality and the consequent refusal to scapegoat the Other as the carrier and agent of death, as death is indeed part of all of us.

With regard to the confrontation of death that touches all, including the doctor of dying patients, and the revisionary uses of American modernist aesthetics, Lázaro Lima provides readers of his *The Latino Body: Crisis Identities in American Literary and Cultural Memory* (2007) with a cogent analysis of the way in which Campo's poem "The Good Doctor" (60) from the middle section of his volume *What the Body Told* (1996) revises the poem "The Cuban Doctor" from Wallace Stevens's collection *Harmonium* (1933). Stevens's poem features a Cuban doctor whose "enemy is the Indian who brings death, like the virus that brought death (AIDS) in Campo's poem" (Lima, 160). Stevens has his Cuban doctor going to "Egypt to escape / The Indian" (as quoted by Lima, 160). Campo's revision "The Good Doctor" presents a doctor who cannot escape death and instead dies of the same disease that afflicted his patients: "When he died of the disease, / They left him where he fell" (60). Lima suggests that Stevens's poem expresses a fear of death and a modernist questioning of the sufficiency of language for dealing with it through the telling of the Cuban doctor's flight to Egypt to get away from the Indian (161). In contrast, Lima argues, Campo's poem questions the focus of concern in Stevens's poem, which is the gap between the imagination and reality and the insufficiency of words ("linguistic insufficiency," 161) to overcome that gap. Campo's poem shifts its tactics to the pursuit of "a corporeally grounded recourse to meaning" (161) and a call to "ethical action" (161) in the face of the death-bringing disease. I would add to Lima's analysis that Campo's poem "The Good Doctor" eschews the somewhat disturbing ambiguity of the ethno-racial politics of Stevens's poem that associates an Indian, a Native American, with stealthy death and a Cuban doctor with potential cowardice in not wanting to face up to death. In Campo's poem, no human is made to stand in for physical death (rather, there is a "city / Full of dying men and women," 60), and the "Cuban doctor" may well be Campo himself. Campo's poem closes the gap between self and Other. In the collection *What the Body Told*, night is the medium for that transference.

In Campo's third collection of poems, titled *Diva* (1999), night appears closely connected to issues of race and Cuban identity, the presence of Africans in Cuba, and the Cuban American poet physician's relationship to African American culture in the United States. The first poem, "The New World's History in Three Voices," concatenates African to slave to rebellious escaped slave to night: "part-slave, part-royalty, part-Caliban" (3), "the proud black slave / in me" (3), "renegades by night" (4), "black as night" (4), "men / More black than brown, whose children played and starved / And waved the Cuban flag" (5). Though the title of the collection, "*Diva*," is the Italian word from the Latin for female deity (*divus* being the masculine form), besides being the poet's narcissistic image of himself writ large, the muse who "rides" the poet and inspires his poetry of the night is, in turn, African American or black divas of U.S. popular culture named in the poem "Diva": Whitney Houston and Janet Jackson. Paula Abdul and Madonna make appearances, as well. Though the latter two are not African American (Abdul's heritage is Syrian and Canadian Jewish, and Madonna's is Italian American and French Canadian), Abdul's music often fuses African American rhythm and blues and Middle Eastern instruments, and Madonna has performed the part of black diva surrounded by her numerous African American vogue dancers (32–33). Though not female, the poet Derek Walcott also occupies the position of the black diva for Campo, teaching a Cuban American to "reinvent the lost Caribbean" (35) and its "swallowed gold" (40). He is claimed as one of the poet's black diva fathers.

But the most striking (yet classically Caribbean) parental substitution occurs in the poem "Night Inexpressible," dedicated to the African American lesbian poet Audre Lorde, who died in 1994. Rejected by his own Cuban, presumably "white," mother for being a gay son ("Madonna and Child," 15), the poet narrator takes as his "true" mother Audre Lorde and her body, "black as it was true" (16). The poem imagines her afterlife body as a "dark wind" the poet breathes in to speak, to express, and which simultaneously embraces him as "night inexpressible" (16).

The collection *Diva* is full of such moments—of black diva goddesses, their voices, possessing, invading, "riding" the poet in the presumed self-containment and impenetrability of his Cuban parents' "well-appointed house" (32) or, for that matter, closed models of culture that disavow what they consider Other. The poem "Night Inexpressible" represents the culmination of the incomparable night of intratextuality in *Diva*—a night of dark, revelatory engulfment and palpably visceral ghosting of one's own voice by another's. If Campo claims to be writing English circulating to the beat of a Spanish heart—that elusive inner language of his childhood—this double voicing is mediated time and time again by the figure of a black diva who is West Indian Caribbean or African American. In Shakespeare's *Tempest,* Caliban is a "thing of darkness." Judging from *Diva,* the "part-Caliban," like the "part-slave" of Campo's new world history, is African or black. While blackness is not always African any more than the night can be pinned down to race (being as it is melancholia as well), the collection *Diva* suggests that at the heart of the incomparable night of intratextuality, where Spanish beats inside English, is African-ness. This connection should come as no surprise given the long tradition of associating the Caribbean (of which Cuba is a part) with blackness. Antonio Benítez-Rojo's image of the Caribbean as a black woman is a latter-day manifestation of that tradition.[53] *Diva* includes a poem titled "The Repeating Island" in honor of Benítez-Rojo, a U.S.-based Cuban poet and literary scholar. Furthermore, during his time in New York City, García Lorca, Campo's idol, made similar claims and added that "negro" culture and the midnight blues were the most vital aspects of U.S. culture. Is it any wonder that *Diva* is, among other things, an homage to blackness, a mixture of African-ness and melancholia of the night?

Is it suspiciously appropriative for an ostensibly "white" Cuban American man to be grafting difference onto his work in this way? At what point does the graft in a Derridean sense begin to seem like a graft of another kind, intertextuality as intratextuality as dishonest acquisition or, at best, dubious appropriation in the face of socially imposed class, race, and gender inequalities between "white" males of the upper and upper middle classes and most Afro Cubans and African Americans? Scholar Vera M. Kutzinski cogently dissects the Cuban national myth of "*la mulata*" and of invocations of *cubanidad* and *cubanía* through African heritage, particularly through the body of a part-African and part-white woman, in several centuries of Cuban poetry and general discourse beginning with the early nineteenth century.[54] Kutzinski observes,

> In fact, by the early twentieth century, terms such as *cubanidad* and *cubanía* . . . were, for all intents and purposes, synonymous to *mestizaje.* Most saliently contradictory about such discursive entanglements is the symbolic privileging of a socially underprivileged group defined by its mixed race or phenotype, its gender, and its imputed licentious sexuality. In the case of the mulata, high symbolic or cultural visibility contrasts sharply with social invisibility. (7)

Later, Kutzinski summarizes, "The iconic mulata, then, is a symbolic container for all the tricky questions about how race, gender, and sexuality inflect the power relations that obtain in colonial and postcolonial Cuba" (7).

I see some differences between, on one hand, Campo's references to black divas and the poetic and more general, national mythologized discourse of *mulatez, mestizaje,* and *cubanidad* via African heritage and, on the other hand, "critical projections of the desire for a 'black aesthetic'" (7–12) that Kutzinski traces and takes apart with rigorous acumen. Though one can discern strains of continuity between Campo's idealization of black divas and iconic deployments of *la mulata* (including his portrayal of himself as a *mulato* of sorts), his poetry appreciatively emphasizes blackness more than *mulatez* or the black elements of *mulatez;* his divas, such as Whitney Houston, Janet Jackson, Paula Abdul, Derek Walcott, and Audre Lorde, are named and not nameless; and his figures of blackness are not socially invisible—rather, they are the opposite. They are visible figures in U.S. popular and literary culture, and their reputations are by no means confined to U.S. culture but instead are transnational. His poems render homage to the cultural impact of African American and—in the case of Derek Walcott—West Indian Afro Caribbean contributions to the Americas and to the United States. The poems of *Diva* are often aimed at underscoring the foundational importance of African American and Afro Caribbean histories and cultures to the making of the United States and certainly to the making of Campo himself as a poet.

To give the poems credit, they announce their indebtedness just as they announce, echoing Roberto Fernández Retamar's 1971 essay "Caliban: Notes toward a Discussion of Culture in Our America," their multi-voicedness, their "part-slave, part-royalty, part-Caliban" quality, except that, unlike Retamar, Campo does not subsume Caliban's racial difference under a working-class status. Caliban is a variant of a cannibal. The announcement also amounts to a confession of cannibalization, of ingestion—but, ironically, even Caliban has been cannibalized. A vampire (69)—a favorite queer icon because of its connotations of an alternative mixing of blood and, hence, technology of (re) production—is another figure for the poetic persona. What does it mean for a pale vampire Caliban to cannibalize, to ingest, others—those black divas, goddesses of the night, for instance? If, to quote Audre Lorde, "the master's tools will never dismantle the master's house," what are the implications of not only borrowing but incorporating the subaltern's tools and claiming to be inspired by the subalterns? If one of the tools is blue-black melancholia, what are the political valences of the poet's enhanced melancholia?

In *The Psychic Life of Power,* Judith Butler reminds readers that Freud characterized the melancholic by his or her shameless self-exposure and insistent communicativeness, both symptoms of the poetic persona in *Diva.* Postcolonially imperialistic, the book's incomparable night of intratextuality contains within it and is composed of Others culturally suppressed within a conservative *emblanquecida* (enwhitened) Cuban culture, a homophobic post-revolutionary Cuban culture, and jingoistic Anglo-America. One might not think of the introjections of melancholia as anything but an egoistically colonizing move "to occupy every position to preclude the loss of the addressees," the Others.[55] Homi Bhabha, however, links melancholia to a form of rebellion against the master to the extent that it inverts against itself the indictment it would level against that very master. In this case, that master can be understood as whatever dominant ideology or master text is attempting to close its borders to the fundamental historical and cultural contributions of people of color and queer folks.[56] In *Diva*, Campo uses night to overcome and overwhelm these borders. The fifth and last section of *Diva* is dedicated to the translation of Federico García Lorca's "Sonnets of Dark Love" with verses such as "dark love is all I've ever known" (83), "the night above us . . . / The night beneath us" (85), "my soul's long night eternally devoid of stars" (87), "O boundless night with certain boundaries" (88) that turn out to be nonhuman (a mountain, a dog, silence), and "make for me / a dusk of nightingales with your own tears" (89). These poems seal the use of night in the service of a melancholia or persistent sense of loss that questions and undermines social and ontological boundaries and hierarchies in the name of queer "dark love."

Campo's fourth collection of poetry, *Landscape with Human Figure* (2002), continues a number of the themes of the earlier collections. As the title connotes, however, it is both more panoramic (in terms of geopolitical location and events: wars, refugees, terrorism) and more retrospective, written from the perspective of an older person in the first years of the twenty-first century remembering his college days in the mid 1980s, as in the poem "In Praise of Experience" (23). With regard to accumulated experience, night is variously represented. Sometimes, as in "Nightfall in Asturias" (4) and "What I Would Give" (16), night appears as sanctuary from the ravages of history and from loss itself, from the awful void beneath the beauty of the world (30)—"the night around our bed like timelessness, / like comfort" (16). However, night features most heavily in a much more directly socio-political meditation on troubled race relations in the United States in the third section of the collection, "Afraid of the Dark" (39–48). This section owes a good deal to Toni Morrison's collection of essays *Playing in the Dark: Whiteness and the Literary Imagination* (1992) that explore the denotations and connotations of blackness in the United States. Campo extends these explorations to Cuba's complicity in slavery along with the United States—"my people's owning slaves" (41), and its pigmentocracy, which leaves Cubans on the island and in the United States with unresolved, ambivalent attitudes about their racial heritages: "My father, black and white, / is smoking as he speaks mestizo thoughts" (42). Campo acknowledges his own fear of any inherited blackness, a fear culturally induced by the differing yet overlapping racisms of Cuban and U.S. societies. As a child, having returned with his family to the United States from a temporary sojourn in Venezuela where the "equatorial strong sun" (45) tanned him, he writes that this tanning "left fear / that I might be the blackest one of all" (45). Fear and December's sunless blanching of his skin do not protect him from yet another shade of racism, "the moniker of 'spic'" (45), related to racism against African Americans. Hispanophobia affects the perception of most Latina/os in some measure. Realizing that they share in this "fear of the dark" / fear of the night cast against them, Campo sings the praises of strong black women who have had to endure racism, misogyny, and, in the case of someone like Audre Lorde, homophobia: "I'm seeing Amazons and Audre Lorde, / Aretha Franklin, Nefertiti, crazed / Old Tituba, the nameless women slaves / escaping North to change their destinies" (47). The verses run the risk of participating in the stereotype of the strong black woman who gives strength to others. However, the emphasis is on "their destinies," and his admiration, read through the lenses of empathy, also functions as a call for both internal and social transformation on the part of other Americans and Cubans who fear the dark without understanding that it is an inextricable part of their lives and their destinies, that they themselves might be what they fear.

The fifth and latest collection of poetry, titled *The Enemy* (2007), expands on the inter-relation between fear and the creation of an internal enemy and the pain and suffering that results from this dynamic. As the back cover of the book states, *The Enemy* "considers what it means to be the enemy" in the United States today.[57] The last poem of *Landscape with Human Figure*, "Questions for the Weather," was written in memory of the victims of the terrorist attacks of September 11, 2001, but it does not employ fear or hate mongering. It is elegiac. *The Enemy*, published five years after *Landscape with Human Figure*, laments the degradation of civil and human rights in the new age of the terrifying war on terrorism. It charts ongoing conflicts as well as changes for the worse: Palestine, Israel, criminalized Hispanic males (8), wartime fumes (10), "the war against Iraq" (18), the feeling of "the world . . . too broken to repair" (13). This collection of poems is marked by a profound sense of loss, melancholy, rage, and black despair: "sense of loss . . . blackness" (14) and "staring in the blackness" (14). The poet physician admits that he sometimes does not know what to do in the face of so much rage and despair (14). Night is deployed to express his progressive disenchantment with "America's promises" (15). In this "time of terror" (21) and brutal amputations that happen without warning (85), he feels deep depression, uncertainty, and malaise. In a poem titled "Sestina

Dolorosa," blackness, like night, becomes a way of expressing his disenchantment and sorrow, his angry sense of loss: "Outside, I'm sure of it, the street is
wet, / a slick black tongue, always telling its lie. / . . . / I'm sure it had to do with
distant wars" (19).

The most salient poem of night in *The Enemy* is "Night Has Fallen" (6), an
apostrophe (a turning away from the living to the absent or dead) to the Cuban
sexile novelist, poet, and playwright Reinaldo Arenas (1943–1990), who, in his
battle with AIDS, committed suicide. Campo's title references Arenas's picaresque memoir *Antes que anochezca* (1992), the English translation of which is
Before Night Falls. Arenas's memoir is a testament to his experience of living as
a gay man and a dissident despite repression of homosexual artists and intellectuals in Cuba and unfriendly exile in the United States. The verb tense of
Campo's title is significant. Whereas Arenas's account takes place before night
falls, implying the life that breathes before some government-imposed curfew
or snuffing out, Campo's poem signals from its title onward that "night has
fallen": the darkness, the political and social repression, has descended and is
here. He calls on the dead Reinaldo Arenas to guide him through this time of
restriction, pain, insomnia, and despair: "You would have loved the irony: The
dark / persists, Reinaldo, even as / you helped to conquer it" (6). A bit later on
in the poem, Campo writes, "Night / was falling everywhere, and everywhere
/ I looked I saw my own black memories; / I learned what cannot be recovered
teaches" (6). In the memory of Reinaldo Arenas and his confrontation with
night, Campo finds courage and tenacity to live in the face of the despair generated by the cold "white, stench-smeared walls" (6) of fortresses and hospitals—
or, rather, the fortress-hospital, the Foucauldian punishing institution, which
he suggests the fear-mongering American society has become. Campo uses
the figure of Cuban writer Reinaldo Arenas, who experienced sexual and ideological repression in Cuba and an uneasy exile in the United States, to remind
readers that the Caribbean and the United States are linked, that they share
colonial and diasporic histories on account of the millions of human beings
who have shuttled between the two locations. It is also his way of reminding
readers that no place, not even the United States with all its promises of freedom and democracy, is immune to socio-political repression. In *The Enemy,*
Campo addresses the contemporary moment—over half of the first decade of
the twenty-first century in the United States. He does so through potent and
portentous glimpses of how he feels post-millennium, after the year 2001, with
night having fallen. In doing this, he conscripts "night" as the expressivity that
resists the darkness of the despair he chronicles. This conscription of night as a
mode of expressivity—of rage, sorrow, and creativity—against socio-political

oppression, against "the dying of the light," may be, as Lázaro Lima suggests in his own terms (not with regard to tropes of night but with regard to Campo's rewriting of two of Stevens's poems: "Academic Discourse at Havana" and "The Cuban Doctor," 151–61), one of the fundamental ways in which Campo uses, critiques, and revises the more genteel, detached, idealist modernist aesthetics of the Anglo-American modernist poet Wallace Stevens.

Projecting a Queer Tropics of Night from the Voodoo Ballroom of His Skull

I titled this chapter "Queer 'Tropics' of Night and the *Caribe* of 'American' (Post) Modernism." All the poets whose work I analyze are engaged with each of the elements in this title and with these elements in relation to one another: queer, tropics, night, the Caribbean, the contested meanings of "American," a pronounced interest in and revisionist use of modernist poetry, and an active sense of being cultural commentators of their contemporary postmodern, deracinated, diasporic condition and yet of finding reasons to make specific use of writers, texts, and concerns of the earlier part of the twentieth century. With regard to the contemporary postmodern, deracinated, diasporic condition, the poets of this chapter are not equally at home with the term "postmodern." I suspect that some would find it too academic or abstract to suit their interests. Despite Umpierre's deconstructive lesbian feminist approach to language, Algarín's polymorphous dematerializations of the body and materializations of the invisible, and Campo's persistent sense of diaspora and permeable transfer between internal and external realities, these writers do not have the same self-declared and unabashed relation to the term "postmodern" as the late Rane Ramón Arroyo, who in his 1998 collection of poems *Pale Ramón* uses the term "postmodern hymns" in a poem about the Amherst writer Emily Dickinson.[58] He deploys the term again in a poem titled "Imitations of Bruce Springsteen" in his collection *The Portable Famine* (2005): "Postmodern / car locos."[59] He is by far the most "postmodern" of these diasporic Caribbean Latina/o poets—and he is proud to admit it, as well.

Rane Arroyo (November 15, 1954–May 7, 2010) was a professor of English and creative writing at the University of Toledo, Ohio, a performance artist, a playwright, an essayist, a short story writer, and especially a poet. He was or is the most obviously postmodern of the poets I discuss here, not just because he uses the term but because his poetry has all the technical hallmarks of postmodernist work: hyper-allusive pastiche; irony; a low quotient of sentimentality; performativity that confounds the difference between depth and surface, the natural and the artificial, the real and the put-on, and the heavy and the light;

self-referentiality; a strong tendency to eschew fixed origins or anything fixed that might serve as a single origin point; a meta-narrative approach to story-telling in all genres including his poetry; a performative approach to identity in which identities are worn as a series of costumes or disguises or masks;[60] a voracious interest in popular culture and in mixing what has traditionally been considered high-brow and elitist (literature, philosophy, cultural references going back to the classics) with popular culture references to musicals, movies, TV series, pop songs, and MTV videos; and the practice of subversive, usurping mimesis or imitation that confounds original and copy and supplants the master with the subaltern.

This last technique dovetails in significant ways with a postcolonial modernist Caribbean as well as Latin American—specifically Brazilian, in the figure of the poet Oswald de Andrade, 1890–1954—aesthetic of cultural anthropophagy or cannibalism in which cultural references from a dominant "external" European or Anglo-American culture are greedily devoured by the subaltern subject and then spit up again and recycled back into the textual, visual, or performative environment. A number of Arroyo's works, but especially his collection of poetry *The Singing Shark* (1996), create the poetic persona of a singing shark of Puerto Rican, Caribbean, heritage. In a form poem titled "The Singing Shark Dream, or Toto, I Don't Think We're in Tegucigalpa Anymore" that is remindful of late modernist (1950s) Brazilian concrete poetry by Carlos Drummond de Andrade and Augusto de Campo, he writes, "I'm a shark / with a man's mind ever so hungry."[61] The singing shark gobbles up U.S. popular culture (for example, musicals such as *West Side Story*, about two rival teenage gangs, the Anglo Jets and the Puerto Rican Sharks) along with American and European literary culture and spits them back out to make a space of shifting geography for himself as a diasporic Puerto Rican "freak" (83) subject—with all the connotations of difference that implies, including queerness.

Despite his meta-narrative, performative approach to identity, in his own introduction to one of his latest collections of poetry, *The Buried Sea: New and Selected Poems* (2008), he "profiles" himself almost the way someone would in a personal advertisement in a newspaper or on the internet (an example, perhaps, of the contradictory impulses at work in our postmodern times, both more fluid and yet also more electronically categorical, like digital media at large):

I'm a Puerto Rican, gay, Midwestern, educated, former working class, liberal, atheist, humanist, American, male, ex-Mormon, ex-Catholic, pseudo-Buddhist, teacher, reader, global, and popular culture-informed poet. These are a few of the adjectives I've come to own and that inform my poems.[62]

The words "former," "ex," and "pseudo" suggest a significant degree of change, fluidity, and volatility in his identity and identifications, and they introduce a tongue-in-cheek, provisional quality to a description that might seem over-determined to a committed postmodernist. But it is also significant that he is willing to label himself to this extent—that he wants to posit certain coordinates for his readers to ponder, such as Puerto Rican, gay, and Midwestern. In terms of the Puerto Rican diaspora, his coordinates are significant because they are different from those of Luz María Umpierre or Miguel Algarín and from a vast number of East Coast, upper-mid-Atlantic, Southern New England Puerto Ricans. Arroyo is a Chicago-riqueño (born in Chicago of Puerto Rican immigrant parents), and he spent most of his life living between Illinois and Pennsylvania. He received his Ph.D. from the University of Pittsburgh in Pennsylvania. He was a visiting professor at Slippery Rock University in Pennsylvania, an assistant professor at Youngstown State University in northeastern Ohio, and an assistant, associate, and finally full professor at the University of Toledo in northwestern Ohio. Having gone east from Illinois in the early 1990s, he made a slow journey northwest along the bottom of Lake Erie back toward Chicago.

The various places he lived, worked, and traveled show up rather autobiographically in his poems despite his postmodernist aesthetic, which brings his poetry closer to the work of the other poets examined in this chapter, which tends toward the autobiographical. Furthermore, in the introduction to *The Buried Sea* (2008), Arroyo reveals a number of his literary muses whom he borrows and bends with little remorse—a mixture of English, continental European (with one Russian), Latin American, and U.S. writers mostly of the nineteenth and twentieth centuries.[63] In *The Buried Sea*, a collection of old and new poems, and in other collections of poems, he makes explicit reference to more writers, most of them Anglo-American and a number of them modernist, though not all.[64] Harlem Renaissance writers Langston Hughes (whose sexual orientation has remained a mystery, though Isaac Julien's 1989 film *Looking for Langston* suggests he was gay) and the gay James Baldwin make appearances in Arroyo's poems, with a special poem titled "Nights without Dawns" being reserved for the latter.

One of Arroyo's projects is to blend, like a disc jockey, strands of the aesthetics and labor and class dynamics interests of the Chicago Renaissance writers of the 1910s–20s with the early ethno-racial and larger civil rights concerns of Harlem Renaissance writers such as Hughes and Baldwin. This blending furthers a musical blending of the modernist traditions of the Americas (and of Spain) that Langston Hughes had already commenced with his interest in the literary production of the Caribbean—especially that from Haiti and Cuba—and of

Mexico, not to mention of Spain, with the translation of the poems of Federico García Lorca ("A Chronology of the Life of Langston Hughes," *Collected Poems,* 10–15). Extending some of the voices and concerns of the Harlem Renaissance, Arroyo throws into the mix references to pop music singers, with a particular concentration on African American and Latina/o musicians, singers, and performers.[65] The dead and the living are all his conjured specters for the borrowing, his ghosts.

Patterns do emerge that are central to the argument of this chapter. A concentration of writers cited are American modernists, Anglo and/or African American (with the exception of the partly Puerto Rican William Carlos Williams), and a significant portion of their writing is engaged with the Caribbean in some fashion, including the work of William Carlos Williams, Wallace Stevens, Hart Crane, Langston Hughes, and Ernest Hemingway. The two writers with whom Arroyo's poetry engages most extensively are Wallace Stevens and Hart Crane, as is evident not only in the numerous passing references to them but in the titles of entire collections of poetry, such as *Pale Ramón* (1998)—"pale Ramon" (without the proper accent mark that Arroyo restores) being the name of a character from Wallace Stevens's well-known poem "The Idea of Order at Key West." Like Wallace Stevens, Arroyo dedicates any number of poems, more ironically and post-colonially than Stevens by far, to Spanish explorers of the Caribbean, of Cuba and Puerto Rico, in particular Columbus (in *Pale Ramón*) and Ponce de León (in *Home Movies of Narcissus,* 40–55). Arroyo constructs a part-woebegone, part-mischievous *picaro* persona for himself as "Columbus's orphan / so often out of place" ("The Last Rumba in Toronto" from "Columbus's Orphan" in *The Buried Sea,* 36). He counters Stevens's generally Platonic enwhitening idealism with skewering skepticism and irreverent subaltern mimicry, positioning himself as a bastard child of Columbus, "a little brown boy," "Lost Muchacho," lost Hardy Boy transformed into a Puerto Rican descendant of fatal explorers (from "Write What You Know" in *Home Movies of Narcissus,* 71).

Similarly, Arroyo allows Hart Crane's ghost to permeate his poetry in the form of references to Crane's Brooklyn Bridge from *The Bridge* (1930) ("The Singing Shark Dream," *The Singing Shark,* 82), dreams of and apostrophes to Hart Crane (Arroyo's introduction to *The Buried Sea,* 3), blatant borrowings of Crane's desirous imaginings about "mermen" ("A Bolero, But Not for Dancing," in *Home Movies of Narcissus,* 29–34), homoerotic sailor role-playing encounters with a lover ("Homesick for America" in *Pale Ramón,* 3), and an extended imagining on Arroyo's part of himself as Hart Crane full-fathom five "coral-pillowed" on the bottom of the sea ("Hart Crane's Caribbean" in *Pale Ramón,* 82–84). In the spring of 1932, a drunk and despairing Hart Crane committed suicide by jumping overboard into the Gulf of Mexico from a steamer headed back to New York from Mexico. The language and images of Arroyo's poem—"holiness of our weakness" (82), "apocalypse of air bubbles" (82), "coral-pillowed" (82), "pearled lights" (83), "peerless depths" (83), "a boneless monument of loneliness" (83), and "Archipelago of pigeons crumble in marble sky" (84)—capture some of the neo-romantic, mythically modernist grandeur of both Crane's and Stevens's language and vision (Arroyo hybridizes the two poets) while ending on a much more postmodern note marked by an unsettling, recycling repetition: "The sea won't stop throwing up sick gods" (84).

In this complex context and panoply of cultural allusions and commentaries, what of Arroyo's uses of the night? Whereas the poet himself calls attention to his uses of specters or ghosts (and they are everywhere in his work), his night work happens unannounced, without editorial comment or critical notice. It happens stealthily, like his passing reference to Christ's "promises / to come back as a thief" in "Litany in Time of Plague" from his early poems, 1985–1993 (*The Buried Sea*, 28). The crucial missing part of that image of Christ's return is the phrase "in the night" from St. Paul's letters to the Thessalonians, I. Thessalonians 5:2, which reads "For yourselves know perfectly that the day of the Lord so cometh as a thief in the night."[66] Arroyo's uses of night function similarly, coming as a thief in the night to the solar plexuses of his poems. There are many references to the solar plexus region, or upper abdominal center of the body, in Arroyo's work. In Hindu mysticism, the solar plexus is associated with the connection between spirit and matter, ideas and reality (in other words, creativity). Thus, I refer to the thief of night stealthily laboring in the solar plexus, in the creative heart, of his poems.

But the metaphor I like best is the one represented by the title of this section on Arroyo: "Projecting a Queer Tropics of Night from the Voodoo Ballroom of His Skull." I favor this heading because it captures the widest gamut of uses of night in Arroyo's poems, from his early ones (1985–1993) to his 2009 collection *The Sky's Weight*. The term "projecting" has photographic, cinematic, and psychological/psychoanalytic connotations. It signals the business of projecting images into the external environment. The images are registered on some medium for their retention—the human mind, plates, celluloid, digital memory cards, and so forth. "Projecting" has psychoanalytic connotations in that it implies a relation of mimesis (imitation) and potentially subversive counter-mimesis, reflecting back into the environment the internalized image to alter that environment. Furthermore, "projecting" is suitably postmodernist inasmuch as both humans and machines have the capacity to project. The verb calls to mind that we live in the age of code, a fact of which Arroyo's poetry, with its eye for all kinds of genres and codes, reminds readers. As for "queer tropics of night," I have explained it in the introduction to this chapter. The phrase "voodoo ballroom" I picked up from his poem by that title from the collection *Columbus's Orphan* (1993) included in *The Buried Sea: New and Selected Poems* (2008). The "I" of that poem describes himself in the following terms: "People want from me / what I gave away years ago. / I'm their electric matador, / my head a voodoo ballroom" (*The Buried Sea,* 47). The images "electric matador" and "voodoo ballroom" flirt with stereotypes of Hispanic cultures and the Caribbean. Specifically, "voodoo" refers to Haiti, but the Hispanic Caribbean customs of Santería have been analogized to it, and "voodoo" has come to be seen as Caribbean, not just Haitian. With the phrase "voodoo ballroom," Arroyo touches on the dynamic of the demands readers make of a Caribbean Latino poet that he fulfill certain exoticizing expectations. At the same time, he states that his head is a "voodoo ballroom," which is an image that condenses a great deal of what his poetry does through its alchemy of elements: it conjures spirits, involving the readers in the spectacle of the poet being ridden by his *loas,* by the spirits and gods (or demons) that possess him. "Ballroom" evokes dancing, and many of the spirits literally dance in these poems just as the poet dances or moves about on the streets of many different towns and cities and in his bedroom ("Angel Striptease" from early poems in *The Buried Sea,* 19) or "we [he and his now dead uncle] danced to Aretha, / and you taught me to scream for the joy of / a song on the radio" ("My Transvestite Uncle is Missing" in *The Singing Shark,* 46). "Ballroom" also suggests something involving special lights and music, the ceilings, walls, and dance floors of a discothèque or a dance hall: "I'm hungry for music, for / nights when I'd put on my Tom Cruise codpiece / and rock & roll in my Keatsian anguish / on dance floors that have mapped out my desires" ("Island to Island" in *Pale Ramón,* 55). Nighttime is usually the time for dancing. And dancing in clubs at night, especially as a regular practice, was and still is central to the creation and maintenance of queer cultures as well as African American and Latina/o cultures, as Tim Lawrence's book *Love Saves the Day: A History of American Dance Music Culture, 1970–1979* documents through the 1970s.[67] Finally, I have invoked "ballroom of his skull" rather than "head" because it serves the same purpose as head—as the seat of thought and of all the images and spirits Arroyo conjures and projects—but it has the advantage of connoting mortality and death. In Arroyo's last books of poems, most of the references to night are tinged with thoughts of death as a black hole of extinction.

Though Arroyo's poetry recycles its own images and personae within and between collections of poems, frustrating any easy claims about evolution or development, I find an evolution and a deepening in his uses of night. In the early poems, 1985–1993, night is largely a time for rebelling against the dominant mainstream order of the day. It is a time to stay up past midnight, bribe the "night to stay one more day," and write a "blank check" for the moon ("Old Checks" from early poems in *The Buried Sea*, 17). In another early poem, "boys in dresses won't stop dancing . . . they are the wind-up / keys to the night" ("Juana and Joanna" from early poems in *The Buried Sea*, 21). In "The Last Rumba in Toronto" from the 1993 collection *Columbus's Orphan*, night unfolds as a gay leather man's party and floor show to crown "Mr. Leather Toronto . . . king of midnight" (*The Buried Sea*, 36). Night is a queer time of performance, theater, and carnival. The verses "Tonight, I will demand / that the front desk / fix the porno channel, because / tonight I'm tired of reading" (*The Buried Sea*, 38) reinforce the "carnality" of "carnival"—a celebration of the living flesh and not just words on a page (reading). The poem calls for Mr. Leather Toronto to "rule his dark kingdom," or his kingdom of night, and for "the bongos [to] bring the sun back from the dead" (*The Buried Sea*, 39). The combination of "dark kingdom" and "bongos [to] bring back the sun from the dead" intimates Orphic rites, a pagan celebration of life over death. Arroyo gives this scenario an Afro Caribbean twist with the mention of bongos. The fact that bongos provide the beat for a leather party in the cold northern clime of Toronto enacts the singing shark's queer torsions and tropics of night.

In successive books of poetry, night becomes more aligned with the notion of double exile—with queer and diasporic ethno-racialized Puerto Rican experience that entails paeans to the island of Puerto Rico but also an equally strong sense that the island exists for him in a romance of yearning spurred by his very distance from its actual soil. His is the voice of the diasporic subject long since cast out of a ravaged garden, though he can still emblazon its qualities. In "Santiago in San Juan" from *The Singing Shark*, the poet describes San Juan as a "garden . . . full of flames" (probably a reference to the brilliant red flowers with yellow stamens of the flamboyan tree so characteristic of Puerto Rico) and "Midnight . . . with a black eye" who has had a few lovers as has the poet (11). The eye is not black just because of the time of day but because of the phenotype of many of the people who will "never be / blonde" (11). The poet celebrates this fire and this darkness: "Let's enjoy the moon. / Sounds of wings in the night" (11). References to night often accompany his descriptions of Puerto Rico: "Fireflies in San Juan / around El Morro are gardens / with feet and wings" (29). Here he sounds like Luz María Umpierre celebrating Puerto Rico's flora and fauna to counter the patriarchal, colonial, military presence of El Morro. Like Umpierre and in a fashion more removed from the island, Arroyo embraces loss, a kind of postcolonial and queer negative capability: "Loss / has, in the past, been his source of / knowledge" (29). Night brings hints of loss and sometimes stands in for loss, for that which knows the wounds of history and has survived them even so. "The Carlos Poems" from the last third of *The Singing Shark* (in the section "Existentialist with Conga Drum") equates all the production of this queer, Caribbean singing shark with the public and collective remembrance of a memorable night that is wasted, dissipated away from stable signifiers (the island of Puerto Rico included): "What is / poetry if it isn't the public / memory of a night wasted singing?" (64). This emphasis on "public" is important because aside from registering the poet's hopes to be known (to be singing to a public and not just to himself) the term "public" also implies a collective endeavor among participants, a collective resistance against the normalizing, homogenizing, conformist-assimilationist order of the day. Perhaps this is the resistance that is available to the poet when other resistances—such as the *independentista* ones of Umpierre's poetry—have not yet materialized.

Pale Ramón (1998) steps up a doubled postcolonial queer resistance to Columbus and to an "America" unaware of its complex colonial and neocolonial history: "Tonight, I'm your sailor, Chicago, / a sea-orphaned one who will drown / you in my saltern legs" (from "Homesick for America," 3). It is "tonight" that the bastard orphaned child of exploitative explorers will challenge the big, industrial, hyper-capitalist, post-industrial city with his subaltern "saltern legs" and with all these innuendos about colonialism, imperialism, class inequalities, and labor conflicts. At the end of this collection, the eponymous hero—or rather mock hero—Pale Ramón "borrows / a stepladder from the moon / for a better view of his tropics" (85). When he "falls off the stepladder" he lands on an angel's back and is "hijacked to a ruined castle inside / mountains of cumulus clouds. / It is peopled by crows in leather / who demand he recite the history / of literate Heaven" (85). The poem pokes fun at explorers and conquistadors, taking aim at their tropics of the new world and their metaphysics (invocations of heaven and God). When Pale Ramón does not give these black crows what they want to hear (he is out of his depth in this kingdom in the clouds), they shove "black feathers" into his mouths (plural). He is "feathered" (without being tarred) by these birds the color of night. His "opulent palms"—this phrase could be interpreted as a dig at Wallace Stevens's "palms at the end of the mind"—do not restore him to his proper depth. The crazy, disorienting experience goes on until it suddenly breaks off in ellipses. The poem is, after all, titled "A Fragment" (85–87). Night figures in various ways, though obliquely. Pale Ramón's borrowing of a stepladder from the moon to get a better look at his "tropics" cleverly collapses colonial exploration of the new world with space-age explorations of the moon and the heavens more generally. The black crows and their black feathers connote black angels. Black angels are often associated (as in Algarín's poems) with the night, not the day. They blacken Pale Ramón by stuffing him with their feathers. The motif is one of comic yet real revenge against the now explorer/conquistador/colonizer who appears pitifully hapless and foolish when stripped of his powers. The crows, moreover, are dressed in leather remindful of the garb or costume of S&M, which is considered a queer or non-normative practice regardless of its practitioners' sexual orientation. In this way, the poem introduces not only what might be considered a subaltern postcolonial revenge against the former master but, moreover, a queer postcolonial revenge with reverse-lynching ethno-racial and sexual overtones—this stuffing of the mouth of the "pale" Ramón with black feathers. Though the word "night" is not mentioned, the poem began with the moon, a celestial body most visible at night and a mirror of the sun's light that is, hence, imagistic shorthand for imitative practice or mimesis. The poem takes advantage of this nocturnal mimesis of the sun's light and makes it subversive: both moon and stepladder fail Pale Ramón, and he is hijacked—a turning or tropic action in itself—to the kingdom of the black crows. The tropics are no longer his; they are no longer under his masterful, controlling gaze.

Beginning with *Home Movies of Narcissus* (2002), "night" challenges the poet's own powers as well, not just those of his mock heroes or historical fools. Here night functions in the counter-narcissistic vein Kevin Bell elaborates in *Ashes Taken for Fire: Aesthetic Modernism and the Critique of Identity* with regard to the void out of which language is born and to which it returns. In "Night Ignores an SOS," the poet himself is "Falling off a dream ladder" (59). He thinks of a new book to write, but he also confesses that "My bed is full of bad poems," a line that suggests a questioning of his own creative powers and the limits of his strength: "How dark my cooling limbs / against glowing bedsheets" (59). In a later poem titled "A Dark Rain," the night finds him sleepless (63), remembering the dead, and wishing to sit "in my underwear next to a drunk lover / looking at constellations on the white ceiling" (63). The feelings expressed are of vulnerability, loneliness, and, potentially, despair.

These feelings, however, are given specific social coordinates and politicized in the last poem of the volume titled "That Flag," a reference to the Confederate flag. The poet witnesses two "white, shirtless men" engaged in a drug deal. One of them has a Confederate flag in his truck window. He is attracted to their physiques, to their muscular youth, despite himself, and he thinks to himself that they are "America's perfect heirs" while he is an "aging Puerto Rican / homosexual poet exiled / to a borrowed bed [his Motel 6 bed]" (75). He walks past the hotel clerk and sings "Buenas Noches" but tells his readers that it is not a good night because he has nightmares about the Confederate flag and "a terrible army

/ of soldiers in uniforms of skin" persecuting Puerto Ricans and Latinos more generally (75). The phrase "buenas noches," which means "good evening" (hello) and also "goodnight" (goodbye) functions as a double-edged sword, revealing the nightmare in the American dream that spawns such "perfect heirs" as these "white, shirtless men." *Home Movies of Narcissus* ends with trenchant cultural critique exposing the disturbing depths of the poet's double exile, his sexile.

The Portable Famine (2005) is full of dreams and nightmares, many of them occurring at night, about traces and wounds of war, empire, colonialism, neo-colonialism, diaspora, and globalization. The poems are bursting with ghosts of the dead and shadows of the dying. The sense of loss is acute as the poems move from place to place in an odyssey that never will return the poet home: New York City, Texas, New Orleans, Miami, Puerto Rico (to which the poet returns "as a stranger," 22), Ohio, Chicago, Utah, Mexico, Iceland, Italy, Greece, London, and other places that are not mapped out for the reader but that suggest that the poet is still traveling, taking leave and never arriving.

The most significant role played by night comes in the poem "Nights without Dawns" dedicated to late modernist writer James Baldwin (1924–1987), African American and queer novelist, playwright, essayist, poet, and civil rights activist who, among other things, marched with Martin Luther King Jr. to Washington, DC. Baldwin's work openly and unapologetically deals with issues of sexual orientation and race/ethnicity and with the facts of being homosexual and black both in the United States and as an American expatriate in Europe. Arroyo's poem "for James Baldwin" mentions "[a] jazz eclipse," "noisy bar-closings," "Europe," "secret saxophones," "streets as crooked as the teeth of unowned musicians on stage," "undressings," "kissing a foreigner back," pulling "down the shades," and defining "nations tonight" (48). The poem creates the impression of the poet's being in European, old-world bars with jazz combos, meeting and picking up a stranger (another foreigner like himself) there, and taking that stranger/foreigner back to his room where they will have sex, pull down the shades, and define nations—or rather, de-define them, deconstruct them. On the surface, the poem could be taken to be about cruising in jazz bars and picking up a stranger for sex. However, the dedication to James Baldwin and the last line involving night—"We define nations tonight" (48)—expand the reach of the poem, suggesting an intersection of numerous identities, localities, and activities (African American letters, jazz, Europe, expatriates, cruising, and encounters between foreigners) with defining nations. The central irony of the poem is that the kind of nation-defining it would seem to advocate defies the definition of nations as they are currently mapped. The poem hints at an open-ended network of associations between people not in their countries of birth or their home countries. The nations defined are diasporically created. They defy the known world; they exist at the edge of knowledge.

In keeping with this defiance of the known and mapped world, the uses of night in Arroyo's poems written after 2005—"Ghost Island: New Poems" in *The Buried Sea* (2008), *The Roswell Poems* (2008), and *The Sky's Weight* (2009)—are increasingly connected with "the great black [of the nocturnal skies] / that surround this blued Earth."[68] The coordinates of night are in space, the last frontier, more than on earth. In Arroyo's poetry, the conjuring of space provides an opportunity for a complex, tragicomic, skeptical yet serious investigation of the continuation of myths, dreams, and nightmares about the Americas, the New World, and about what is deemed alien and thus feared—human "illegal" aliens, space aliens, and queer people—projected into the expanding universe or cosmos. In "Ghost Island: New Poems" of *The Buried Sea,* night manifests in glimpses as the stars that "require exquisite heights in order to fall" (181) and UFOs (185), a prelude to *The Roswell Poems.* These stars become associated with "starry books" (186), the very starry books that Arroyo, with an eye to mortality, posited as "the opposite of graves" (186) even though some of the starlight that reaches us on earth is from stars that have burnt themselves out long ago.

In *The Roswell Poems,* black, nocturnal space is everywhere. The poems keep it from being disconnected from shades of black on earth, from Arroyo's own lyrical voodoo—"horses beg to be ridden where darkness / turns silver hooves into hard sparks" (excerpts from *The Roswell Poems* in *The Buried Sea,* 189). Talk of space aliens in New Mexico is mixed in with references to the Mexican celebration of the Day of the Dead, a reminder of the vast presence (dead and living) of Mexicans and other Latina/os in the Southwest and the United States as a whole (excerpts from *The Roswell Poems* in *The Buried Sea,* 191). One of the poems from "Ghost Island: New Poems," "Don Quixote Goes to the Moon," has the quintessential Hispanic chivalric knight errant going to the moon, tilting with "cruel constellations," and being buffeted by solar winds (*The Buried Sea,* 192). The poet is half laughing at and half identifying with this knight errant of Spain who is so divested from his La Mancha and who, unaccompanied by his Sancho Panza, has nothing to keep him grounded.

The Sky's Weight (2009), and especially "II: Solar Constant," takes uses of night in new and potentially disorienting directions for Latina/o writers, especially diasporic Caribbean Latina/o writers and Puerto Ricans in particular. Although many Latina/os have contributed to U.S. space missions since the establishment of NASA in 1958, California-born astronaut Joseph M. Acaba was the first Latino of Puerto Rican heritage to be sent into outer space, an event that occurred on March 15, 2009.[69] At the beginning of "II: Solar Constant" the queer Chicago-riqueño poet, who has suffered the "black plunge" of a physical coma, plunges, albeit metaphorically, into "black skies."[70] What unfolds is a series of poems that explore contributions to the exploration of night skies by historical figures from Plato (between the fifth and fourth centuries BC) to Albert Einstein and beyond in the twentieth and twenty-first centuries.[71] These poems are followed by one devoted to the 1990 deep space probe Project Ulysses, which contained 24.2 pounds of the highly toxic plutonium dioxide: "Ulysses will never come home, but / instead circles the neared sun" (81) and "Ulysses is a worker never to be mourned" (81). The collection also contains two afterwords, "The Sun Speaks" and "What is Here." The sun, consuming itself, speaks of how humans "are always looking for narratives" to produce order and meaning. The sun, a postmodernist in Arroyo's hands, recommends that we follow the Caribbean shark's anthropophagic behavior: gobble up those human narratives and "leave the soul to turn / into honed flotsam" or, if lacking such teeth, "mourn that we mourn and return / to music far from deathbed dancers" (The Singing Shark, 60), to those dance halls, those discothèques. The emphasis is on avoiding the narrative traps of nostalgia and, instead, living in the here and now. This idea is reinforced by the last image in the second afterword: "He's greedy for fires that dangle like damaged / fruit offering what is here. That is enough" (84). The Sky's Weight, with its pointed reference to "the planets inside skulls, and the sun's / race around the eye's provenance" (63) and "the affect of / the eternal against his imperfect / skull" (66), concludes with an affirmation of life here and now suspended in the black night skies of an expanding universe that will make the blackness all the more profoundly dark: "Light is just a byproduct, a stage whisper" (82). This affirmation lends itself to being read existentially as the cry of life in the face of death and extinction. But it can also be read as an affirmation of the poet's presence as a queer Puerto Rican diasporic intelligence. Some of the concluding verses of The Sky's Weight read: "My / shadows will be austere cargo / . . . They'll / embrace me before asking of / our home. I'll tell of gold, held / grins, and noon when naked" (85). The words "cargo" and "gold" resonate with the history of slavery; transplantation of humans, flora, and fauna; and the conquest, colonization, and exploitation of the New World, including Puerto Rico among other places. To be embraced unconditionally suggests a home-coming absorption into and reunion with the cosmos despite the disconcerting nightmares of the long history of colonialism and neocolonialism that extends into the night skies, which are fathomed bit by bit by numerous space probes and by the Hubble Space Telescope, launched in 1990—coincidently, around the time that scholars were focusing serious attention on Latina/o cultural production. With the powers of the voodoo ballroom of his skull, the poet has absorbed the history of astronomy and cosmology and projected this history back outward in a philosophically critical way for his multicultural, multi-ethnic readers to learn from and ponder, expanding their own horizons of knowledge and experience, making their own attempts at defining nations in an era of postnational globalization, and drawing their own maps of orientation, which are informed by a willingness to confront their own scatterings and their own disorientations.

Thus I conclude this chapter entitled "Queer 'Tropics' of Night and the *Caribe* of 'American' (Post) Modernism." Rane Arroyo's poetry—as it has evolved from the mid 1980s to the latter part of the first decade of the twenty-first century—is probably one of the most postmodernist expressions of queer, diasporic, Caribbean Latina/o aesthetics written in English by a U.S.-based poet. Arroyo is the one who leaves the shore of an island community, whether it be Puerto Rico or the island of Manhattan, furthest behind, with all the attendant loneliness and disorientation that this odyssey entails. In the introductory pages of this chapter, I wrote,

> The chapter is dedicated to outlining and elaborating the connections among the ingredients signaled in the title: *Caribe* or Caribbean, queerness, modernism, postmodernism, and especially the tropics of night, a fluid, dark sea in which all these other particles are suspended, emitting effects upon one another.

I have considered three poets of Puerto Rican descent and one of Cuban descent because I wanted to keep the emphasis on the Caribbean and not simply on Puerto Rico or the Puerto Rican diaspora. Despite the distinctiveness of each poet's project and voice, I have traced some powerful commonalities between very different texts by focusing on their tropics of night, a tropics effecting complex uses and revisions of *modernism(o)s*, especially Anglo-American modernism, to lyrically render their historical experiences, as queer Caribbean diasporic subjectivities, of the last three decades in the United States. Their renderings entail some powerful expressions of how it feels to ground themselves, as U.S.-based Caribbean sexiles, in the places where they are and also, as part of their respective projects of grounding themselves, to un-ground, unsettle, deconstruct, and redefine major social constructs of belonging, such as hegemonic overlapping categories of race, ethnicity, nationality, sexuality, class, and rhetorical affiliation. In her study *Cuban-American Literature of Exile*, professor of Spanish and Cuban American Studies Isabel Alvarez Borland cites Timothy Weiss's study of West Indian exile writer V. S. Naipaul and Weiss's invocation of the concept of "exotopy," "vision from outside through which a writer can see what those on the inside cannot,"[72] according to Russian literary critic, semiotician, and philosopher Mikhail Bakhtin (1895–1975) and Russian scholar, activist, and friend to Bakhtin, Pavel Nikolaevich Medvedev. Following Alvarez's lead, I return to Weiss's study *On the Margins* (1992), where he argues that the exotopic vision developed in relation to Naipaul's exile both from the West Indies and especially from the motherland India "allows him to see what Indians themselves sometimes do not see about their country [India]."[73] The positions of the U.S.-based Caribbean poets whose work I have examined and Naipaul are not parallel. The poets of this chapter are concerned more with conditions in the United States than in the Caribbean islands of their heritage. However, the notion of exotopy—vision from outside as queer, Caribbean-descent sexiles—does pertain to their ways of seeing and feeling with regard to the United States. I do indeed claim that the aesthetics of the queer tropics of night and the *Caribe* of "American" (post) modernism in the works of the four poets I have examined exemplifies exotopic vision that sees what those on the inside cannot, and makes new cultural maps accordingly.

CHAPTER THREE

POSTCOLONIAL PRE-COLUMBIAN COSMOLOGIES OF NIGHT IN CONTEMPORARY U.S.-BASED CENTRAL AMERICAN TEXTS

Then, the four hundred boys whom Zipacná had killed, also ascended,
and so they again became the companions of [the boys]
and were changed into stars in the sky.

—*Popol Vuh*

The Invisibility of U.S.-Based Central American Cultural Production

Central America is the invisible sleeping giant or the eclipsed celestial body in the study of U.S. Latina/o culture, Latin American culture, and American (United States) culture. I deploy the phrase "sleeping giant" to remind U.S.-based critics and readers of the ideological framework of a particular "Latin Americanism" (to borrow Román de la Campa's phrase)[1] that afflicts consideration of Central America, especially in the United States. An American Cold War against land redistribution and liberation movements in Central America and the proliferation of government-sponsored counterinsurgency operatives in many Central American countries (including Nicaragua, El Salvador, Guatemala, and Honduras) have over-determined U.S. consideration of Central America. This framework has played a significant part in creating an occlusion of U.S. vision with regard to both the living presence of Central Americans here in the United States itself (for example, over one million Central Americans live in Southern California around the Los Angeles area) and to the socioeconomic, cultural, and political complexity of each country and of the countries in relation to one another (the significant presence, for instance, of Salvadorans living in Honduras). Diaspora in relation to Central America is varied. It involves

Central Americans in one Central American country moving to another Central American country as well as to other countries such as Mexico, the United States, and Spain.

In his study *Taking Their Word: Literature and the Signs of Central America* (2007), U.S.-based Guatemalan scholar and writer Arturo Arias minces no words when he describes the "neocolonial" subjugation of these Central American countries to an ongoing, now neoliberal U.S. imperial agenda and the marginalization and silencing of people who dare to express themselves inside their own countries as well as within the United States. At the same time, Arias points to the very important role of Central American and U.S.-based Central American literatures (the genre of the novel in particular) in the project of addressing and beginning to undo this occlusion:

> In Central America, cinema and other visual media productions are in their infancy. The images that people in the region see on television, in the movie theatre, or on the Internet very rarely represent their reality. These people are also unable to project their personal vision onto the worldwide screen. For this reason, the novel's ability to give heteroglossic representations of its people and to assert their identity and history remains of primary importance. This is true as well for a significant portion of the Central American population living in the United States, who need a representation to become visible and "crawl into the place of the human." [With this latter phrase Arias quotes Gayatri Spivak from *Death of a Discipline*.] The interactions between the United States and the Central American nations and societies it has dominated (and invaded, aiding in the slaughter of their best and brightest) since the early twentieth century can best be examined through a study of literature, which can frame and contextualize those "neocolonial" forms of subjugation that result from expanding capitalism and globalization.[2]

In the introduction to his study of Central American and U.S.-based Central American literature, Arias makes a strong case for the cultural work being done by the novel in particular, which is a form of expression simultaneously accessible enough, complex (heteroglossic) enough, and weighty enough to begin to make visible Central Americans and U.S.-based Central Americans in the Americas and, more specifically, in the United States.

As a scholar of Latina/o cultural production, I am, like Arias, interested in the status of Central American cultural production, especially literature, in the United States itself, related as it is to cultural production in Central America. Central American cultural production, both from within the region and diasporic, has played virtually no part in American studies. For the most part, American studies scholars have ignored it. Even Latina/o studies has only recently begun to deal with Central American cultural production, although Central American writers, artists, activists, and organizations within and outside of Central America, as well as a number of non–Central American Latina/o ones, have been calling attention to Central American issues unfolding within and diasporically beyond the geographical boundaries of Central American countries and across the region of the isthmus since at least the early 1980s. Salvadoran American critic Ana Patricia Rodríguez documents and analyzes these issues in "The War at Home: Latina/o Solidarity and Central American Immigration" from her 2009 book *Dividing the Isthmus: Central American Transnational Histories, Literatures & Cultures.*[3] Rodríguez's book is exemplary within Latina/o studies for breaking the silences and bridging the ignorances within the U.S. academy as a whole about Central America and Central American diasporic histories, cultures, self-representations, and peoples. While judiciously acknowledging the groundbreaking work of other Central American and U.S.-based Central American critics, Arturo Arias among them (10), she also unequivocally states the prime motive of her book: "I wish finally to read beyond the endings that would ultimately seek to erase, silence, destroy, and scatter to the winds the narratives, cultures, and peoples of Central America" (18). To "the endings" I would add the problem of limited knowledge horizons produced by the imbrication of the U.S. Cold War and neoliberal ideologies that also affect the academy.

Under the pressure of historical and demographic forces, the discipline of Latina/o studies in the United States has developed beyond its traditional close association with the three main Latina/o populations in this order: Mexican Americans, Puerto Ricans, and Cubans. About the influx of Central Americans to the United States, Rodríguez informs her readers that "well over one million Central Americans had immigrated to the United States . . . making Central Americans (after Mexicans) one of the fastest growing subgroups of foreign-born Latinos/as in the United States" (130). El Salvador, Nicaragua, and Guatemala, the three Central American countries torn apart by civil wars, "generated the greatest number of immigrants in the United States" (Rodríguez, 130). Latina/o studies has become more self-declaredly transnational in focus and more obviously concerned with immigration and the flow of people, labor, and capital back and forth across borders.

A telling example of this more recent orientation within Chicana/o studies, not even the broader Latina/o studies, is that in 1997, the Chicana/o studies department at East Los Angeles College (ELAC) in Monterey Park,

California, proposed a new class titled "Central Americans: The New Chicanos." The campus curriculum committee did not approve the course because
the Social Science department blocked it. This department challenged the right
of a Chicana/o studies department to propose such a course combining the
experiences of Central Americans and Mexican Americans. Presumably, such
a combination violated the traditional boundaries of Mexican American studies. According to the ELAC Chicana/o studies department chair Sybil Venegas,
the course has never been taught.[4] However, the course proposal generated turf
wars that brought to the fore important evolving debates about the common
ground among Chicana/os and Central Americans in relation to U.S. imperialism, neocolonialism, and global economies and the need for intersectional
studies within and among Latina/o ethnic groups. As Sonia Saldívar-Hull
chronicles in her 2000 book *Feminism on the Border,* Chicana feminism together
with Third World feminism provided a strong platform for making connections
between Central American liberation movements and Chicana/o liberation
movements.[5] In her monumental 2008 bilingual *500 Years of Chicana Women's
History / 500 Años de la Mujer Chicana,* anti-war and social justice activist Elizabeth "Betita" Martínez documents, through summaries and extensive photographs, the multi-decade involvement of many Chicanas with Central American liberation movements.[6]

To return to the situation at ELAC, the controversy over the course "Central
Americans: The New Chicanos" also raised the question, which is still being
debated, of whether the Chicana/o studies department should re-name itself
the Chicano/Latino studies department to signal its inclusion of Latina/o studies more generally without losing sight of its traditional mission to Chicana/o
studies.[7] As with Chicana/o studies in the ELAC case, Latina/o studies is recognizing that it must go beyond the three or four traditional groups (Dominicans
often constitute the fourth group) typically included within its purview.

I focus on the work of resisting the occlusion of Central American perspectives performed by an element of narrative, not the grander structure or
genres as Arias does. I focus on the conceptual labor done by tropes of night.
I look at descriptive fragments and cameo moments of scenes. These descriptive fragments of texts occur in novels but also in short stories, novellas, and
non-fictional accounts. Tropes of night in these U.S.-based Central American
narratives function as looking-glass portmanteaus of time. They blend two or
more time periods—specifically, a pre-Columbian or ancient time and a contemporary one. The references to night pulsate with two or more times and
spaces. I compare these tropes of night in these U.S.-based Central American
narratives to the stars of the night sky. In the depth of the dark, moonless night,

the stars are visible to star-gazers. However, the real-time sight of them constitutes an optical illusion. They are transmitting light from millions of years ago.
Many stars have long ago burned out and disappeared. And yet they are with us
still—an appearance of what has been disappeared.

Pre-Columbian Mesoamerican Night

Coming from the previous chapter of this book, Midwestern Puerto Rican Rane
Arroyo's concentration on night skies takes us by association of ideas to an overlooked historical hot spot and repository of night sky studies: Mesoamerica
(Yucatan Mexico and Central America) and the works of cultures descended
from and inflected by the world views and practices of the Aztecs and, especially,
the Maya. These civilizations and cultures valued agriculture, geomancy, and
astronomy (the study of solar and lunar eclipses and the night sky). As scholar
of Mesoamerican religions Davíd Carrasco points out, the "surviving precon-
quest pictorials drawn and painted on bark or deerskin" show that "Mesoamerican people conceived of *time and space* as thoroughly intertwined" and attest
to a "powerful obsession with the cycles of agriculture and stars (macrocosmos
and microcosmos) and the forces and meaning of sacred time and sacred place."[8]
Geomancy (the study of the earth and its dirt and minerals) and astronomy were
especially intricately interrelated. For instance, the dark-as-night obsidian, which
was formed from volcanic activity and referred to by the natives as "the stone of
lightning," possibly because sand struck by lightning sometimes turned to glass,
was used for scrying, which implied time-travel, and for the observation of solar
eclipses.[9] Earth and the underworld were understood as connected to the skies.
According to Mary Miller and Karl Taube's *An Illustrated Dictionary of the Gods
and Symbols of Ancient Mexico and the Maya,*

> In the Maya region, the Milky Way is conceptualized as the road to Xibalba, the
> Underworld, and the entire night sky may replicate the Underworld and the move-
> ments of its denizens. In Yucatec, it is termed *zac beh,* or "white road." Another
> Yucatec Mayan word for it was *tamcaz,* a curious term that also signifies seizures.[10]

The Milky Way of the sky was thought of in relation to the *inframundo,* the realm
below the earth. The concentration of stars in the night skies, construed as a
path, led to another realm of the night, Xibalba, or, as Carrasco informs his readers, "the Mayan underworld" (16).

Study of solar eclipses and the night skies informed the Mayans' most fundamental beliefs and their calendric technologies of space-time keeping. Study of

the night skies informed the recording, via hieroglyphic writing, of the lives of royal families or dynasties, of the prescribed labors and sacrifices of the people on behalf of the rulers and gods, and of the labors and sacrifices of the rulers on behalf of the gods. The Mesoamericans of Yucatan Mexico and Central America read eclipses and night skies for signs of historic destiny or fate, looking for good or ill omens for the lives of the rulers and peoples. As evidenced in the *Popol Vuh* or Council Book, the sacred book of creation of the ancient Quiché Maya—which was not in itself a pre-Columbian text, as it was authored shortly after the Spanish Conquest by "a Quiché Indian who had learned to read and write in Spanish" but which served as a compendium of the ancient cosmological concepts of the Maya[11]—nocturnal elements (sky, earth, water; certain animals such as bats, jaguars, coyotes, wolves, and owls; supernatural beings such as gods, demons, and demon gods; and the underworld) feature heavily. The Quiché Maya warriors who died a violent death were changed into stars in the night sky.[12] This belief belonged to their cosmological acceptance of the ordeals of sacrifice and self-sacrifice for the sake of "defeating death through rituals of transformation" (Carrasco, 117). The same *Illustrated Dictionary* informs its readers, "Most Mesoamerican calendars included a separate count of the Nine Lords of the Night, who ruled over the nighttime hours" (57). Pre-Columbian cosmologies hinged as much on night as on day and any worship of the day-star, the sun. "Night" receives its own separate entry in *An Illustrated Dictionary of The Gods and Symbols of Ancient Mexico and the Maya*. The entry reads:

> In traditional Mesoamerican thought, the night was widely regarded with a certain amount of dread and fear. At night, formchangers and demons from the perimeters of the social world would wreak havoc upon humans. During the time of darkness, spooks and demons of the underworld rose to the surface of the earth and the heavens. It was commonly believed that the soul traveled about while one slept, exposing the individual to great danger. Dreams were often considered to be memories of the soul's nocturnal journeys and exploits. Thus in most Mayan languages, the term *uay* often bears connotations of sleep, dream, form-changer, or spirit companion. The forces of the night often diametrically oppose the ordered world of the sun and daylight. Thus for example, during the New Fire vigil (see fire), the Aztecs greatly feared that the stellar demons of darkness, the Tzitzimime, would plunge the entire world into darkness and chaos. (124)

Many cultures have regarded and still regard night with dread and fear. Mesoamerican cultures are not unusual in this respect. However, what does emerge as a more distinctive feature of Central American pre-Columbian cosmologies is the extent to which night is conceptualized as a time of animate forces of chaos, of fearful and often violent transformation—a plunge into darkness. Night assumes a negative value remindful of its portrayal within much later European and Euro-American Gothicism. Yet Mesoamerican pre-Columbian representations of night are different and distinctive to the extent that the forces of havoc are not so much to be suppressed as deemed part of the order of things and certainly part of a sacrificial warrior code. Confrontations with night forces were considered rites of passage to new life. This is clear from the *Popol Vuh,* where the two divine Hero Twins (Hun-Hunahpú and Vucub-Hunahpú, whose mother is the female trickster Blood Moon) must brave the House of Gloom, the House of Jaguars, the House of Bats, and the House of (Obsidian) Knives among other places in the underworld generally associated with night (117). Those who died a violent death through trials by night or in relation to forces of the night were often heroized, metaphorically and literally changed into "stars."

These patterns of belief and thought found in the geographical area known today as the Yucatan Mexican Peninsula, Belize, Guatemala, El Salvador, and Honduras but also in Nicaragua, Costa Rica, and even Panama emanate from the distant past, from pre-Columbian times.[13] I mean times before the Spanish conquests, the colonial era, the complicated incursions of and negotiations with other Old World powers such as Britain, France, and Germany, and, of course, with the United States. Regarding the latter, consider the historical pressure of the strategic and economic interests of the Monroe Doctrine of 1823, the mid-nineteenth-century expansionist adventures of William Walker, the 1904 Roosevelt Corollary to the 1823 Monroe Doctrine, the building of the Panama Canal in 1914, the imposition of U.S. rule in the Canal Zone, and unequal, neocolonial dependency trade between various parts of the Americas.[14] Also to be figured in the calculus of pre-Columbian times versus what followed are the struggles for independence from Spain and from other Old World powers such as Britain, in the case of Belize or British Honduras; post-independence military coups, dictatorships, and turmoil throughout the twentieth century—the dirty wars of the 1980s are far from finished—that were aided, abetted, and instigated by covert U.S. CIA operations; and the violent domination of the wealthy elite over the vast poor, a situation exacerbated by the lending policies of the World Bank and the International Monetary Fund.

Why bother to invoke or revisit Mesoamerican pre-Columbian beliefs and myths about night? Is this not an ahistorical move? One response lies in the related claims that beliefs and myths undergird history and the telling of history. People and whole cultures act out the stories they collectively tell themselves. Psychoanalyst Sigmund Freud, depth psychologist Carl Jung, and historian and textual analyst Hayden White concur from various angles that beliefs

and myths undergird history.[15] Each in his work demonstrated a strong dialectical feedback loop between belief/myth and history.

One danger in this claim for the analyst (whether psychoanalyst, historian, or
literary and cultural critic) is that evidence for the dominance of a certain paradigm can have an over-determining effect on understandings of the past and on
present and future possibilities. The cycle becomes a spell—a sentencing. Even
the U.S.-based Central American Guatemalan Jewish American contemporary
writer and journalist Francisco Goldman, despite his self-professed narrativiza-
tion of history and his desire to write anti-realist prose—for example, his novels
The Long Night of White Chickens (1992), *The Ordinary Seaman* (1997), and *The
Divine Husband* (2004)—occasionally dips into well-worn tropes about Central American countries. The spellbinding narrative appeal of certain tropes
exercises what U.S. literary theorist and philosopher Kenneth Burke described
as "terministic screens." By this Burke meant the power of language, symbols,
and paradigms—ways of describing things—to orient us to see some things
about the world and not others, to create a selection of reality and therefore
also a deflection of it.[16] Here is the second paragraph from Goldman's supposedly non-fictional account of the murder of Guatemalan Bishop Juan Gerardi
Conedera in *The Art of Political Murder: Who Killed the Bishop?* (2007). In the
process of recounting his investigation of the human rights activist bishop's horrific murder, Goldman also describes Guatemalans thus:

> Guatemalans have long been known for their reserve and secretiveness, even
> gloominess. "Men remoter than mountains" was how Wallace Stevens put it in
> a poem he wrote after visiting "alien, point-blank, green and actual Guatemala."
> Two separate, gravely ceremonious, phantasmagoria-prone cultures, Spanish
> Catholic and Mayan pagan, shaped the country's character, along with centuries
> of cruelty and isolation.[17]

These sentences conform to a Black Legend about Guatemala, a colonial
extension of the Black Legend against Spain.[18] Guatemalans are represented
through the eyes of Anglo-American modernist poet Wallace Stevens, whose
tropes about the Caribbean, Hispanicity, the Spanish Americas, or the Other
Americas we have already seen other Latina/o writers take on, deconstruct, or
re-construct in an effort to de-centralize their authority or weight. The opera-
tive phrase here is "phantasmagoria-prone cultures." The historical meaning of
phantasmagoria is an optical illusion display achieved with the aid of a magic
lantern used to project images on to fabric, smoke, or walls. The images were
frightening or exotic or both (as the exotic was often deemed menacing). The

shows required darkness, save for the light emanating from the magic lantern, and were frequently performed at night. Phantasmagoria is an activity associated with the terrors (the fantasies, fears, and dangers) of darkness and the night. The claim that Guatemalans are especially prone to phantasmagoria—when phantasmagoria was invented in France and popular in England and Germany—is obviously problematic. However, the association of Guatemalans with phantasmagoria and the terrors of the night by a U.S.-based Guatemalan Jewish American writer brings us to a second response to the question of why we should revisit Mesoamerican pre-Columbian beliefs and myths about night.

Whether these beliefs have any historical explanatory power or not and whether they are over-determined or not, Central American writers and U.S.-based Central American writers themselves deploy pre-Columbian Mesoamerican tropes of night derived from pre-Columbian cosmologies: Mayan prophecies, obsidian mirrors and knives, black jaguars, night serpents, and conical volcanoes casting dark shade or shadows. This particular passage from Goldman's *The Art of Political Murder* (2007) notwithstanding, I contend that the uses of night by U.S. based Central American writers such as Arturo Arias, Héctor Tobar, Goldman himself in his novels, Sylvia Sellers-García, and Cristina Henríquez do cultural work that moves against the grain of mere reiterations of pre-Columbian Mesoamerican tropes of the terrors of night seen through colonialist European or Euro-American and specifically U.S.-ian neocolonialist lenses. These U.S.-based Central American writers' deployment of pre-Columbian Mesoamerican tropes of night is akin to what Davíd Carrasco talks about in his chapter on the contemporary continuance of pre-Columbian Mesoamerican sensibilities in the Chicana/o movement:

> One of the most interesting responses to the changes of the modern West comes from the Chicano movement in the United States. This response includes the utilization and celebration of the pre-Hispanic past in the aesthetic and political expressions for Chicano liberation in the United States. Chicanos are Americans of Mexican descent who have formed a movement to liberate themselves from Anglo stereotypes, political oppression, poverty, unequal opportunity, and spiritual doubt. (155–56)

In the works I examine, the references are more Mayan than Aztec, and they pertain to different geopolitical events and circumstances. The decolonial impetus, however, is comparable to that demonstrated by the works I discussed by Chicana/o cultural producers. As Chicana/o studies scholar Rafael Pérez-Torres notes, Chicana/o evocation of indigenous, "pre-Cortesian cultural elements proclaims a pre-European relationship to the New World," and thus constitutes "a strategy of empowerment and entitlement."[19] Like Davíd Carrasco, critic Ana Patricia Rodríguez notes an overall similarity between Chicana/o deployments of Aztec concepts and U.S.-based Central American uses of pre-Columbian Mesoamerican and specifically Mayan cosmologies. She does so in her analysis of Guatemalan writer Gaspar Pedro González's novel *Return of the Maya,* which was published in Spanish in 1998. Focusing on the novel's representation of Yichkan, a Mayan liminal place for world-centering and renewal in the face of hardship and trauma, she writes,

> Yichkan, thus, reminds us of Nepantla, as the Aztecs called their postconquest state of being and condition of neocolonialism. Yichkan, like Nepantla, is the reference and subjective point where the past and the future are held in balance, or imbalance, and the space-in-between where different forms of knowledge and practices of time, life, and beliefs and modes of cultural survival coexist. (109)

Central American and U.S.-based Central American writers, like Chicana/o writers, deploy their pre-Columbian cosmology to underscore postconquest conditions of colonialism and neoliberal neocolonialism as well as resistance to those traumatizing conditions and forces. Rodríguez offers detailed readings of the uses of pre-Columbian Mayan cosmology in González's *Return of the Maya* and Héctor Tobar's *The Tattooed Soldier.*[20] However, she does not concentrate on the centrality of night as I do.

More General Uses of Night in These U.S.-Based Central American Texts

Not all representations of night in the work of these U.S.-based writers are specifically inflected with traces of pre-Columbian cosmologies. Some of them appear rather culturally or regionally unmarked or, if specific, not pre-Columbian Mesoamerican, at least not at first glance. "[E]normous black clouds" hiding the sun, an association of nightclub proprietors protesting a 9:00 P.M. military curfew, the uncanny image of "black umbilicus," and recurring nightmares crop up in Arturo Arias's novel *After the Bombs,* which was first published in Spanish in 1979 and translated into English in 1990.[21] *After the Bombs* opens with the bombing of Guatemala City in 1954, a bombing that was part of the CIA's and the Eisenhower administration's coup against the democratically elected government of Jacobo Arbenz. The novel's narrative style matches such an event with its hurried, chopped, and hallucinatory prose; broken syntax conveys both frantic and jumbled actions and emotions. The opening chapter shows an upper-middle-class married heterosexual couple with a baby having their world torn apart by the bombs and this coup. The social dismemberment continues throughout the novel, affecting all levels of Guatemalan society, which has been forcibly taken over by U.S. interests: "As soon as the bombing ended a new government was in. The distinguished man of arms, Colonel Castle Cannons [an American], was in the Big Chair" (12). The rest of the narrative is concerned with the "education" of Máximo Sánchez, the son of the couple. He is left to deal with the world and the political situation into which he has been born. His is a war-torn consciousness that refracts the post-1954 turmoil of Guatemalan society: "When Máximo entered third grade, a new government came to power. . . . The assassination of five of the candidates had caused some delay" (34). His father, an Arbenz supporter who rebelled against the generals and joined the Guatemalan revolution, was disappeared in the 1954 coup. Máximo tries to piece together what happened, but disappearances, silences, and continual disruption foil his attempts to find answers. Multiple images of night signify the black void of fear, silence, disappearance, dismemberment, and death. Tropes of night become more horrific as Máximo progresses into the heart of the political darkness around him and into his own bourgeois, irresponsible apoliticism, as reflected in his first lover, an American named Karen Johnson who is the daughter of the president of the Monsanto Company's Guatemalan branch. Karen's father also works as the U.S. ambassador to Guatemala. Máximo slowly evolves, partly on account of his involvement with a unionized prostitute Amarena, into someone aware of his own complicity in and responsibility for the political dynamics that are apocalyptically pulling his country apart: "our cities will go on burning" (118), with blooming black smoke darker than the night skies and corpses everywhere. When he decides to write about his new awareness and revolutionary commitment and exposes the local chief of the CIA, he becomes a "menace to society" (155) and must flee the country for his life with the help of Amarena. He makes his escape in disguise. The narrative, despite its blackness, ends with the possibility of life. But the tale's nightmarish quality lingers in the reader's mind.

"[H]aunting mountain darkness," "dark shadows," "evening falling," "hovering nightfall," a sky of "black, fulminating violence," "a crazy star projector in a planetarium" rotating on its axis and spinning out of control, more nightmares, and a darkened sun emerge in Arias's later novel *Rattlesnake*, finished in Spanish in 1998, translated into English, and published in 2003.[22] This novel, set in 1980s Guatemala during the height of the military repression and the "civil war," takes the tactic of being written (with much irony) from the perspective of U.S. CIA agent Tom Wright, who is sent to Guatemala to rescue an Australian banker kidnapped by a guerrilla group named the Guerrilla Army of the Poor. Wright's heart is not in this mission; rather, he is distracted by a former lover (Sandra de Herrera) who has married into the Guatemalan oligarchy. She has multiple contradictory connections—to the guerrilla group who has kidnapped the Australian banker, to the military, to the international drug trade, to powerful Guatemalan entrepreneurs, and to Wright, the CIA agent. The renewed entanglement of Tom Wright and Sandra de Herrera exposes both of them to a host of dangers (at each other's hands and at the hands of others). This exposure results in Sandra's gruesome torture, rape, and murder by Guatemalan military Captain Pacal. His "justification" for this treatment of Sandra is that she betrayed the military's cause with some of her other connections. Meanwhile, Tom Wright escapes back to the United States to re-join his wife and children and hide behind a façade of normalcy in suburban Virginia with its "shiny green lawns" and "white, wooden" houses (242). Via a televised newscast, agent Wright learns of the mutilation and murder of Señora Sandra de Herrera. The American anchorman relays the official story—that the murder has been attributed to "a terrorist organization, the EGP, Spanish acronym for Guerrilla Army of the Poor" (244). Readers of the novel know otherwise. The military, not guerrillas, murdered Sandra. Despite his amorality, Tom is haunted by Sandra's murder and by his own complicity in the ugly unfolding of events in Guatemala. Though technically the narrative is delivered via an omniscient narrator and relays the thoughts and feelings of other characters in addition to Tom Wright's, the presentation of the novel's situations through Tom Wright's point of view compels readers to inhabit the mind of a CIA agent. Readers are encouraged to experience and recognize their own complicity—to step into a space of supposed privilege and "immunity" only to wind up like a snake darkly devouring its own tail. This narrative technique complements the one in the earlier novel of having a privileged bourgeois subject slowly awaken to the nightmare of history and of Guatemalan/U.S. relations in particular.

"[T]he Los Angeles sky stretched in a vast blackness empty of stars, constellations erased by the glowing lights of too much city," "the only stars the lights of skyscrapers that come on at dusk," night school, "a moonless night . . . infinite darkness," and the total darkness of a black tunnel characterize the son of Guatemalan immigrants in Héctor Tobar's 1998 novel *The Tattooed Soldier.*[23] This novel concerns the fateful crisscrossing of the lives of Guatemalan immigrants to the Los Angeles area of the United States. Guatemalan refugee Antonio Bernal, whose wife and child were massacred in the 1980s by the death squad Jaguar Battalion of the Guatemalan army, crosses paths with a retired sergeant from that very death squad: Guillermo Longoria. The poor, evicted, and homeless

Antonio, who wanders the streets, steals into Guillermo Longoria's apartment. There, he finds enough photographic evidence to realize that this tattooed soldier (trained to kill at Fort Bragg, North Carolina) was responsible for killing his wife and child. Antonio, now into his seventh year in Los Angeles, jobless, dispossessed in every way, and without recourse to the law or to meaningful social support except from a few of his other homeless companions, decides to take the law into his own hands and kill Guillermo Longoria to avenge his wife and child and the other innocents who were massacred. Antonio risks his life but is willing to make the sacrifice, as he views this act as his last chance to give his nearly destroyed life existential validity. Though his initial attempt is foiled, his second one—conducted during the L.A. riots of 1992, in which South Central Los Angeles erupted in racial and socioeconomic tensions of all kinds in the wake of the acquittal of the policemen who beat Rodney King—is successful. The L.A. riots (characterized by looting, arson, assault, and murder) resulted in over fifty reported deaths. Probably more occurred. The novel scripts one of those deaths as that of Guillermo Longoria at the hands of Antonio Bernal, a Guatemalan fighting against a Guatemalan in a continuation of the U.S.-supported Guatemalan civil war.

As Los Angeles burns and black smoke fills the air, Antonio Bernal manages to shoot Guillermo Longoria (not without Longoria seeing his avenger face-to-face) and drag him into a dark tunnel to die. Images of darkness, blackness, and night dominate the last pages of the novel, but Antonio Bernal emerges from this experience feeling reconnected to his wife and child and with a renewed will to live. He also finds himself reflecting on the continuum between his act of revenge and those of the rioters and looters during the L.A. riots. He recalls Argentine pan–Latin American revolutionary Che Guevara's words: "The revolutionary is guided in all his actions by great feelings of love" (306). The narrative more or less concludes with: "[i]t was absurd to mistake rock throwing and looting for an act of love, but Antonio was willing to allow for the possibility" (306).

In the baroque and Proustian prose of Francisco Goldman's 1992 novel *The Long Night of White Chickens*, there are references to "nightmares," an orphaned Guatemalan girl sitting awake late at night in a New England house, nights in Lord Byron's bar in Guatemala City, phantasmagoric shadows and the pursuit of shadows, long nights of insomnia, neon city lights stretching down avenues at night, repeated references to "the Long Night of White Chickens," "fateful night[s]" of murders, volcanoes "absolutely black and conical," lying on one's back in a yard and "trying to imagine the end of the stars," and refugees moving by the "[t]ens of thousands" at night, night school, night clubs, and a "Times

Square of spangled lights."[24] This story tells the tale of a part–Jewish American, part-Guatemalan narrator, Roger Graetz, who was raised in a Boston suburb in the company of an "orphan girl" from Guatemala named Flor de Mayo brought to serve the household as a "maid" (3). Flor de Mayo exceeds the limitations of this role, excels in school, wins a full scholarship to Wellesley, and returns to Guatemala in 1979 to be the director of "a private orphanage and malnutrition clinic" in Guatemala City. Four years later, in 1983, during the "civil war," "Flor was found murdered" (4). The Guatemalan authorities accuse her of illegally purchasing and stealing babies and arranging for them to be adopted out of the country (4). The novel moves backward and forward in time before and after Flor's mysterious and horrific murder. Her throat was slashed like that of a sacrificed chicken. The story is told through the conflicted and obsessive consciousness (363) of Roger Graetz, whose own relationship to Flor is anything but simple; it is remindful of Quentin Compson's to his sister Caddy in William Faulkner's *The Sound and the Fury* (1929). Roger's love/hate relationship with Guatemala echoes Quentin Compson's love/hate relationship with the South. Roger's quest to make sense of what happened to Flor de Mayo entails many stories within the larger story—about U.S./Guatemalan relations, Jewish/Mayan ethnic identities, small-town New England provincialism and regional class and ethno-racial prejudices, life in Guatemala City during the 1980s, complicated romantic and familial relations between people, and meditations on Guatemalan history from the murders and cruelties perpetrated against the indigenous people by the Spanish conquistador "Don Pedro de Alvarado" (243) onward. The novel makes a number of pre-Columbian references to Mayan civilization and explicitly mentions the *Popol Vuh* (201). As the novel concludes, instances and images of darkness, blackness, and night accumulate. Though the novel, like all of Goldman's novels, reads like a mystery, Flor de Mayo's murder remains unsolved. Roger Graetz's narrative is an attempt at remembrance and memorialization in the face of the black "defeat" and despair of being unable to know who was responsible for Flor's ghastly sacrifice (376–377).

Goldman's second novel, *The Ordinary Seaman* (1997), opens at night in the airport of Managua, Nicaragua. Much of the novel's activity—among the Central American crew marooned, like slaves and refugees, aboard the *Urus* ship docked the entire narrative in Brooklyn with no electricity or plumbing—takes place at night. A number of nocturnal dream sequences and waking ruminations fill the pages. So does a persistent sense of haunting by both human and animal dead, whether murdered by Contras, as in the case of Esteban's first love Marta, or terminally missing, as in the case of the ship's cat Desastres (Disasters). The main protagonist, Esteban, one of the members of the Central American crew marooned on a boat never destined to depart from the Brooklyn docks, steals off the boat and gets a night-shift job in a small chair factory, earning just enough money to feed and clothe himself and stay in New York with the help of his *novia* la Joaquina.[25] The novel reads like a mystery story and a ghost story. It is a ghost story about being haunted by the murdered and disappeared and about living, in life itself, the death of the social subject. During the time that the Central American crew are marooned on the *Urus*, they are more or less dead to the world, a condition that only exacerbates the death of or separation from loved ones that many have already gone through as well as their socioeconomic displacement. The dominance of night as the central time of much of the significant activity in this novel, including the movements of consciousness, reinforces its ghost-story quality.

On the subject of specifically nocturnal ghost stories, Cuban revolutionary, the "Apostle of Cuban independence" from Spain, writer, poet, translator, diplomat, journalist, orator, and painter José Martí (1853–1895) haunts Goldman's third novel, *The Divine Husband* (2004). Martí penned the famous poem "Dos patrias" (Two Homelands") with lines that translate "Two homelands have I: Cuba and the night / . . . silently / Cuba like a sad widow appears to me. / . . . The night is good / for saying good-bye. Light hinders / as does the human word. Universe speaks / better than man." Goldman's novel is shot through with the verbally conjured spirit of a major Latin American, Cuban, and Cuban American poet of the night as a powerful rhetorical symbol of political engagement and sacrifice—"the night is good to say good-bye." The novel repeatedly reminds readers of Martí's 1895 sacrificial death, which involved riding into a dark hail of Spanish bullets for the cause of Cuban independence. In the novel, Martí's dreams of liberation for the Americas (and for the Indios of "the young American republics") are rendered through his contact with Central America: "Though Martí was only twenty-four when he came to Central America, his life was already following a path that, from the perspective of his heroic martyr's death in battle eighteen years later, would seem as predestined as any saint's."[26] Martí's silhouette as shadow is conveyed through the passionate attachments to his rhetoric and persona that Goldman's novel depicts him to have inspired in various women who appear in the novel. These women include María de las Nieves Moran, Francisca (Paquita) Aparicio (modeled on the wife of the nineteenth Guatemalan dictator, Justo Rufino Barrios), María García Granados (the daughter of the first president of the Liberal Republic), Carmita Miyares de Mantilla, and his actual wife Carmen Zayas Bazán before their relationship cooled and failed. According to the novel, Martí inspired these attachments through his night-inflected verse that was part mystical Spanish baroque and part Romantic Byronic. The "Divine Husband" of the novel's title begins as the hidden God of cloistered nuns locked away from the world in their dark habits but winds up being the "revolutionary-hero-martyr-poet-saint" (253) of "Reina[s] de la Noche" (264), "unexpectedly blossoming flowers as evening falls" (265). Some of the blossoming flowers are former nuns whom Goldman's narrative transforms into "unforeseen 'niñas' of destiny" (250) giving birth to dark-versed (*versos oscuros*) love children of the Americas—none other than Martí's children. The gendering of this transformation testifies to a secularization but continuation of patriarchal ideology. Goldman's novel retells history through the romantic longings of female protagonists such as María de las Nieves, thus seeming to give the upper hand to apocryphal versus official history, the latter usually an androcentric story of accomplishments and victories. Following the tropes of night and day, dark and light, what was previously invisible or barely so comes to light, but only in relation to a famous man who passes through the body of the novel like a reanimation of Anna Hyatt Huntington's statue of José Martí in New York City's Central Park, which is rendered in shadowy form on the cover of *The Divine Husband*.

It might seem inappropriate to talk about "tropes" in Goldman's work in relation to his non-fiction account *The Art of Political Murder* (2007), but as scores of literary scholars have pointed out, writing is not a transparent medium. It entails all kinds of choices (conscious and unconscious) evident in the patterns and organization of the text, whether fiction or non-fiction. Literary analysts have questioned hard-and-fast distinctions between these two categories, as already seen, for example, in the work of Hayden White and Kenneth Burke. Night does play a central part in *The Art of Political Murder*. Most obviously, the murder of Bishop Juan Gerardi Conedera occurs at night, so night is continually referred to in relation to the immediate sequence of events surrounding and involving the murder. Phantasmagoria, an art of the night, in this text associated with the "art of political murder," shows up prominently in the second paragraph of the book as a lens through which to view the unfolding narrative of what Goldman later refers to as the blend, in Guatemala, "of paranoia, stealth, ruthlessness, betrayal, corruption, violence, and cunning that characterize the exercise of real and secret power" (325). During the 1980s, the torture of civilians opposed to the military regime and to the fascist power of the army takes place at all times of day but especially at night (17). Some of the tortured managed to escape their tormentors "at night, under the cover of darkness" (18). Goldman's account suggests that these patterns of repression persist through 1998, the year of the bishop's murder, into the twenty-first century. The story describes the fear and cover-up that accompany the investigation and the trial of the military men responsible for the death of a bishop who spent the last part of his career generating a report titled

> *Guatemala: Never Again,* a four-volume, 1,400-page report on an unprecedented investigation into the "disappearances," massacres, murders, torture, and systematic violence that had been inflicted on the population of Guatemala since the beginning of the 1960s, decades during which right-wing military dictators and then military-dominated civilian governments waged war against leftist guerrilla groups. An estimated 200,000 civilians [many of them Mayan Indians] were killed during the war, which formally ended in December 1996 with the signing of the peace agreement monitored by the United Nations. The Guatemalan Army had easily won the war on the battlefield, but making peace with the guerrillas had become a political and economic necessity. (4–5)

Guatemala, Never Again was part of the Recuperación de la Memoria Histórica, the Recovery of Historical Memory Project (5). Goldman's account suggests that Bishop Juan Gerardi Conedera's project was designed to bring to light what the Guatemalan Army and those supporting military dictatorship, both inside and outside Guatemala, wanted to confine to the perpetual night of forced historical amnesia. His death was a "politically motivated act of state-sponsored murder," an act of vengeance and punishment for exposing those in power as the criminals they were and are (258). According to *The Art of Political Murder,* the relatively young reporters, investigators, lawyers, and judges who dared to bring members of "the Guatemalan Army's Presidential Guard and the Estado Mayor Presidencial (EMP), or Presidential Military Staff" (28) to trial and conviction "were too young to have been corrupted, demoralized, or made cynical" (259). Goldman concludes his account thus: "For half a century the military's clandestine world had seemed impregnable. The Gerardi case had *opened a path into that darkness* [emphasis mine]" (357). Those who made the case possible risked and continue to risk their lives. These lives could still be claimed by that darkness, that perpetual night.

In the same year that Goldman's *The Art of Political Murder* appeared, Sylvia Sellers-García's novel *When the Ground Turns in Its Sleep* was published. In 2007, Sellers-García, a self-described Boston native with family in Guatemala who was, at the time of publication, a Ph.D. candidate in Latin American history at the University of California, Berkeley, came out with a novel set in Guatemala in 1993. This temporal setting is significant: it is one year before "[t]he truth commission established in 1994 through the Accord of Oslo published a report that relied principally on first-person accounts of the armed conflict" in Guatemala.[27] The armed conflict to which Sellers-García refers is that between the U.S.-backed Guatemalan military and the guerrillas. This is an armed conflict that has been ongoing since 1954, when "the CIA and the Eisenhower administration orchestrated a coup to overthrow Jacobo Arbenz, Guatemala's democratically-elected president" because, among other reasons, those in power in the United States were opposed to Arbenz's reforms, especially his redistributive land reforms.[28] Because she chooses to set her novel in 1993, before such reports were available to those wishing to find out about the military repression and human rights abuses in Guatemala, Sellers-García has the liberty to present readers with a Guatemalan American protagonist who knows very little and will find out more than he ever wanted to know. He is a priest named Nítido Amán whose father has died of Alzheimer's at the story's commencement and whose mother dies of a heart attack at its conclusion. The well-intentioned Father Amán goes to serve a parish in a small Guatemalan town called Río Roto (Broken River) and becomes engrossed in piecing together the personal histories of the people there in an attempt to learn about his own Guatemalan history; he was born in Guatemala but taken to the United States when still a young child. Through fragmented confessions of some of the townspeople, Nítido Amán discovers that they are simultaneously covering up and trying to express the trauma of their involvement with and against the brutal military repression and the armed struggle of the guerrillas opposed to the military's rule.

Sellers-García's narrative, with a largely unknowing but curious and committed narrator-protagonist, reads like a mystery novel. It is a kind of mystery novel and psychological thriller written from the perspective of a historian turned anthropologist of gesture, expression, and various kinds of discourse. Sellers-García's text openly acknowledges its debt and borrows from "many books and works of scholarship":

> John Perry's *Practical Sermons*; J. Eric Thompson's *The Rise and Fall of Maya Civilization*; Barbara Tedlock's *Time and the Highland Maya*; Murdo MacLeod's *Spanish Central America*; and the translation into English of *The Popol Vuh* by Delia Goetz and Sylvanus Griswold Morley.[29]

Sellers-García's prose distinguishes itself for its attention to bodily gesture and facial expression, often in lieu of dialogue. The novel does contain dialogue, but it is marked by silence. It heightens the sense of silence not only to illustrate the townspeople's reticence to talk about their traumatic history but also to convey Nítido Amán's contemplative consciousness as well as the absorbing cognitive work he must do to grasp the complex reality he has entered by accepting his pastoral post in Guatemala.

Given the repressive silence and erasure of the townspeople's experiences, a silence which is both imposed on them and imposed by themselves as self-censorship, the modicum of knowledge that Nítido Amán acquires is highly mediated by silence. This knowledge is often represented in terms of darkness and by what, from a Western "rational" perspective, is deemed at best "alternative" and usually "apocryphal" kinds of knowledge—dreams, memories, impressions easily confused with one another. Amán is many times portrayed as meditating on and piecing together clues at night and in his dreams (198) as if he were divining and deciphering (186, 235) through a glass darkly or an obsidian mirror. He time-travels from 1993 backward to both the recent and the distant past, willing to lose track of present time (137–39). This journey is represented as arduous; it is likened to sitting not on "the mountain [where the past is buried] but in it, at its volcanic core, surrounded by its dark walls, beside its dying fire" (202). The more Father Amán figures out about the recent historical and ongoing trauma of the townspeople, the more he himself becomes not only cognitively but physically involved—just as the image of sitting in the volcano and not just on top of the mountain foreshadows. At one point, Nítido Amán is physically attacked and suffers a blackout: "[Noé] spun around and pushed me up against the wall. . . . I kneed him in the stomach and he grunted but kept pressing his fingers into my throat. . . . The room blackened from the outside in" (247). At another point, Father Amán finds himself in the mountains at sunset and then at nightfall, with the bodies of the mutilated and dead all around him; they are doubly shadowed by the trees and the wings of buzzards (275–276).

The "ground" that "turns in its sleep" of the novel's title begins to yield some of its nightmarish secrets: "The ground seemed to disintegrate beneath me inch by inch, and I imagined that it wouldn't be long before the bones would begin to show" (269). However, this dialectic—Father Amán's increased involvement with and commitment to the people he encounters in Guatemala and the yielding of buried secrets—constitutes the basis for the ground of connection tacitly presented as a non-utopian alternative to the deadly U.S. military interventions in Guatemala. The acts of reading a passage from his dead father's journals and meditating on its silences and expressions comprise Nítido's own recognition of his past and present connection to Guatemala as a Guatemalan American who was removed to the United States but who chose to return:

When the sun sets [in the desert, not in Guatemala] the world goes blind. On the mountain, in places like Naranjo [ancient city of the Maya civilization in

Guatemala], it's completely different. The ground turns in its sleep, stretches, and comes awake after dark. It sits back and watches. (287)

Night is alive in Guatemala.

In this book, night predominates as the time of seeing and, furthermore, of undergoing a psycho-cultural transformation, of yielding to forces that make one stumble "into another world" (253) and become someone else:

> Everyone has experienced how day and night seem to inhabit different spheres. Sensations and thoughts that take firm hold in the middle of the night seem, by day, unimaginable, and likewise awakening in the dark, as I [Nítido] did, can sometimes temporarily erase the ordinariness of daylight. The experience is so universal that we can speak of it without explaining. (251)

The novel emphasizes the universality or non–culturally specific transformative experience of night, but the novel also transparently and deliberately represents night through the filter of pre-Columbian cosmologies of night. And it does so, I argue, as part of a postcolonial recuperative project to recover historical memory in the face of cognitive and cultural oblivion. Alzheimer's in this text is not merely a physiological problem. It functions symbolically—allegorically—relative to Guatemalan cultural memory and U.S./Guatemalan relations.

The authors of these texts I have just discussed—Arias, Tobar, Goldman, and Sellers-García—are Guatemala-born and U.S.-based or are, one way or another, Guatemalan Americans. This chapter on U.S.-based Central American writers' uses of night is Guatemala-dominant. This Guatemalan predominance raises certain issues about the valences of the postcolonially pre-Columbian cosmologies of night in contemporary U.S.-based Central American texts. Am I justified in using the term "Central American," or do I really mean Guatemalan? I do employ the term "cosmologies," plural, but do I mean just Mayan pre-Columbian cosmologies of night? And if I do mean largely Mayan-derived pre-Columbian cosmologies of night, does that emphasis prevent me from including writers working out of other cultures whose imaginary realms cannot be so emphatically traced to the Maya material—as, for example, a U.S.-based Panamanian writer? I did point out that not all representations of night in the work of these U.S.-based writers are specifically inflected with traces of pre-Columbian cosmologies. Some of them appear rather culturally or regionally unmarked or, if geographically specific, not seemingly pre-Columbian Mesoamerican. In the next section of this chapter, however, I will show to what degree these seemingly uninflected representations of night are inflected by the pre-Columbian.

Meanwhile, to address the former questions about the Guatemalan dominance in this chapter on literature already marginalized even within Latina/o
studies, I point out that the tropes of night I have been discussing thus far are
not confined to specifically Guatemalan referents. This is true with respect
to the culturally unspecific uses of night, but it is also true to the extent that
these generalities cross or resonate with pre-Columbian cosmologies of night,
Mayan-derived as many of them may be. Current-day Guatemala was only a
part of the Mayan cultural extension, which included other modern Central
American countries. However, Mayan pre-Columbian cosmology was only one
of many pre-Columbian cosmologies, though it is one about which much more
is known on account of the Mayan system of record keeping that, as anthropologist Dennis Tedlock points out, had been practiced "long before the Europeans brought the roman alphabet" to the Americas:

> By the seventh century, when English literature made its first tentative appear-
> ance, Mayans had a long tradition of inscribing ornaments, pottery vessels, mon-
> uments, and the walls of temples and palaces, and they had also begun to write
> books. The pages of these books were made of a kind of paper that is native to
> Mesoamerica . . . literature existed in the Americas before Europeans got here—
> not only oral literature but visible literature. . . . Despite the best efforts of the
> invaders [the Spaniards], Mayan authors went on writing even when their books
> were in danger of being burned, and they themselves were in danger of falling
> into the hands of the Holy Inquisition.[30]

The fact that some pre-Columbian cosmologies were better documented than
others makes the traces of the better-documented ones easier to detect.

How are we to detect pre-Columbian cosmologies of night in a U.S.-based
Panamanian text? The criteria are not clear-cut. I rely on the U.S.-based Guatemalan texts to guide me. I find some similar pre-Columbian elements in
key night passages from the text of the Panamanian American writer Cristina Henríquez.[31] I justify inclusion of Henríquez's *Come Together, Fall Apart*
(2006) along with that of U.S.-based Guatemalan writers because this chapter is about U.S.-based Central American (and not just Guatemalan) cultural
production. Critic Ana Patricia Rodríguez grants Panama a very representative
Central American status as a "transisthmian region" (74) and a nation divided
against itself by the various "plantation economies and neocolonial cultures of
the Black Atlantic" (74), including the U.S.-run "banana-canal industrial military complex" of the Canal Zone (66–75). I would add to her argument about
the Central American–ness of Panama that the liminal transnational status of

Panamanian cultural production both questions and underscores the viability of the term "Central American."

Henríquez's 2006 *Come Together, Fall Apart* draws on night in most of its nine sections, or eight stories and a novella: "Yanina," "Ashes," "Drive," "Mercury," "Beautiful," "Chasing Birds," "The Wide, Pale Ocean," "The Box House and the Snow," and "Come Together, Fall Apart." "Yanina" concerns a heterosexual couple, Yanina and René, who decide to "split Panama City" and live near the beaches of El Rompío, Panama.[32] They have an unequal commitment to one another. Yanina has asked René "to marry her forty-five times" (1), but he prefers to philander. Brief mentions of night signal the emotional distance between the two people in this couple and the colonized, predictably gendered inequality of their power dynamics (18, 29, and 30–31), as evidenced in the last "nocturnal" situation of the story. The couple spends the night on a beach. When Yanina falls asleep, René finds a stick and writes in the sand: "YANINA, WILL YOU MARRY ME?" He then goes to lie down beside her. He thinks to himself: ". . . if it's still there in the morning [if the waves do not wash away the writing] . . . then that will mean something. Then I will ask her" (31). Like a heedless colonizer, the man inscribes the land, but in a way that absolves him of responsibility for his relationship with the woman.

In the second story, "Ashes," the protagonist's mother dies, and the narrator is left to deal with her grief. The narrator rides a bus home from work "that night," passing "strip malls with blinking neon signs" (38). Among other things, she thinks of a line translated into English from a poem by the modernist Peruvian poet, writer, and journalist César Vallejo (1892–1938), who was exiled to France, where he died: "And now a shadow falls on the soul" (39). The line references shadows and the night of the soul, as does the entire collection of his first book of poetry, *Los heraldos negros* (1918, published in 1919), *The Black Heralds* or *Messengers,* a modernist avant-garde work expressing in striking experimental language and structure a profound affective and political melancholy. Henríquez's inclusion of this reference to a famous poet of shadows, night, and unresolved mourning connects "Ashes" to a long history of similarly freighted Latin American works. Loaded allusions to night continue through the end of the story. The narrator's father "cleaned government buildings at night" (40), and her unreliable boyfriend wakes her up "in the middle of the night" to tell her that he misses her (52). At the end of the story, the narrator is sitting on the rocks by the sea with her mother's ashes in an urn, ashes that presumably she intends to scatter "into the gathering darkness" (56). The story references multiple injustices and colonizations at once: economic subordination in a neoliberal Americanized landscape of strip malls, power inequality in a romantic relationship, and the death of a mother or the loss of one's origins. Together these suggest cultural erosion and psychological trauma. The deployments of night function as a strong cry of protest against these silencing, defeating forces.

"Drive," divided into eighteen short scenes, concerns the painful distance between dreams of movement, freedom, and happiness versus barriers, emotional distances between people, and the actual economic and socio-political stagnation under the U.S. domination of Panama. Brief references to night (61, 62, 68, 69, 70, 75, and 81) appear throughout the story and culminate in the narrator's declaration about her night walks in Panama City:

> No one knows I go, or maybe they do and they don't mention it, but I do it because it's the time when I feel the most alone in the world but it's also the time when I feel most intimately connected to it. Like the hour confers some kind of clarity of vision in which everything appears to me in its true, naked state, and everything in this city makes sense to me, at least for a while. (70)

Night here signifies an existential connection on the narrator's part to Panama City, an acceptance of that place despite the hardships and disappointments, the heartbreaking abysses between dreams and harsh realities, and the troubled history of the domination of U.S. interests in Panama.

"Mercury" is a multi-layered story about three generations of a transnational, diasporic Panamanian family with grandparents in Panama and parents and children in the northeastern United States. Life in the United States has taken its toll, and the parents are getting a divorce. During this time, they send Maria, their child, to spend part of her summer vacation with her grandparents in Panama. The story is told through Maria's eyes and is composed of memory fragments of her relationship with her parents (and their strained relationship with each other) and her attempt to connect with her Spanish-speaking grandparents. Communication is the fundamental issue of the story. Maria discovers that she has more in common with her grandparents, despite the language barrier, than she does with her estranged parents or than they with each other though they speak "the same language" (113). Maria and her grandparents communicate with more than words—with gestures, whispers, and body language. The implication is that they understand each other despite the limited words they share; they are Spanish speakers, and Maria is an English speaker who is hesitant in Spanish, her second language. Importantly, Maria and her grandparents share some key images of the night—a sensual, visual imaginary communicated via Maria's bilingual mother when Maria visited her grandparents with her mother as a young child:

Maria and her grandfather used to . . . gaze at the sea [off Panama]. Black silk, he would say, on the nights when the moon was new. Liquid mercury, when the moon was waning or waxing. A layer of butter melting in a frying pan, when the moon was full. Descriptions Maria gathered from her mother. This is what he's saying, Maria. . . . They never spoke directly. (89)

The language Maria and her grandparents share pertains to the phases of the moon seen at night. These phrases connote change but also what returns, what persists, despite all the diasporic, displacing change that Maria and her family have experienced in Panama, in the United States, and in mercurially intersecting places, as the title of the story "Mercury" suggests. The story ends with Maria tracing "*Goodnight,* in Spanish, on her grandfather's arm" and whispering "*Buenas noches*" to "her grandmother in the dark" (113).

"Beautiful" involves the story of a family in denial about the incest a drunken father commits against his daughter and her own struggle to defy this violation and be herself. The incest takes place at night when the father is drunk: "It's almost like he's a ghost, swimming through the dark. Maybe he's walking in his sleep like the people on the streets at night . . ." (123). After being violated by her father, the daughter abruptly decides to cut her hair, thinking that if she defies prevailing beauty standards she can discourage further advances from her father. She must endure her parents telling her that she has "ruined everything" (128). Night signals a pattern of inversion here where what seems one way is quite another, and "normal" family life is shown to be a façade concealing a dark secret. As her parents add insult to injury, she resists quietly but defiantly by just standing "there feeling more beautiful than ever" (128). Night is associated with the nightmarish truth of incestuous, internally destructive domestic social conditions in the home and, by extension, in colonized patriarchal societies, which include not only Panama but also the United States and certainly Panama under neocolonial, U.S-dominated economic and military relations.

"Chasing Birds" is about another heterosexual couple (this time married) who are emotionally out of touch with one another. As with the couple of the first story, the woman is aware of the estrangement and the man is not. The couple is from Appleton, Wisconsin, but is visiting Panama City and Gamboa, the latter so that the husband can bird-watch. The wife is not interested in bird-watching. She just wants to have a romantic time with her husband. When she is unable to reach him emotionally, she takes an interest in a hotel employee (138) who takes an interest in her. One night, feeling especially neglected by her husband, she pads "down the dark hallway" (146) to the hotel employee's room, where she has a brief encounter with the Panamanian employee, Diego.

The encounter involves "only a kiss" (147), but it is a kiss that the wife replays in her head. The kiss comes to embody for her the romance she was seeking—"something graspable but beyond your grasp, something fluttering in the distance, something surprising and new and rare" (152). The story is bittersweet in that it provides the reader with enough information to create an awareness of the ironies of this brief romance between an American tourist and a Panamanian hotel employee. Though purveying a sense of surprise, newness, and rarity, this relationship is over-determined by the neocolonial relations between the United States and Panama. The story's title, "Chasing Birds," suggests an analogy between the American wife's infatuation with the Panamanian hotel employee and the American husband's pursuit of rarity via exotic birds; both Panamanian birds and Panamanian people become the exotic objects of the gazes of bored tourists from the United States. Boredom passes into fascination. The difference between the husband's object choice and the wife's is that the latter contains a glimmer of a threat to the neocolonial U.S.-dominant power structure, somewhat like the wife's behavior in "The Adulterous Woman" from Camus's *Exile and the Kingdom* (1957). Night in Henríquez's "Chasing Birds" functions as a medium of alterity, of a different order than that of the daylight-dependent, bird-watching husband.

Henríquez's stories generally deploy night to reveal an obscured or repressed but essential state of contradictory emotions and conditions between people—a dual dynamic of division and connection communicated by the book's title, *Come Together, Fall Apart* (2006). This dual dynamic of division and connection, often communicated most potently through night scenes, corresponds to the underlying historical forces being negotiated by Central American literature and Panamanian literature in particular, both in Panama and abroad, as discussed by Ana Patricia Rodríguez in her chapter "Nations Divided" (66–75).

A similar use of night occurs in the next story, "The Wide, Pale Ocean," about a strong mother-daughter bond that is challenged when the daughter acquires a boyfriend of whom the mother does not approve and who, in fact, leaves the daughter at the end of the story. The strained but elementally close bond between the mother and the daughter is encoded in a striking nocturnal image: "bands of moonlight stretched across our stucco ceiling like tiny highways, like the ones they had in the city" (165). Much is conveyed in that one compound image about the forces that pull apart and produce diaspora.

The eighth and final story, "The Box House and the Snow," reads like a Russian fairy tale mixed with a creation/sacrifice story from the *Popol Vuh*. It is emphatically not written in the realist style of the other stories. It concerns a family (father, mother, and daughter) who live in a "tropical country" in a house built by the father himself (180)—a "perfect house" (180), though this epithet is as ironic as any that might be found in a story by Tolstoy or Gogol. One April, the unthinkable in a tropical country happens. A huge snowstorm falls on the town where the perfect house is. The snowstorm arrives at night:

> The snowstorm came at night while everyone was sleeping. . . . The moon was masked behind thick clouds. The world was black, caked on and opaque. Then, all at once, millions of snowflakes burst from the murky sky and fluttered to the earth. It was a pillow ripping open. It was a silent, exploding firework. It was as if God had been collecting mounds and fistfuls and armfuls of snow for centuries and, finally, could hold the white flakes no more. (181)

The father of the house cannot handle the catastrophe. He takes it as an affront to his pride. He panics that the house will collapse under the weight of the snow. He enlists his daughter and forces her to hold up the ceiling and, thus, his house. His mother protests his treatment of the daughter but goes along with it against her better judgment. She caves in to his patriarchal obsession with his house as a reflection of his own worthiness. The daughter continues to hold up the "perfect house" (193), becoming a sacrifice. The mother, disturbed but not openly rebelling against the father, has trouble sleeping. Strange dreams surge in her mind at night. In one dream, the untropical snowstorm, which lends itself to being interpreted as the presence of North America in Central America in that the snowstorm invades the tropical town, turns into a "volcano rumbling beneath her":

> She could feel the vibrations traveling through her toes to her knees to her hips to her shoulders. And then the volcano exploded. She was thrown out. And what it spewed wasn't lava and ash. It was snow. . . . She dreamed she was choking on snow. (194)

The daughter continues to hold up the ceiling and, therefore, the house, "too exhausted to speak" (198). The story is complexly allegorical. One of its implications is that patriarchal ideology contributes to the enslavement of the generations to something as freaky, unnatural, and bizarre as the consequences of a North American–style snowstorm that invades a tropical Central American country. Night plays a pivotal role as an expressive device to reveal the affective and socio-political conditions of the writer's societies, conveying what it may feel like to be Panamanian in U.S.-dominated Panama and also abroad in the United States.

This eighth short story about the oppressiveness of a massive snowfall in the tropics provides a pointed prelude to the last item in the book, the novella "Come Together, Fall Apart" (199). The novella opens on October 23, 1989, with the words, "We were all scared in those days. Noriega [General Manuel Antonio Noriega, former head of Panama's secret police and CIA informant] was on his way to collapse and already the chaos had started" (199). The novella begins two months before the December 20, 1989, United States invasion of Panama to oust Noriega, who was in power partly because of connections with the CIA and U.S. Department of State, and to perpetuate, under the guise of liberation, U.S. control of the canal-related lands of Panama. On December 31, 1999, a decade after the invasion, the United States handed over these lands to Panama. The narrative—divided into journal entries subtitled by month, date, and year—extends from October 23, 1989, to January 8, 1990, and then jumps forward more than a decade to April 24, 2000. During this time, a Panamanian family suffers multiple traumas. An aunt is injured in the explosion of a homemade bomb (199) and talks all night, every night about her injury (200–201), although the men in her family fall short in empathy for her pain (203). At night, the narrator's father takes fantasy-refuge in songs from American comics and musicals: "My father was in the bathtub, humming 'Popeye the Sailor Man.' I could hear him through the door. That and 'The Impossible Dream' [from *Don Quijote de la Mancha*] were his favorite songs" (206). His reflexes have been colonized by American culture and, in the case of "The Impossible Dream," by U.S. culture's appropriation of Spanish culture, the original colonizing culture of the Americas. The irony of the situation is extreme—a Panamanian shortly before a U.S. invasion singing about Popeye the Sailor and dreaming of being Don Quixote, making his son enact scenes from the novel, and calling his wife Dulcinea until she tells him "enough" (207). The family lives in a rented house that everyone in the father's family back to the narrator's "great-grandparents had occupied" (209). The sense of permanent impermanence is greatly heightened before and during the invasion, as is "a certain lawlessness to everything" (212). Under President Ronald Wilson Reagan (1981–1989), the banks in Panama are closed as part of economic sanctions. U.S troops occupy Panama City "in force" (212). The actual invasion, which overlaps with the start of President George Herbert Walker Bush's presidency (January 20, 1989–January 20, 1993), only precipitates the socioeconomic and psychological disintegration alluded to at the beginning of the novella. A few weeks before the bombing of Panama City, the family receives an evacuation notice from the Zoña Construction Company (232, 235). The owner of their rented house has signed away the house where the family lives. The father refuses to leave the "Velasco family home" (245). In the middle of this dilemma, the narrator Ramón falls in love with a young woman whose affections he discovers his best friend has already claimed.

Places, people, and things are all up for grabs and yet out of this family's reach, adding to the vertiginous feeling of uncertainty and displacement and the implacability of loss. Though the family does move to a "new house"—"smaller than our other one" (251)—the father never accepts the move any more than Don Quixote accepts defeat. Instead, shockingly, the father places himself in the path of the bulldozers and wrecking ball that demolish the old home, allowing himself to be destroyed along with the house where he was born and grew up. After relaying this incident and the subsequent funeral, the novella leaps a decade ahead to April 24, 2000, opening with the sentence "Our lives fell apart after that [after the invasion of Panama and the father's suicide], crumbling in on us like the house, like buildings all over Panama in the aftermath of the invasion" (300). The narrative reports the death of the family's mother. The narrator speculates that life's heartbreak killed his parents, but he vows to tell his story "about my mother and my father and me—and how in that story was all that I knew about love" (306). The story ends with an image of faith: "God's arms growing infinitely longer so as to be able to hold all of us in His embrace" (306). This image of togetherness hauntingly counters the situations and images of disintegration and destruction offered to readers throughout the novella "Come Together, Fall Apart." The novella's ending is in exact chiasmic relation to the title. Whereas the title finishes on falling apart, the novella concludes with the image of holding things together; this is what, as an act of creation emanating from so much destruction, it attempts to do, at least on a symbolic level.

In "Come Together, Fall Apart," references to night appear in relation to an ever-increasing insomnia as the U.S. military's invasion of Panama looms nearer and nearer: "I had trouble sleeping" (255). Night also plays an essential part as the time when people take refuge in fantasies against an unacceptable, encroaching reality. At night, Ramón's father insists on sitting on the narrator's bed to read out loud the tale of Don Quixote (207), a tale that gives the father both courage and respite. At night the narrator, Ramón, stays up thinking of Sofia, the young woman with whom he is in love and who commits herself to his best friend Ubi (239, 255–56). Two uses of night stand out as especially important to the overall effect and emotional impact of the novella. One involves the father's declaration that he fell in love with his old house (the one for which he sacrifices himself) at night during an electrical blackout:

[T]hat's when I fell in love with this house. It was like being blind. I experienced everything differently. The shock of the cool floor as I moved my feet over it was something I had never noticed to that degree. The rough feel of the walls as I trailed my fingers over them, trying to steer my way down the hall. (250)

As previously mentioned, night telegraphs the essential emotional state of affairs—the real feelings behind the roles that people are compelled to play to keep up appearances of normalcy in a state of emergency. The official meaning of "state of emergency" applies to the neocolonial takeover and dispossession of the Panamanian populace who are not part of the elite power structure. The father's declaration about falling in love with the house foreshadows his sacrifice at the end. The second significant reference to night comes on Christmas Eve during the U.S. military invasion of Panama in December of 1989. The family decides to brave the perils of going to church for Christmas Eve Mass. The church pianist plays "O Holy Night." The church is portrayed as "a cavern, much larger and darker than our old church" (278). It provides a temporary "holy night" sanctuary against the desecration of the bombs of light and sound falling everywhere over the city. These textual arrangements of night demonstrate the extent to which night, in Henríquez's work, serves to transmit an undeniable emotional charge. Night is almost as "sacred" as God and, at the very least, serves as both touchstone and Geiger counter.

Postcolonial Pre-Columbian Cosmologies of Night

Tropes of night in these U.S.-based Central American works function not only in the more general or culturally unmarked fashion but also in a more culturally specific way: they are informed by pre-Columbian motifs (whether Mayan, Aztec, or other) of night as described in the second section of this chapter. I deliberately insert the adjective "postcolonial" here to mean not just that the works were produced after colonialism or in the wake of the colonial histories, in this case, of Central American countries but also that they are part of a tactic of resistance against that history and against the neocolonial presence of the United States. Almost all the works discussed thus far—by Arias, Tobar, Goldman, Sellers-García, and Henríquez—refer extensively to the socioeconomic, political, military, and surveillance interventions of the United States in Guatemala, Panama, Nicaragua, El Salvador, and other Central American countries. They do so beginning with the nineteenth century, taking, for instance, Goldman's *The Divine Husband* with its reminders of the Monroe Doctrine of 1823. However, most of the representations of the United States in relation to Central America range from the 1950s into the first decade of the twenty-first century with a concentration on the decade of the 1980s—the early 1980s in the case of

Guatemala and the late 1980s to early 1990s in the case of Panama. The 1980s and 1990s correlate to the Guatemalan civil wars and the height of U.S.-backed military repression of the populace. The late 1980s and early 1990s correspond to the U.S. military's invasion of Panama.

Most of the texts I have analyzed could be described, and some of them have been described, with terms such as "the new [in these cases, U.S.-based] Guatemalan novel" or "the new Central American novel." Critics employ the term "new" to signal the work of one to two generations now, from people such as Arturo Arias and Francisco Goldman, onward (that is writers in their fifties and younger) but also to signal a critical and questioning perspective on the "civil wars," U.S. intervention, the condition of being Central American in the Americas, etc. So, for instance, none of these writers comes across as a card-carrying member of the guerrilla movements or of the repressive forces, though I would say that they all exhibit a strong aversion to the history and presence of U.S. backed repressive military forces. These texts are not interested, as far as I can see, in being neutral or being politically removed. All of these texts are political and critical, but that does not stop them from being skeptical about the use of violence to address blatant social injustice. On the other hand—and here is where these texts are complicated performances and why I do not find the term "new" critically descriptive enough—the texts themselves describe situations of violent repression and revolt. Certainly, Héctor Tobar's *The Tattooed Soldier* does not condemn Guatemalan refugee Antonio Bernal for avenging himself against Guillermo Longoria, murderer of Bernal's wife and child. Tobar's novel leaves the reader to decide how she or he feels about Bernal's actions and to consider what she or he might do if confronted by the torturer and killer of loved ones.

Furthermore, the rhetorical image patterns of these texts produce their own opposition. The tropes of night are not mild—quite the contrary. These tropes of night are literally dark and confrontational, even in their general or culturally unspecific forms. Factor in their pre-Columbian cargo—tropes of night that link night to journeys into the underworld, violent transformation, and sacrifice—and the term "new" requires another more descriptive term. I have chosen "postcolonial" to signal both a particular temporality and a resistant stance against colonial and neocolonial forces. I realize that the term "postcolonial," like many other critical terms, is used in so many different contexts that its edge is hardly assured. I might have chosen the term "decolonial" as more trenchantly connected to a project of indigeneity—after all, these pre-Columbian motifs are usually indigenous ones. This is not to say that the term "decolonial" is limited to a project of indigeneity. According to Chicana historian Emma Pérez, that is only one possible understanding and application of the term as a practice—to write a story that takes into account the agency of those indigenous subaltern lives and imaginations.[33] Nevertheless, for the texts I am considering here, the term "decolonial" might be a bit premature, especially given the authors' own awareness of the fact that the conflicts and power struggles of cultural domination continue into the present day in many different permutations. That is clear, for instance, in works such as Tobar's *Tattooed Soldier* or Goldman's *The Art of Political Murder*.

In my use of the term "postcolonial," however, I do not rule out a strong decolonial impulse—a decolonial desire to visualize and narrate spaces and agencies between and beyond the "colonist and that which is colonized," to reference Emma Pérez's description of the "decolonial imaginary" (6–7). Pérez theorizes the decolonial imaginary in relation to a "time lag between the colonial and the postcolonial" (6). I would amend that model to suggest that the postcolonial of which I write lies in the interstices between the colonial and the decolonial. "Postcolonial" as I am deploying it here lies in relation to a decolonial desire, working as a resistance against the colonial and neocolonial and a striving toward the decolonial.

This difference between my conceptualization and Pérez's aside, I find significant the fact that she imagines the "decolonial imaginary" as "intangible" and compares it to a shadow: "it acts much like a shadow in the dark. It survives as a faint outline gliding against a wall or an object. The shadow is the figure between the subject and the object on which it is cast, moving and breathing through an in-between space" (6). My investigations have led me to conclude that this shadow manifests, among other ways, through figurations of night. Night is the in-between space, the space-time opening up between colonizer and colonized that Pérez describes as the "decolonial imaginary." The chief question of this third chapter is: "What role do pre-Columbian cosmologies of night—involving Mayan prophecies, obsidian mirrors, black jaguars, night serpents, and conical volcanoes, casting dark shade before *La Noche Triste* (the night of Don Pedro de Alvarado's massacre of Mayan *indígenas*), and persisting even after subsequent *noches tristes* of government-planned massacres of indígenas—play in these narratives?" Are they serving merely as nostalgic markers of authentic Central American cultures, as cultural flavor, in the era of military-industrial dictatorships and transnational global capitalism? Or is there something more being achieved? If so, what is produced, and why is it produced via appeals to night? How are these pre-Columbian cosmologies of night deployed postcolonially—and decolonially—in the context of ongoing neocolonial realities of socioeconomic inequalities and political atrocities? Let me examine that question in some detail for each text I have discussed thus far, beginning with Arturo Arias's *After the Bombs* (1979/1990).

After the Bombs, as I pointed out earlier, contains multiple images of night that signify the black void of fear, silence, disappearance, dismemberment, and death. The narrative connects some of these images to the ancient, pre-Columbian presence of volcanoes in Guatemala by switching between images of darkness and images of volcanoes: "a tiny little volcano of ashes fallen from his cigar" (10); "[t]he wind was blowing away flakes of ash" (55); "[o]n the wall a faint image of a volcano, upside down" (59); "[h]e remembered that she wanted to climb a volcano in eruption" (60); volcanoes, old age, and references to an insomniac Thomas Mann (author of *The Magic Mountain*) seeking answers to questions with no answers in the dark (95); and "boiling lava" and "the picture, blacker, soggier, unbearable, constrictive, vomitive" (100). The effect is to link the volcanoes with the darkness of night. Darkness, night, and shadows become potentially explosive—and they are explosive in a way that no human agency, not even the repressive U.S.-backed Guatemalan army and military intelligence, can control. Thus, through association with the ancient volcanoes that have been around since before European and U.S. dominations, night in *After the Bombs* is akin to hurricane references in postcolonial Caribbean texts. Volcanoes and night are forces of nature that defy colonial and neocolonial orders, that defy human orders period. *After the Bombs* takes perverse pleasure and consolation in such forces despite their fearsomeness. It opposes these forces to the military-industrial neoliberal order of the U.S.-backed military and of Monsanto, a corporation known for its genetic engineering and manipulation of agricultural plants and seeds. If, as Carrasco observes, the "most creative cultural event in the pre-urban history of Mesoamerica was the control of food energy contained in plants" (28), then Monsanto represents a genuine threat to centuries-old Central American and Mexican ways of life. With regard to contemporary history, Monsanto's manipulation of agricultural products echoes the destruction wrought upon the crops and seeds of the Guatemalan people, especially of the Maya, by the Guatemalan military during the Guatemalan civil war.[34] Night and the deep, dark shadows cast by the volcanoes, charged as they are with the explosive power of nature in Arias's novel, are two forces represented as being able to swallow up or engulf Monsanto's control over the historical agricultural vitality of Mesoamerica.

After the Bombs also makes specific references to the nocturnal cosmology of the Quiché Maya *Popol Vuh*. They may appear in the form of a passing allusion:

Máximo remembered that the road to Xibalbá [the underworld] was one way on Monday, Wednesday, and Friday and the other way on Tuesday, Thursday, and Saturday. But nothing was said about Sunday. (98)

Or the references may be much more extended, though fragmented, as with the hallucinatory scene of the military's and the Church's execution with "long obsidian kni[ves]" of supposedly politically subversive prostitutes in a stadium under "the sky completely black" (115–116). The scene of the punishment of prostitutes suspected of helping the guerrilla forces against the military evokes a Mayan and/or Aztec sacrifice—a blood sacrifice with the aid of the forces of night (obsidian knives, black skies) and on behalf of the forces of darkness. Readers may wonder what is postcolonially pre-Columbian about this involvement of tropes of night with such unjust sacrifice. The scene functions as a reminder that the Mayan and Aztec empires were hierarchical and were hardly models of justice for the poor, the disenfranchised, the slaves, or the servants. The lives that truly mattered were those of the ruling class. Other lives were disposable. However, I suggest that this dreadful scene of the prostitutes sacrificed under obsidian knives and black skies be read in the context of Máximo's slow awakening to the political nightmare around him and his decision to do something about it—to expose the local CIA chief and thus risk losing his own life. The encounter with oppressive aspects of pre-Columbian cosmology involving the forces of darkness and human sacrifice intruding into the contemporary time period spurs Máximo to defy the complicity between authoritarian agents that is making life impossible in modern Guatemala. So, without idealizing all aspects of the indigenous past, the novel manages to conscript unsettlingly violent aspects of pre-Columbian cosmologies of night to defy the neocolonial domination of Guatemala by the military, by the church of the wealthy (as opposed to the church of and for the poor), and by the U.S. CIA and its operatives.

The later novel *Rattlesnake* (1998/2003) creates and handles references to pre-Columbian cosmologies of night similarly. It contains allusions to "volcanoes" that re-appear in nightmares (12) and whose darkness is associated with "loss of visibility" (105), "a black, fulminating violence" (133) and death; ancient landscapes of "haunting mountain darkness" (29); eclipses (36); "the night-serpent" or "cosmic serpent, akin to a Maya goddess called Ixchel" who brings about the meeting of opposites and turns tyranny and humiliation into "liberty" and "the universal fraternity of all people" (78–79); and multiple allusions to a serpent, resonant with ancient Mayan associations, that returns a "shadowy, ominously black" (243) presence back to Tom Wright's bright, sunshine-saturated suburban Virginia existence at the novel's conclusion. The main function of these modified fragments of pre-Columbian cosmologies of night is to suggest that history—Guatemalan as well as that of the Americas—is not linear or progressive but cyclical and cataclysmic. It repeats and is not necessarily getting better. Its disastrousness, behind the well-manicured lawns of the Virginia suburbs that serve as luxurious bedroom communities for many who work at the U.S. Department of State in Washington, DC, will not be denied by this novel, which deploys a pre-Columbian, indigenous, elemental, cyclical sense of space-time and history to shadow a rationalist, Enlightenment-derived, Euro-American idea of history and destiny. Significantly, the legislation that provided the foundation for the formation of the United States Department of State was formulated in 1789. To a well-ordered Enlightenment imaginary about this endeavor, Arias's novel counterposes the dark, coiling, self-devouring figure of the rattlesnake that might, at best, be a night-serpent as described above but that, for the most part, acts as a destructive and self-destructive nightmarish Quetzalcoatl Ouroboros, or snake devouring its own tail. The postcolonial, pre-Columbian resistance of these night tropes is evident. They constitute a rejection of the pretensions of the Euro-American Enlightenment assumption of rational and improving intervention in foreign affairs that is reiterated in so much policy, including of course, the Monroe Doctrine of 1823.

Although Tobar's novel *The Tattooed Soldier* (1998) is mostly set in Los Angeles and not in Guatemala, it also subtly but forcefully bends its tropes of night toward a pre-Columbian cosmology. I am not the first critic to point this out; Ana Patricia Rodríguez provides a succinct, but detailed, analysis of how the story of "two embattled Guatemalan sons, Guillermo Longoria and Antonio Bernal" (121) re-enacts the Mayan pre-Columbian "jaguar cosmology" (124) linked to "the hero twins' vanquishing of the lords of Xibalba through the killing of the jaguar" which brings about regeneration out of death (127).[35] By concentrating on tropes of night, I trace other aspects of the use of pre-Columbian Mayan cosmology in *The Tattooed Soldier*. The recurring image of "the Los Angeles sky stretched in a vast blackness empty of stars, constellations erased by the glowing lights of too much city around him" (13) is a fascinatingly resonant image. It can be taken at face value as a description of the contents of the night sky occluded by electric light pollution. Denotatively, that is what it is stating. However, the early foregrounding of this occlusion of the stars and constellations in the context of a story about a refugee (Bernal) from the Guatemalan military oppression of the 1980s and a representative (Longoria) of that oppression and about the ties in the United States to that repression in Guatemala pushes the image onto complex connotative planes. I have spent some time elaborating pre-Columbian cosmologies of night, especially those of the Maya. As I mentioned, the study of the night skies was central to Mayan cosmology. The ancient Maya saw their history and destiny written in the stars and conceived of their hero warriors who died violent deaths in battle being transformed into stars and thus memorialized in the night skies. Antonio Bernal, a man so ordinary that his ill fate seems to lie with the world's millions and millions of refugees and homeless people, struggles to discover a purpose for himself. He does so when he crosses paths with Longoria, another Guatemalan and the torturer and killer of his wife and child. Stripped of almost all his possessions and alone under the skies of Los Angeles (except for a few homeless men with whom he bonds), Antonio, through what I contend may be read as a very Mayan warrior code of sacrifice (a code which Longoria has used for nefarious purposes far from any justice whatsoever), transforms his status as a passive victim by taking the life of the man who robbed him of his loved ones. He achieves this transformation through his willingness to sacrifice himself in the attempt to avenge the lives of his wife and child. I suggest that beneath the seeming "general" uses of tropes of night to connote loss and despair is the substratum of pre-Columbian Mayan tropes of night and the stars at night. The realization of this substratum helps to explain the recurrence throughout *The Tattooed Soldier* of this image of the absence of the stars in the nocturnal skies of Los Angeles, an absence that pulsates all the more strongly in the face of U.S. and worldwide notions of Los Angeles as the city of the stars (the Hollywood stars). Early in the narrative, Antonio thinks,

> *Elena [his wife] is gone too many years. She has left me alone in this city of food lines and plastic cheese. Elena did not live to see this Los Angeles that I know; the empty sky, the only stars the lights of the skyscrapers that come on at dusk and watch over me like a thousand glass eyes.* One moment he might be a normal man, someone with hopes and desires like anyone else, and the next he wanted to curl into a ball. To lie down and let his body seep into the ground. (39)

Against this suicidal despair, Antonio clings to his memories of his wife Elena and her loving belief in him: *"Elena loved me because she knew I could be a brave fighter"* (183). Eventually, driven beyond his meager means and running on his last emotional reserves, he works up the courage (or the madness, depending on how the reader interprets his actions) to fight and kill the representative of his and his family's horrifying repression. He transforms himself into a guerrilla fighter on U.S. soil, fighting the wars that have extended onto U.S. soil in a mimetic reversal and continuation of the U.S. interventions in Guatemala. The novel subtly but powerfully associates Antonio's transformation into a guerrilla fighter with the Mayan warrior whose destiny is connected with the night stars. Antonio may live *"in the streets, under the starless sky"* (228), but he burns as brightly as any star with a passion to effect the justice that neither the U.S.

judicial system, nor the U.S. police, military, or paramilitaries, nor the Guate-malan authorities, nor, of course, Longoria himself will bring to a continuing history of horrific human rights violations. Whether Antonio Bernal is a star of sorts or a crazed homeless man turned criminal is something that the reader must decide.

Goldman's first novel, *The Long Night of White Chickens* (1992), advertises its mythological and cosmological resonances in its very title. I argue that those connections are part of a pre-Columbian cosmology of night. The title is so strik-ing that from the beginning readers are likely to ask, "What is this long night of white chickens? To what does it refer?" The most obvious answer is that the long night of white chickens refers to an incident in a Guatemala City restaurant between Flor de Mayo and one of her suitors, Luis Moya, with whom she will have a brief affair. During this dinner, at which Luis Moya is trying to seduce her, "three Indian men rapidly pass by, in straw cowboy hats, each carrying live white chickens by the feet in both hands" (314). The phrase "long night of white chickens" is a reference to the manual transportation of chickens from their coop into the restaurant kitchen for slaughter and consumption. Given the type of death inflicted on Flor de Mayo by her unknown murderers—having her throat slit like a sacrificed chicken—this scene and the peculiar phrase that emanates from it—"the long night of white chickens"—must be taken symbolically and not merely literally. The "long night of white chickens" connotes the sacrifice not only of animals but also of human beings. The sacrifice takes place in the dark, shrouding it in mystery and dread. The fact that the night is long and the chick-ens are many only heightens the feeling of dread. The lack of specificity (which night?) and the anonymity of the chickens (all that is known is their color, which stands out in contrast to the dark night) lend a certain quality to the notion of sacrifice—it is serial and most likely ritual. Goldman's novel explicitly alludes to the *Popol Vuh*, the sacred book of the Quiché Maya, in chapters 11 (185), 12 (201), and 20 (319). The *Popol Vuh* contains salient instances of human sacrifice.

The result of these layered references within *The Long Night of White Chick-ens* and to the *Popol Vuh* is that night becomes associated with human sacri-fice; neither night nor this kind of sacrifice is naturalized or taken for granted. Instead, they are underscored as something that must be explored, and Gold-man uses this exploration to begin tracing the complicated lines of entangle-ment between the United States and Guatemala and among sectors of Gua-temalan society. He underscores the cosmological to explore the history of individual people in relation to larger social forces. The postcolonial aspects of this investigation lie in the often uncomfortable and disturbing exposures of the entanglement between these agents, factors, and forces. Furthermore,

Goldman's novel underscores this dark and multi-layered entanglement to propose that the characters, the narrator included, have been born into "a kind of labyrinth" (185). While the notion of the labyrinth of life and history is hardly original and was a trope much exploited by Argentinean writer and well-known giant of Latin American letters Jorge Luis Borges, Goldman uses his version of the labyrinth—the long night of white chickens—to push against positivistic notions of history as a narrative of progress. The following passage from chapter 11 illustrates the kind of resistance I am highlighting:

> I [Roger Graetz, the narrator] even owned a slim volume called *The Guatemalan Positivists*, about the influential circle of native scholars who, in the last century, proposed as a cure for the country's total backwardness a systematic belief in the progress of man through his own efforts and the study of logical philosophy. . . . The Positivists paved the way for the Liberal Reforms of the Great Reformer, General Justo Rufino Barrios, who discerned the export potential of coffee and took the logical next steps of terminating traditional Indian land rights and inviting ambitious German pioneers from across the ocean to come and own and operate the new, giant coffee plantations. Decades later another positivist dictator built imitation Pantheonlike temples to the Goddess of Wisdom, Minerva, all across the countryside. (186)

Positivism—or the belief in the methodical and materially, empirically measurable progress of human beings—in any form, whether Guatemalan or U.S.-ian, is one of the targets of satirical criticism in *The Long Night of White Chickens*. Positivism and despotism (colonial and neocolonial) are shown to go hand in hand. In fact, *The Long Night of White Chickens* implies that the adoption of positivism is a colonial (not a decolonial) project—a symptom of some kind of coloniality-induced inferiority complex (here I am referencing Aníbal Quijano's concept of coloniality) that leads to uncritical mimesis of European and Euro-American models. The adoption of positivism provides a civilized-seeming justification for dispossessing indigenous populations of their land— "the logical next steps of terminating traditional Indian land rights" (186). This first novel by Goldman employs tropes of night to subvert logical positivism as being neither particularly "logical" (except in a kind of instrumentalist way) nor "positive." This critique of positivism also advances a critique of colonial and neocolonial relations, though the critique is in no way systematic in this novel that is a labyrinth of stories.

Night in Goldman's second novel, *The Ordinary Seaman* (1997), is not as obviously connected to pre-Columbian cosmologies of night, though night dominates the novel from the opening sentence. In it, the chief "ordinary sea-man" Esteban finds himself in Nicaragua's Managua airport, on his way to the United States (to New York City via Miami) at three in the morning—the darkest and quietest time of night. Perhaps this lack of specifically Mayan pre-Columbian cosmologies of night makes sense in a novel where the main refer-ence point back to Central America is Nicaragua and not Guatemala. Further-more, the novel engages in a pan-*Latinidad* with characters from any number of Central American countries as well as Cubans, Colombians, Dominicans, Mexicans, Puerto Ricans, and Ecuadorians, all Latin Americans and Latina/os found in New York City. For instance, the novel quickly but pointedly flags the existence of different Latina/o neighborhoods of Brooklyn:

> Marilú tells him about her life too: she lives with her three children and sister on Smith Street, a street he knows from his nocturnal prowling; her husband left for a boricua and is living with her in another neighborhood that's mostly Dominican; he works as a doorman. The neighborhood is mainly Mexican now, but it has people from all over Latin America. (245–46)

The pan-Latinidad of the novel is also expressed in the way that it keeps any one set of cultural references from dominating, even though the experiences and memories of Esteban, the Nicaraguan, do prevail, as does his grief for his girlfriend, Marta, who was killed by the Contras (203).

The novel offers a brief but significant metaphor for Esteban's grief. This metaphor also applies to the grief of the other members of the *Urus*'s crew who have been stripped of their status as citizens of a particular country and are caught in limbo on the ship that does not sail. The ship is part of the failed neocolonial adventure of two men: Elias Tureen, a sort of multi-national global-ized subject raised in Mexico City with a British father and a Greek-American mother (281), and Mark Baker, an Anglo-American: "Grief stays hidden like an alarm clock with no hands set to go off at the bottom of sleep" (159). The sense of timelessness or suspended time coupled with night and night at sea or chained to the Brooklyn docks for nearly the entire length of the novel produces a sense of living underwater in an underworld. This is where one can begin to see the correlation between this novel and pre-Columbian cosmologies of night that involve journeys to the underworld—to a place such as Xibalba. In *The Ordinary Seaman,* a highly oneiric novel where from the first page sleeping and waking blend into one another, as do movement and stasis, the living crew trapped on the *Urus* ship docked in the Brooklyn harbor remember the human and animal dead and departed, usually at night. A number of the seamen are in mourning for people from whom they have been separated by all kinds of events, including wars and ongoing militarized conflicts. They experience "[m]elancholy in the evenings" (249) and "nightlong hauntings" (248). The seamen, in their becalmed state, not only remember the dead but also talk to them, see them, or feel their presence in some way. Thus, the *Urus* ship, whose name has a rather underworld sound and is, after all, a wreck without electricity (light) or plumbing (movement), becomes the site for the crossing of paths of the living and the dead. It is also the site for the gradual transformation of the living into the dead, either literally, as with the old seaman Bernardo, or figuratively, as with the rest of the crew who are socially dead to the world, trapped in a dark limbo.

This version of the underworld is not exclusively Mesoamerican pre-Columbian; it shares features with classical Greek notions of the underworld (Hades, the Plutonian shore, etc.). However, the extent to which the narrative invites readers to imagine this degree of convergence between the living and the dead opens onto ways of seeing that are not typically European or Euro-American rationalist ones and that exceed the models inherited from classical Greek traditions. Representations of the relation between the living and the dead in Goldman's novels draw on Jewish mystical traditions and Mesoamerican pre-Columbian cosmologies. In these traditions and cosmologies, night plays a crucial role as the time of conversation between the living and the dead; night is not so much one time as a passage to other times and places, to the supposedly multiplanar nature of existence. In Goldman's *The Ordinary Seaman*, night functions as a trope conveying multiple times and locations, as is evident in the focus on the pan-Latinidad of the Brooklyn *barrios* that Esteban wanders when he escapes the ship. Night is a zone of uncanny temporal, spatial, and cultural melding, a melding specifically among people from different Latina/o groups that suggests that such congress is taking place beneath the radar of the still-dominant Anglo-American culture. Night as both the time and metaphor for such melding is a topic that I explore in the fourth chapter of this study.

The 1997 novel *The Ordinary Seaman* deploys night to this effect in a way that subtly resonates with Mesoamerican pre-Columbian cosmologies of night in relation to the ongoing convergence of the living and the dead, the transformations to which both are subjected, and the combination of epic journeying and stasis. If Mesoamerican pre-Columbian cosmologies of night entailed a belief that the soul traveled about while one slept at night, this novel shows a number of the *Urus* shipmates, trapped and isolated on that ship moored in Brooklyn, traveling in their dreams and memories back to their respective Central American countries and to the people and socioeconomic and political situations that shaped their lives. Via this dream-state night traveling, these characters become repositories of the alternate Central American realities that are brought home for U.S. readers through the characters' thoughts and feelings.

Goldman's third novel, *The Divine Husband* (2004), is set in the late nineteenth century. Through the lives and romantic longings of former novice nuns forced out of their convents, it examines the revolutionary legacy of José Martí, the orator of Cuba and the night, in relation to Central American history and politics as well as to U.S. / Central American imbrications. The novel emphasizes the motifs of generally nocturnal ("[d]eep in the night," 229) time and space travel by alluding to bilocationism, the supposedly paranormal ability to be in more than one location at the same instant in time:

> For the past week, María de las Nieves had been reading the *vida* of Sor María de Agreda during her afternoon periods of directed study in the novice cloister library. Nothing she had ever read before had so impressed or stimulated her, or awoken such concentrated yearning. In deep prayer trances, Sor María de Agreda had traveled from her convent in Spain to the other side of the world, to remotest New Mexico, where she went among the Indians to go in search of Spanish priests to come and baptize them, walking hundreds of miles, for days and weeks, often across the territory of the Apache, unredeemed and murderous spawn of Satan. Sor María was often wounded on these missionary journeys, and more than once she received holy martyrdom from our Lord. *Yet because she was in both places at once, in New Mexico without leaving her convent in Spain, she never broke her vow of perpetual cloister* [emphasis mine]. (41)

In this passage, a mid- to late-nineteenth-century Central American novice nun is reading about the lives of Spanish sixteenth-century nuns and admiring their allegedly miraculous heroic exploits on behalf of God among the indigenous people of the Americas, in particular what was once a part of Mexico and then, forcibly, became U.S. territory or the American Southwest. This and other passages like it are both historically ironic and tonally satiric—to the point that I would characterize them as deliberately "preposterous," outrageous, and outré—yet all the while are fastidiously and fantastically historical. History, for Goldman, is clearly preposterous, and it elicits from him an ironic gaze and a satirical treatment. How ironic that a partly indigenous, partly Yankee (167) Central American nineteenth-century nun should be admiring the exploits of a sixteenth-century "Golden Age" (Age of Conquests) Spanish nun in the midst of a Central American country that is never quite identified but that textual material, including multiple direct references to "Justo Rufino" (78, 81, 440), suggests is Guatemala during its dictatorial "Liberal Reforms" phase. Guatemala gained independence from Spain in 1821, but only to become, for a short time, part of the Mexican Empire and then part of the United Provinces of Central America. The reference to "New Mexico" is as colonial and imperial as the reference to Spain, not only in relation to Spain but in relation to Guatemala's satellite status vis-à-vis the rest of the Americas.

To return to bilocationism, "a supernatural state, brought about by prayer, and an act of Divine Will by which God helped people who otherwise were prevented by earthly circumstances from bringing comfort or doing good" (339), *The Divine Husband* depicts belief in its possibility as part of an inheritance in Central America from mystical traditions of the Spanish colonial era—for example, from Sor María de Agreda (1602–1665), Santa Teresa de Ávila, San Juan de la Cruz, and others. But *The Divine Husband* also suggests that this type of time and space travel, which is associated with night as in *The Ordinary Seaman*, has precedents other than Spanish colonial ones. The clues to these other precedents are embedded in sentences such as "The Spaniards had conquered the Indians but had not, of course, vanquished their religion. Instead the Indians had adapted Christianity as a system of symbols and rites within which to hide their own beliefs" (332) and "The Indios place their great Tree of Creation in the Milky Way, its roots in the Underworld and in ritual, but where should they look for the Tree of Knowledge? In the symbolism of some of our Hebrew folk..." (333). The novel situates these statements in the mouth of Rubén Abensur, a Hebrew teacher from Tangier living in Central America and making common cause with "Indian rebels opposing the Supreme Government and the new coffee oligarchy" (329). Like all views and characters in this novel, these statements are presented with an ironic gaze and a muffled satiric tone, so no one character's voice or point of view emerges as authoritative. Thus, Abensur's point of view cannot be equated with the author's or even with the narrator's. Nevertheless, the effect of both the deployment of the thematics of a generally, though not exclusively, nocturnal mystical bilocation and the inclusion of the *Popol Vuh*–like image of the "Tree of Creation in the Milky Way" (the Milky Way can only be seen at night) with its "roots in the Underworld" (associated with night) is to offer an occluded but substantial syncretism of Central American belief and perspective that owes as much to Mesoamerican pre-Columbian cosmologies as it does to Spanish Golden Age mystical traditions.[36] The novel also implies that Spanish mystical traditions are partly derived from the contact of the Spaniards with the indigenous peoples and their beliefs. Cultural acquisition is not uni-directional but dialectical. When the Spanish mystics went into trances, those trances and the modes of mind-altering consciousness may well have been learned from those Others not deemed Spanish or properly so but who were part of the Spanish Empire and Spanish explorations—Jews, *indios*.

In this novel, as in *The Ordinary Seaman,* tropes of night are complicit with the phenomenon of cultural syncretism—not between Latina/os in the United States but between Catholicism, Mayan belief systems, and Judaism, a syncretism that is also about the creation of certain Central American identities. Furthermore, the specific tropes of night in *The Divine Husband*—the "phantasmagoric" (353) nocturnal bilocation achieved by the mind either dreaming, in a trance, or insomniac (229), and the Tree of Creation with its roots in the Milky Way of the night skies (333)—create a resistance against "positivist materialism of the Liberals," to quote the novel itself (373) and, I would argue, against its descendant in more contemporary times, neoliberalism. Somewhat nostalgically, the novel counterposes to this positivist materialism the Romantic, Emersonian transcendentalist (210–11) and the mystical oratory and personality of the Cuban revolutionary and would-be liberator of parts of the Americas José Martí, poet of Cuba and the night, magician of words who emerges in this long tale like a figure from "the nocturnal magic of a fairy story" (120). As mentioned earlier, the historical personage of Martí is a silhouette-shadow (the secular version of the Divine Husband) who passes through the body of the narrative in a journey analogous to his own one to Central America (Guatemala, in particular) where, according to Goldman's narrative, he viewed "an indigo twilight horizon of darkening volcanoes and mountains" (102).

The postcolonial implications of these complex twists and turns of tropes of night, which include Mesoamerican pre-Columbian coordinates, are not manifestly evident. It might seem puzzling to readers and critics that the novel should engage in a resistance against positivist materialism until that movement's colonial Euro-centric and Euro-American inflections are appreciated. Positivist materialism in the Americas often betrayed a sense that the former European colonies of the Americas were not advanced enough, that they were behind assumed historical progress and had to catch up. Goldman's novel even pokes fun at Martí's investment in some aspects of this positivist materialism:

> Martí was optimistic about the Liberals' programs for the Indios. Great changes were occurring in their little country, which might turn out to be exemplary for all the young American republics. True, the Indios were now required by law to provide manual labor on the new coffee plantations on demand, but in the long run even that draconian measure could be a good thing, if it inculcated modern work habits and virtues. Similar praise might be rendered to the policy of

> expropriating the Indios' fallow ancestral lands and putting them into the ardent
> hands of young coffee pioneers, who created wealth and employment. (217)

The passage implicates positivist materialism in blatant exploitation of the indigenous populations and the poor of the Americas. Although this novel is set in the mid to late nineteenth century, it resonates with Pierre Bourdieu's critiques—in *Acts of Resistance: Against the Tyranny of the Market* (1998) and *Firing Back: Against the Tyranny of the Market 2* (2001 in French and 2003 in English)—of technocratic neoliberalism that poses as a solution to the world's problems when in fact it is producing and perpetuating a predatory "center-periphery" globalization (to use Nelly Richard's terms).[37]

In *The Divine Husband,* invocations of night and especially of night in relation to Mesoamerican pre-Columbian cosmologies provide a counterpoint to the belief in historical progress and the rush toward the ever-receding horizon of modernity. Goldman's novel demonstrates a keen awareness of the complexities of José Martí's relations to the ideology of positivist materialism. Goldman chooses to depict Martí the mystic, the Romantic, the transcendentalist, the poet of the light that "seemed entirely animate" of "the supreme masterpiece of all sunsets in the history of the Americas" (210) and, of course, the poet of "Cuba and the night," as a romancer of the former novice nuns who form part of his "evening class in Literary Composition for Women" (212) during his sojourn in Central America.

All these references to evening, sunsets, and night may seem like mere poetry devoid of any further effect than that of inducing a passing state of beatific or haunted fancy. But I argue that taken all together and in relation to one another—once again, as a constellation of associations—they serve interrelated purposes. They underscore a deep-structure cultural syncretism and, especially, the persistence of indigenous cosmologies in Central America. They employ the elements of native cosmologies, along with those of other people in Spain and the Americas whose world views have been marginalized or excluded from official or dominant national identities of said places, to question and resist the "progress"-obsessed project of modernity. And they resist, by all the previous means stated, imperial and neocolonial assumptions of European or Euro-American (U.S.-ian) superiority.

While Goldman's deployments of Mesoamerican pre-Columbian cosmologies of night are ideologically complex, some are more ambivalent, conflicted, and contradictory than others. I argue that such is the case with his non-fictional account *The Art of Political Murder* (2007). I have already suggested as much in my earlier discussion of this book's second paragraph, which describes

Guatemalans: "Two separate, gravely ceremonious, phantasmagoria-prone cultures, Spanish Catholic and Mayan pagan, shaped the country's character, along with centuries of cruelty and isolation" (3). Here Mesoamerican pre-Columbian culture becomes associated with the generally nocturnal arts and terrors of phantasmagoria. This hardly seems to have any redeeming valence. Neither does the implied association of "Mayan pagan" (the word "pagan" in this context already tips the balance into a zone of negative valuation) with a culture of sacrifice as an interpretive frame in which to situate the murder of Bishop Juan Gerardi Conedera and the subsequent government-sponsored punitive cover-up. This approach to the murder potentially sensationalizes Guatemalan culture, a puzzling decision in the context of the complicity between certain power structures in the United States and in Guatemala. However, complicating this negative valuation of Mesoamerican pre-Columbian cosmologies of night and cultures of sacrifice is Goldman's own rhetoric about the young reporters, investigators, lawyers, and judges who risked their lives to bring members of "the Guatemalan Army's Presidential Guard and the Estado Mayor Presidencial (EMP), or Presidential Military Staff" (28) to trial and conviction. Goldman stresses the extent to which these people were demonstrating a willingness to sacrifice themselves for justice and in the name of human rights. He concludes his own long investigation with the sentence: "The Gerardi case had opened a path into that darkness," meaning the darkness of the military's "clandestine world" but also, one gets the sense, the nocturnal phantasmagoria of Guatemalan culture (357). I would like to point to the curious rhetorical mirroring in *The Art of Political Murder* (2007) between the initial description of "Mayan pagan" culture and the descriptions of the stakes as well as the effects of the exposé work done by the reporters, investigators, lawyers, and judges. I am hard-pressed to call this mirroring, which could be understood as an appropriation of certain well-worn tropes about Guatemalan culture in particular and Central American cultures more generally, postcolonial. However, the mirroring does have the effect of redeeming acts of sacrifice and the willingness to plumb the darkness of that nocturnal murder for the cause of justice and human rights. The implication seems to be that counterforce equal in some, though not all, "extremes" must be exerted to open a "path into that darkness" of military counterinsurgency.

Sylvia Sellers-García's novel *When the Ground Turns in Its Sleep* (2007), published the same year as Goldman's *The Art of Political Murder,* offers a more sympathetic view of Mesoamerican pre-Columbian cosmologies of night. The novel makes early and frequent mention of the *Popol Vuh's* stories and images, which include many references to night, darkness, the human dead as stars and constellations in the night sky, gloom, obsidian knives, night watchmen, and the various kinds of darkness associated with sacrifice, servitude, and slavery. The stance of the narrator (Nítido Amán) toward Guatemala and its history and culture combines that of a contemplative and scholar with an element of the mystery-novel detective. Throughout *When the Ground Turns in Its Sleep*, the narrator interweaves allusions to and whole passages from the *Popol Vuh* (44–45), the post–Spanish conquest collection of the ancient pre-Columbian beliefs of the Quiché Maya. Moreover, readers witness the narrator attempting a space-time experiment with himself based on his readings of the *Popol Vuh* and other anthropological and historical texts such as Eric Thompson's *Rise and Fall of Maya Civilization* (94). Gradually, it becomes apparent that the experiment forms part of the narrator's attempt to stay linked to his own past, including to his father's pursuits (Nítido Amán owns his father's copy of the *Popol Vuh*, 22) and to become a more effective priest both in a transcultural and in a specifically Guatemalan context. He takes an interest in Mayan shamanistic practices of divination and healing the sick and in the Mayan calendar's concept of cyclical time. Via his reading of Thompson, he familiarizes himself with the supposed Maya understanding of "time as a series of burdens, carried one after another by the gods" with "the night god" taking over "when the day is done" (136–37). He delves into the ancient stories of creation and destruction and of the regeneration of life after experiencing a deep dark hole (as did the hero Zipacná, 45), sitting at the imagined volcanic core of a mountain (202), or actually losing consciousness among the bodies of the massacred on a remote, densely forested mountainside at night (276).

Most significantly, the novel shows the gradual transformation in Nítido Amán's consciousness from that of a relatively ignorant outsider sent to minister to the Guatemalan town of Río Roto to a priest who has also recognized the fragmented limits of his own Western knowledge. He does this by confronting face-to-face and in his very body the complicated history that the townspeople have had with the armed conflict lasting since the 1954 overthrow of the democratically elected president Jacobo Arbenz. Father Amán witnesses the pain and turmoil the people have experienced and sees how that pain and turmoil have shaped their consciousness, their words, and their silences. The priest comes to minister, but there are many messages waiting for him to absorb. The text demonstrates a reversal in the flow of knowledge and experience from that of the usual colonial and neocolonial model whereby the colony, former colony, or the periphery country is the recipient of whatever the colonizer/metropole/center brings and becomes marked by that knowledge. I mentioned earlier that the novel *When the Ground Turns in Its Sleep* attempts to effect a postcolonial recuperative project to recover historical memory in the face of cognitive and cultural oblivion. But for that project to come into being, the North American or Americanized, partly Guatemalan outsider who is separated from his roots must listen, watch, and feel for what he does not yet know and has not yet taken into himself firsthand—not as a native informant (another colonial role, after all) but as one who experiences and empathizes with what crosses beyond his attempted self-protections and immunities.

Of all these texts I have analyzed, Panamanian American writer Cristina Henríquez's 2006 novel *Come Together, Fall Apart* is the most difficult to characterize in terms of the operations of postcolonial pre-Columbian cosmologies of night. This is true for several reasons. One is that it is a U.S. Panamanian text and, thus, it does not exhibit the same patterns as these Guatemalan American texts I have been investigating. Whatever traces of pre-Columbian cosmologies of night there are to be found in *Come Together, Fall Apart* are not obviously or necessarily Mayan-derived. For example, there are no direct references to the *Popol Vuh*. Instead, readers find allusions to the night work of early twentieth-century avant-garde Peruvian poet (exiled to France) César Vallejo (39), to the Christmas carol "O Holy Night" (180), and to Christmas Eve Mass (276–82). "O Holy Night" may be traced back to mid-nineteenth-century France, where it was composed by Adolphe Adam and became an international favorite among carols. Christmas Eve Mass said on *Noche Buena* in Panama, at the beginning of the Christmas liturgical season, would have had origins in Panama roughly conterminous with the Christianization (via Roman Catholicism) of that country a few decades before it became an official part of the Spanish Empire in 1538. In Panama, *Noche Buena* and liturgical celebrations of it go back to the sixteenth century, post-Columbus. With regard to Henríquez's novel *Come Together, Fall Apart*, the historical references to night—such as the lines from Vallejo's poetry, "O Holy Night," and Christmas Eve Mass—are derived from other places and periods than pre-Columbian Mesoamerica: Peru in the early twentieth century, France in the nineteenth century, and the post-Columbian sixteenth century. This in itself is revealing, particularly given the transnational history of Panama as a place and society that was treated from the beginning of colonization as a throughway (a canal and a channel) from the Atlantic to the Pacific and that also belonged to South America (Colombia), adding to the liminality of its status as part of Central America. Panama City is today highly globalized, with all that implies in terms of the impact of outside forces on its "internal" workings.

However, despite this apparent lack of allusions to pre-Columbian Meso-american cosmologies of night, the novel does share some features with the other texts I have investigated. It couples allusions to night with references to natural forces such as oceans or water more generally (30–31, 89), storms (129, 179–98), giant rocks and volcanoes (75, 194), and raw emotions as well as heightened sensations received by the five (or more) senses that break through social roles and veneers (250). Night is represented in conjunction with and often as part of primordial forces that resist, defy, or do not conform to the expectations of socio-political structures such as patriarchal colonial and neocolonial orders. In Henríquez's *Come Together, Fall Apart*, as in Arias's *After the Bombs*, night serves a postcolonial purpose with a decolonial desire embedded in it.

As for pre-Columbian Mesoamerican factors, Henríquez's collection contains one story—the eighth one titled "The Box House and the Snow"—that is constructed with elements that, while not specifically pre-Columbian, resonate with the pre-Columbian elements in the other texts I have analyzed. In this story, night is associated with volcanoes, with a storm that overwhelms civilization such as it is, and with the sacrifice on behalf of a hero who in this case is presented as the daughter of the family. As I observed earlier, the story reads like a Russian fairy tale mixed with a creation/sacrifice story from the *Popol Vuh*. This mixture symptomizes the globalized hybridity of Panamanian culture of which Henríquez provides pointed glimpses for her readers. However, the story also deploys remnants of an indigenous and culturally subaltern sensibility coupled with a specifically feminist critique of a patriarchal neocolonial order. The untropical, un-Panamanian snowstorm (typical of northern climates and symbolic of domination from the north—i.e., the United States) falls on "the perfect house" at night. The father of the house, who takes such pride in its supposed perfection, panics at the thought that the weight of the snow will overwhelm his house. He coerces his daughter into the hard labor, or slavery, of holding up the ceiling against the weight of the snow. The slave labor done by the daughter resonates with indigenous history under Panama's multiple colonizers as well as the history of Africans and Afro Caribbeans who were recruited to Panama to perform hard labor. Many Panamanians who worked on the Panama Canal, in the Canal Zone, and also on the banana plantations were (and still are) of African descent.

In "The Box House and the Snow," the snow is compared to a "boa constrictor" (187), a Latin American snake to be found from Colombia to the Sonoran desert of Mexico, and also to the ash from the lava of an erupting volcano (194). Ancient elements of the Central Americas appear in this story, and invading northern-clime snow is compared to them, suggesting that the family is caught between a socio-political allegorical version of "a rock and a hard place." The snow that comes at night overwhelms the patriarchal neocolonial structure of the "perfect houses," and yet the advent of the nocturnal snowstorm also reveals the essential dynamics of that society—with the daughter caught in the role of the enslaved indigenous person made to do the work of a master (her father, hybrid subject of empire) who is not master of his own house but is affected by greater coercive forces—the invading snow of an alien civilization and the snow that is also remindful of the destructive forces of nature native to Panama.

Although Henríquez's story "The Box House and the Snow" does not contain obvious references to pre-Columbian cosmologies of night, it does partially work with a constellation of elements similar to those of the other texts, such as night in conjunction with volcanoes and other forces of Central American geography and topography. The spatio-temporality of Henríquez's story is distinctively mixed, suggesting both a contemporary time period of "the box house" and a much older mythic or cosmological time that leaves the daughter holding up the house, like Atlas holding the world on his shoulder or like the twins Hunahpú and Xbalanqué sacrificing themselves for the lords of Xibalba, the underworld associated with night and the Milky Way, in the *Popol Vuh* (158): "The daughter . . . her tears long since dry was too exhausted to speak. She simply stared at the father and held up the ceiling" (198). The postcolonial aspect of this story emerges in its critique of those in power and in its demonstration of the forces of nature overwhelming a questionable colonial and neocolonial human order.

Regarding some of its more fundamental techniques and its aims and purposes, Henríquez's text belongs with the others I have been investigating. From this sample of nine texts of U.S.-based Central American writers from the late 1970s onward, it is evident that these writers share some distinctive concerns. These concerns involve processing and representing the dirty wars in Central America and their own double displacement and occlusion both within and outside of Central America as culturally critical Central American subjects and as U.S.-based Central Americans living inside the very country that has had such a disturbing, yet covert, relationship to the unfolding of events in their or their families' countries of origin. Though easily overlooked as part of the atmospherics of these texts about the processing and representation of the trauma of the dirty wars and counterinsurgency in Central America, postcolonial uses of pre-Columbian Mesoamerican cosmologies of night play a crucial role in the cultural critiques that these texts offer. Not only do they strikingly deploy night in globalized ways but they also pointedly harness these less specific uses of night to much more culturally specific tropes of night that are Central American, and, moreover, inflected by the indigenous pre-Columbian.

In the introductions to this book and to this chapter, I posed the question of whether such deployments of night serve merely as nostalgic markers of authentic Central American cultures or whether something more is being achieved. I have endeavored to show that the texts' treatment of these pre-Columbian cosmologies of night are postcolonial by being resistant to colonial and neocolonial orders, critical of nineteenth-century liberalism and twenty/twenty-first-century neoliberalism that make possible the confusion of coloniality with progress, and expressive of a cultural syncretism and transculturation among empire's Others and among various Latin American and Latina/o populations both within particular Central American countries and in the United States. This is so especially in relation to issues pertaining to cultural displacement, exile, homelessness, and shared marginalization. With this latter observation, I do not mean to imply that some kind of utopian pan-Latinidad is at work in these texts. Here I am thinking of Francisco Goldman's *The Ordinary Seaman* and *The Divine Husband* as well as Héctor Tobar's *The Tattooed Soldier* and Cristina Henríquez's *Come Together, Fall Apart*. But these texts from various U.S.-based Central American vantage points do demonstrate the transcultural night work that I focus on in the next chapter of my book.

CHAPTER FOUR

TRANSCULTURAL NIGHT WORK
OF U.S.-BASED SOUTH AMERICAN
CULTURAL PRODUCERS

On full moon nights, I sit alone near the piers, reaching across the waters
to commune with my sisters. Each standing on her own pier, shore,
or river's edge, we extend outward our spiders' webs until our thoughts
meet and our spirits touch once more.

—Mariana Romo-Carmona, "The Web," in *Speaking Like an Immigrant:
A Collection* (1998 first edition and 2010 second edition)

"Transcultural" is the adjectival form of "transculturation." The latter term was originally coined in Spanish more than half a century ago by Cuban anthropologist and ethnographer Fernando Ortiz Fernández (1881–1969) to describe a bi-directional if not multi-directional convergence of different cultures that changes all cultures in the process, creating new hybridized cultures. He deliberately coined the term and elaborated the idea of "transculturation" as an alternate paradigm to coloniality, the dominant paradigm in the Americas including the United States, that assumes and attempts to enforce the acculturation and assimilation of what are deemed non-hegemonic nationalities, ethnicities, or cultures to what are deemed hegemonic ones.

Ortiz elaborated this paradigm of transculturation in his 1940 book on Cuban culture titled *Contrapunteo cubano del tabaco y el azúcar* and translated into English as *Cuban Counterpoint: Tobacco and Sugar*. Starting in the early 1990s and with intensifying critical attention in the twenty-first century, numerous scholars in Latin American, Latina/o, New Americas, empire, and postcolonial studies have adapted Fernando Ortiz's paradigm of transculturation to their particular field of research and teaching. Take, for example, Mary

Louise Pratt's book *Imperial Eyes: Travel Writing and Transculturation* (1992), Frances R. Aparicio and Susana Chávez-Silverman's edited volume *Tropicalizations: Transcultural Representations of Latinidades* (1997), Agustín Laó-Montes and Arlene Dávila's *Mambo Montage: The Latinization of New York* (2001), Luis A. Ramos-García's edited volume *The State of Latino Theatre in the United States: Hybridity, Transculturation, and Identity* (2002), Walter Mignolo's article "Capitalism and Geopolitics of Knowledge: Latin American Social Thought and Latino/a American Studies" in *Critical Latin American and Latino Studies,* edited by Juan Poblete (2003), Alberto Sandoval-Sánchez and Frances R. Aparicio's special issue of *Revista Iberoamericana* dedicated to "Hibridismos culturales: la literatura y cultura de los latinos en los Estados Unidos" (2005), and the section subtitled "Transcultural" from Gabriela Baeza Ventura's anthology *Latino Literature Today* (2005). All, in various ways, call upon the concept of transculturation as a multi-directional crossing of cultures and cultural forms into one another across borders or boundaries to produce a contact zone comprising both lived experience and the representational forms that rhetorically and visually encapsulate these lived convergences and complexities.

I employ the terms "transcultural" and "transculturation" to showcase works by U.S.-based South American writers and one U.S.-based Peruvian photographer. I use the terms with specific reference to the ways in which these works—a collection of short stories, a volume of poems, a novel, and a series of photographs—extend, stretch, and break from the conventional boundaries of *Latinidades.* Their various challenges to the representational paradigms of Latinidades come first and foremost in a fundamental representation of Latinidades that does not use the United States as the main reference point for Latina/o identity. Night figures as a key device in works that challenge the geopolitics of Latinidades, of whatever is deemed "Latina/o."

To the extent that these verbal and visual productions do this kind of cultural work, I distinguish them from the larger vernacular baroque category of night-steeped literature of South America. The latter has a long history back into the colonial period but is also strongly evident in culturally rebellious twentieth-century writers, such as the highly ideologically ambiguous crypto-fascist Bolivian poet Jaime Saenz, with his night-obsessed poems—see the collection *The Night* translated by Forrest Gander and Kent Johnson (2007)—or a permanent exile such as the Chilean Roberto Bolaño (1953–2003) with his many eponymous nocturnal works, such as, following the titles from the translated New Directions series, *By Night in Chile* (2003), *Distant Star* (2004), *Last Evenings on Earth* (2007), and even—less directly at first glance but no less so in the details of its scenarios—*Amulet* (2008). These South American works may exhibit a strong degree of exilic transnationalism, as do Bolaño's novels and short stories, many of which reference various places such as Chile, Mexico, Argentina, and Cuba as well as Spain, France, and the United States, particularly in its proximity to Mexico (see the story "Anne Moore's Life" in *Last Evenings on Earth*). By saying that these works exhibit exilic transnationalism I mean that they traverse many national borders and often inhabit more than one place at any given time. However, this definition does not assume or expect that the work in question will exhibit a sense of belonging to any of these places. I use the term "exilic" to signal and highlight the fact that a sensibility of displacement and alienation is strong.

Exilic transnationalism, though related to the transcultural night work of South American writers and visual artists on which this chapter focuses, does not necessarily result in transcultural night work. With regard to the latter, socio-politically driven exile and socioeconomically driven immigration from one country to another are representationally converted into nocturnal scenarios that do particular cultural work. The nocturnal scenarios of this chapter challenge U.S.-centric geopolitical paradigms of Latinidad at the same time that they figure the United States in their transmuting calculus. As such, they cultivate and maintain a strong identification with immigrants as outsiders in societies (not only U.S. society) that tend toward deep-structure xenophobia and fear and oppression of immigrants. These nocturnal scenarios function to valorize the culturally non-dominant or non-hegemonic in the context of encounters between one culture and another—for example, the traces of indigenous populations of the northern Chilean desert despite the conquest and attempted Christianization of that area in the 1500s, or specifically female immigrants, or homosexuals and lesbians and others who do not conform to heteronormativity. Furthermore, these night scenarios are often part of an experimentation with modes of abjection including not being visible, dissolving or dispersing, and being formless rather than fighting for or defending one definite shape or identity. Consequently, these nocturnal scenarios resist an assimilation that suppresses difference and otherness. These nocturnal scenarios effect a powerful politicization of night that, despite its co-option as a time of colonial and neocolonial terror designed to maintain the status quo through fear and punishment, turns night into spatio-temporal social and psychic dimensions of resistance, rebellion, and, potentially, the construction of other ways of seeing, feeling, thinking, acting, and being.

Despite the wide range of references to Chicana/o cultural production in the first chapter, none of the chapters of this book aims to be exhaustive in its investigation of the uses of night by the respective "groups" upon which I focus:

Chicana/o cultural producers; contemporary, queer, partly Anglographic poets of Hispanic Caribbean heritage; U.S.-based Central American writers; and U.S.-based South American writers and visual artists. This last chapter is narrowly focused on three contemporary writers (the Chilean Mariana Romo-Carmona, the Colombian Jaime Manrique, and the Peruvian Daniel Alarcón) and one contemporary Peruvian photographer (Carlos Jiménez Cahua). Why these four cultural producers and, in particular, Romo-Carmona's *Speaking Like an Immigrant* (1998 / 2010), Manrique's *Twilight at the Equator* (2003) via *My Night with / Mi noche con Federico García Lorca* (1995), Alarcón's *Lost City Radio* (2007), and Jiménez Cahua's twenty-first-century photographs of Lima, Peru, at night? I concentrate on these works as notable examples of transcultural night work.

The uses of night by South American cultural producers who are either U.S.-based or evidently U.S.-conscious are much wider. Take into account, for instance, cameo passages in Uruguayan essayist José Enrique Rodó's famous essay "Ariel" (1900); Peruvian poet César Vallejo's night poetry; Bolivian poet and onetime U.S. embassy clerk Jaime Saenz's poems in *The Night*; Chilean painter Robert Matta's paintings such as "Invasion of the Night," which was created in 1940 shortly after his emigration from Chile to the United States; the murdered Salvadoran poet Roque Dalton's selected poems *Small Hours of the Night*; Argentinean exile Julio Cortázar's short story "La noche boca arriba" ("The Night Face Up") from the collection *Final del juego* (1956) or the essay "Background" from the collection *Salvo el crepúsculo / Save Twilight* (1984), in which he writes *"Todo vino siempre de la noche"* / "Everything always came from the night";[1] Argentinean exile Manuel Puig's *La traición de Rita Hayworth* (1968), *El beso de la mujer araña* (1976), and *Cae la noche tropical* (1988); some of the shadow-filled images of the Chilean photographer Oscar Wittke and the nocturnal conceptual art intervention pieces of the Chilean Alfredo Jaar (see especially the 1987 "A Logo for America" that disabused viewers of the well-entrenched notion that the United States equals America); Uruguayan exile (to Spain) Cristina Peri Rossi's novel *La última noche de Dostoievski* (1992) / *Dostoevsky's Last Night* (translated and published in 1996) or her collection of poetry *Aquella Noche* (1996); Uruguayan London-based conceptual and performance artist Ana Laura López de la Torre's "Night Salons" series about people living and working in London boroughs at night and also exploring darkness more generally;[2] and the cultural production of many other South Americans. Whereas some aspects of these works may align with my basic description of transcultural night work, none of them does so to the extent that the works I have chosen do. Furthermore, the fundamental difference between the texts and the visual images I have chosen and the others I have mentioned is that they challenge U.S.-centric geopolitical paradigms of Latinidad while at the same time figuring the United States in their transmuting calculus.

Mariana Romo-Carmona's *Speaking Like an Immigrant* (1998/2010) and the Extended Practice of "Living at Night"

Mariana Romo-Carmona, born in Santiago, Chile, in 1952, emigrated to the United States over forty-five years ago on October 3, 1966, with her father and her younger sister.[3] She taught in the MFA program at Goddard College in Plainfield, Vermont, for twelve years and currently teaches at Queens College (the JSM Center for Worker Education and Labor Studies in Manhattan). She published her first novel, *Living at Night*, in 1997. She co-edited *Cuentos: Stories by Latinas* (1983) with Alma Gómez and Cherríe Moraga, and she edited Spanish-language coming-out stories by and for parents of Latina lesbians and Latino gay men titled *Conversaciones: relatos por padres y madres de hijas lesbianas y hijos gay* (2001). Her own work has appeared in many anthologies—notably *Compañeras: Latina Lesbians* (1987) compiled and edited by Juanita Ramos—and periodicals. Aside from her debut novel, *Living at Night*, she has published two book-length works of her own writing: *Speaking Like an Immigrant* (first edition 1998 and second edition 2010) and a collection of poems titled *Sobrevivir y otros complejos: Narrative Poems in Engllano* (2011), in which some poems are written in Spanish and others translated into English or Spanish. I focus on *Speaking Like an Immigrant* and its night work.

In an article titled "Night Becomes 'Latina': Mariana Romo-Carmona's *Living at Night* and the Tactics of Abjection," which was published in *Centro: Journal of the Center for Puerto Rican Studies* in spring of 2007 along with a series of photographs I composed to accompany the article and underscore the aesthetics of her novel, I analyzed the powerful deployment of nighttime in the novel whose title so obviously calls attention to night:

> [I]n the novel "nighttime" is made to perform diasporas and borders, exilic memory, sexual, ethnic, and racial identities, and social positioning in terms of power or agency, deterritorializing these variables from conventional or dominant values. Specifically, this deep-structure redefinition is accomplished by confronting culturally induced shame, fear, and repudiation and deliberately embracing the abjection inherent in transculturation or in the "contaminating" ("not-me") contact zone between identities and cultures that transgresses their limits.[4]

The novel *Living at Night* makes night the condition for living. It turns night into the very ontology of and for the narrative. With regard to questions of the "location of culture," to borrow Homi Bhabha's phrase,[5] the novel *Living at Night*, for all its innovation and its peculiarities, is more of a conventional Latina/o story in that it takes place within the borders of the United States, as do so many Latina/o stories. Of course, it is unconventional for situating the action in New England in the late 1970s—and not in any major city or port city (such as Boston) but rather partly in Storrs (where the main branch of the University of Connecticut is) and mostly in Willimantic, Connecticut, with briefer periods in Manchester and New Britain, Connecticut, as well as in Provincetown, Massachusetts. Yet the novel reads very much like a typical Latina/o text. It focuses on experience within the United States of America and is narrated by a member of one of three major Latina/o groups in terms of national origin (Mexican, Puerto Rican, and Cuban). The narrator of *Living at Night* is a young Puerto Rican woman on the U.S. mainland. My *Centro* article explores the important socio-political representational work of this choice of narrator—a young, Puerto Rican, working-class lesbian woman—on the part of a now middle-class (once working-class) Chilean lesbian writer. The general setting of the United States may conform to expectations of a Latina/o text even though the choice of narrator—a Puerto Rican U.S.-based Latina—on the part of a writer of South American (Chilean) origin does not.

Speaking Like an Immigrant: A Collection (1998 / 2010), in contrast, pertains to the kind of texts and other cultural productions that challenge the geo-politics of the location of culture of Latinidades, of whatever is deemed "Latina/o." The first edition of this text was published in 1998, but many of its stories were written in the 1980s. In fact, a first draft of the book existed in 1991. My analysis follows the order of the material in the 1998 first edition. However, because the 2010 second edition is most likely the one that readers will find more readily available now and in the future, I have quoted from it and not from the first edition. The fact that a second edition of *Speaking Like an Immigrant* has been issued more recently attests to a growing interest in its paradigms, which may have been a little ahead of their time in 1998. At any rate, texts such as *Speaking Like an Immigrant* do not only show Latina/os to be between two nations and/or continents; the strongly transcultural productions analyzed in this chapter extend, stretch, and break with the conventional boundaries of Latinidades. This challenge to the representational paradigms of Latinidad comes first and foremost in a fundamental re-orientation of Latinidades away from the United States as the main reference point for identity. Rather than becoming a "Latina/o" through contact with the United States, the narrator of some of the first-person pieces of *Speaking*

Like an Immigrant asserts her or his Latin American and even more specifically South American identity despite longtime contact with the United States. The first piece with the eponymous title "Speaking Like an Immigrant" begins, "You must know I'm South American, though I live here [in the United States]. A lifetime denying I'm exotic, a lifetime to become one with my own eyes."[6] The phrase "[a] lifetime denying I'm exotic" indicates just how much time has passed in the United States, and yet the fifth word of the first sentence very deliberately uses the term "South American" and not "Latina/o." I argue that this move is not a refutation of "Latina/o" but a bid for specificity and for alterity that refuses to assimilate to categories imposed by the dominant culture in the United States. Most especially, it is a challenge to U.S.-ian indifference to both the variety and the specificity of the South American continent. The narrator continues in an ironic tone:

> it's what I'm fated to do, being South American. A million jobs and a million questions, but it doesn't matter what country I'm from, to you they're all the same. Uruguay, I tell you, and you light up and say, oh yeah, my cousin, he has a dentist, and his wife is from Brasil! (2)

In this ironic way, the narrator highlights the tendency in the United States to conflate one Latin American country with another and—heedless of history, geography, politics, and the like—recklessly substitute one for the other. One could argue, and scholars and cultural commentators have certainly pointed this out, that both the terms "Latina/o" and "Latin American" encourage these misinformed conflations. However, the narrator does not harden identity in the face of this misrecognition but rather uses the dominant culture's misrecognition as an incentive to identify with others and underscore "South American" as a reference composed of many places, many conditions opening onto something akin to the loss of bounded identity which, though perhaps disturbing or abject, this piece celebrates: "I blended with the darkness that isn't dark" (2) and "the more I look. I could be anyone, the old man, the old woman, Santa María Madre de Dios—Shoeshine! . . . The more I look. The darker they [the narrator's eyes] become" (3). I ask readers to notice how much "darkness"— with so many connotations both phenotypic (as in dark people) and existential—plays a part in this transformation of misrecognition, of taking a South American from one particular country for a South American from any number of countries, into a darkness implicitly connected via the title of the story and the narrator's account of jobs held, holes dug, math taught, and buses driven (mundane, everyday tasks of survival) with "speaking like an immigrant."

The various darknesses mentioned are, in subsequent stories, associated with night. In contrast to *Living at Night*, *Speaking Like an Immigrant: A Collection* does not deploy night obviously and continuously. However, night plays a set of associated cameo roles throughout many of the stories in *Speaking Like an Immigrant*—particularly in "The Virgin in the Desert," "Contraband," "Orphans," "Cuento de Jalohuín," "The Web," "La bruja pirata de Chiloé," and "2280." In some of the other pieces, night appears at the end of the story almost as the verbal equivalent of the fade-to-black technique in films. This is so, for instance, in "Love Story" and "Idylls of a Girl" or what was entitled, in the 1998 edition, "Idilio." Is this technique in any way related to the identity-challenging project of *Speaking Like an Immigrant*? Yes. This simple fade-out technique is used in stories about a Spanish-speaking woman who is late for work on a spring morning in Boston, Massachusetts, partly on account of missing her long-distance lover in the case of "Love Story," or about a narrator remembering her girlhood existence and crushes (on other girls) in Santiago, Chile, in "Idilio."[7] These stories about being both here (in the United States) and there (somewhere else, either in the sense of remembering a long-distance lover or being in Santiago, Chile) close with the darkness that in the first piece is strongly associated with being an immigrant and remaining one—a transcultural subject that resists grounding. Not only do darkness, night, and evening (with "Idilio") provide an open or indeterminate kind of closure for these stories about being "here" while thinking or dreaming of "there," but darkness and night grace the endings of stories subtly encoded with difference. The narrator of "Love Story" is rebelling against the diurnal business day of the New England city of Boston: "I imagine the route I must follow to reach that sterile place, the holes on Mass Ave, the stretch of construction lined by raincoated burlies making more holes in the street" (implying the setting of the cold New England spring) (34). When night is invoked at the end of the story, it appears along with "a warm wind and radios blaring" (more Latin-like) and visceral thoughts of the absent female lover anticipated by the female narrator to be arriving soon: "I know you'll be here tomorrow" (36). Under the sign of night, the narrator turns this absence of the long-distance lover (and everything the lover stands for, including, potentially, an elsewhere of the Other America) into an uncanny but powerful presence: "I finally feel your absence surrounding me like mist, taking shape, like the depth of your eyes and the scent of your body" (36). This image of the "depth of your eyes" resonates with the one of the dark eyes at the end of the piece "Speaking Like an Immigrant" (3), which just keep getting more deeply dark the more the narrator moves toward them. Though it appears for only a fraction of a short passage at the end of "Love Story," "[t]he night" (36) transports the narrator and the reader into a paradoxical space where absence becomes presence, where mist, the vague and formless, takes "shape" (36), and where difference and Otherness—however much they are suppressed by the dominant order of the day (the diurnal business world of Boston, for instance)—emerge, via Romo-Carmona's descriptions, to leave an impression. This emergence of difference to leave an impression also summarizes the function of the brief mention of night or "summer evenings" (138) in "Idilio," the last piece in the 1998 edition of *Speaking Like an Immigrant,* or "Idylls of a Girl," the fourteenth out of nineteen pieces in the 2010 edition:

> Summer evenings glide on evenly past girls swinging on a swing with brown limbs and hair shorn off at the nape, no more braids, no more ribbons. On the clothesline, the sheets flutter, and on the horizon the moon rises ghostly still, no edges to its roundness yet. . . . A net is cast far from herself; a girl who will fly away as surely as summer ends, days turn, rains come, market days are yellow, wash days are blue. (117–18)

This paragraph, like the rest of the piece, is best understood as prose poetry. Many differences are compacted into this small space of prose inaugurated by the phrase "[s]ummer evenings." Readers get the image of brown girls—perhaps South American girls, as earlier in the story readers will find a reference to "Avenida Catedral" in Santiago, Chile—divested of traditional signs of femininity: braids and ribbons. They swing in more ways than one. They shape-shift and thus resist the proper image assigned to them under patriarchy. Furthermore, the moon is ghostly as it rises, introducing uncanny transformation into the scene. And the last lines conjure the image of a girl flying away from where she once was—leaving her home, immigrating perhaps. Given the context of the collection *Speaking Like an Immigrant,* the implication is that this girl will be flying from Chile to the United States. The net cast far from herself, an image reminiscent of one toward the end of Zora Neale Hurston's novel *Their Eyes Were Watching God* (1937), reminds readers once again of the fundamental diasporic, transcultural experience and subjectivity being conveyed by Romo-Carmona's collection of stories. Most importantly, the net is cast both ways—not only toward the United States from Chile but also away from the United States back toward South America. The primary effect of "Idilio" or "Idylls of a Girl" is to remember that Chilean girlhood, not to forget it or let it lose its vibrancy in the momentum of a traditional process of assimilation. "Summer evenings" are those of that girlhood, after all, that is still vivid and important to the narrator's identity and identification.

As mentioned previously, in yet other stories such as the 1998 "The Virgin in the Desert" or the 2010 "La virgen en el desierto," "Contraband," "Orphans," "Cuento de Jalohuín," "The Web," "La bruja pirata de Chiloé," and "2280," references to night play even more prominent cameo roles that extend the project of transculturation of the collection *Speaking Like an Immigrant*. The second piece of the 1998 collection, "The Virgin in the Desert" (originally published in Spanish in 1982 and then republished in Spanish in the 2010 edition), concerns a young girl (the narrator) and her mother journeying by truck back and forth across the Pampa of the Atacama Desert, which is one of the driest places on earth and is sparsely populated. I quote from the 2010 Spanish version but provide an English translation found in the 1998 edition.

Mother and daughter make brief stops in villages such as Calama, Toconao, and San Pedro. As the story unfolds, a woman who is riding at one point with the mother and daughter is revealed to be seriously ill. The young girl prays to the Virgin on the woman's behalf. However, it is not the Virgin of the Spanish colonizers and Jesuits that she prays to but rather "una virgen viva y morena" (29) or a "virgin dark and alive" of her own imagining that the narrator associates with the words of a folk song by Clara Solovera, "Niña en tus trenzas de noche" (31) or "Girl of the braids as dark as night." Much of the narrator's praying to the dark virgin is done at night, a time that is considered "traicionera" (27) or "treacherous" in the desert "porque oscurece de repente y la temperatura baja mucho" (27) or "because darkness comes suddenly and the temperature drops." The effect of these brief but concentrated references to night is to associate it with the haunting vastness of the northern Chilean desert that was inhabited by the Indians long before the Jesuit order tried to Christianize the area in the 1500s (25). The combination of night and a vast desert either once inhabited or currently inhabited (or both) by people different from the dominant order of Western European and U.S. culture (European, Euro-American, Christian, and so forth) produces the strong sensation of another place, as in Albert Camus's story "The Adulterous Woman" from *Exile and the Kingdom* (1957), a work published three years into the Algerian War of Independence (1954–1962), which I discussed in the introduction to this book. In "The Virgin in the Desert," Romo-Carmona employs an existentialist approach—situating her story in the northern Chilean desert, much of it during the night—and infuses this existentialist scenario of a desert crossing with specific geo-cultural references. These particular references include the names of the Chilean towns, the narrator's nocturnal conjuring of a "virgin dark and alive" from a rocky pool in Toconao to whom she prays, the story within a story of a woman who had been in jail because "no tenía certificado de nacimiento" (24) or she "didn't have a birth certificate" and "no podía probar a las autoridades que era chilena y que no había cruzado el desierto desde Bolivia" or she "could not prove to the authorities that she was Chilean and hadn't crossed the desert from Bolivia" (24), and the ongoing narrative thread about the woman who is seriously ill and needs medical attention but in the end (at the town of Calama) does not receive it because the orderlies and doctors at the hospital are more concerned with finding out to which political party she belongs (30). These references, which are mixed in with reminders of nighttime in the desert and, in turn, pervaded by night, politicize night to locally, regionally, and hemispherically specific ends that particularize and expand concepts of Latinidad. For example, readers who pick up *Speaking Like an Immigrant,* a text mostly in English by U.S.-based writer Romo-Carmona, find themselves in South America or northern Chile rather than in some part of the United States. Then, readers are encouraged to think about South Americans moving around their own countries and between countries (between Bolivia and Chile, for instance) potentially in various states of political exile (as with the seriously ill woman whose life is sacrificed to party politics). Readers are also asked to contemplate a cast of characters living in and traveling across the desert, this frontier-like place that is not the U.S. West or Southwest but northern Chile. Among the characters readers find a military man, a blond Dutchman who sounds like a "yanqui" (22) or Yankee, the narrator and her mother, the sick *señora* who dies, another woman who may be Bolivian, and Spaniards and Indians (when the story shifts into descriptions of the historical past of the desert). The characters come from several nations and ethnicities, and the location of the story is not the usual one in a U.S. text—the United States. The location is, transculturally, northern Chile, and it is presented as a location of confluence, conflict, suffering, and possibility equally deserving of attention as the United States. Furthermore, as with most of Romo-Carmona's work, location—transcultural in different but related ways in *Living at Night* and *Speaking Like an Immigrant*—is, in this story, bound up with gender. The character whose life is sacrificed in the geopolitical conflicts is a woman. The narrator consoles herself by singing to her dark virgin, whom she has conjured as a symbol of succor and strength, and also by singing one particular song, the folk song "Niña en sus trenzas de noche" (31) or "Girl with the braids dark as night." Night marks a locational transculturality represented through gendered inflections of exile (internal to one's native country as much as between countries), immigration, and survival.

Subsequent stories such as "Contraband" extend both the variables and locations of Latinidades without losing certain particularities. For example, the narrator of "Contraband" is a U.S.-based Chilean old man who, readers discover at the story's conclusion, is teaching a young Puerto Rican woman to play jazz clarinet (145). The body of the story concerns this old man's memories of his years "on the road" (144) in Europe, especially southeastern Central Europe and Eastern Europe, after leaving Chile as a young man. The narrator's account of his experiences in Bucharest (Romania), Moscow (the Soviet Union), and Budapest (Hungary) are characterized by descriptions of his nocturnal performances and minglings with musicians and other people from each of these cities. It is during these evenings and nights that the U.S.-based Chilean narrator remembers establishing a camaraderie with the people of countries that at the time of his sojourn were part of what the United States deemed, during the Cold War, "the Communist Bloc." Though the narrator is often close to starvation during his time in Romania, the Soviet Union, and Hungary, he feels connected to the people—people who took little for granted and struggled for what they had, people whose experience, "Contraband" implies, was not so very different from that of many immigrants and even émigrés to the United States. At one point the narrator recalls thinking:

> The faces of the people became mine, a memory, a grandmother's face, an uncle, and strangely, I thought, would I ever go home? Is there home anymore? And why, why on earth did I ever think I knew where it was? (140)

This questioning of the location of home dovetails significantly with the deployment of night in the story. Night is represented as the time when the narrator and his companions, other South Americans (Jorge and Jaime) and Eastern Europeans, perform in jazz clubs and move about the streets of Eastern European cities encountering and interacting with the inhabitants. The experiences, though clearly involving hard work, hunger, and poverty, are described with a deep empathy rather than through the lenses of a U.S.-inflected Cold War mistrust and contempt for "Communist Bloc" countries. Night is international, internationalist, and, furthermore, transnationalist to the extent that the narrator, an old man living in the United States and teaching a young Puerto Rican woman to play jazz clarinet, reflects on his adventures as a young man in Central and Eastern Europe and emphasizes the coalitions and networks of support between displaced South Americans and Eastern Europeans. The solidarity felt between these groups of people rests on more than jazz—this music of the night—as entertainment, but, in the spirit of something like Toni Morrison's novel *Jazz* (1992), on a complex mixture of joy and suffering, freedom of expression and political persecution (from Pinochet in Chile, from Ceaușescu in Romania): "Sergei had disappeared, too, had been arrested one day during

Ceaucescu [*sic*] when he was teaching guitar at a school, never heard from again. I cried when I heard this . . . not for him . . . but for me" (144). The narrator cries for himself when he hears of Sergei's disappearance via arrest because it quashes the possibility of further productions of solidarity through Sergei's night music: "I cried for . . . for all the people who would never hear them [Sergei and his comrades] play" (144). At the end of this story, the narrator's hope for the survival of some remains of his experiences as a Chilean in Central and Eastern Europe lies with the young Puerto Rican woman from New York City who is studying jazz clarinet with him: "she may not want all these memories passed on from an old man, but maybe, maybe she will. And she'll play jazz" (145). In the face of questions about the location of home, the ending brings the story back from Central and Eastern Europe to the Americas, to the United States in particular.

This narrative itinerary is important to the implications of the story and its night music—wandering jazz—aesthetics for new conceptualizations of Latinidades and Latina/o identities and identifications. Pieces of music classified as jazz usually do not resolve where they began. Jazz eludes the symmetry of classical or more conventional, less experimental kinds of music. Likewise, this story "Contraband"—with its curious title referring to something stolen and sold or bartered on a black or invisible market—does not really end where it began, unless one counts the old man's memory and the brief reference to "Amsterdam Avenue" (133) on the first page. Amsterdam Avenue is a long, 129-block avenue running from West 59th Street to West 190th Street in Manhattan. Its name indexes the fact that a portion of current-day New York was once a Dutch colony and that the immigrants of the early seventeenth century to the island of Manhattan were Dutch. The implication, particularly as conveyed through the consciousness of an old Chilean man, is that successive waves of different immigrants have been arriving ever since then. In terms of named places, the story finishes not in Chile, South America, where the narrator was born, but in the United States and with a Chilean and a Puerto Rican rather than with Chileans and/or Chileans and Eastern Europeans. The story concludes with a pointed reference to the Lower East Side[8] southeast of Amsterdam Avenue, the dwelling place (if not the home) of so many immigrants for over two hundred years especially of Latina/os and Puerto Ricans, who have become Nuyoricans. Jazz, which is represented in the story as being played in the evening and at night, connects the Chilean exile narrator living in the United States with Central and Eastern Europeans who are often exiled and wandering from place to place in their own countries and, of course, who have a long history of migration to the United States. New York City in particular saw waves of Eastern Europeans arriving in the 1870s. And, through the music lessons that he gives, the night music of jazz connects the narrator to more recent non-European immigrants, such as the young Puerto Rican woman. The effect of "Contraband," a reference to that which circulates on a black or hidden market, is to encourage readers to think of being a South American immigrant in the United States in connection with other parts of the world often not considered under the rubrics of "Latina/o," "Latin American," or "Latinidades." Latina/o studies is a transdisciplinary field involving, among other approaches, the intersection between geography and comparative ethnic studies. A story like this one stretches the boundaries of the geopolitical locations and ethnicities that inform Latina/o subjectivities, as can be seen through the experiences of the U.S.-based Chilean narrator and one of the recipients of an account of his remembered experiences via oral storytelling, the young Puerto Rican woman.

Another story that also stretches concepts of Latinidades in a transcultural fashion, though it concentrates on a smaller scope of space and time, is "Orphans" (103–11). It does so partly through the use of night to convey a time when a sister and brother who have emigrated from Guayaquil, Ecuador, to New York City find themselves once again reminded of their bond as orphan immigrants after long days of trying to survive in New York by peddling their wares—handmade jewelry, wood carvings, and pencil-drawn as well as cardboard-cut miniatures of New York City and other places around the world—on the street:

> At night, Daniel [the brother] slept soundly while Serena [the sister] stayed awake, stroking the amber, looking at the full moon through their dusty windows, planning a future with Daniel, perhaps even with Doreen [Serena's newfound girlfriend]. . . . One day there would be a woman who would take him away, who would make him forget the years in the orphanage, their journey to a new land, but that was life. And she had always known that someday she, too, would search for her own happiness, not just money, or a home. But for the moment, it was too soon to dream. (110–11)

Night here forms a privileged moment that re-asserts the bond between these two relatively poor orphans from Ecuador, from Guayaquil, "the city of soft colors, tropical and rich for others, not for orphans like themselves" (103). Night here plays the opposite role as night in "Contraband." It is a time of bonding between family members from one South American country rather than for the mixing of non-consanguineous people from a plurality of nationalities and ethnicities. In "Orphans," mixing of non-consanguineous people happens mostly

during the day and afternoons on the streets and in the parks and squares of
New York City. However, night still serves a function similar to that in "Contraband" by being a medium for the subjectivity of a South American (in this case
an Ecuadorian) based in the United States, a South American who is becoming
Latina/o but is not from one of the three representationally dominant Latina/o
groups: Mexican American, Puerto Rican, or Cuban American. By "becoming
Latina/o" I do not mean that these characters forget their country of origin.
Becoming Latina/o, unlike as in the traditional U.S. melting pot model of assimilation, does not require this foregoing of the past, at least not in these stories or
in the cultural productions with which this chapter is concerned.

Mariana Romo-Carmona's *Speaking Like an Immigrant* contains a third
group of stories—neither the ones in which night is confined to the end of the
story ("Love Story," "Idilio," and even "Orphans") nor the ones in which night
runs through the story like the primary element of a folk song or a repeating
jazz riff ("The Virgin in the Desert" and "Contraband")—that both extends
and particularizes the boundaries of the geopolitical locations and ethnicities
informing Latina/o subjectivities. The titles of the stories in this third group-
ing—"Cuento de Jalohuín" (which could be translated "Halloween Story), "The
Web," "La bruja pirata de Chiloé" (The pirate witch of Chiloé), and "2280" (after
a year in the twenty-third century)—correspond even at a titular glance to the
genres of fantasy and science fiction. The stories do not adhere to the conventions of realism as do the other ones (with the partial exception of "Idilio" or
"Idylls of a Girl"). This tendency toward fantasy and especially science fiction is
interesting in itself because Latina/o writing does not usually fall into these categories. Latina/o writing looks unapologetically at numerous historical pasts,
concerns itself very much with material conditions both in the past and the
present, and may also be particularly invested in alternate epistemologies that
question Western rationality or, more to the point, rationalism. Latina/o writing usually does this, however, by blending realism with that which defies it, not
by departing more wholeheartedly into fantasy or sci-fi worlds.

To summarize each story briefly, "Cuento de Jalohuín," set three days before
Hallows Eve 1959, concerns a coven of witches, "my sisters and I . . . our language
. . . subtle" (13), who live beside a town where they are "foreigners among the
locals, though our ancestors have inhabited this continent for centuries" (14).
One of the sisters gives her heart to a young man of the town who, in the end,
does not return her love, breaking her heart: "she gave her heart to another and
received emptiness in return" (14). To avenge her sister's pain at being jilted, one
of the witches poisons a thorn from roses that the young man gave to her sister,
pierces his hand with this thorn, and kills him. The story ends with the line: "In

three days' time, at midnight on *hallows eve*, he will die" (15). Though no nation-alities are mentioned and night is not specifically associated with an alternative to the more dominant conception of "Latina/o" (for instance, a South American Latinidad), the story creates a strong sense of a dominant culture (the town) and a subaltern culture (that of the witches). It envisions payback for an unequal exchange between lovers, that is, between a man of the town and a witch of the outskirts. These figures serve as vessels for a repeating dynamic between center and periphery, to invoke Chilean-based cultural theorist Nelly Richard's terms.[9] Thus, the revenge could be interpreted as one not only by a witch on an insensi-tive man but also by the colonized on the colonial order.

"The Web" features a kind of spider woman who considers herself to be from another planet: "Soy un ser de otro planeta" (125) and "I am the daughter of a comet from a southern latitude that extends its tail between two oceans and then is lost, disintegrating in a thousand islands glowing in the night" (125). That comet would seem to correspond to the long, thin shape of Chile and the southern tip of the country, which indeed fragments into hundreds of small islands. The spider woman has a special relationship with full moon nights near water: "On full moon nights, I sit alone near the piers, reaching across the waters to commune with my sisters" (126). These spider women weavers draw strength from communing with "older women immigrants who tried to leave me clues" (126) and from their sisters elsewhere, on other shores. Strongly implied is the idea that these spider women must remain in transnational, inter-spatial com-munication with each other or they sicken and die, losing themselves: "I knew they were calling me, and I learned to listen, especially at night" (126). At one point, the narrator describes herself as a "small and brown" spider (127) and says that in the early days after arriving at the new shores of this terrestrial world where she is now, she was not "ashamed of being small and brown" (127). But as time wears on in the new place (the corollary with the United States is left for readers to draw), the immigrant spider woman from another planet experiences hardship, rejection, and complicated romantic relations with other "sisters" (here the word takes on connotations that exceed consanguinity, suggesting the intimacy of lovers, not blood relations) who may be too "earthbound" (127), interested in conforming to where they are and uncomfortable with the narra-tor's difference as an immigrant, alien spider woman who still wishes to main-tain webs of communication with her mother ("that distant flickering spider lost in a shower of meteorites," 127) and with sisters in other cities (128). Never-theless, the spider woman narrator tries to maintain her lines of communication with other outsiders, sister spiders: "On nights like these, I wandered by the black water of the river, gathering strength from the deep velvet of the sky, and willed myself to call a meeting of the sisters who live in cities near to each other" (128). The narrator's entanglement with an earthbound woman, who does not want the narrator to wander the piers at night, presents a barrier to her ability to communicate like the spider woman alien/immigrant that she is: "The earthbound woman has taken my sister away, and she has severed the connection" (131). However, the night remains the narrator's ally; it is the proper medium for spinning those transnational, inter-spatial webs of connection that do their transcultural night work to defy the artificial borders and boundaries created by the conforming earthbound people.

"La bruja pirata de Chiloé" underscores the theme of transgression against the earthbound, in particular the earthbound conquistadors greedy for ownership of land and sea. Though the story has a very historical theme—that of defying conquistadors—some of its main characters are witches and ghosts, who are traditionally considered the staple of fantasy and ghost stories, not historical fiction striving for verisimilitude. The first paragraph of the story reads as follows:

> This is the story of Jacinta, the witch who knew my great grandmother Chillpila, and who communed with ghosts in her old ship, a creaky schooner anchored in a rugged cove of the southern Chilean archipelago below the island of Chiloé. Perhaps this is also the story of the great Indian witch Chillpila who was known for changing shapes, and for grounding in dry land the ship of the Spaniard Moraleda, when he attempted to match his powers with hers in 1787. She was the ancestor for whom my great grandmother was named. (65)

The story focuses on the adventures of Jacinta, "an orphan from the island of Quinchao, who had never married and had no children" and who "was a weaver who travelled from island to island with her portable loom" (66). One day she is sequestered aboard a smuggler's schooner, is attacked by bandits, fights for her life, and kills one of the pirate bandits with the help of a ghost. The events that follow lead her to meet Doña Chillpila, a witch who informs Jacinta that the ghost has come for her. Jacinta, who now lives outside the law for having taken the life of a man, must become a powerful witch to survive. She will learn how to become that powerful witch through her conversations with Chillpila and her encounters (which turn sexual) with the ghost of, Jacinta learns, a female pirate (69–70).[10] In this way, Jacinta herself becomes an adept witch and female pirate whose life span seems to extend indefinitely:

> In the 50's and 60's she was involved in the Indigenous uprisings of the southern regions. Wearing her usual black leather men's clothes and puffing on a red

clay pipe, she was often seen at night near the bars where smugglers, sailors, and government informers drank.... She was persecuted for years by the authorities during the dictatorship, but it was very simple for Jacinta to blend in as an old woman and make people believe she had died. (70)

Jacinta becomes a legendary outlaw who takes revenge on those who persecute the indigenous populations and who oppress anyone opposing the dictatorship (70). She also successfully romances the women of Chile: "Jacinta was a favorite with the women" (70). Nighttime and thick fogs are her element and her alibis (70). Not only a weaver and a female pirate but moreover a witch who communes with ghosts, Jacinta approaches night as the ideal medium for her exploits. She travels from place to place undetected, invisible, so as to continue her work, even though the last image is of her schooner rounding a cove during the day, "sails billowing and snapping" (71).

Finally, "2280" also belongs to the third kind of story I am outlining. The number refers to a year in the future on an environmentally ruined planet Earth plagued by a widespread illness referred to simply as "the Disease" (51). The scenario that the narrator presents—a city of "the northern continent" (an allusion to North America) in which the air "feels used up, tired" and the "horribly deformed and malodorous" human beings "barely had a thin layer of grayish light around their physical bodies" and "hardly any psychic energy" (51–52)—is remindful of Camus's existential 1947 novel *The Plague*. As in *The Plague*, there are numerous descriptions of eerie night-related darknesses that convey a historical or future historical malaise related to the politically and socially toxic evolution of society. Take, for instance, these sentences from Romo-Carmona's "2280":

> The red glow in the sky seems to be dimmer. I hear it never really gets dark in this village, that the mercury illuminators glow perpetually because it is never really light. Through the plexigate I can still distinguish some of the shapes of the eroded architecture of the 20th century. I have no access to any history before that. There is a great iron structure that extends across a foul gorge they call the East River. (54)

The reference to the East River coupled with an earlier reference to "this old New York town" (52) locates "2280" in New York City at that time—in the year 2280. In that year, the city exists as a massive jumbled collection of buildings, composed of a "mixture of granite, molten metal, cement, organic material, wood, and thousands of other particles processed and reshaped after several nuclear meltdowns, earthquakes, laser blastings, and many other urban catastrophes" (55), in a perpetual twilight of reddish, grayish, greenish, and bluish glows. At a place called "the Medical College" (56) power-hungry researchers and physicians conduct medical experiments presumably to find a cure for the Disease. The narrator-protagonist, who is also a *curandera* herbalist in opposition to the medical establishment, does not trust the enterprises of the Medical College and suspects, correctly, that they are part of a governmental and corporate conspiracy to manage the population (and especially to reduce the numbers of "brown-skinned human beings," 59) and to hoard resources: "it was also discovered that reactionary factions all over the globe had begun the great infection [*sic*] in an effort to control the remaining resources" (59):

> The Brownskinned people were blamed for the transmission of the Disease and the now clearly despotic regime sought to control its spread by testing every human being with brown skin for the antibody. . . . Experiments were conducted on human beings who were used to incubate serum [against the Disease], while ignoring the great progress healers were making in other parts of the globe. (59–60)

Romo-Carmona's story employs a sickly twilight to underscore environmental devastation, political repression, and the corruption of medical and social services by the worst aspects of Western conventional medical practice that involves a dehumanizing split between subject and object, observer and observed, the globe partitioned by ideology and practice into "first" and "third" worlds, and center/periphery power dynamics regarding the acknowledgment of which ontological and epistemological practices constitute viable knowledge. The work of healers in other parts of the globe is ignored, while the practices of institutions such as the "Medical College" in New York City are elevated and deified. This twilight of civilization in the "northern continent" that has "cut itself off from the rest of the globe" (52) is a dark and terrifying version of H. G. Wells's utopian ideas about the supposed benefits of a "New World Order" in his 1940 book by that title. Wells envisioned the New World Order as a progressive, cosmopolitan world socialism constructed upon the intersection and merging of governmental and non-governmental organizations that would address and vastly ameliorate the destructive divide between the haves and the have-nots. In Romo-Carmona's story "2280," a similar though capitalist convergence coupled with the isolationism of the "northern continent" (by which she means North America and specifically the United States) results in precisely the opposite effect: a deeper and deeper abyss between the haves and the have-nots and environmental devastation of the whole planet, including the northern continent.

The story "2280" is divided into four unnumbered parts signaled by several blank spaces between the parts. The fourth and last part begins, "It was night again. The sky glowed a dark red and the mist became more dense" (60). During the night, the narrator protagonist comes upon an outdoor musical concert in a large open plaza and telepathically performs a healing on some of the people who have gathered there. Then the narrator, having surreptitiously gathered more information about the Medical College—information that confirms that the institution is engaged in "[m]urder as population control" by inducing "massive immunodeficiency from many viral combinations" (61)—decides to return there to hack into its computer systems and shut down its eugenic operations, including the "remote source of [electrical] energy" that keeps the Chief Physician, her guards, and "the elders" (part of the government) alive despite the radiation to which their bodies have been subjected in this futuristic dystopia (63–64). With its focus on a fatal disease induced in part by radiation from holograms combined with a politically persecutorial social environment, the story is remindful of Argentinean writer Adolfo Bioy Casares's 1940 novella *La invención de Morel* (*The Invention of Morel*), a tale concerned with death-inducing holographic recorders and projectors of an unscrupulous scientist named Morel who aimed to colonize an island with his idea of the perfect artificial paradise. *La invención de Morel* was itself inspired by another of H. G. Wells's works, the 1896 novel *The Island of Dr. Moreau*. One of the hallmarks of "2280" as a specifically Mariana Romo-Carmona story is the use of night to unambiguously confront and liberate oneself and others from oppression, as the narrator protagonist does in the fourth part of "2280":

> [A]lerted by the sudden drop in power, they [the Chief Physician, the guards, and the governmental elders] advanc[ed] like glowing ghosts through the darkened corridors. They all seemed inconsequential then, so unreal and feeble, because at the end of the sequence on my screen their power source would shut off without a sound, and they would all be most certainly dead. (64)

As in Camus's novel *The Plague,* night is complicit in the breakdown of the colonial order, in this case the neocolonial machine. In contrast to Camus's novel, Romo-Carmona's story suggests a distinction between the sickly twilight of the gods of the neocolonial order and the night of the rebellious *curandera* who manages to hack into the system and shut it down.

With regard to the intersection of uses of night by South American U.S.-based Latina/o cultural producers and the stretching of the boundaries of the geopolitical locations and ethnicities informing Latina/o subjectivities and identity construction, "2280" does actually name particular geographical locations in the course of its unfolding. In naming various places, it creates, from its beginning, a strong sense of a there and a here that corresponds to South America versus the "northern continent" and especially the United States. For example, consider the following sentences:

> Back in Venezuela City, none of us ever guessed it would be so sad here. Naturally, my people and I are not naïve enough to think of the northern continent as that glowing, polished "land of opportunity" as it was known in the 20th century. (51)
>
> . . .
>
> At first, I thought this was the urban village called Chicago in the 1990s, but it isn't. It's one that was thought to be uninhabited by mid-21st century; this is old New York town. (52)
>
> . . .
>
> It was surprising, then, when we heard talk of a vaccine cure being developed in the northern continent. I was sent from Venezuela City to investigate. (53)

As the narrator begins her narrative already on her mission in New York City, the United States, the "there" is South America and Venezuela City in particular, and the "here" is the northern continent, the U.S. cities, and New York City. The important feature to notice is that from the first paragraph onwards an interplay is set up between a "here" in the environmentally, socially, and politically devastated United States and a remembered and cherished "there" represented as what is definitively not the northern continent and what can be inferred from place-names such as Venezuela City (51 and 53) and "Macchu Picchu" [sic] (59) to be South America. The story locates other kinds of medical practices—a respect for alternative medicine—in places such as Venezuela City, whence the narrator departs to the United States as an emissary from the "Global Association of Curandesas," or healers (53). This polarization of South America versus "the northern continent," in which the Southern continent, South America, or more broadly *América Latina* is represented as both the more philosophical and more organic of the two Americas, dates back to the early to mid nineteenth century in Latin American cultural production. It can be found in the revolutionary rhetoric of the Venezuelan Simón Bolívar and the writings and speeches of the Apostle of Cuban Independence, José Martí. It culminated in the famous 1900 essay titled *Ariel* by the Uruguayan essayist José Enrique Rodó. Drawing on William Shakespeare's play *The Tempest* (1610–1611), the essay casts Latin America in the role of the airy spirit and servant to Prospero, and North America in the role of Prospero's deformed slave Caliban. The essay represents Ariel / Latin

America as more spiritual and creative than Caliban / North America, which is represented as earthbound, materialistic, spiritually underdeveloped, utilitarian, and lacking in creative vision. When I say "culminated" I do not mean that the construction of this contrast between América Latina and what Romo-Carmona calls "the northern continent" came to an end in 1900, two years after the Spanish-Cuban-American War of 1898. Rather, this contrast became a staple of much of Latin American modernism and, as attested to by Romo-Carmona's story "2280," has survived in some U.S.-based Latin American or Latina/o cultural production. The difference between Rodó's essay and much Latina/o cultural production that pursues this thematics is that the latter rescues Caliban from negative connotations.

Furthermore, in Romo-Carmona's work night is associated with the creativity of this Other America as opposed to the dismal twilight daytime order of "the northern continent." The many links to this Other America and to its remaining alternate systems of value despite Americanization or what José Enrique Rodó referred to as "*nordomanía*" (literally translated as "Northern-mania") are what Romo-Carmona's 1998 *Speaking Like an Immigrant* refuses to trade away to fit into a United States context. Though "2280" is set in a New York City, a United States, of the future, the underlying geopolitical and geocultural orientation of the story bears out the opening lines of *Speaking Like an Immigrant*: "You must know I'm South American, though I live here" (1). By the end of the collection of stories, this statement has accrued emotionally charged cultural and historical substance, especially through the tactical uses of night that extend the familiar boundaries of "Latina/o" beyond Mexico, Puerto Rico, and Cuba and beyond assimilation to U.S.-centricity.

The third group of stories—these fantasy and sci-fi ones—that are so heavily encoded with night also extends the familiar boundaries of Latina/o subjectivity and identity construction by moving into both the past and the future with equal ease, thus expanding the temporal as well as the spatial deictics of Latinidades based in the United States. By "deictics," I mean those references in any given text (whether written or spoken) to temporal or spatial position relative to a narrator's or speaker's current location in space or time. Those references in these fantasy and sci-fi stories from *Speaking Like an Immigrant* continually reinforce a transculturality and transnationalism that emphasizes the present and future tenses of "speaking like an immigrant" rather than the confinement of that kind of "speaking" to a past moment when one first made the journey from South America or, more broadly, *América Latina* to the United States. In 1998 (the publication date of *Speaking Like an Immigrant*), thirty-two years after Romo-Carmona emigrated to the United States from Chile, she offers readers models and scenarios for how to keep speaking like an immigrant and socio-political reasons why such continuity is valid and important. Night courses through all this immigrant speaking to the extent that it represents, visually and viscerally, an acceptance of the productive dis-orientation and relative bound-lessness of a live and ongoing transculturation and transnationalism that, if any-thing, is becoming a stronger and stronger force in the United States despite xenophobic isolationist or unilateralist genocidal tendencies.

The Delirium of Oncoming Night
in Jaime Manrique's Novel *Twilight at the Equator* (2003)

What is deemed mad operates by a different kind of logic—a deviant logic that does not function according to recognized rules of the game—argues French philosopher Gilles Deleuze along with Félix Guattari in *Anti-Oedipus: Capital-ism and Schizophrenia* (1972) and by himself in *L'Immanence: Une Vie* (1995). Following Nietzsche, Deleuze (1925–1995) called for philosophy to critique and unmoor established values—especially the very anchoring concepts of self, God, and the world—and create new values "not yet recognized."[11] He attacked the notion of the individual self and any assumed unity about it. He insisted the self was not a stable given but only a fiction or artifice in which, through habit, we come to believe. Is it irresponsible to de-personalize the self, to focus on the impersonal of the personal? Can this perspective and praxis lead to a greater commitment, to a new collective awareness or, more precisely, awareness through multiplicity that allows for collectivity but not under the usual strictures of a totalizing or monadic unity? What does such radical revi-sion have to offer Latina/os in the United States who are dealing with problems of marginalization and socioeconomic injustice, not only under-representation but moreover lack of cultural authority and control and lack of credibility?

How might this impersonal in the personal be recognized, cultivated, and accepted, and what political implications does it have? Of what value is the will-ingness to be indefinite, formless? To be anybody (*nadie y cualquiera*) instead of somebody? What value does a mad process of impersonalization (one might call it de-personalization) have for people struggling against the presumptuous hierarchies of coloniality and potentially fascistic counter-responses based on appeals to difference or unity (nation, *raza*) from or against the oppressors? Can the dissolution of boundaries and the loss of identity serve as methods of decolonization? Or do such tactics just unproductively simulate boundary disorder and identity confusion? What does such plasticity of identity have to offer? Can a Latina/o subject afford to see the self as a fiction? Or is such an approach eroding what is trying to be constituted even before it has a chance to come into being?

Can one have a consciousness without a self, and what are the implications of this state of affairs for a Latina/o decolonial politics? This might be another way to ask some of the questions posed in José Muñoz's book about disidentifications. Rather than suture oneself into a majoritarian phobic sphere, does one aspire to lose oneself in a new unfolding polis, the polis of Latinidades, a deliberate fiction? What madness is required for this experiment? What is the relationship between Latinidades and fiction, artifice, institutional inventiveness? And how does this artifice, fiction, poetry, invented institution move participants beyond the limited partialities of their own passions and identifications? I focus these questions on and through U.S.-based Colombian writer Jaime Manrique's 2003 novel *Twilight at the Equator*, which opens with the lines, "I arrived in Madrid [capital of the former Spanish Empire] to become a poet. The year was 1976 [the bicentennial of the American Revolution] . . . I also went to Madrid to self-destruct . . . I wanted to split from this world with a shattering cry."[12]

Poet (author of several poetry collections, *Los adoradores de la luna*, *Scarecrow*, *My Night with / Mi noche con Federico García Lorca*, *Mi cuerpo y otros poemas*, and *Tarzan, My Body, Columbus*), memoirist (*Eminent Maricones: Arenas, Lorca, Puig, and Me*), novelist (*El cadaver de papá*, *Colombian Gold: A Thriller*, *Latin Moon in Manhattan*, *Twilight at the Equator*, and *Our Lives Are the Rivers*), translator (with Joan Larkin of *Sor Juana's Love Poems*), and critic (*Notas de cine: Confesiones de un crítico amateur*), Jaime Manrique was born in Barranquilla, Colombia, in 1949 of a wealthy white father and a mixed-heritage (African, native, and white) mother. As described in Manrique's memoir *Eminent Maricones* (1999), the relationship between his unmarried parents of different socioeconomic and ethno-racial strata in Colombian society was strained for many reasons. His relationship with his father, who did not acknowledge him fully as a son, was problematic. Manrique emigrated to the United States (Lakeland, Florida) at seventeen with his mother, who took a job as a domestic. He grew up in Florida, became a naturalized U.S. citizen, and attended the University of South Florida, earning a B.A. in English. He has lived in New York City, where, for some years, he taught in the MFA program at Columbia University. Most of his material is self-confessedly autobiographical (though often fictionalized), and much of it is obviously—even in the very titles—concerned with night, as evidenced by the books of poetry *Los adoradores de la luna* (*The Worshippers of the Moon*) and *My Night with / Mi noche con Federico García Lorca*, his picaresque debut novel, *Latin Moon in Manhattan* (1992), and the much more somber novel *Twilight at the Equator* (2003).

Of these various nocturnal ventures, *Twilight at the Equator* (2003) presents readers with the most intense intersection of seemingly autobiographical material, tropes of night, and the critical crossing and multi-directional mixing of cultures (transculturation) that draws distinctions among groups of Latina/os and Hispanics. I say "Hispanics" because Spain and Spaniards appear in Manrique's work. Ultimately, these techniques challenge those distinctions and lay out other bases for the construction of Latinidades that question assumptions and expectations about nationality, sexuality, class, ethno-racial categories, and so on. Other bases for the construction of Latinidades are created through manipulations of the representation of the narrative "I," the seemingly autobiographical self, in the chapters of this novel, especially as the narrative "I" appears in relation to night and nocturnal scenes. By assumptions and expectations with regard to Latinidades I mean, for example, that even while the novel does what many other Latina/o cultural productions do—that is, delineate how it feels to be a member of a particular Latina/o national and/or ethnic group, in this case, a Colombian exile and more specifically a Colombian American—*Twilight at the Equator* places particular individual and ethnic identities (the Colombian exile "I" of the narrative) under the sign and effects of what I am calling "the delirium of oncoming night."

"The delirium of oncoming night" as technique is already evident in Manrique's 1995 book of poems *My Night with / Mi noche con Federico García Lorca,* in which tropes of night signal and form intense and sometimes sudden metamorphoses[13] beyond language or linguistic categories ("and there is no language / that can capture / the transcendence of this fire," 77) in half of its twenty-two poems. Many of the references to night partake of a neo-Romantic sensibility. They draw on the work of British Romantic poets such as Coleridge, Wordsworth, "Shelley and Keats" (named outright in the poem "Memories," 119); American transcendentalist writers such as William Cullen Bryant and Ralph Waldo Emerson; and painters such as Frederic Edwin Church of the Hudson River School (95) and Martin Johnson Heade. But Manrique also constructs these references of night by mixing, like a disc jockey of poetry, this neo-Romanticism with late nineteenth-century (1870s–1890s) and early to mid-twentieth-century modernist accents taken from the visual and verbal work of the French painters Henri Rousseau and Paul Gauguin, the Dutch painter Vincent van Gogh, the Russian painter Wassily Kandinsky, the Spanish poet Federico García Lorca (featured in the collection's title), and the more contemporary Chilean poet Pablo Neruda.

The uses of night in the earlier *My Night with / Mi noche con Federico García Lorca* (1995) that most foreshadow the delirium of oncoming night as technique in the later *Twilight at the Equator* (2003) arise in the rather Nerudian poem

"Toadstools." In this poem, the poet imagines himself in a thick forest or "track-less woods" (67) in "the burning twilight" (67) of a brewing thunderstorm with claps of thunder, lightning, and rain beginning to fall (67–69) through the penumbra. He comes across "a concentration camp of dead toadstools" (67) but spots among them a "dozen red toadstools" living and sprouting. He breaks off a bit of red toadstool cap and eats it. The poem suggests that the toadstool contains hallucinogenic substances that carry him "toward the other" and toward "profound terror" (69). Though he is frightened, the poet seeks and welcomes this sublime experience of being taken beyond his familiar self—beyond the self altogether. The break between two stanzas, with the last stanza of the poem beginning with the verse "When I open my eyes the rain has stopped" (69), implies that the poet has fallen into a trance induced by the hallucinogenic toadstool. Important to note is that this encounter with the toadstools in the dark forest takes place at twilight deepening into night. When the poet opens his eyes after ingesting the bit of toadstool cap, "the forest is dark" (69). The last lines of the poem read, "Like a firebreathing dragon / I move through the darkness / radiating a crimson delirium" (69). The passing of the poem, one image flowing into another in quick succession, and the closing lines resonate with Gilles Deleuze's description of the mind in his treatise *L'Immanence: Une Vie* first published in France in 1995, the same year as the original publication by The Groundwater Press of Manrique's *My Night with / Mi noche con Federico García Lorca:*[14]

> Left to itself, the mind has the capacity to move from one idea to another, but it does so at random, in a delirium that runs throughout the universe, creating fire dragons, winged horses, and monstrous giants. (41)

Deleuze's description of the mind, like the whole of *L'Immanence: Une Vie* or *Pure Immanence,* is aimed at questioning the unity and stability of the individual self and at substituting in place of assumptions about unity and stability concepts of motion, change, and multiplicity—all of which come across in his brief but vivid description of the mind or consciousness. Jaime Manrique clearly establishes a pattern of associating this delirium of motion, change, and multiplicity with twilight and oncoming night. Twilight functions as an in-between stage of liminality, as a harbinger of night and its metamorphoses. Night in this volume of Manrique's poems is represented as the time of delirium and metamorphoses to such a degree that the poet no longer appears as human but as mythical animal, "a firebreathing dragon" moving "through the darkness / radiating a crimson delirium" (69). In Deleuzian fashion, the self becomes other.

This is not a cause for lamentation as in Dante's reference to being lost in "the middle of a dark wood" (113), an allusion that surfaces unequivocally in a later poem in the collection but that subtly pertains to the dark forest of the earlier "Toadstools" (69). Rather, this delirium of un-becoming oneself, surpassing or going beyond one's familiar identity, is described in ecstatic terms—even if that ecstasy is deeply tinged with the sadness of elegy, as is frequently the case in Jaime Manrique's work.

The implications of this delirium of oncoming night for conceptions of ethnic identity or disidentification—of aspiring to lose oneself in a new unfolding polis, the polis of Latinidades, a deliberate fiction, rather than suturing oneself into a majoritarian phobic sphere—are incipiently appreciable in *My Night with / Mi noche con Federico García Lorca*. The title already suggests a transference between self and other and between two or more Latin and Hispanic cultures and space-times, that of the contemporary, living, U.S.-based Colombian poet Manrique and the early modernist and dead Spanish poet Lorca. The choice of a Spanish poet is important to consider. Though a poet from the Old World colonial power vis-à-vis the Americas, Lorca has long been cast as the artistic martyr who dared to challenge the revival of the Spanish colonial project in *Franquismo*. That challenge included a queer resistance against the heteronormativity and general social conformism of Spanish fascism. Furthermore, as the eponymous poem "My Night with Federico García Lorca" suggests, Lorca took a decolonially inflected interest in horizons beyond his own—in the Americas, in "New York and Cuba" (83). For a U.S.-based queer Colombian poet to identify with Lorca—or at least cast his lot in with him ("my night with . . . Lorca")—amounts to a declaration of rebellion against similar fascist and conformist tendencies in the Americas and in other so-called Latin societies. The identification with Lorca extends Colombian identity beyond a more narrow tribal or circumscribed identification solely with other Colombian exiles or transplants living in the United States.

The extension of identification with other Latin peoples—even with a Spaniard in the figure of Lorca—takes place under the sign of night. Poems such as "Mambo," with its references to the Caribbean and generally Cuban mambo (31); "The Nat King Cole Years," with its celebratory remembrance of African American lyrics and tunes (those of Nat King Cole) and specifically Mexican movies and movie actors (Cantinflas and María Félix) (37); "Saudade," with its Portuguese title that the poem anchors in Brazil with its allusion to "Copacabana beach" (85) and its continued hybridization of places in "Jamaica beige petals" (85); and "Barcelona Days," which returns the poet to Spain but via a line from an Argentine tango (103), link the U.S.-based Colombian poet's unfolding autobiographical persona to many other Latin American countries. The people from these countries are also in the United States as Latina/os (in the broadest sense) from all these places: Cuba, Mexico, Brazil (whose people are sometimes counted as Latina/os and at other times not), and Spain. *My Night with / Mi noche con Federico García Lorca* produces its own version of pan-Latinidades as well as trans-Latinidades. A spectrum of Latina/o identities is invoked but, more in keeping with the delirium of oncoming night, the U.S.-based Colombian writer incorporates elements of other Latina/o cultures into his own lyrical narrative about himself. Consequently, boundaries blur between what is Colombian and what is other Latin American and Latina/o.

This incorporative blurring might seem too easy, like a suspiciously romanticizing and commodifying tropical cocktail blend of Latina/o cultures. The danger of hybridizing Cuban, Mexican, Brazilian, and Spanish cultural elements with Colombian is the potential effect of encouraging an uncritical consumption of Latin cultures, particularly on the part of non-Latina/o readers who might already be predisposed to think that one Latin culture is like another. I argue that the context of an extended meditation on the Americas—and on Latin America or the Other America—seen through the eyes of nineteenth-century Anglo-American landscape painters such as the directly referenced Frederic Edwin Church (94–95) and the inferred Martin Johnson Heade (in the poem "Oda a un colibrí / Ode to a Hummingbird," 46–51) gives a more pointed and politicized value to the characterization of pan-Latinidades as trans-Latinidades of the poems as a whole. Jaime Manrique's allusions to elements of other Latin American and Latina/o cultures create a map of references that extends and transmutes, in his own Colombian Latina/o image, the nineteenth-century Anglo-American landscape painters' acknowledgment of the existence of another America besides that of the United States.[15] The poems *My Night with / Mi noche con Federico García Lorca* deploy the genre of landscape rendered in poetry rather than paint (*ut pictura poesis*) to produce a pan/trans-Latina/o-centric geography of relations—a hallucinatory, delirious geography conveyed in vivid descriptions that appeal to the senses. Manrique's writing is highly descriptive. And, in at least half of his descriptions, night appears as the time of maximum sudden change or metamorphosis between one state and another or between one space-time identity and another. So, for instance, at night the poet remembers the lyrics of a Nat King Cole song, the strains of a mambo, an imagined encounter with Federico García Lorca, or the identity-shifting communion with the crimson toadstools of a night forest deep in the heart of the South American wilderness, which is as much a frontier of knowledge and experience as any U.S. Wild West (much of which was expropriated from Mexico, after all).

The delirium of oncoming night—as both consciousness of the autobiographical, ethnically particularized self and the undoing of this seemingly unitary, particular self into multiplicities that challenge the stability and solidity of identitarian formulations (such as "Colombian writer" or "queer Colombian exile writer")—is narrated in more fully developed form in *Twilight at the Equator* (2003). As in the collection of poems *My Night with / Mi noche con Federico García Lorca* (1995), the various parts of the book are held together by a title invoking night or its onset (twilight). If night in Jaime Manrique's work signals intense change or metamorphosis, the title "Twilight at the Equator" gestures to a double liminality—one of time (twilight between late afternoon, technically part of daytime, and evening, technically part of night) and another of place, the equator dividing the northern and southern hemispheres from one another. Taken together, the elements of the title also operate in purposeful tension with one another. What does twilight at the equator look like? At twilight, lines of demarcation between one place, person, or thing and another begin to fade. Where does the equator, the imaginary line more or less equidistant from the north and south poles that divides the planet into northern and southern hemispheres, begin or end? What does twilight do to such mappings? What effect does its rapid deepening into oncoming night have on such bearings? The equator has the quickest rates of sunrise and sunset. Twilight is shortest at the equator, a fleeting half-light darkening into night. The opening lines of the first chapter, "To Love in Madrid," suggest that, in great measure, this novel is about losing one's bearings: "I also went to Madrid to self-destruct. . . . Madrid was a place lost in time" (3). In relation to the title of the novel, these opening lines constitute a double form of dis-orientation: readers who pick up a book by a Colombian or U.S.-based Colombian writer with "Equator" in the title hardly expect to be reading about mid-1970s Madrid, Spain. However, the first chapter of the novel titled "To Love in Madrid," is set in Madrid, Barcelona, Cadaques, and Barcelona once again, returning to the United States only in the last two paragraphs of that chapter.

The opening chapter concerns the adventures of a twenty-five-year-old Colombian-born man named Santiago Martínez. Like the remainder of the novel, it is written in the first person—as if it were at least partly autobiography, a feature centrally related to the enterprise of challenging the expected coordinates of the constitution of this particular Colombian Latino self. Whether this novel is autobiography, autobiography disguised as fiction, or fiction disguised as autobiography is not the question most important to the challenge directed at a horizon of expectations about Latina/o autobiography or Latina/o fiction. What matters more, I argue, is the content offered to readers. From the start,

Twilight at the Equator deliberately surprises and disorients. A Colombian-born Latino man goes to "Madrid to self-destruct," all the while drawing inspiration from U.S. non-Latina/o icons of poetry and popular music—"Sylvia Plath, Jimi Hendrix, Janis Joplin" (3). This combination of cultural elements alerts readers to take little for granted. The Plath-like confession "I wanted to immolate myself while writing dazzling scorching poems; like Janis Joplin, I wanted to split from this world with a shattering cry" (3) signals to readers that some break with precedent, both personal and transpersonal, is afoot . . . that the compass needle is spinning around and around in this *Twilight at the Equator.*

In keeping with the book's title, Madrid, Barcelona, and Cadaques are often portrayed at a time between day and night, either at twilight or right before dawn. The first chapter even manages subversively to conscript Franco's early-to-mid 1970s Spain into a queer living at "twilight" and night on the part of this Colombian-born young man beginning to come out and explore his sexuality as a gay man: "Best of all it [Madrid] was safe: one could walk Madrid's streets, avenues, and boulevards at 3:00 AM without fear of any kind of danger" (3). This tentative coming out is not without its problems, however, as the young man Santiago Martínez and his male lovers still cannot be open in Franco-influenced Spain, and their relationships suffer on account of this secrecy. Actually, 1976 Spain, the time at which this first chapter is set, was more a part of the Transition to democracy, as Franco had already died in November of 1975. However, laws regarding the expression of homosexuality and especially social attitudes toward homosexuality had not yet changed much since the Franco years. Despite the remains of the oppression of homosexuality, Santiago writes a first novel, mostly at night, titled, in a Plath-like mode, *Papa's Corpse* (10) that takes revenge on his fascist Colombian father and, furthermore, on his conservative Catholic bourgeois family. The narrator confesses gleefully,

> I worked hard to make the book as sacrilegious as possible: I not only wanted to kill my father, but also to shit on the Catholic Church, Colombian society, and my bourgeois family. The book had the mad insolence of the would-be suicide who has nothing to lose . . . I didn't mind burning all my bridges behind me. (10)

With the exception of the angry tone of revenge, this paragraph and much of the novel *Twilight at the Equator* enact Gilles Deleuze's call for philosophy (and art) to critique and unmoor established values (especially anchoring concepts of Self, God, and the World) and create new values "not yet recognized" (*L'Immanence* 75) or at least not part of dominant culture(s).

At the same time that the character Santiago Martínez is shown rebelling against the fascist father with his impious novel *Papa's Corpse*, he is also teaching English "as a second language" (3) posing as a "Chicano from Texas" (4):

> The director [of the Instituto Inglés in Madrid] hired me with the condition that I impersonate a native speaker, a Chicano. Monday through Friday, from 10 to 2, I posed as a Chicano from Texas to my highly suspicious students (Madrid matrons and middle-aged businessmen) who bombarded me with questions about Texas. . . . I learned to improvise quickly, fearlessly, since all I knew about Texas I had learned from the [the James Dean] movie *Giant*. (4)

A Colombian-born young man posing as a Chicano from Texas for matrons and businessmen, some of whom want to learn Texan English so that they can work for Exxon in Texas (8), cuts a complicated cultural figure. On one level, it parodies those members of the Spanish middle and upper-middle classes who have bought into a U.S. capitalist value system in which profit at the expense of other issues is the bottom line. Santiago Martínez finds these students repulsive (8). Eventually he cannot bring himself to sustain, on their behalf, his pose of a Texan Chicano. One morning in class he snaps at them "I'm Colombian, not Chicano" (8) and declares that he hopes never to visit Texas, "a hideous place" (8).

The episode of a Colombian-born man posing as a Chicano from Texas becomes even more culturally complicated in terms of how *Twilight at the Equator* intervenes in the understanding of what constitutes "Latina/o" and in a new unfolding polis, the polis of Latinidades, a deliberate fiction. On first examination, Santiago Martínez's exasperated revelation to his Madrid students that he is not a Chicano but a Colombian would seem to contradict and fly in the face of the identity-blurring plasticity, multiplicity, and liminality I have been emphasizing as part and parcel of the delirium of oncoming night as technique. The episode would seem to defy and negate altogether the concepts of pan-Latina/o and trans-Latina/o Latinidades. The narrator appears to be drawing a line in the sand between Colombian and Chicano—asserting that he is not Chicano, but Colombian. The episode might actually have the effect of offending some or many Chicana/os who might conclude that the depiction of them as Texas-drawling English speakers not only parodies the conservative bourgeois ESL students in Madrid soon after Franco's death but also casts Texas-based Chicana/os in a dubious light as potentially too assimilated, as *vendidos*. Detectable in Santiago Martínez's rejection of his Chicano pose—and the possibility of being confused for a Chicano—is a Latin American's distaste for being confused with those U.S.-ian Latin Americans termed "Latina/os." The narrator does not refer to himself as a Latino but rather as a "Latin American": "For a Latin American writer there was no more attractive place than Barcelona in those years" (19). The evidence would seem to amass against the construction of pan-Latinidades or trans-Latinidades in this chapter of *Twilight at the Equator*. Even Latin American writers are shown not getting along. The narrative reports that it was in Barcelona, Spain, that the Peruvian Vargas Llosa gave the Colombian García Marquez a black eye (19). Santiago Martínez's desire to "immolate [him]self while writing" and "to split from this world with a shattering cry" (3) manifests itself in a strong misanthropic, deconstructive tendency.

However, there are other ways of reading the episode in which a Colombian taken for Chicano asserts his Colombian identity as well as the remarks about the rivalries between Latin American writers from different countries and, moreover, with different politics. The novel *Twilight at the Equator* underscores the heterogeneity of Latinidades, the existence of Latinidades that cannot be represented by any one group. Even Colombians differ from one another in terms of class, gender, sexuality, politics, ethno-racial categorization, geographical location, and so forth, as is patently obvious in the rest of the narrative, particularly in chapters 2 ("Papa's Corpse") and 4 ("Twilight at the Equator"). The novel emphasizes heterogeneity to such an extent that one may well wonder if one can speak in terms of pan-Latinidades as trans-Latinidades because these terms would seem to imply some kind of collective awareness or making of a common cause despite difference. Despite the splitting and strongly differentiating tendencies as well as the full-blown rebellious, suicidal gestures (even the evidence of the self is thrown into question), the novel extends awareness of varieties of Latin American presence in Europe and the United States—and of Latinidades, whether primarily or only occasionally U.S.-based.

"Latin American" shades into "Latina/o" when the United States is involved. Of the five chapters, chapter 3 ("The Documentary Artist") and chapter 5 ("The Day Carmen Maura Kissed Me") are set exclusively in New York City, and the other three chapters all mention the narrator's connection to the United States. For example, chapter 1 ("To Love in Madrid") contains the sentence, "A few years later, we met again in Gotham [New York City]" (37). Chapter 2 ("Papa's Corpse") recounts that the narrator was in a "boarding school in Connecticut" and spent an afternoon in Manhattan (42). The narrator has a wife at one point although he is also a homosexual, one of the many details that complicate notions of a unitary, stable identity in this novel. His wife Beatrice has a grandfather who was named ambassador to Washington, DC (54), and a cousin who was a student at Georgetown University (55). Beatrice's mother is an American psychiatrist (56). The narrator served as Colombian consul in Florida with the help of his wife's family's connections (61). Back in Colombia, caught between his secret life as a homosexual married man and pressure from Beatrice's family, who have made much of their fortune on the drug trade between Colombia and the United States, the narrator, by the end of the story, seems poised to run off to the United States to escape the roles his wife's family wants him to play. Chapter 4 ("Twilight at the Equator") begins in Jackson Heights, the particularly Colombian part of New York City, with the suicide of the narrator's "sister" (his mother's half sister), Rosita. The narrator's grief over both the death of his lover Ryan from AIDS and Rosita from "scores of Valiums" (107) and slashed wrists prompts him to reconnect with his Colombian past. He flies from New York City to Barranquilla, Colombia, where he spends time visiting family in Barranquilla (on the north coast of Colombia) and then takes a "tiny two-engine plane" (141) to El Banco, "the ancestral home of [his] mother's family" toward the interior "along the Magdalena River" (141). From there, he travels to Barranco before returning to Barranquilla and finally to New York City. In each place in Colombia that he visits, Santiago the narrator sees members of his extended family. He states that his "American exile was obliterated" and he "experienced a happiness unlike any other I had ever known" at the sight of "the snow-capped peaks of the Sierra Nevada . . . as if out of the vision of a luminist, transcendental painter" (149). The line simultaneously cancels out the narrator's experience and transculturates one "America" into the other by invoking the Central and South American landscapes of Anglo-American painters such as Frederic Edwin Church and Martin Johnson Heade who employed luminist techniques.

Chapter 4, with the same title as the novel itself, is the longest chapter of all. It portrays an epic voyage from New York City back to various personally significant places in Colombia and ends with the anticipation of returning to New York City. The narrator's relationship to both the United States and Colombia is complicated and fluctuates depending on mood and socio-political circumstances. The most revealing moments of his liminal, in-between, transculturating relationship to both places as a Latin American and a Colombian Latino are bound up with startling representations of night. His ambivalence toward Colombian and South American histories more generally comes across in his childhood memory of the fate of a woman in Barranquilla "who died in a doctor's office during an abortion" (124) and whose body the doctor hacked into numerous pieces and dumped out of a car on the way to the coast:

> In fact, I hadn't thought about it since it [the incident] happened thirty-five years ago. *But as night fell from the Caribbean to the Equator* over the Amazonian jungle, above the icy peaks of the volcanoes of the Andes, all the way to Patagonia, to

the bleak, glacial regions of Tierra del Fuego, this image, this memory, burst through the fortress of denial with such violence that I sat on the rocking chair in a trance, shivering, sweating a cold sweat. [emphasis mine] (124)

Traditionally, nations have been and still are figured as women. In the Spanish language, even the word "fatherland" is gendered feminine: *la patria*. Jaime Manrique's invocation of a woman—in this case, the literally and horrifically fragmented body of a woman—to express his grief over the history of socio-political oppression in his native country and the continent of South America as a whole is a conventional move, however suddenly the image seems to arise. What I find especially significant, however, is that this image of horror—the disemboweled and dismembered woman to signify socio-political oppression in South American—occurs to the narrator at twilight turning into night, during the delirium of night. In fact, the only antidote to this terrifyingly dark memory is night itself:

I could not break the spell until some time later when the tropical sky glowed with shimmering stars the size of planets, and a moon as gigantic and luminous as the midnight sun of artic [*sic*] summer poised herself in the night sky, not just as a light fixture, a deity to be worshipped, but as an object of desire. (125)

This transformation of horror to romance and promise—the moon an object of desire as bright as a midnight sun—fore-illuminates, rather than foreshadows, the ending of the longest chapter, "Twilight at the Equator." Toward the end of this chapter, the narrator visits his uncle Carlos before returning to the United States. This uncle Carlos, who lives on the outskirts of Barranquilla, is very wealthy. The narrator, in the process of visiting so many of his relatives, discovers that his uncle made his money not only "with his refining factories" (174) but through the drug trade, as part of the Colombian drug cartels (176). His visit to his uncle's place turns into a confrontation with this violent and homophobic man. The narrator barely escapes his uncle's compound, but he is glad that he risked his life to confront his uncle with what he really feels about him—that he is indeed an evil man, not admirable. Walking away from the compound, the narrator thinks about how he will soon be returning to New York City, "to the place that for the first time looked like home to me" (188). The last sentence in this chapter reads,

As I loped down the road, under the starry equatorial sky, I knew that coming back home had freed me from the tyranny of dreaming of returning to the sullied paradise I had left as a boy, for which now I could cease to yearn. (188)

This other intense image of night—under a starry equatorial sky, loping away from the compound of the evil uncle—partially resolves the ambivalence toward both Americas or toward New York City and the northeast section of Colombia in favor of an existence in the United States or at least in New York City, a Latin American city outside of Latin America.

The fifth and last chapter, "The Day Carmen Maura Kissed Me," further materializes this ambiguous resolution, as the United States could certainly be considered yet another "sullied paradise." The last chapter intimates as much with its references to class stratification (196), crack addicts, and puddles of piss in the streets (198). Nevertheless, the chapter and the novel end after the magical moment of having seen the Spanish actress Carmen Maura taping a program on the streets of New York and after having had drinks with Colombian film buff friends. The narrator walks home in the New York City twilight with "night not far behind" (197). In the slipstream of oncoming night, the narrator feels himself transculturated between happiness and sadness, "happy and sad in the same breath" (198). The sadness is for "all that was sad in this wide, mysterious world we tread upon" (198). The "unreasonable happiness" is "produced by the tinsel gleam of the glamorous dreams that had brought me to America" and that continue to bring so many others, from Latin America and the rest of the world, despite betrayals of those dreams, despite their "heartbreaking ... fleetingness" (198).

By the end of the novel, the narrator is not unequivocally a Latin American exile. Instead, he thinks of the United States as a place that while not necessarily home, "for the first time looked like home to me" (188). This "looked like home" is a significant phrase that could be interpreted as an attempt to move away from the mental self-conception and stance of a nostalgic exile pining for the country he has left to become someone able to adapt a variety of places to his or her needs. Both the first chapter ("To Love in Madrid") and the last chapter ("The Day Carmen Maura Kissed Me") place the narrator and readers in contemplation of Spain (Madrid, Barcelona, and Cadaques of the mid 1970s) and of a Spanish actress who became very well known the world over for her starring roles in gay, post-Transition Spanish film director Pedro Almodóvar's films in the 1980s and 1990s: Carmen Maura. By prominently introducing Spain, a third geopolitical/geo-cultural space apart from the Americas but historically related to the Americas as a former colonial power, as a medium through which the narrator works out some of his conflicts both with his home country (Colombia) and his other home or what "looked like home" (the United States), the novel *Twilight at the Equator* widens the scope of and for the formation of Latina/o subjectivities. First of all, on the most obvious level, it widens the scope of Latinidades by concentrating on the historical, cultural, and geopolitical experience of Latina/os who are not part of the three groups of Latina/os who have received the most attention under the rubric "Latina/o"— Mexican Americans, Puerto Ricans, and Cuban Americans. Instead, *Twilight at the Equator* focuses on the experiences of a Colombian-born person who is no longer a permanent resident of Colombia. Historically, many Colombians have emigrated not only to the United States but to Spain as well. The novel underscores these two sometimes intersecting Colombian diasporas to the United States and to Spain in chapters 1 and 5, the first and the last. This double axis for the destinations and experiences of Colombian exiles complicates conceptions of "Latin American," "Latina/o," and "Latinidades," especially for the U.S.-based reader, who may be accustomed to reading narratives about Latin Americans coming to the United States and partly assimilating to or at least accommodating to U.S. Anglo dominant culture. Or if the stories are not about Latin Americans transitioning to the United States, then they are generally about U.S.-born Latina/os attempting to negotiate a particular ethnicized (usually Mexican, Puerto Rican, and/or Cuban) "minority status" generally in the southwest border zones (including California), Chicago, or the cities of the Northeast (usually New York City). *Twilight at the Equator* does not follow the familiar templates of the Latin American negotiating the United States or the U.S.-born Latina/o struggling against her or his marginalization and eventually gaining a place for her/himself in relation to the promises of the American dream. Although the novel concludes with a long sentence that alludes to the American dream or at least to dreaming in "America" (by which the narrator means not the Americas plural but the United States)—"the unreasonable happiness produced by the tinsel gleam of the glamorous dreams that had brought me to America" and that in "heartbreaking . . . fleetingness . . . became real" (198)—most of the novel has not taken place exclusively in the United States despite the scattered references to it.

Although all the chapters mention the United States, and chapters 3 ("The Documentary Artist") and 5 ("The Day Carmen Maura Kissed Me") are set entirely in the United States, the chapter most intensively centered in the United States, chapter 3, manages to build a surprising resistance to traditional assimilation (that of Latina/o to Anglo-American culture) into its scenarios. In chapter 3, the narrator is a professor teaching film-directing classes at a university in New York City. Details form close autobiographical parallels with Jaime Manrique's actual life as a professor, for a time, in the MFA program at Columbia University. The focus of the account is on one of his students—not a Latino, but rather, a young man from New Hampshire with an Anglo-sounding or Anglicized name

(Sebastian) from blue-collar parents who pin all their hopes for economic bet-terment and social advancement on their son. Instead, Sebastian, though bril-liant and potentially an excellent student, becomes homeless and a drug addict. Yet he also produces an experimental autobiographical film, an adaptation of the early twentieth-century Austro-Hungarian writer Franz "Kafka's *The Hun-ger* [sic] *Artist*" (95), about his own dropping out of society and dropping away from a bourgeois pursuit of the American dream. The narrator confesses his fas-cination—even somewhat pedagogically taboo romantic obsession—with this student dropout and admires the student's refusal to assimilate into or conform to the system. The narrator's admiration constitutes a significant twist on either assimilationist or accommodationist narratives about Latina/o experiences in the United States. Readers witness a now middle-aged, relatively successful Latino professor at a U.S. university identifying with a non-Latino dropout and experimental artist rebelling against the pursuit of success, property, financial security, and a life commonly associated with the American dream of upward mobility. Not only does the dropout rebel against and reject the American Dream altogether, he also produces an experimental and form-imploding docu-mentary titled "THE HUNGER ARTIST, BY SEBASTIAN X. INSPIRED BY THE STORY OF MR. FRANZ KAFKA" (103). The documentary is "autobiographical" in a perfor-mative way. It fuses performance and autobiography by filming Sebastian during a hunger strike he embarks on, a hunger strike that literally kills him. The film captures his deterioration from starvation as well as his self-chosen homeless-ness. Other characters appear in the film: a woman with "long green hair" and "lots of mascara," a man in a three-piece suit, and a buxom blonde "bedecked with huge costume jewelry" who eats and drinks throughout her time on screen (104). They are like characters from a John Waters film. They are his audience, preposterously watching his very real performance of starvation and showing their approval. Actually, Sebastian plays all the parts (104). This act of playing all the characters demonstrates just how experimental this "autobiographical" documentary is. It also reveals another implosion of boundaries and the crossing of demarcations between self and other, including the Deleuzian transformative dissolution of the Self that readers glimpse throughout *Twilight at the Equator* in different forms and situations, beginning when the narrator himself proclaims, "I also went to Madrid to self-destruct . . . I wanted to split from this world with a shattering cry" (3). The narrator's strong identification with as well as desire for Sebastian ("I could not deny anymore that I had been in love with Sebastian," 103) coupled with the fact that he too creates a documentary about homeless-ness "shown by some public television stations to generally good reviews but low ratings" (102) further reinforces, at multiple levels, a boundary-dissolving transculturation between self and other—in this case, between a middle-aged Colombian-born U.S. resident who is by now a well-established professor and a lower-middle to middle-class Anglo student who refuses to conform to the dominant culture's signifiers of success.

In terms of models of Latinidades, the identification of Santiago with Sebastian, who questions and critiques the American dream and assimilation that disregards the situation of millions for whom the dream is not plausible or possible—for whom the dream exists only as a horror film or a nightmare—introduces new, subversive definitions of assimilation not posited on conformity, fitting in, belonging, or integration, but rather, quite literally, on disintegration. If the Anglo young man chooses homelessness, chooses "not to integrate" (101), and Anglo is the cultural default to which Latina/os have been expected to conform, then what are the implications of a Latino or a Latina choosing not to integrate by, among other tactics, exposing the discontent and nay-saying within Anglo-American culture? Chapter 3 of *Twilight at the Equator*—"The Documentary Artist"—gives readers a glimpse of what that refusal on the part of a Latin American–cum–Latino feels like, how resisting the mollifying promises of the American dream and pointing up its heartless contradictions might play out. Santiago, the narrator, concludes his account with this nocturnal image: "As I passed them [the homeless] in the dark streets . . . the phantasmagorical lament of the arctic wind sweeping over the Hudson, powerless over the mammoth steel structures of this city [New York]" (105).

The narrator's night walk through the late-autumn streets of New York City brings chapter 3 to a close. This nocturnal walk on which the narrator encounters the homeless on the dark, cold streets of the city is preceded by a viewing of Sebastian's film "The Hunger Artist" while evening turns into nighttime. It is this night viewing of Sebastian's film of his own demise, homelessness, and eradication of self, which is further accomplished by mixing in "footage of people in soup lines and the homeless scavenging in garbage cans" (105), that brings the narrator to a shattering realization that recalls an initial self-immolating motive in chapter 1, "To Love in Madrid": "I felt shattered by the realization that what I don't know about what lies in my own heart is greater than anything else I do know about it" (105). This statement lends a particular conceptual content to the delirium of oncoming night already transmitted in the episodes of watching Sebastian's film during evening and night and walking the icy late-autumn streets of New York City. That conceptual content deconstructs the semi-autobiographical mode of the novel *Twilight at the Equator* by suggesting that what is not known about oneself (and others) is much more powerful than what is known. This realization keeps open, unfinished, and beyond fixed positions self, other, and any group or collective identity such as a particular version of Latinidades. Metamorphosis entails an unfolding darkness of the unknown. In this unfolding darkness, Santiago, as both subject and subjectivity, maintains a volatile interstitiality. No one place, even the United States to which he returns, claims him completely. He reserves the right to "self-destruct," "to split from this world [any given place] with a shattering cry," and to be multiple selves: a Colombian exile in Spain, Colombia itself, and the United States; a young man trying to live as a homosexual; a homosexual married man trying to figure out what he must do with his life so as not to be a prisoner of other people's expectations; a professor identifying with a dropout and a rebel instead of with an academic success story; and a Latino who is not Chicano, Puerto Rican, or Cuban American but Colombian and yet for whom that subject position cannot be taken for granted among either Colombians or non-Colombians. Santiago, or rather Jaime Manrique through Santiago, like Sebastian to a great extent, has plural selves. Like Sebastian, he takes a perverse pleasure in the risk of immolating himself for the sake of the greater cultural and aesthetic experiment that is *Twilight at the Equator.*

The cultural producers whose work I have discussed up to the present moment in this study have been based within the geographical boundaries of the United States. Their narratives have either stayed within the confines of U.S. territory or, if they have unfolded elsewhere, have returned to or ended up in the United States. However, this last chapter on "Transcultural Night Work of U.S.-Based South American Cultural Producers" is fundamentally about challenges to more established and traditional moorings of Latinidades with the United States and with Mexican Americans, Puerto Ricans, and Cuban Americans within the United States. Thus far, the chapter has demonstrated how U.S.-based Chilean writer Mariana Romo-Carmona's 1998 collection of stories *Speaking Like an Immigrant* extends the practice of "living at night," amply illustrated in her earlier 1997 novel by that title, to challenge the geopolitics of the location of culture, to break with the conventional boundaries of Latinidad, and to extend the familiar boundaries of "Latina/o" beyond Mexico, Puerto Rico, and Cuba and beyond assimilation to U.S.-centricity. Her work offers readers models and scenarios for how to keep "speaking like an immigrant" and sociopolitical reasons why such a project is valid and important. Meanwhile, Colombian U.S.-based Jaime Manrique's 2003 novel *Twilight at the Equator* and his earlier 1995 collection of poems *My Night with / Mi noche con Federico García Lorca* both, in their respective and related ways, pass identity, nationality, ethnicity, and cultural affiliation through the "delirium of oncoming night." They cultivate this delirium of night as a counter-strategy against assimilation into or even accommodation to a majoritarian, phobic sphere that insists on know-able and enforceable boundaries among nationalities, ethnicities, and other kinds of positionalities. Instead, this delirium of night entails losing oneself in a new, unfolding polis: the polis of Latinidades, a polis assembled by the books themselves. Both the collection of poems and the novel extend awareness of varieties of Latin American presence in Europe and the United States and of Latinidades, whether primarily or only occasionally U.S.-based. This extension is not merely mimetic—reflecting already existing realities—but, rather, also projectively constructivist in widening the scope of and for the formation of Latina/o subjectivities. *Twilight at the Equator* (2003) manages to build surpris-ing resistances to traditional assimilation (that of Latina/o to Anglo-American culture) into its scenarios, as when Jaime Manrique, through his alter ego narra-tor Santiago (for whom the rebelling Anglo Sebastian is yet another nested alter ego), takes a perverse pleasure in the risk of immolating the self for the sake of the greater cultural and aesthetic experiment that is *Twilight at the Equator.*

The works of U.S.-based Chilean writer Mariana Romo-Carmona and U.S.-based Colombian writer Jaime Manrique break with the precedents established by many Latina/o texts (usually Mexican American, mainland Puerto Rican, and/or Cuban American) and, of course, with the expectations of the dominant Anglo-American culture. They elaborate and, I claim, advocate a transcultural aesthetics that conveys a politics of not letting go of an immigrant and "out-lier" stance. Their conception of Latina/o identity resists the gradual process of Americanization that entails any number of socio-cultural changes, such as those shown in Puerto Rican writer Esmeralda Santiago's *When I Was a Puerto Rican* (1994), Cuban American writer Oscar Hijuelos's *The Mambo Kings Play Songs of Love* (1990), or Mexican American writer Richard Rodriguez's *Hunger of Memory: The Education of Richard Rodriguez* (1981). In each of these works, the primary cultural movement is one from Mexico, Puerto Rico, or Cuba to the mainland United States, where the protagonists struggle to achieve success and inscribe themselves in the American dream as Latina/os of particular ethnicities but not necessarily as subjects who continue to identify as immigrants or who actively rebel against or deconstruct the dominant culture's codes of acceptance or success. This is not to say that a work such as Esmeralda Santiago's *When I Was a Puerto Rican* glosses over the high price and the losses entailed in such assimila-tion. Even Richard Rodriguez's narrative attests to a profound sense of pain and loss. Esmeralda Santiago's memoir is geopolitically pointed, however. It contains a critique of the neocolonial policies of the United States toward Puerto Rico.

Night works by Latina/o cultural producers are much more likely to rebel against or deconstruct the dominant culture's codes of acceptance and success.

The ones that I examine in this chapter do so with particular intensity, to the point, in Manrique's 2003 *Twilight at the Equator,* of self-immolation. That is, even among the night work of Latina/o cultural producers with which this book is concerned, Mariana Romo-Carmona's 1998 volume *Speaking Like an Immigrant* and Jaime Manrique's 2003 *Twilight at the Equator* stand out for the degree to which Latinidad is represented through and by a transculturation without the usual U.S.-centric *telos* and also without the usual focus on one ethnic group within the Latina/o umbrella rubric.

That such texts are by Latina/os of specifically South American origin (Chile, Colombia, etc.) might be coincidental. I suggest, however, that this correlation between intensely transculturated texts and Latina/o cultural producers of South American origin is more than coincidental. It is part of a cultural logic constructed by responses to the demographics of diaspora of particular Latina/o populations in relation to other Latina/o populations and to perceptions (or misperceptions) of these populations by the dominant culture. As is well known, Mexican Americans, Puerto Ricans, and Cuban Americans have been the most demographically numerous groups of Latina/o Americans on U.S. soil. People from other "Latin American" countries (this term is misleading as, technically, Mexico is part of North America) have been less numerous and less concentrated in the United States—though that is changing, especially with respect to Dominicans from the Caribbean and Salvadoreños from Central America as well as other Central Americans, such as Guatemalans and Nicaraguans. South Americans from countries such as Venezuela, Colombia, Ecuador, Peru, Chile, Argentina, Paraguay, and Uruguay constitute the minority of Latina/os in the United States taken country by country. Furthermore, their countries do not lie adjacent to the United States as do Mexico and Cuba. After all, a third of the United States was once Mexico before the termination of the Mexican-American War of 1846–1848. Nor are these countries part of U.S. territory as is Puerto Rico, a commonwealth of the United States. Finally, the countries of "South America" have not been occupied by U.S. troops and intelligence units to quite the same extent as countries such as Guatemala, Panama, Nicaragua, and El Salvador, though Colombia and Bolivia see their fair share of U.S. intervention under the aegis of the so-called war on drugs. South Americans and South American countries are more distant on any number of counts from the U.S. mainland and its border zone and extended offshore politics. As of the early twenty-first century, South Americans are also less represented by rubrics of more typically U.S.-centric Latinidades that are inflected by the interests and concerns of Mexican Americans, mainland and island Puerto Ricans, and Cuban Americans. On the whole, this entails a greater invisibility and a less recognizable group identity in the United States both as "Latina/os" and by dominant Anglo-American mainstream culture. While in some cases South Americans living in the United States may enjoy a higher socioeconomic status than many Mexican Americans or Puerto Ricans, from the perspective of factors pertaining to cultural representation, they may be less established, left to their own experimental devices. Texts such as Romo-Carmona's *Speaking Like an Immigrant* (1998) or Manrique's *Twilight at the Equator* (2003) furnish evidence that South American U.S.-based cultural producers are indeed compelled toward the experimental expression of an intensified transculturality that does not resolve itself in becoming American (U.S.-ian) Latina/os. Instead, the transculturation these texts offer is one in which the audience must immerse itself in experiences of various parts of South America as well as of other inter-related cultures, sometimes more so than in experiences on U.S. soil. I hasten to add, however, that the representation of these other experiences (not on U.S. soil) are written with U.S. audiences in mind—that is, for an American reader/viewer. This U.S.-ian addressee is implied in details of various sections of the works by Romo-Carmona and Manrique—for instance, in the piece "Speaking Like an Immigrant" that I analyzed as challenging U.S.-ian indifference to both the variety and the specificity of the South American continent, or in the way that Manrique eventually brings the voyaging Santiago Martínez to the United States in order to comment, through his interactions with other characters, on the limitations of the American dream or the emptiness of assimilation.

I should clarify that this transcultural night work functions as a particular aesthetic intensification of a broader phenomenon that is apparent in Latina/o writing from the late 1990s onward with the vast increase of recent immigration from Latin America, South America included. More people in the United States are arriving from a plethora of Latin American countries and maintaining ties with their countries of origins in the form of spoken and written language; internet, television, and radio venues; remittances (money earned in the United States and sent back to the country of origin); and multiple border crossings for work and to maintain personal connections. As this occurs, U.S.-centric models of and for Latinidad cede their pre-eminence as a praxis for the construction of an American or hyphenated American identity within the United States.

The Refracted Night of the Transculturated Study of Latinidades

This chapter has been concerned with an intensification of transculturation both in the objects of study (Romo-Carmona's, Manrique's, Alarcón's, and Jiménez Cahua's work) and also in the paradigm of analysis proffered by the chapter itself.

By the phrase "refracted night" I seek to call attention once again to the principle of refraction. The basic action of refraction involves deflection of a propagating wave (in this case, of the deployment of night rather than light or sound) at the boundary or border between different mediums (in our case, geographical/geopolitical locations) with different refractive indices (cultural contexts). Whether speaking in terms of physics or astronomy, refraction involves deflection—a deviation from a previously charted or expected course. Indeed, departing from the geographical boundaries of the United States within U.S.-based cultural productions constitutes a deflection from the more traditional, U.S.-centric elaborations of Latina/o identities and concerns discussed in other sections of my book *Buenas Noches, American Culture: Latina/o Aesthetics of Night*. Yet a careful analysis of the full transculturality of signs, verbal and visual, reveals that rather than a deflection away from U.S.-based Latina/o studies, the examination of these productions incites questions that simultaneously complement and extend more U.S.-focused Latina/o studies. This type of examination opens up an opportunity to understand the uses of night in a transnational context that nevertheless reflect back on Latina/o uses of night in a U.S.-centric context. One of the more important insights to emerge from a refracted night of transculturated Latinidades in a novel such as Daniel Alarcón's *Lost City Radio* concerns the historical, socioeconomic, and cultural experiences of coloniality that different Latin American groups have acquired or accumulated within their countries of origin even before they reach the shores or inlands of the United States. Awareness and knowledge of this refracted night are crucial for gaining a more nuanced and wide-ranging appreciation of the intersecting spectra of Latina/o experiences, cultural productions, and political concerns in the United States. The paradigm I have been elaborating in this section on the refracted night of the transculturated study of Latinidades may propel scholars and observers more generally to view the interrelation of history, sociology, and cultural production of regions of the Americas in new lights and shadows. When thinking of migration to the United States from the global south, scholars and other interested parties will also have in mind internal migrations within Latin America and within and among the countries of South America in particular. Questions will arise as to the complex interactions between these geopolitical movements.

Two of the more salient examples of this refracted night of the transculturated study of Latinidades that manifest a strong departure from the geographical boundaries of the United States are Daniel Alarcón's 2007 novel *Lost City Radio* and the portion of Carlos Jiménez Cahua's photographs of twenty-first-century Lima, Peru, that were shot at night. These works do more than depart from the geographical boundaries of the United States. They are set elsewhere, very deliberately elsewhere, though, I argue, this displacement is one calculated in relation to U.S. viewers and readers. The city of Alarcón's novel is unnamed, but many of the narrative details suggest that it is modeled on Lima, Peru, and that the country in question is Peru. Some of the districts of this unnamed city as well as the surrounding environs are remindful of other parts of the world such as West Africa, Palestine, and Bosnia. One district of the vast, sprawling city of Alarcón's novel is called Tamoé, a name with a real-world counterpart in Guinea, West Africa.[16] Not only is *Lost City Radio* set beyond the geographical boundaries of the United States with locations that take U.S. readers out of their comfort zone but, moreover, the novel mostly focuses on the lives of ordinary and poor people in a vast war-torn city and in a thick jungle. The descriptions of upper-middle class and upper-class people's lives are few and far between. Places and people of *Lost City Radio* are not in hegemonic positions vis-à-vis the United States, Western Europe, or even the unnamed globalized city of an unnamed South American country.

Likewise, not only are Jiménez Cahua's 2007–2010 photographs of Lima located outside of the United States but, furthermore, the subject matter pertains largely to what lies outside the city center or the "Cercado de Lima," outside "what Pizarro saw of the city or even . . . the city at the beginning of the 20th century."[17] The slightly more than five percent of the photographs that were shot at night contrast heavily with those done during the day, in which an opaque white veil of a sky renders the scenes strangely monotonous. The approximately fifty photographs in the series *Ciudad de los Reyes* generally depict the city's peripheries or edges, that which does not pertain to the city's monuments and landmarks of colonial and neocolonial wealth, power, and prestige. As Jiménez Cahua has indicated to me,

> The images were made mostly in the periphery of Lima, but still within the city limits. Most of the images come from the southern areas of the city like Villa María del Triunfo, Chorrillos, San Juan de Miraflores and Villa El Salvador, but I've also made images in the other parts of the city, as far east as Pachacamac, in the north, Los Olivos and even the (only recently) autonomous city of Callao. The above names the districts (*distritos*), but the neighborhoods (*urbanizaciones*) vary perhaps even more. In any case, many whole districts like Villa El Salvador, despite containing many *urbanizaciones* and being a city in every way except technically, are collectively considered *pueblos jóvenes*.[18]

Pueblos jóvenes translates into "young towns." They compose Lima's peripheries, the outskirts of the outskirts, where the city meets the desert. These young towns sprang up in the 1970s or later as a result of the migration of vast numbers of people from the overcrowded areas of Lima's inner city and also from the places in the country beyond the city. As Jiménez Cahua has described to me,

> The district of Villa El Salvador [for example] was inhabited only in the early 1970s, before which it had simply been an expansive desert as still surrounds today's Lima. People from the more crowded areas of the inner city "invaded" the area overnight (literally, in some cases) and refused to leave when threatened by police and government officials. Ultimately, the efforts of these squatters were successful (if measured by the simple goal of having property unto themselves), and the district grew into what it is today. This is generally the pattern other *pueblos jóvenes* have followed, and it still exists today: one can still go to the edge of the inhabited area of a *pueblo jóven* (that is, the outskirts of the outskirts of Lima), build a small home made of a plywood-like material, demarcate the border of property and it's his (all but officially, that is). Certainly, this is prohibited by both the law and suspicious neighbors, but it doesn't stop it from happening still. Indeed, Limeans often comment on how quickly the hills and areas surrounding them become occupied (even from one year to the next).[19]

According to Jiménez Cahua, the center of Lima is "dwarfed in size and population by the center's periphery, largely composed of these *pueblos jóvenes,* where the city's population is concentrated (a figure that has nearly doubled in the last thirty years to nine million)."[20] Not everyone living in the *pueblos jóvenes* is poor. Jiménez Cahua clarifies, "the people living there range from penniless to (upper) middle class, but, in any case, today's typical *Limeño* is a denizen of these areas, a fact surprising to no Limean himself, but only to the visitors with cosmetic knowledge of the city, thinking that the limits of their guided tours were limits of the city."[21] However, as I will discuss in further detail later on in relation to his nocturnal images, Jiménez Cahua's photographic representations of a supposedly third-world city in the twenty-first century challenge U.S.-centric notions of urbanism. As Jiménez Cahua has remarked about the dominance of the earth, the desert, and the hills in and around the urban peripheries so much larger than Lima center, "The earth remains visible if not nearly unaltered despite their development. . . . The people of Lima quite literally merely scratch the surface—their relationship to the ground is not one of dominance, but of acquiescence."[22]

Perceiving Night in Daniel Alarcón's Novel *Lost City Radio* and Carlos Jiménez Cahua's *Ciudad de los Reyes*

Alarcón's tripartite, fifteen-chapter novel about an unnamed South American city transformed by an ongoing civil war between its government and insurgents whom the government deems terrorists contains over twenty key scenes of night—an average of six or seven night scenes per section. The novel concerns the denizens of the war-torn and traumatized city of missing, murdered, and lost people. With its strange white "opaline glaze" (40) of sky during the day that washes out the colors of the environment; its "sprawling and impenetrably dense" districts given names such as "Newtown" reminiscent of the term "*pueblos jóvenes*" (72); its "desolate" city beaches with its "lonely expanses of windswept sand beneath crumbling bluffs" (105); its "Great Blackouts spread across the capital" (148); its militarized, embattled condition remindful of the repressive government response to the most active years (1980–1992) of the militant Maoist Marxist organization *El Sendero Luminoso* or The Shining Path and its allies, who were willing to employ violence to oppose capitalism and revisionist socialism; and the constant reminders of the striking relationship between the city and the land beyond it, the "lost city" of *Lost City Radio* closely resembles Lima, especially Lima of the 1980s and early 1990s. While conveying a sense of conditions affecting millions of people, the novel focuses on the way the ongoing civil war has shaped a cast of deeply interconnected characters. These characters include the radio announcer Norma, who runs a talk radio show commemorating the missing and reconnecting people separated by the war and by the human rights violations perpetrated by both the government and the subversives; Norma's missing young botany professor husband Rey who gets caught up in subversive activity against the government and has a double life not only as another person but in the jungle; Rey's mistress in the jungle, Adela, with whom he has a son, Victor; Adela, the other woman, who slips on the jungle river's rocks one dark night, loses consciousness, and drowns; Victor, who appears at Norma's radio station as a penniless orphan in need of someone to care for him; Elmer, who runs the radio station and has a long-standing unrequited crush on Norma; Elijah Manau, Victor's mediocre and weak-willed teacher who brings him out of the jungle where he was born and abandons him in the city; Zahir, the government informant who fancies himself a poet and who is ultimately responsible for Rey's capture and murder; Yerevan, a radio personality at the station where Norma works who is accused "of treason and collaboration" (169) with the subversives and is disappeared; and Blas, the artist who draws portraits of the missing by listening to verbal descriptions given to him by those desperate enough to believe that his draw-ings will make a difference.

The more than twenty night scenes form the emotional spine of the book. They jump backward and forward in time and are presented out of chronologi-cal order. The first scene involves the first night Norma and Victor, Rey's son by another woman, are thrown together and wind up in a part of the city that the ongoing war has rendered unrecognizable (12–14). The second night scene pertains to the night that Norma and Rey first met "through mutual friends at a dance" (15). The third encapsulates all the nights since his disappearance that Norma lies awake, caught "in that netherworld between life and death" (38) remembering her husband Rey and being filled with dread. The fourth is not a night scene in the usual sense but rather an extended description of the government-run prison that is named none other than "the Moon" (40) and that harbors many captured members of the insurgency movement (40–48). The fifth returns readers to the nocturnal solitude of Norma's apartment height-ened by the unexpected presence of the abandoned orphan Victor (48–49). The sixth travels back in time to Rey's early teen years and "the moonless night" (51) when he and some other boys got drunk and threw rocks at their school, which resulted in Rey's being accused of exploding a homemade bomb inside the mayor's office (51) that same night because he was spotted near the scene of the crime stumbling around drunk "with a dark bandanna covering his nose and mouth" (56). This night scene foreshadows his eventual murder for his undercover, somewhat unwilling and furtive, collaboration with the insurgents later in his life. The seventh night scene unfolds when Rey takes Norma on an extended walking tour of some of the city's poor neighborhoods outside of her more middle-class socioeconomic bracket. The novel's descriptive language underscores the relation between these neighborhoods and the earth along the lines of Jiménez Cahua's photographs of the *pueblos jóvenes:* "Neighborhoods like these are networks of impulses, Rey said, human, electrical, biological, like the forest . . . [l]ike in the mountains" (65). The eighth night scene concerns the evening that Elijah Manau, Victor's teacher, obliquely seduces Adela, Rey's mistress and the mother to his child (92–93). The ninth scene involves some of Manau's memories of Adela and, in particular, the river at night in which she drowns (144). The tenth nocturnal reference is to the "Great Blackouts across the capital" during the war years (148). The eleventh is to the "night strolls" that Rey takes "beneath the city's yellow streetlights" (149) after he has become involved with the insurgents and no longer feels safe because he fears discovery by government informants and further embroilment with the insurgents: "He was afraid no one would speak to him, and equally terrified that they might"

(149). Night strolls through the city provide him with respite from the alienation of paranoia. The twelfth reference is to "evening in America, past midnight in Europe, already tomorrow morning in Asia" (152) and has to do with the sense of nightfall as the "end of a working day" and the time to call and check in with loved ones to make sure they have not forgotten you. Again, the associations are of respite from exploitation, distance, absence, and severance. Nightfall here functions like the radio of *Lost City Radio,* collapsing distances (152) and filling in the abyss between the missing—and between the living and the dead—by calling on both "imagination" and "concentration": "The whole world had scattered, but there they were, so close you could feel them" (152). The thirteenth reference is to Norma walking at night on "the empty streets" of the city (157). She knows that during the ongoing civil war "many terrible things had happened all at once" (157), but the night offers her some respite from alienation. The fourteenth night scene re-introduces dread and sweeps away respite when Norma is working at the radio station and an anonymous caller on the radio threateningly inquires about the whereabouts of her colleague Yerevan, who was disappeared for his alleged involvement with "terrorists" (177). The fifteenth nocturnal scene entails Rey's psychotropic root trip in the jungle, where he ingests a hallucinogenic plant substance to foresee the future (especially that of his son Victor). Under the influence of this plant root, he wades into the river at night and in the darkness feels colors: "he felt them all around, a fantastic brightness bubbling within him: reds and yellows and blues in every shade and intensity" (183). This scene foreshadows his death at the novel's end. The sixteenth night scene is once again of the Great Blackouts. The city is described as "a city of sleepwalkers" (199) who have become accustomed to having their reality altered by endless war. The seventeenth night scene involves the betrayal of Rey by the informant for the government Zahir who fancies himself a poet. He gives his government contact information about Rey that will lead to his murder and then goes to drink in a bar until night falls (207). The eighteenth night scene switches to a large party in the home of a wealthy couple who own "a stake in the radio station" (209), a party at which Norma and Rey find themselves much to Rey's discomfort, as his secret entanglement with the insurgents lies in direct opposition to the interests of this class and to what his own middle-class wife would deem wise. The nineteenth night scene takes readers back to the radio station, to "the first night" of the "Lost City Radio" show for missing persons (221) when Norma must screen calls to make sure no one mentions the war and must operate under the injunction of "neutrality" that is not to be confused, according to her boss Elmer, with "indifference" (221). The twentieth night scene is just a single image, a nocturnal view seen from the radio station's conference room of the eastern part of the city. Government troops have set that district of the city on fire in retaliation for its supposed participation in the insurgency, a fire that will not be "mentioned in the newspapers or on most radio stations" (234). The twenty-first night scene is of Norma, Victor, and Victor's teacher Manau driving at night across the city "still under curfew" and riddled with government checkpoints (237–38). This episode of driving across the vast city under military curfew is the last night scene per se. A symbolic echo of a night scene concludes the narrative and the novel. Rey is captured by boy soldiers, blindfolded with a "black cloth" through which he cannot see—"There was only darkness" (254)—and shot in the chest. Behind this black blindfold and the relative darkness of closed eyelids, the golden sunlight in the middle of the river where the trees of the jungle do not reach, illuminates—moments before his murder—mental "scenes and images of people and places he loved and would never see again" (255).

This last scene, though one of artificial night or darkness created by a blindfold, encapsulates a fundamental quality of most of the night scenes in *Lost City Radio*. The night scenes are clusters of nerves along the emotional spine of the novel. The night scenes themselves function as Rey describes the poorer neighborhoods of the city: "Neighborhoods like these are networks of impulses . . . human, electrical, biological, like the forest" (65). The night scenes comprise nodes of intense connectivity during which people and events, presumably distant and far-flung from one another, meet up, collide, and change each other's pathways forever. As networks of impulses, these night scenes contain and transmit sensory information that both codes and conveys how it feels to live in a country and a city undergoing civil war, insurgency, and repressive counterinsurgency. I have subtitled this section of chapter 4 "Perceiving Night" because the focus of these scenes is on the way characters perceive nights, as in "She [Norma] remembered this night: the dancing and the drinking, their easy and light conversation in the early morning hours, so enthralling they didn't even notice the bus ease to a stop, or the idling rumble of the motor, or the flashing lights. It was a roadblock . . ." (17–18). The verbs Alarcón chooses continually reference the process of perception: "remembered" (17), or "it was an awareness, sudden and stark, of her solitude" (48), or "Everything had the air of urgency, of that long-wished-for, long-awaited trouble" (56). The novel's night scenes compel readers to align their vision (and, through their vision, their other senses) with the characters' inhabitation of their felt thoughts (which are not reducible to mere sensations). In this way, readers are invited to step into, with regard to each of the novel's characters, what French Marxist phenomenologist Maurice Merleau-Ponty describes as "the incarnated *cogito*" in "The

Primacy of Perception and Its Philosophical Consequences."[23] What Merleau-Ponty underscores with this concept is that all consciousness is perceptual and our perceptions depend on our embodied situatedness and resulting blend of perspectives. He emphasizes the contingent nature of perception (16) and its temporality, the fact that it never occurs all at once, but rather develops over time (42), and that it is relational as is history itself—"History is other people" (25). By the time readers have finished *Lost Radio City*, they have stepped into the incarnated *cogito* or embodied consciousness of ordinary people, becoming aware of the civil war tearing their society apart, active insurgents, and active counterinsurgents. Proportionally, a greater amount of novelistic space is given to the perceptions of so-called ordinary people caught in the crossfire of the civil war and to the perceptions of a relatively ordinary, though educated, person, Rey, who eventually develops a double life as a collaborator with the insurgents, a role that classifies him as a "terrorist" by the government.

Most of the U.S. newspaper blurbs included in the front matter of the book make no mention of the political parallels with late twentieth-century Peru. Some, as with the blurb from the *Chicago Tribune*, note, with evident relief, that Alarcón "sees no heroes here, not the rebels nor the soldiers, not the government. Instead, he uses his considerable literary gifts for a merciless meditation on the selfishness of both sides and the victims they left behind" (front matter of the novel). The review from the *Washington Post Book World* echoes a similar sentiment: "[Alarcón's] words express, eloquently and exactly, the self-destructiveness of violent insurgency and official retaliation" (front matter of the novel). Reading these framings of *Lost City Radio*, I am reminded of the injunction to radio announcer Norma from her boss Elmer: maintain "neutrality," not to be confused with "indifference" (221). State-sponsored repression in the world of this novel provides the ironic context for taking these words of advice literally as a guiding rule for people with careers in the media, including writers who produce award-winning, well-selling novels such as *Lost City Radio*. The novel is not indifferent. That it is as neutrally balanced as the *Chicago Tribune* and the *Washington Post Book World* reviews describe it to be is not clear to me. Nor is it clear to me that engaged (as opposed to indifferent) neutrality is an aim of the novel. I caution against confusing one character's advice with an interpretive key to the overall tenor of the novel. To take Elmer's advice as a key is to confuse one character's situated perspective with the overall novel's perspectival gestalt. The novel is dedicated to Alarcón's uncle, his father's disappeared and murdered younger brother, whom the writer describes as "an activist on Peru's radical political left" in the novel's back matter and whom the government evidently considered some kind of insurgent.

The novel's dedication reads "Q.E.P.D. Javier Antonio Alarcón Guzmán." The capital letters followed by periods are an acronym for *"Que en paz descanse,"* Spanish for "May he rest in peace." Like the character of Rey in the novel, the uncle was a university professor—not of botany, but of engineering. Javier was a "professor and union leader" (novel's back matter, 8). According to Daniel Alarcón, Javier left home in December 1989 and never returned. When he had been dead for years, people for whom "his disappearance was politically more useful to them than his death" lied to his immediate and extended family that he was "missing" (novel's back matter, 9–10). Daniel Alarcón emigrated with his parents to the United States from Lima, Peru, in 1980 when he was three years old. His immediate family received the call about the uncle's disappearance in 1989 when they were living in Birmingham, Alabama. In 1999, Daniel and his family were still asking questions about the uncle's whereabouts. Eventually, they pieced the story together and figured out he had been dead for years, dead since the night in Birmingham they had received the call about his disappearance (novel's back matter, 9–10). Daniel Alarcón, who has been living in Oakland, California, in "a predominantly Spanish-speaking neighborhood" and in "a community of immigrants" (novel's back matter, 3), wrote *Lost City Radio* in part to deal with the impact of his uncle's murder passed off as an extended disappearance and to convey, in fictionalized form, the experiences of those war years in Lima, Peru, but in a deterritorialized way that would not limit their association to Lima and that would intersect with similar experiences in other parts of the world.

How do the night scenes relate to questions about the allegiances of the book and Elmer's injunction to strive for neutrality not to be confused with indifference? The novel has been published in more than a dozen countries, and it has gained the attention of the U.S. press at a time when this country is traversing its own obsession with terrorism, terrorists, and subversion and when radicalism of any kind is met with deep suspicion by the right wing and by neoliberal centrists. The novel is transnational and transcultural in the way that it crosses borders by being modeled on late twentieth-century Lima, Peru, and yet never confines itself to a precise location. The night scenes reinforce the novel's transculturalism through their highly perceptualist approach that asks readers, and originally U.S. readers in English, to feel and think the intensely emotional experiences of insurgents, counterinsurgents, and ordinary people caught in the cross fire in an unfamiliar setting that nevertheless contains plenty of echoes of the familiar. These night scenes transport U.S. readers on networks of felt and thought impulses beyond certain ideological comfort zones. Thinking of the overall aesthetico-political effect of the novel *Lost City Radio*, I suggest that what at a more cursory level might seem to be engaged neutrality is in fact a technique of highly effective transculturation in which readers in the United States feel the perceptions of millions of ordinary people in the Other America or in the periphery as their own perceptions. One of the chief results seems to be to encourage readers to entertain, at least for the duration of the novel, a deep aversion to war, no small accomplishment in the context of the seemingly endless imperial and neocolonial military intervention in which we presently find ourselves. Furthermore, the novel draws attention to the suffering of millions of people caused by state-sponsored wars justified in the name of terrorism.

Jiménez Cahua, who read Alarcón's novel (a novel that was published the same year he began taking his photographs of Lima), has remarked that it has been works of verbal and visual art that have drawn the most attention to the human rights abuses perpetrated by the government's "bloody over- or mis-reaction" to insurgency and terrorism.[24] At the same time, Jiménez Cahua emphasizes that Lima and Peru as a whole have a host of other pressing problems besides "terrorism and past government abuse": "these concerns, now that the worst of terrorism [one might say both state- and -insurgent-sponsored] is over, are the very pressing problems of poverty, a lack of proper education, civic works, delinquency, corruption, etc."[25] Traces of some of these problems, particularly poverty and the lack of civic works, are visible in his photographic images of Lima, especially in the daytime ones in which *pueblos jóvenes* that look as if they were made out of cardboard lie exposed on their desert-like land under, to borrow his phrase, an "amorphous, white sky."[26] He and his family moved from Lima, Peru, to New Jersey when he was "about a year of age" and then moved to Greenville, South Carolina, when he was ten, where he remained until he returned to New Jersey to attend college at Princeton University (chemistry major, visual arts minor). However, when he was a child, his mother and his siblings went to Lima fairly often to visit family. During his time at Princeton, Jiménez Cahua went to Lima alone for the first time to make photographic images focusing on construction sites. He writes, "I made such images, but I was immediately seduced by the environment/atmosphere of Lima."[27] The result of this seduction has been an intense focus on the relationship between urban space and land. The photographs feature the exponentially expanding edges of the city in relation to the desert landscape and both the white and, contrastively, the night skies of Lima. Jiménez Cahua wishes to demonstrate that the relationship Limeños have with the earth is "radically different" from that of the people of "the Eastern U.S." where he has spent much of his life. He currently lives in Boston, Massachusetts.[28] As I mentioned earlier, the thesis statement for his series *Ciudad de los*

FIG. 4.1. Carlos Jiménez Cahua, *Untitled #21,* from series *Ciudad de los Reyes,* 2007, archival inkjet print, 35 × 44 in. *Courtesy of Carlos Jiménez Cahua.*

Reyes extends the implications of his photographs to suggest that they challenge U.S.-centric notions of urbanism. The question I would like to close this section with is how his night photographs perform transcultural night work and pose a perceptual challenge to U.S.-centric notions of urbanism. I consider three images from his series *Ciudad de los Reyes* in this order: #21, #37, and #28.

Untitled #21 (fig. 4.1), shot in 2007, shows a section of the periphery of Lima under a foggy, smoggy sky. The general tones of the image are a slightly violet gray overcast sky descending to the sparse brown earth of flat plains and hills that are partly covered by what looks like fairly new but bare, incomplete, plywood-like, largely horizontal rather than vertical construction. Myriad orange streetlights coming on in relation to this twilight dot the urban panorama. The image is fairly monotonous except for these orange streetlights and four or five colorful facades of the low buildings. The brown, dry, rocky earth dominates the foreground and reappears at the horizon beyond the expanse of city caught between the hills. The city seems to be in the process of being blanketed by the sky and absorbed into the earth as twilight turns to evening. The many unlit windows in the middle to foreground suggest that this part of the city may have no electricity. The only visible electric light comes from the orange streetlights. When night falls in this district of the city, it will be dark indeed.

This impression is reinforced by *Untitled #37* (fig. 4.2) also made in 2007. This shot, angled uphill, is of a curving asphalt road at the edge of the city flanked by what appears to be relatively new construction (again with no interior lighting) and illuminated by bright orange-white street floodlights like starbursts against the twilight, early evening sky. The darkness in and under the buildings on the left side of the photograph is profound and, potentially, ominous. U.S. viewers who take electricity in their cities for granted as a default condition are immediately confronted by the absence of interior lighting. The only light comes faintly from the sky and strongly from the brilliant orange-white street floods presiding over the road like rafter lighting over a stage set and lending a surreal quality to an otherwise gritty, realistic scene. Temporal disorientation coexists with spatial disorientation. The tarred road, the streetlights, and the architecture of the buildings signal contemporaneity. But the angle of the shot points uphill toward land and sky whose time coordinates are hard, if not impossible, to gauge from this photograph. Furthermore, some of the construction, like the stonework pillars, has a megalithic quality defiant of contemporaneity.

FIG. 4.2. Carlos Jiménez Cahua, *Untitled #37*, from series *Ciudad de los Reyes*, 2007, archival inkjet print, 35 × 44 in. *Courtesy of Carlos Jiménez Cahua.*

The more seemingly timeless appearance of the hillside's earth would seem to dominate over the more measurable temporalities of human construction. The image suggests the present, but it is a present challenged by other temporalities and even by atemporalities. This aspect also challenges U.S. viewers generally accustomed to less temporal dissonance.

Both *Untitled #21* and *Untitled #37* present pictures of rapidly proliferating urbanization—almost as if out of nowhere—without, as Jiménez Cahua has pointed out, "a long sequence of history" in which, along a more U.S. model, "an urban area is the final manifestation of an inhabited area that began as a sparsely populated village or neighborhood."[29] These photographs show the exponential growth of Lima's peripheries without urban planning and without, Jiménez Cahua observes, "ample capital" to build the infrastructure that would address civic needs, such as adequate plumbing and electricity, that are the usual first-world or Global North standard for making an urban zone habitable and minimally safe. Inhabitants of the United States looking at these photographs are likely to see an alien-looking urban sprawl, the product not of gradualism, urban planning, and vertical stacking of city buildings to maximize space but of population explosion, overcrowding, "literally overnight" piecemeal growth, and "horizontally destined growth surfaces."[30] With regard to the night views of *Ciudad de los Reyes,* Jiménez Cahua emphasizes the horizontal expansion, a sharp contrast to many U.S. cities, particularly of the Eastern seaboard, with their skyscrapers or vertical buildings: "So what might surprise a U.S. viewer of especially the night photographs in my series is just how flat everything is in the city, even when it's hilly. The topography really comes out at night with the ubiquitous presence of light-posts serving as surface markers, very often the highest structures in their vicinity."[31]

Untitled #28 (fig. 4.3), done in 2009, is the most arresting of Jiménez Cahua's after-sunset and nocturnal photographs. According to him, it "was made on the higher slopes of an undeveloped hill similar to those seen in the photograph. It was made just as twilight was giving way into pure night."[32] The city flows and spreads out, almost like white and orange gold lava, between black hills under a vast sky graduating upward from an afterglow pale pink and amber combination to Prussian blue and cobalt. The image is hauntingly beautiful; black hills in the foreground and middle distance remind viewers of alien geological forces looming up in the midst and all around this evident urbanism. The striking topography attests to telluric forces that humans have not altered. One is reminded of Jiménez Cahua's statement for the series *Ciudad de los Reyes:* "For the people of Lima, their relationship with the earth is fundamentally different [from that of the people in the United States]. They do not sculpt the land, for the earth

FIG. 4.3. Carlos Jiménez Cahua, *Untitled #28,* from series *Ciudad de los Reyes,* 2009, archival inkjet print, 35 × 44 in. *Courtesy of Carlos Jiménez Cahua.*

remains visible if not nearly unaltered despite their development." Viewing such a different relationship challenges U.S. viewers' assumptions about the effects of urbanism. Jiménez Cahua's photographs remind viewers of the power of the earth as opposed to that of human enterprise, development, and neoliberal assumptions about control through technological progress and built environments. For U.S. and Global North viewers who wish to learn more about this image, further assumptions may be challenged. According to Jiménez Cahua,

> *Untitled #28* looks upon Nueva Esperanza . . . located in the district of Villa María del Triunfo. . . . Nueva Esperanza is a typical lower to middle class neighborhood of Lima. It snakes along a thin valley following a main road whose only purpose before people came was connecting a more distant cement plant to the city for semi-trailer trucks. This road is now filled with restaurants, stores, salons, etc., with purely residential areas surrounding it. It's a moderately safe place during the day (though really only peopled by residents) but can be (quite) unsafe at night especially for non-residents, mostly due to the near-ubiquitous presence of teenage gangs as in any other poorer area of the city. I don't think even lifelong

residents of Nueva Esperanza would immediately recognize that this photo-graph's subject is their home. The image was made from high enough to make its exact identity pretty obscure, but with knowledge of this, a resident could easily then recognize parts of the neighborhood.[33]

This explanation provokes a certain cognitive dissonance for viewers. The image of the city as molten gold between the black hills is so alluring that the explanation with its socioeconomic underpinnings, in addition to the defamil-iarizing features of the scene, serves as a corrective to viewers who might have assumed they were gazing upon a U.S. city or, conversely, a mythical city of the Americas such as El Dorado. The view is ravishing, but the socioeconomic reality is complicated—tied deeply to Peru's history of coloniality and to the ways in which global forces impinge upon the local. Even without knowledge of which neighborhoods of Lima are captured in the photograph, *Untitled #28* conveys, through its powerful contrasts of light and dark and of the seemingly familiar and the unfamiliar, that it belongs to the refracted night of transcultur-alism, taking U.S., first world, and Global North viewers beyond the panoramas and geo-cultural coordinates to which they are most likely accustomed.

Coda on Transcultural Night Work in the Cultural Productions of Latina/o Writers of the Three Dominant Ethno-National Groups

These mutually informing movements from south to north and from north to south on the part of U.S.-based South American cultural producers and the way in which these movements are encoded and dramatized by verbal productions and visual works involving many aspects of "night" serve to remind readers and scholars that Latina/o cultural production in the United States has become increasingly oriented toward the Latin American countries that lie south and southeast of the United States border aside from Mexico, Puerto Rico, and Cuba. This increased orientation toward other Latin American countries than the three that have traditionally been dominant marks a shift in the geo-cultural mappings of Latinidades that is very evident in the works I have analyzed on the transcultural night work of U.S.-based South American writers and the photog-rapher Carlos Jiménez Cahua. The works that I have examined in this chapter are contributing to the exploration by Latina/o cultural producers of other Latin Americas in addition to Mexico (technically part of North America), Puerto Rico (a commonwealth of the United States and the oldest colony in the West-ern hemisphere), and Cuba (that island ninety miles off the coast of Florida). This pattern of cultural production gives new and more nuanced significance to

Chicano poet, essayist, and short story writer (1938–1991) Arturo Islas's claim about Chicano literary production:

> The Chicano writer falls between the Latin American and the Anglo-American literary traditions, and at this stage in the development of Chicano literature, he displays an uneasy relationship with both traditions. The uneasiness is at times reflected in the writing problems that arise in his work. Sometimes he sides (or is made to side) with the view that expects its writers to devote themselves directly to the social and political problems of their community; sometimes he strikes out in the direction of the view of the writer as solitary explorer of domains beyond the social and political.[34]

Islas made this claim in the mid 1970s. I contend that rather than being an accurate description of Chicana/o literature, this statement encapsulates certain assumptions about not only Chicana/o cultural production but more generally Latina/o cultural production in the United States—for instance, that it exists in an often fraught, misrecognized, and under-appreciated in-between space between U.S. and Latin American cultures and that it is torn between allegiances to the context of the United States and the context of particular countries of the Other America.[35] But the works analyzed in this chapter demonstrate that a number of U.S.-based South American cultural producers have managed to handle allegiances and priorities so as to confound such expectations and assumptions. The transculturality of their cultural productions entails a multi-directional bridging rather than falling between categories, places, and so forth.

Furthermore, this transcultural, multi-directional bridging is increasingly evident in work over the last decade or two by Latina/o writers of the three main ethnic groups: Chicana/os, Puerto Ricans, and Cubans. Certainly, Juanita Heredia, scholar of Latina/o and Latin American literature and popular cultures, has underscored and analyzed this trend in her critically and historically rich 2009 study *Transnational Latina Narratives in the Twenty-First Century: The Politics of Gender, Race, and Migrations*.[36] Not surprisingly given the patterns identified in my study, cultural productions involving tropes of night and darkness play a key role in this intensified—and, according to Heredia, Latina feminist—transculturalism and transnationalism. Take, for instance, Chicana writer Graciela Limón's novel *In Search of Bernabé* (1997) about the civil war in El Salvador, the disappearance and murder of thousands of Salvadorans from 1989 to 1992, and the connections via a tide of human refugees between El Salvador and Southern California, the Los Angeles area in particular. Night and darkness as primary tropes for the terror and disorientation created by this civil war play a pronounced, though scattered, role in this novel that addresses the realities of communities beyond Mexican and Mexican American ones in Southern California and the Americas more generally.[37] Night and darkness play an even more prominent role in her later novel *Erased Faces* (2001) about the Chiapas rebellion in the Yucatan Peninsula of indigenous forces against the tyranny of the neoliberal Mexican government. Though this novel is about Mexico and that subject matter is within the map of expectations for a novel by a Chicana writer, the novel exceeds the assumptions about a Chicana text by placing its emphasis on experiences outside of the United States, in southeastern Mexico. It also presents readers with a specifically Afro Chicana protagonist, Adriana Mora, who leaves Los Angeles to journey from north to south, from the United States to Chiapas, where she becomes involved in a struggle for liberation on multiple fronts—economic, ethno-racial, and sexual. Night in *Erased Faces* is scripted as a psychological, spiritual, and practical/tactical part of that multi-fronted liberation, as evident even from a few sentences such as:

> She [Juana Galván, the woman who becomes Adriana Mora's comrade-in-arms and lover] knew also that she was going in the direction where the Lacandón Jungle became the thickest, where the trees and growth grew so dense that in some places not even sunlight could penetrate its cover. Her people called it the place of eternal night.[38]

This last sentence—her people (the indigenous people of Chiapas) "called it [the thickest part of the Lacandón Jungle] the place of eternal night"—firmly associates night with the transformation of darkness, disorientation, and invisibility into a "methodology of the oppressed" tactics of resistance against the neocolonial incursions of the Mexican government in league with developers and corporations and the attacks of the federal government's military.[39] Notable about this novel by a Chicana novelist based in California at the time of its composition and publication is that it transports its protagonist Adriana Mora very far south beyond U.S. borders, much farther south than the location of characters in a previous nocturnally informed novel titled *The Day of the Moon* (1999).[40] Not only does it transport its Afro Chicana protagonist southward outside of U.S. territory, but, furthermore, it dedicates most of the novel to experiences in Chiapas, not the United States. This type of work shifts the center of gravity of the exploration of Chicana/o and, by extension, Latina/o imagined and lived experience beyond the boundaries of the continental United States and ideologically expands, in the case of Limón's novel, what can be considered to be part of Chicana history and culture.

Puerto Rican, Cornell-educated writer Mayra Santos-Febres's night-interwoven novel *Sirena Selena Vestida de Pena* (2000) performs a similar transcultural function in relation to Puerto Rican cultural production both on and off the island, but it does so somewhat more complicatedly, as it was originally written in Spanish with one single chapter in English (chapter 36), a feature that is also making a bold transcultural statement in that it is a bilingual novel of sorts, but not in the expected ways.[41] The novel, written by a bilingual writer based on the island of Puerto Rico, is mostly in Spanish, though in its translated version it appears in English with Spanish words peppering the text. This night-steeped novel of nightclubs, dark bars, and nights of fantasy-desire amid harsh neocolonial realities concerns itself with the queer, transvestite, drag-artist sex trade/tourism and performance circuit among the Dominican Republic, Puerto Rico, and the United States. The novel emphasizes the human traffic and circulation from one island of the Caribbean to another—between the Dominican Republic and Puerto Rico. While the United States is mentioned—particularly New York City—the focus remains on the Caribbean islands themselves and the sexual/tourism trade between them, a focus that is different from that of much Puerto Rican literature, both on and off the island, which is centered on the relationship between Puerto Rico and the continental United States.

With regard to an example of a Cuban American text that performs this kind of transculturation, I would point to Cristina García's 2007 novel *A Handbook to Luck* that I mentioned in the introduction of my book. This novel is not only about Cubans and Cuban Americans like García's previous novels. It is also largely about Salvadorans fleeing civil war in El Salvador as well as Iranians opposed to the Shah and trying to escape political persecution. The novel draws upon other places (such as Panama, the Dominican Republic, Colombia, Argentina, and the Caribbean islands) through marriage, friendship, and the histories of a magician's and a gambler's careers[42] and even more places (such as Brazil, Mexico, and China) through various acts of cultural acquisition and performance (15, 43, and 63). Night plays a small but powerful role in the story. Whenever it appears, it signifies the ability to hide, as in the case of Marta escaping from El Salvador and crossing the border through Mexico into the United States under the cover of night. It signifies the ability to disappear into the mystery of darkness—"What can we expect of the night but mystery?" (47)—and to survive and transform despite acute hardship, pain, and loss. The last image of the book involves the Salvadoran Marta Claros's brother Evaristo back in El Salvador as he thinks about the people who were killed during the Salvadoran Civil War and as he listens to the woeful song of canaries at dusk turning into night (258–59). The fact that the canaries are singing is important: it lends to the images of darkness descending a note of resiliency and hopefulness despite their encoding of loss and disappearance through death. Though night plays a cameo role in this novel, I contend that the intensity of that role, associated as it is with mystery, transformation, and endurance, is not accidental in this transnational and transcultural novel that ventures into subjects and histories beyond those of Cuba and Cuban/U.S. relations. The placement of Cuban American experience in relation to other diaspora experiences and, consequently, its pan-Latinidad are quite deliberate. Though it does not deploy tropes of night the way that *A Handbook to Luck* does, her next novel, *The Lady Matador's Hotel* (2010), continues this exploration of pan-Latinidad and pan-Americanism. It takes place not in Cuba or in the United States but in the unnamed capital of an unnamed Central American country characterized by a long civil war and ongoing political turmoil. Most of the action unfolds at the hotel indicated in the title: Hotel Miraflor. The hotel serves as a space for the convergence and clash of its guests' cultures, ideologies, life trajectories, and the actual messy entanglement, within the neoliberal order of the twentieth century, of their countries' histories: a Japanese Mexican American matadora; an ex-guerrilla from the country's civil war waitressing in the hotel's coffee shop; a Korean manufacturer and his underage mistress Berta whose name and behavior recall the supposed insanity of Edward Rochester's first wife, Bertha, in Charlotte Bronte's novel *Jane Eyre* (1847); a Cuban poet and his American wife who have come to the unnamed Central American country to adopt a local infant; an international adoption lawyer of German heritage; and a colonel, possibly from the unnamed Central American country in question or another one like it, who has committed human rights atrocities during the civil war. Each chapter of *The Lady Matador's Hotel* is prefaced by a line or two of poetry—mostly from Latin American male poets. Meanwhile, the novel enacts its own kind of prose poetry. With regard to night, the most striking passages of the book occur in relation to ex-guerrilla waitress Aura's remembrance of rainy night surprise attacks on the dictator's soldiers and informers and her long-awaited re-enactment of such attacks on the colonel, committer of atrocities, as he lies having nightmares in his hotel bed.[43] This kind of transnational, transcultural production is more and more characteristic of Latina/o cultural production, and it remains to be seen to what extent tropes of night continue to play an aesthetic role in conveying the socio-political import of these productions.

TWO HOMELANDS HAVE I:
"AMERICA" AND THE NIGHT

Night works among Latina/o cultural producers demonstrate that "assimilation" does not have one meaning but several, some of them opposed to one
another. "Assimilation" is a commonly used term in U.S. society and has been
both an expectation for and practice of the society's construction since the mid
to late nineteenth century, between the Mexican-American War of 1846–1848
and the Spanish-Cuban-American War of 1898, during which time the United
States became a world empire. Being so central to U.S. culture (at least thus far),
it is an under-examined term and concept because it has been taken for granted
by U.S. culture at large and even within academia. Latina/o studies, however,
has a history of questioning insufficiently critical uses of the term "assimilation" and its companion term "immigration." Take, as a salient example, the
conceptually astute introduction on "the decolonization of the U.S. empire
in the twenty-first century" to a book on Latina/os in the "world-system" by a
cluster of Latina/o studies scholars: Ramón Grosfoguel, Nelson Maldonado-
Torres, and José David Saldívar. They critically deconstruct expectations about
assimilation in relation to immigration as well as the equal-opportunity myth
of "America" as "immigrant nation" by pointing out the "complex ways in which
race and ethnicity combine with colonization and migration" to produce many
conflicting kinds of immigrant experiences and positionalities.[1] They posit,

> If we apply the coloniality perspective to the history of U.S. migration studies we
> would need to distinguish between three types of transnational migrants: "colo-
> nial/racial subjects of empire," "colonial immigrants," and immigrants (Gros-
> foguel 2003). Latin@s are no exception to this history. Within the Latin@ cate-
> gory there are multiple experiences of incorporation inside the United States. (8)

From my perspective, not only have Latina/os had multiple and diverse experiences of incorporation inside the United States but, moreover, Latina/os, despite differences among ethno-racial and socioeconomic groups under the umbrella rubric "Latina/o," have been both subtly and blatantly resisting a traditional model of assimilation. As mentioned in my introduction to this book, assimilation under the sign of night entails a far more multi-layered exchange between various minority or sub-cultural groups that challenges the dominant and the normative.

I do not foresee any contemporary or near-future abatement of tropes of night in Latina/o cultural production. Rather, I see an increasing accumulation of those tropes, particularly in relation to the Latina/o-phobia that many Latina/os face in the United States on account of the xenophobic, anti-immigrant feelings of the general population who fear that their "American" (read Anglo-oriented) culture is being hybridized, diluted, and even destroyed by the increasing presence, on account of births as much as immigration, of Latina/os everywhere in the United States and not just in the expected places such as the Southwest, California, and southern Florida. Night is a way for Latina/os to represent and talk about what I term their/our simultaneous "invisibilization" and "hyper-visibility" in all kinds of genres and media. Invisibilization and hyper-visibility occur because people are cued to not see or not imagine through the grid of over-determined stereotypes that rely on certain patterns of physical and mental visualization. Postcolonial psychoanalytic critic Kalpana Seshadri-Crooks reminds us of feminist philosopher, socio-political theorist, and activist Teresa Brennan's association (in her book *History after Lacan*) of "the dominance of the visual" with the objectification and dominance of others. Seshadri-Crooks writes of racialization and its imbrication in the visual,

> Perhaps we can consider race itself as a symptom of what Brennan terms the "ego's era," when objectification and dominance of others and of the environment are paramount. Among the many insights she offers about the historicity of such a subject of knowledge, Brennan suggests that the dominance of the visual is a symptom of such "social psychosis": "Visualization, whether in the form of hallucination or visual perception, observes difference rather than connection."[2]

Resisting and confounding certain visualizations, turning invisibilization against dominant visualizations, night is, I have argued, a way for Latina/os to express the complexities of being considered and being the Other Americans, *los otros americanos,* or "strangers among us," to reference the title of Roberto

Suro's 1999 book on how Latina/os are changing "America" (by which he means the United States).[3]

Since 2003 in Latina/o cultural production, the number of titles involving night or some nocturnal element has grown. In addition to the twenty-first-century works I have discussed in this book, consider Sandra Benítez's novel divided between Minnesota and Oaxaca, Mexico, *Night of the Radishes* (2003), in which the main protagonist arrives at midnight in Oaxaca to begin her journey of self-discovery; Michael Jaime-Becerra's interconnected short story collection set in the blue-collar town of El Monte, Southern California, *Every Night is Ladies' Night: Stories* (2005), with many references to Latina/os working and educating themselves at night; Mary Castillo, Berta Platas, Caridad Pineiro, and Sofía Quintero's book *Friday Night Chicas: Sexy Stories from La Noche* (2005); Cecil Gómez's account of how and why his parents came to the United States from Mexico, titled *A Mexican Twilight* (2006); horror, surreal science fiction, and thriller writer J. F. Gonzalez's short story collection *When Darkness Falls* (2006); Mexican screenwriter Guillermo Arriaga's first novel published in the United States, *The Night Buffalo* (2007); Yuyi Morales's tale for children *Little Night* (2007); Amy Costales's children's book *Hello Night / Hola Noche* with illustrations by Mercedes McDonald (2007); and Manuel Muñoz's noir-within-noir novel set in late 1950s Bakersfield, California, *What You See in the Dark* (2011), with its re-writing of Alfred Hitchcock's 1960 film *Psycho* and its carefully crafted, nested references to sinister nights of unsettling truths, the artifice of art (especially of the dream factory of the movies), and the deadly harshness of socioeconomic and gendered ethno-racial realities shadowing and exposing "American" daydreaming.

Several aspects of this list become apparent upon closer inspection. Though searches for titles involving "night," "noche," "darkness," and "nocturne" generally call up a great many works that fall under the rubrics of horror, Gothic thrillers, science fiction, noir fiction, murder mysteries, and harlequin romances crisscrossed with Gothic thrillers (as in the vampire genre), most of the titles I have just named do not fall under these categories. In the first chapter of this study on Chicana/o cultural production, I did explore a Chicana/o interest in noir. Recall, for example, Carla Trujillo's *What the Night Brings* (2003) and Lucha Corpi's *Crimson Moon* (2004). This noir interest is indeed also manifested in *Night Buffalo* (2007), by Mexican screenwriter publishing in the United States Guillermo Arriaga, and Manuel Muñoz's *What You See in the Dark* (2011). J. F. Gonzalez's short story collection *When Darkness Falls* (2006) combines horror with surreal science fiction. But the majority of the titles discussed here cannot be classified as noir, horror, or surreal science fiction, though they may contain noirish elements or confront the horrors of history. Most Latina/o cultural production centrally involving night or darkness is more focused on the historical struggle of people dealing with the injustices created by invisibilization, hyper-visibility, marginalization. and stereotyping stigmatization. As I endeavored to demonstrate especially in the first chapter on Chicana/o cultural production and in the third chapter on U.S.-based Central American texts, even the Latina/o texts that are predominantly noir have been adapted to represent a struggle for justice in terms of an intersection of socioeconomic, ethno-racial, gender/sexual, and national identities, especially in regard to the overall issue of being Othered as the Other Americans, *los otros americanos*. Although one can certainly find examples of noir from the dominant Anglo-American culture that employ noir to represent social injustice, the fundamental identification with ethno-racial minorities as underdogs is often transmuted into a stereotyping fear and stigmatization of those underdogs as simply part of the underworld or the dark side of society. This is much less the case with Latina/o noir produced in the United States—at least with regard to the representation of Latina/os in these works.

The other works I have listed traverse a number of genres, from young adult literature to queer autobiographical fiction to "chick lit" to "true" accounts of immigrant experiences to fictional recreations of relatively recent history (the Guatemalan Civil War, for example) to children's literature. Striking is the variety of literature (including noir, surreal science fiction, and horror) that deploys tropes of night to the point of associating the work from the outset with night by including the actual word or some word that connotes night or a nocturnal space-time in the title of the work. This variety of genres—even within textual production (not to mention those that pertain to the audio, visual, and performance arts)—implies that for many Latina/os, the first few lines of nineteenth-century (1853–1895) Cuban revolutionary and visionary José Martí's famous poem "Dos patrias" may have a strangely prophetic significance. The first line and a half reads: "Dos patrias tengo yo: Cuba y la noche. / ¿O son una las dos?"[4] The verses translate: "Two homelands have I: Cuba and the night. / Or are the two one?" The vast amount of material in this book that attests to the existence of Latina/o aesthetics of night could be summarized as a slight twist of Martí's words involving the substitution of "America" (meaning the Americas and, especially in the United States, the United States itself) for "Cuba," like this: "Two homelands have I: 'America' and the night. / Or are the two one?"

Both utterances—Martí's and my adaptation of his words—have an aphoristic, riddle-like quality that prompts the question, "What is meant?" What I mean is that I am thinking of Martí's words in relation to the title of this book,

Buenas Noches, American Culture: Latina/o Aesthetics of Night. I have shown the ways in which Latina/o aesthetics of night function to both confront and transform "American" culture such that the word and concept "American" cannot be understood to have the stable, fixed range of significations that a dominant Anglo-American culture has taken for granted or attempted to perpetuate in its supremacist drive, both conscious and unconscious, for legitimacy as properly "American." As I mentioned in my introduction, *"buenas noches"* has a dual function in the Spanish language and in this study, signifying both hello and good-bye, an acknowledgment and a change of scene. Pair this acknowledging hello with a transforming good-bye that gives the "hello" a more volatile quality, and square that dynamic with the idea "Two homelands have I: 'America' and the night," and one begins to sense the import of the aphorism or riddle as I have modified it.

One intriguing aspect of Martí's original words is the combination of duality and unity that simultaneously produces the idea of contrast or at the very least juxtaposition ("Cuba" versus or in addition to "the night") and sameness or equivalence ("Or are the two one?"). This combination of contrast and sameness is similar to that of the phrase *"buenas noches"*—which can be understood both in terms of self-difference (hello versus good-bye) and self-sameness (all one thing, either hello, good-bye, or both simultaneously). Not surprisingly, Martí's poem contains a reference to saying good night and good-bye: "La noche es buena / Para decir adiós" (211). The night is a good time to say good-bye. So, if the poet has two homelands—one of them is Cuba and the other is the night, good-bye, and departure from the known world—then, when I suggest that one can think of many Latina/os as having two homelands (one "America" and the other the night, good-bye, and departure), I am intimating that all these accumulated Latina/o tropes of night point to a simultaneous radical transition from a particular space-time toward another kind of space-time. This simultaneous movement suggests transformation of a given space-time, not a simple departure from it. Latina/o cultural productions show Latina/os moving from one part of the Americas to another, being treated as the Other Americans in the United States, or having to reinvent the notion of "American" in order to live as the socially unrecognized, the socially dead, and, of course—following the logic of texts and films that draw on aspects of horror and noir—as the socially undead. The project of reinventing "American" even extends, as I demonstrated in the last chapter, to the expansion of concepts of "Latinidad."

In Martí's poem, the reference to "good night" is accompanied by an anticipation of death ("Ya es hora / de empezar a morir") or "Now is the time / to begin to die" and several repeated allusions to Cuba as a sad widow, "viuda triste."

Thus, the "good night" in the "buenas noches" of Martí's "Dos patrias" is a multi-dimensional good-bye that crosses the line between the living and the dead and places the poet in the position of the dead or the undead thinking about his sad widow or mourning bride, Cuba. The use of the phrase *"buenas noches"* in relation to having two homelands that may be one and the same—Cuba and the night or, in my formulation, the Americas (the United States in particular) and the night—necessarily involves a considerable capacity for melancholia or what I have described as generative loss. With regard to Latina/o cultural production, I discussed generative loss throughout my book. The notion of loss as generative is hardly new. Many people from many cultures have written about it from many different theoretical and philosophical perspectives. Take, for example, two texts published in the United States within the last two decades, one from a New Age neo-pagan perspective that sounds vaguely Anzaldúan, Demetra George's *Mysteries of the Dark Moon: The Healing Power of the Dark Goddess* (1992), and another from the perspective of self-help psychiatry combined with theology by Gerald G. May, *The Dark Night of the Soul: A Psychiatrist Explores the Connection Between Darkness and Spiritual Growth* (2004). What I would like to emphasize is the culturally transformational aspects of this generative loss and the fact that the process of generative loss does not, as might be expected according to older assimilationist and accommodationist models, result in conformity to a pre-established Anglo-American model of American-ness. This generative loss, in fact, resists such assimilation and establishes other patterns of exchange.

For those people who fear that Latina/os are not properly assimilating according to "the (Anglo) American way," reading or viewing the cultural productions mentioned in this book and reading this book itself with its claims about Latina/o aesthetics of night may elicit a reaction akin to that of the early Puritans if, turning in their graves and time-traveling, they were to become cognizant of a book such as Corvis Nocturnum's *Embracing the Darkness: Understanding Dark Subcultures* (2005). *Embracing the Darkness* looks into the materially and spiritually creative aspects of various "dark subcultures" of the Goths, witchcraft, Satanists, BDSM/Fetishists, and Vampyres. Puritans disturbed from their eternal rest might want to burn, ban, or otherwise suppress the contents of such a book. I offer the analogy partly in jest and partly in earnest. The comparison is historically incomplete, as Latina/os do not face antagonism and antipathy from Puritans but rather from latter-day jingoists, xenophobes, and white supremacists and, more subtly, from anyone who associates Latina/os with immigrants and immigrants with undesirables, conveniently forgetting that their ancestors were once immigrants and that the only "natives" are Native Americans. Of course, some Latina/os fall into the category of those with anti-immigrant sentiment. All the more reason, perhaps, to embrace the darkness, as so many of the works I have examined, such as Mariana Romo-Carmona's collection of short stories *Speaking Like an Immigrant*, seem to be urging. The alternative is to be internally conflicted, divided, and conquered or conquerable, to be afraid of one's own shadow. Ironically, Latina/o tropes of night arose and continue to arise from rejection, marginalization, invisibilization, and stigmatization in the United States or vis-à-vis the United States. This is one of the reasons I predict that tropes of night will not fade but, rather, will persist and intensify—particularly in the face of the national scapegoating of Latina/os as people who steal American jobs, do not pay taxes, drive under the influence of alcohol, are responsible for the decline of American culture, and so forth.[5]

Although tropes of night will surely be produced in response to continued and intensified scapegoating by still-dominant Anglo culture, embracing darkness as a creative practice of generative loss requires much more than reacting to marginalization. It entails cultivating the aesthetics of night as a politics of relationality, of coalition building, across the borders and boundaries of minority and subaltern groups. I explored this politics of relationality in all four chapters of this study but especially in the last chapter, "The Transcultural Night Work of U.S.-Based South American Cultural Producers." To endure "the night" is not enough. It must be embraced, and not only individually, but, moreover, collectively. Lest this injunction seem altogether too vaguely metaphorical, let me state that embracing the night entails a specific set of practices, among them: 1) the adoption of a vigilant and critical attitude toward facile notions of progress and advancement (that is, toward a neoliberalism that demands conformity to a white supremacist military-industrial culture of the United States); 2) the willingness to question, challenge, and devise alternatives to an ethno-racially and class-stratified society in general and among Latina/os in particular; 3) a non-phobic, non-defensive acquaintance with and exploration of loss, personal and collective, and of social abjection; and 4) the desire and ability to practice a kind of Chela Sandoval–like "methodology of the oppressed" tactics of oppositional (or resistant) consciousness through the creation of unpredictable rhizomes of transethnic, transcultural, and transnational "differential" affiliation among Latina/os and between Latina/os and other groups in the Americas and in the world.[6]

Finally, speaking of tactics of relationality and affiliation, what is especially significant about the aesthetics of night in many of the Latina/o works I have investigated is that the effects of these aesthetics point toward rather than away from the social. They often point toward the formation of an alternative polis. In these works, night is not antithetical to the project of transforming an existing polis or creating another one. Samuel Huntington, deceased political science professor at Harvard University who expressed many concerns over the rise of Latina/o cultures in the United States, the increasing racial diversity in the country, and the projection of demographers that "by the year 2050 people of color would be equal in number to whites" (Zinn, *A People's History*, 667) might have considered Latina/o figurations of night in relation to an alternative polis to be a symptom of the "democratic distemper" he described in his portion of the report "The Governability of Democracies." According to historian Howard Zinn, this report was drawn up by a rather conservative group of intellectuals and political leaders from Japan, the United States, and Western Europe just "[a]s the United States prepared in 1976 to celebrate the bicentennial of the Declaration of Independence" (558). Zinn underscores the extent to which Samuel Huntington was troubled by the coalitional consciousness that surged up in the 1960s and 1970s between "blacks, Indians, Chicanos," and progressive whites (559). Huntington's 1976 concerns only grew in the face of the Latinization of the United States and what Zinn describes as the "unreported resistance" of Latina/os who through the 1980s and 1990s "campaigned for better labor conditions, for representation in local government, for tenants' rights, for bilingual education in the schools" (615). Though Latina/o figurations of night do not constitute such direct political and socioeconomic advocacy, they do have the potential to set the stage or provide both the consciousness and the environment for such actions.

This practice of a polis or relation between people forged in, through, and from the darkness of night stands in noteworthy tension with general assumptions about night summarized by Wolfgang Schivelbusch in his 1988 book *Disenchanted Night* on the technological taming of night by the industrialization of light in the nineteenth century. His book also chronicles the effects of various kinds of darkness and light on human consciousness and, particularly, the effects of the transitions from candles to oil lamps to gaslights to electric light on modern (mostly Western European) consciousness:

> Nightfall brings forces very different from those that rule the day. In the symbols and myths of most cultures, night is chaos, the realm of dreams, teeming with ghosts and demons as the oceans team with fish and sea monsters. The night is feminine, just as the day is masculine, and like everything feminine, it holds both repose and terror. . . . Every time the sun rises, the world and light are created anew; in every sunset the world and the light, the sphere of solidity and Apollonian masculinity, again descend into the flux of darkness.[7]

According to Schivelbusch, night is associated with chaos and social instability. He documents this association by taking stock of the uses of light from the medieval period to the present and the close relation between public lighting, surveillance, and the creation of the modern polis of industrial capitalism as well as of twentieth-century communist and socialist urbanized collectivities. Industrialized public lighting of the nineteenth and twentieth centuries expressed itself and culminates in societies of surveillance and organized factory work. Neither surveillance nor factories would be possible without public electric lighting that turned night into day. His study generally features night as the realm of inchoate primeval nature, social unrest, rebellion, crime, and individualistic freedom. Schivelbusch claims that people submitted, sometimes grudgingly, to "a state monopoly on light [in the form of centralized public lighting] and weapons" because this state monopoly "promised to guarantee stability and security. But, although public lighting was welcomed as holding out the promise of security, it was also a police institution"—and a vehicle for the exploitation of labor at all hours (97). Public lighting and lighting up the night in this way and turning it into day are central to the workings of the polis or societies in the wake of the industrial revolution. Furthermore, Schivelbusch suggests that in the wake of the industrial revolution, darkness—either of the un-illuminated night or of the deliberately darkened theater or cinema—cancels out the polis and its social realities and plunges spectators who experience this darkness into an asocial solipsism:

> The spectator in the dark is alone with himself and the illuminated image, because social connections cease to exist in the dark. Darkness heightens individual perceptions, magnifying them many times. (221)

While this may indeed be the case—that night, whether actual or simulated, intensifies asociality and that "social connections cease to exist in the dark" (221), Latina/o aesthetics of night would seem to indicate otherwise. In the texts and films I have examined, night may involve social disruption, disorder, disorientation, danger, and sometimes crime, but it also entails the acknowledgment of social bonds, the formation of new social bonds, and deep-structure challenges to and transformations of existing social orders. "Buenas noches" implies both a farewell and a greeting to the social connections that compose "American" culture.

Julia Kristeva has implied since the mid 1990s that new "maladies of the soul" are the erosion of human rights and the diminished ability to resist and revolt:

> Now, before our eyes, these values [the notion of rights and of human], guaranteed until now by human rights, are dissolving under the pressure of technology

and the market, threatened by what jurists call "the patrimonial person," that is, the human being as an assemblage of organs that are more or less negotiable, that can be transplanted, converted into cash, bequeathed, and the like.[8]

Chela Sandoval reminds readers that Marxist critic Fredric Jameson made what I would term similar observations in his 1984 essay "Postmodernism, or the Cultural Logic of Late Capitalism" (Sandoval, 14–36).[9] I suggest that we link Schivelbusch's description of modern societies of surveillance and around-the-clock labor exploitation dependent on the industrialization of light with Kristeva's critique of contemporary Americanized societies of technologized, corporatized "popular culture" ("TV screens and channel surfing, hard sex and silicone, where thrills are found in murder trials theatricalized to the point of dissolution," 189) and with the callous complacency and political passivity (25) these societies of "privatization" and "marketization" breed, to use Paul Gilroy's phrases for "the destruction of welfare states and the evacuation of the public good" as well as the televised "war on terror" (fueling xenophobia and virulent nationalism) in the United States, a current imperial power, and elsewhere in former empires (Britain, for example).[10] And, let us not forget, in addition to surveillance (including, specifically, border patrol) and mechanized, corporatized exploitation made possible by electric light, the blinding flash, the total illumination, the disastrous nuclear radiation (emanating, as Horkheimer and Adorno would have it, from Enlightenment practice) of the catastrophic, lethal light of atomic weaponry and power (1940s onward) of which Chicano civil rights lawyer and writer Oscar Zeta Acosta shows such fear in his fictional piece "To Whom It May Concern [A Solicitation]."[11] As professor of cinema, comparative literature, and Japanese culture Akira Mizuta Lippit observes,

> Under the glare of atomic radiation, the human body was exposed: revealed and opened, but also displaced, thrust outward into the distant reaches of the visible world. It situated the body between not only two worlds but two universes: two separate orders of all things, or even of the same things. Visibility and invisibility, exteriority and interiority, the living and the dead.[12]

Could the valorization of night, darkness, and shadows in Latina/o aesthetics of night be myriad expressions of what Kristeva calls a still-resistant "culture of the people" (189) in the face of the blinding, fatal light of corporatized, anesthetized "popular culture"? I would answer in the affirmative: Yes, perhaps, and this is one of the reasons I have found these aesthetics of night so compelling.

NOTES

Preface

1. In a poem titled "Historia de la noche," which translates as "History of the night," Jorge Luis Borges reminds readers that no one can contemplate the night without vertigo and that the night, both time-bound and transhistorical, would not exist "sin esos tenues instrumentos, los ojos" (*Obra poética 1923–1977*, 556). The night would not exist "without those fragile instruments, the eyes."

Introduction

1. Baca, *Working in the Dark: Reflections of a Poet of the Barrio*, 20 and 146.

2. I borrow the concept "aesthetico-political" from Algerian-born French philosopher Jacques Rancière. He defines both art and politics as "a recomposition of the landscape of the visible, a recomposition of the . . . relationship between doing, making, being, seeing, and saying" (*The Politics of Aesthetics: The Distribution of the Sensible*, 45). He writes, "Politics and art, like forms of knowledge, construct 'fictions,' that is to say *material* rearrangements of signs and images, relationships between what is seen and what is said, between what is done and what can be done" (39).

3. García, *A Handbook to Luck*, 94.

4. I borrow the phrase "Other America" from Venezuelan public intellectual Arturo Uslar Pietri's essay translated from Spanish into English as "The Other America."

5. *Princeton Encyclopedia of Poetry and Poetics*, 870.

6. See scholarship by Rodólfo Acuña, José David and Ramón Saldívar, Norma Alarcón, Héctor Calderón, and José Limón, among others.

7. See Horkheimer and Adorno, *Dialectic of Enlightenment*, translated by John

Cumming. Also, for a brief but highly informative discussion of various intellectual traditions informing notions of magical realism and *lo real maravilloso,* see Saldívar's section "Some Concepts and Definitions of Magic Realism" in the section "Magical Narratives" of *The Dialectics of Our America,* 90–96.

8. Consult, in particular, Oboler, "'Hispanics? That's What They Call Us,'" in *Ethnic Labels, Latino Lives,* 16, and Caminero-Santangelo, "Introduction: Who Are We?" in *On Latinidad,* 1–35.

9. Adorno, *Aesthetic Theory,* 3–4; hereafter cited in parentheses in the text.

10. Within Chicana/o studies, to name just a few works, I would point to Ramón Saldívar's *Chicano Narrative: The Dialectics of Difference* (1990), José David Saldívar's *Border Matters: Remapping American Cultural Studies* (1997), Sonia Saldívar-Hull's *Feminism on the Border: Chicana Gender Politics and Literature* (2000), María Herrera-Sobek's edited collection of essays *Reconstructing a Chicano/a Literary Heritage: Hispanic Colonial Literature of the Southwest* (1993), Alvina E. Quintana's *Home Girls: Chicana Literary Voices* (1996), and Arturo J. Aldama and Naomi H. Quiñonez's edited collection of essays *Decolonial Voices: Chicana and Chicano Cultural Studies in the 21st Century* (2002). Within continental Puerto Rican studies, I would cite as examples Alberto Sandoval-Sánchez's *José, Can You See? Latinos On and Off Broadway* (1999), Lisa Sánchez-González's *Boricua Literature: A Literary History of the Puerto Rican Diaspora* (2001), Carmen Socorro Rivera's *Kissing the Mango Tree: Puerto Rican Women Rewriting American Literature* (2002), and Eva C. Vásquez's *Pregones Theatre: A Theatre for Social Change in the South Bronx* (2003). Within Cuban American studies, I would underscore sources such as Gustavo Pérez-Firmat's *Life on the Hyphen: The Cuban-American Way* (1994), José Quiroga's *Tropics of Desire: Interventions from Queer Latino America* (2000) though his book also covers non-Cuban Latina/o writers, Ricardo L. Ortíz's *Cultural Erotics in Cuban America* (2007), and Jorge J. E. Gracia, Lynette M. F. Bosch, and Isabel Alvarez Borland's edited collection *Identity, Memory, and Diaspora: Voices of Cuban-American Artists, Writers, and Philosophers* (2008).

11. Muñoz, "Feeling Brown," 67–79. Ironically, this essay calls into serious question the cultural and political efficacy of the term "Latino," but I also see a glimpse of a negative dialectics in which the "term's inability to index, with any regularity, the central tropes that lead to our understanding of group identities in the United States" opens up subversive possibilities later explored in studies such as Antonio Viego's *Dead Subjects: Toward a Politics of Loss in Latino Studies.*

12. Henry, *Caliban's Reason: Introducing Afro-Caribbean Philosophy,* 1.

13. Yúdice, "Rethinking Area and Ethnic Studies in the Context of Economic and Political Restructuring," in *Critical Latin American and Latino Studies,* 80; hereafter cited in parentheses in the text.

14. See Fernández Retamar, *Caliban and Other Essays.*

15. Blum, *Ghost Hunters: William James and the Search for Scientific Proof of Life after Death,* 15.

16. Camus, "The Growing Stone" from *Exile and the Kingdom*, in *The Plague, The Fall, Exile and the Kingdom, and Selected Essays*, 479.

17. Camus, *The Plague*, in *The Plague, The Fall, Exile and the Kingdom, and Selected Essays*, 86; hereafter cited in parentheses in the text.

18. Camus, "The Adulterous Woman" from *Exile and the Kingdom*, in *The Plague, The Fall, Exile and the Kingdom, and Selected Essays*, 363; hereafter cited in parentheses in the text.

19. For a succinct analysis of the gnostic elements of the film *Donnie Darko*, see Eric G. Wilson's study *Secret Cinema: Gnostic Vision in Film*.

20. Auster, *Oracle Night*, 42; hereafter cited in parentheses in the text.

21. Wiesel, *La Nuit*, 34.

22. Hughes, "Negro," in *The Collected Poems of Langston Hughes*, 24; hereafter cited in parentheses in the text.

23. For an in-depth study of the relation of the category "Latina/o" to "Black" and "Afro," see all of *Neither Enemies Nor Friends: Latinos, Blacks, Afro-Latinos*, edited by Anani Dzidzienyo and Suzanne Oboler, but especially their first chapter, "Flows and Counterflows: Latina/os, Blackness, and Racialization in Hemispheric Perspective," 3–35.

24. Hippolyte, *Night Vision: Poems*, 38.

25. Santos, *Places Left Unfinished at the Time of Creation: A Memoir*, 9.

26. See Sontag, *Under the Sign of Saturn*, 111. Susan Sontag's essay "Under the Sign of Saturn" elucidates Walter Benjamin's melancholic solitude as the basis for his work and as his fundamental response to the world. I here adapt Sontag's phrase to form my own—"under the sign of night."

1. Dreaded Non-Identities of Night

1. Acosta, "Autobiographical Essay," in *Oscar "Zeta" Acosta: The Collected Works*, 9.

2. Paredes, "Mexican American Authors and the American Dream," 71.

3. See Camacho, *The Chicano Treatise*.

4. Gordon, *Ghostly Matters: Haunting and the Sociological Imagination*, 72; hereafter cited in parentheses in the text.

5. Generation of 1927 Spanish poet Luis Cernuda (1902–1963), exiled in 1938 first to England and then to Scotland, the United States, and finally Mexico (the one country with which he identified as akin to his native Andalusia yet complementing his Mediterranean world with its "facing" of "a distant Asia"), commented extensively on the similarities and differences between Spain, especially southern Spain, and Mexico (114). See his "Variations on a Mexican Theme" in *Written in Water: The Prose Poems of Luis Cernuda*, 99–151.

6. See Xavier Villaurrutia's collection of poems *Nostalgia for Death*, translated by Eliot Weinberger.

7. See Palmer, "Witches: Europe and America," in *Cultures of Darkness: Night Travels in the Histories of Transgression*, 49–68.

8. For a critical elucidation of Paredes's concept of and scholarship on "Greater Mexico" in general and the Lower Border in particular and their relationship to his creative work, see Ramón Saldívar's *The Borderlands of Culture: Américo Paredes and the Transnational Imaginary*, 53–60; hereafter cited in parentheses in the text.

9. Saldívar, *Border Matters: Remapping American Cultural Studies*, 56; hereafter cited in parentheses in the text.

10. Paredes, "The Hammon and the Beans," in *The Latino Reader: From 1542 to the Present*, 251; hereafter cited in parentheses in the text.

11. Hinojosa, introduction to Américo Paredes, *George Washington Gómez: A Mexicotexan Novel*, 6.

12. Paredes, *George Washington Gómez*, 50–52; hereafter cited in parentheses in the text.

13. For a discussion from a decolonizing perspective with particular attention to gender of the figure of La Llorona in traditional and contemporary narratives, see Domino Renee Pérez's essay "Caminando con La Llorona: Traditional and Contemporary Narratives," in *Chicana Traditions: Continuity and Change*, 100–13.

14. Paredes, *The Shadow*, 1; hereafter cited in parentheses in the text.

15. Stoichita, *A Short History of the Shadow*, 7.

16. I borrow the phrase "secure the shadow" from Jay Ruby, *Secure the Shadow: Death and Photography in America*.

17. Reprinted by permission of the University of Texas Press from "'Darkness My Night': The Philosophical Challenge of Gloria Anzaldúa's Aesthetics of the Shadow," in *Bridging: How Gloria Anzaldúa's Life and Work Transformed Our Own*.

18. About that resistance, Anzaldúa writes, "My Chicana identity is grounded in the Indian woman's history of resistance" (*Borderlands*, 43). This suggests that she thought of resistance to patriarchal, colonial, ethno-racially stratified oppression as grounded in the history of the indigenous people of the Americas and of the Southwest in particular.

19. See the 1982 interview with Linda Smuckler titled "Turning Points" in *Interviews/Entrevistas* (23).

20. Ross, *The Aesthetics of Disengagement: Contemporary Art and Depression*, xvi; hereafter cited in parentheses in the text.

21. Anzaldúa, "now let us shift . . . the path of conocimiento . . . inner work, public acts," in *this bridge we call home: radical visions of transformation*, 551; hereafter cited in parentheses in the text.

22. Kristeva, *Black Sun: Depression and Melancholia*, 145; hereafter cited in parentheses in the text.

23. Castillo, "Un Tapiz: The Poetics of Conscientización," in *Massacre of the Dreamers: Essays on Xicanisma*, 172; hereafter cited in parentheses in the text.

24. Castillo, *Sapogonia*, 354.

25. Castillo, *So Far from God*, 19; hereafter cited in parentheses in the text.

26. Castillo, "Loverboys," in *Loverboys*, 20; hereafter cited in parentheses in the text.

27. Castillo, *Peel My Love Like an Onion*, xv; hereafter cited in parentheses in the text.

28. Bruce-Novoa, "Rechy and Rodriguez: Double Crossing the Public/Private Line," in *Double Crossings / EntreCruzamientos*, 19; hereafter cited in parentheses in the text.

29. On the figuration of the narrator's Latino and specifically Mexican American identity in Rechy's *City of Night*, see my article "Turning Tricks: Trafficking in the Figure of the Latino" in *Trickster Lives: Culture and Myth in American Fiction*, 168–84.

30. Rechy, *City of Night*, 9.

31. Rechy, *The Coming of the Night*, 3.

32. Baca, *Working in the Dark: Reflections of a Poet in the Barrio*, 25; hereafter cited in parentheses in the text.

33. Herrera, *Night Train to Tuxtla*, 13; hereafter cited in parentheses in the text.

34. Montoya, *the iceworker sings and other poems*, 13; hereafter cited in parentheses in the text.

35. Gonzalez, *Turtle Pictures*, 69; hereafter cited in parentheses in the text.

36. Alarcón, *From the Other Side of Night / Del otro lado de la noche*, 20; hereafter cited in parentheses in the text.

37. Martínez, *Breathing Between the Lines*, 7; hereafter cited in parentheses in the text.

38. See Doris Sommer, *Foundational Fictions: The National Romances of Latin America*.

39. Gonzalez, *Cool Auditor*, 11.

40. Palmer, *Cultures of Darkness*, 370; hereafter cited in parentheses in the text.

41. Ginsberg, "Howl," in *Collected Poems: 1947–1980*, 127.

42. William Burroughs, acute cultural commentator behind the persona of a junkie, metafictionally commented on the pervasive national and transnational influence of the Beats in his early 1980s novel *Cities of the Red Night* (13).

43. Morrison, "The Dark American Sunset," in *The American Night: The Writings of Jim Morrison*, Volume II, 139.

44. See Connelly, *The Sleep of Reason: Primitivism in Modern European Art and Aesthetics, 1725–1907*.

45. Romero, "Pito," in *Rita and Los Angeles*, 55; hereafter cited in parentheses in the text.

46. See Todorov, *The Fantastic: A Structural Approach to a Literary Genre*.

47. For assorted details about Kerouac's early to mid 1950s trips to Mexico, see Tom Clark's *Jack Kerouac: A Biography*, 138–39. In *On the Road* (1957) Kerouac describes himself as unusually happy in Mexico with a Mexican woman. Thank you to Linda Wagner-Martin for pointing out the latter.

48. With regard to séances and Leo Romero's description of Jack Kerouac's appearance in the dwarf's apartment in one of the narrator's dreams (67–68), I found a curious reference to Jack Kerouac in practicing medium Elaine M.

Kuzmeskus's book on how to conduct séances titled *Séance 101 Physical Medium-ship* (11–12 and 15). She claims that Kerouac appeared to her in her dreams, encouraged her writing, and attracted her to his writings including those on Buddhism, karma, and reincarnation. In other words, according to Kuzmeskus, Kerouac served as one of her spirit guides from beyond the grave.

49. Purcell, *Weegee*. See also Edward Dimenberg's study *Film Noir and the Spaces of Modernity*, 49–50: "He [Weegee] began to accompany photographers on the night shift, and by the early 1930s he was moonlighting as a news photographer, selling photographs of fires, late-night arrests, and auto accidents to Acme [News Service] and other agencies. . . . Weegee's ability to arrive at the scene of the crime in advance of other photographers contributed to his legend."

50. Weegee's photography has inspired any number of writers, particularly of short stories. Leo Romero is one of them. Robert Olen Butler is another. Read about Butler's *Weegee Stories* (2011) at the online journal *Narrative Magazine*: http://www.narrativemagazine.com/store/book/weegee-stories. Last consulted 26 February 2011.

51. Sontag, *On Photography*, 14–15; hereafter cited in parentheses in the text.

52. Lima, *The Latino Body: Crisis Identities in American Literary and Cultural Memory*, 19.

53. On the relation of photography to the issue of indexing that which once was and is no longer, or on the relation of photography to death, see sections 38–40 of Barthes, *Camera Lucida: Reflections on Photography*, 92–99. See also Prosser, "Roland Barthes's Loss," in *Light in the Dark Room: Photography and Loss*, 19–52; Sontag, *On Photography*, 15–16; Metz, "Photography and Fetish," in *The Photography Reader*, 140–42; and Cadava, "Mortification" (7–11) and "Death" (128) in *Words of Light: Theses on the Photography of History*.

54. The NOVA program *Runaway Universe* describes the repulsive force of dark energy; the accelerating, expanding universe; and exploding stars, billions of light-years away, called supernovae that are charted spectrographically across the visible universe to measure the universe's accelerating expansion: "The most violent scenario occurs when the white dwarf orbits another kind of dying star called a red giant. The giant swells, nearly touching the smaller star. The two then begin a dance of death as the white dwarf draws hot gas from its partner. The dwarf's mass increases but at a certain point it can grow no further, and it goes supernova!"

55. For a brief history of the uses of the term "*noir*" in France, see film and comparative literature scholar James Otis Naremore's essay "A Season in Hell or the Snows of Yesteryear?" in Raymond Borde and Etienne Chaumeton's *A Panorama of American Film Noir, 1941–1953*, vii–xxi. Naremore writes, "At its best, classic or historical film noir had represented for Borde and Chaumeton an intermingling of social realism and oneirism, an erotic treatment of violence, and a feeling of psychological disorientation, as if capitalist and puritan values were being systematically inverted" (xix).

56. Oliver and Trigo, *Noir Anxiety*, xiv.

57. Lott, "The Whiteness of Film Noir," in *Whiteness: A Critical Reader*, 85.

58. On the subject of this nighttime slating of Latina/o actors, see "The Grave-yard Shift" section of the film *The Bronze Screen: 100 Years of the Latino Image in Hollywood.*

59. For a general discussion of images of Latina/os in U.S. film, especially Hol-lywood film, see Charles Ramírez Berg's *Latino Images in Film: Stereotypes, Subversion, Resistance.*

60. American literature and culture scholar Eva Cherniavsky provides an incisive reading of the film *Touch of Evil* (1958) in her book *Incorporations: Race, Nation, and the Body Politics of Capital*, 117–24. She focuses on the ways in which the film visually constructs a "shimmering white woman framed and transfixed by a circle of [menacing] Latino/a bodies" and specifically dark and darkened Mexican male bodies (121). According to her argument, the film plays on the fear that the white wife, who is further whitened by the spotlight upon her, will fall into "possession" by Mexican men other than her husband—a tale that functions as a allegory about ineffectual borders and "domestic interiority" rendered "leaky and contaminated" (121).

61. Lipsitz, *Footsteps in the Dark: The Hidden Histories of Popular Music*, 57, 78.

62. Corpi, *Crimson Moon*, 90; hereafter cited in parentheses in the text.

63. Rodriguez, *Brown Gumshoes*, 55; hereafter cited in parentheses in the text.

64. Corpi, *Black Widow's Wardrobe*, 83.

65. Corpi, *Eulogy for a Brown Angel*, 123; hereafter cited in parentheses in the text.

66. Corpi, *Cactus Blood*, 32; hereafter cited in parentheses in the text.

67. Corpi, *Death at Solstice*, 7; hereafter cited in parentheses.

68. Trujillo, *What Night Brings*, 9; hereafter cited in parentheses in the text.

2. Queer "Tropics" of Night and the *Caribe* of "American" (Post) Modernism

1. Guzmán, "'Pa' La Escuelita con Mucho Cuida'o y por la Orillita': A Journey Through the Contested Terrains of the Nation and Sexual Orientation," in *Puerto Rican Jam: Essays on Culture and Politics*, 209–28.

2. Cruz-Malavé, "Toward an Art of Transvestism: Colonialism and Homosexuality in Puerto Rican Literature," in *¿Entiendes? Queer Readings, Hispanic Writings*, 137–67.

3. See Ávila, "Caribbean Dislocations: Arenas and Ramos Otero in New York," in *Hispanisms and Homosexualities*, 101–19.

4. Negrón-Muntaner, "When I Was a Puerto Rican Lesbian: Meditations on *Brincando el charco*: Portrait of a Puerto Rican," 511–26.

5. See Quiroga, *Tropics of Desire: Interventions from Queer Latino America*, especially chapters 1–6 and 8, though the whole book qualifies. Quiroga concisely summarizes the scope of his book: "the first part is more concerned with gay/lesbian relationships between the United States and Latin America, the second

part focuses more on popular culture in the United States" (232); hereafter cited in parentheses in the text.

6. For example, see Cruz-Malavé and Manalansan IV, eds., *Queer Globalizations: Citizenship and the Afterlife of Colonialism.*

7. For a helpful accounting of scholarship on "transnational queer migration" and its connections to a Caribbean and specifically Puerto Rican context, see the introduction to La Fountain-Stokes's *Queer Ricans,* ix–xxvii.

8. Quijano, "Coloniality of Power, Eurocentrism, and Latin America," 533–80.

9. See Young, *Colonial Desire: Hybridity in Theory, Culture and Race.*

10. Bhabha, "Signs Taken for Wonders: Questions of Ambivalence and Authority under a Tree outside Delhi, May 1817," in *The Location of Culture,* 112.

11. See, for example, Tobar's *Translation Nation: Defining a New American Identity in the Spanish-Speaking United States.*

12. See Lipsitz, "The Possessive Investment in Whiteness," in *White Privilege: Essential Readings on the Other Side of Racism,* 61–84.

13. See Christian, "The Race for Theory," 51–64.

14. Bejel, *Gay Cuban Nation,* xv. Although Bejel is describing the island of Cuba in particular, I would argue, judging from the rampant heteronormativity of their nationalist discourses, that homosexuality haunts the national discourse of many of the Caribbean islands, not just of Cuba. Bejel himself suggests as much (3) when he cites Doris Sommer's analysis of bourgeois heteronormativity in Latin American nationalist discourses in her book *Foundational Fictions: The National Romances of Latin America.* One of the more interesting pre-mid-twentieth-century works that Bejel discusses that dared to represent homosexuality positively is the night-inflected 1940 novel by Cuban feminist writer Ofelia Rodríguez Acosta, *En la noche del mundo* [*In the night of the world*] (Havana: La Verónica, 1940) featuring a gay male couple (see Bejel, 58–65).

15. Bell, *Ashes Taken for Fire: Aesthetic Modernism and the Critique of Identity,* 4 and 9; hereafter cited in parentheses in the text.

16. Crane, *The Bridge,* 6, 16, 52, 65, and 73; hereafter cited in parentheses in the text.

17. Sandlin, "'Poetry Always Demands All My Ghosts': The Haunted and Haunting Poetry of Rane Arroyo," 163; hereafter cited in parentheses in the text.

18. Derrida, *Archive Fever: A Freudian Impression,* 9–13.

19. Campo, *Diva,* 16.

20. Freud, "Mourning and Melancholia," in *The Standard Edition of the Complete Psychological Works of Sigmund Freud,* Volume 14.

21. Viego, *Dead Subjects: Toward a Politics of Loss in Latino Studies,* 4–5; hereafter cited in parentheses in the text.

22. David L. Eng and David Kazanjian, "Introduction: Mourning Remains," in *Loss,* 22; hereafter cited in parentheses in the text.

23. Schiesari, *The Gendering of Melancholia,* 32.

24. Permission to quote granted by Dr. Luz María Umpierre, *The Margarita Poems* (Third Woman Press), 1987 © Exclusive of Dr. Luz María Umpierre.

25. Umpierre-Herrera, "In Cycles," in *The Margarita Poems*, 1; hereafter cited in parentheses in the text.

26. For an even more extended list of writers, modernist and otherwise, with whom Umpierre is in dialogue, see La Fountain-Stokes's *Queer Ricans*, 69 and 85.

27. Lima, *The Latino Body: Crisis Identities in American Literary and Cultural Memory*, 130–40; hereafter cited in parentheses in the text.

28. Luz María Umpierre, "Lesbian Tantalizing in Carmen Lugo Filippi's 'Milagros, Calle Mercurio,'" in *¿Entiendes? Queer Readings, Hispanic Writings*, 306–14. Umpierre has explained to me that with regard to "homocriticism," she created this theory of reading to teach a book of poems by Lezama Lima in the early 1980s in one of her classes. She "then developed it in writing into a theory of reading" which she taught to her students (e-mail from Umpierre to me dated 5 March 2011). For more information, consult her blog at http://luzma-umpierre .blogspot.com.

29. Kristeva, "Place Names," in *Desire in Language: A Semiotic Approach to Literature and Art*, 283.

30. See Chicana writer Cherríe Moraga's essay "A Long Line of Vendidas" in *Loving in the War Years: lo que nunca pasó por sus labios* (1983) on the necessity for Chicana women and all women to learn to love themselves on their own terms and not on the terms of the patriarchy with which they have been indoctrinated.

31. Reprinted by permission of the publishers from "Miguel Algarín's 'Nuyorican Angels' of Night and the Critique of Enwhitened Idealism," in *The Turn Around Religion: Literature, Culture, and the Work of Sacvan Bercovitch*.

32. Algarín, *Love is Hard Work: Memories of Loisaida*, 44–51; hereafter cited in parentheses in the text.

33. Flores, *From Bomba to Hip-Hop: Puerto Rican Culture and Latino Identity*, 9.

34. Kant, *Critique of Pure Reason*, in *Basic Writings of Kant*, 29.

35. Stevens, *The Collected Poems*, 534; hereafter cited in parentheses in the text.

36. Whether "black" was viewed as "nothingness" before it as nothingness came to be associated with people of African descent is a question that pales in the face of the determined European and Euro-American project to reduce "black" people to nothing, to legally and politically non-existent beings. For example, any responsible historical, literary, and cultural analysis simply cannot overlook the glaring fact of what political philosopher Louis Sala-Molins calls "the most monstrous legal document of modern times," the *Code noir* of the late seventeenth century, "the body of laws, statutes, and decrees that codified and regulated the practice of French Caribbean slavery and was promulgated in 1685 under Louis XIV" (see the introduction by John Conteh-Morgan to Louis Sala-Molins's *Dark Side of the Light: Slavery and the French Enlightenment*, x, as well as the entire book by Sala-Molins).

37. Torres-Saillant, *An Intellectual History of the Caribbean*, 74.

38. Miguel Algarín, telephone interview with María DeGuzmán, 3 June 2003; hereafter cited in parentheses as "Interview."

39. Delgadillo, "Singing 'Angelitos Negros': African Diaspora Meets *Mestizaje* in the Americas," 407–30.

40. The Coptic Church of the upper Nile Valley of Egypt is an example of the very long historical presence of Christianity on the African continent.

41. The film *Nowhere in Africa* (2001), directed by Caroline Link and based on an autobiographical novel by Stefanie Zweig, deals with the African-Jewish diaspora out of Germany in the 1930s.

42. One can find both misogyny and homophobia among the Nuyorican voices, but nevertheless there was and still is a refreshing openness about the existence of difference involving all the variables mentioned.

43. See Algarín and Holman, eds., *Aloud: Voices from the Nuyorican Poets Café* for many samples of both Nuyorican poetry and poetry more generally performed at the Nuyorican Poets Café.

44. http://www.rafaelcampo.com/rc_Biography/rc_bio_index.html. Last consulted 20 July 2009.

45. Campo, *The Desire to Heal: A Doctor's Education in Empathy, Identity, and Poetry,* 256 and 264; hereafter cited in parentheses in the text.

46. Ortíz, *Cultural Erotics in Cuban America,* 236.

47. Campo, "America, the Beautiful," in *Landscape with Human Figure,* 10; hereafter cited in parentheses in the text.

48. Campo, "Another Poem in English," in *The Other Man Was Me: A Voyage to the New World,* 15; hereafter cited in parentheses in the text.

49. Campo, *Diva,* 83–94; hereafter cited in parentheses in the text.

50. In *A Lover's Discourse: Fragments* on the discourse of lovers, French semiotician, philosopher, and literary critic Roland Barthes observes that the night of the mystical discourse of St. John of the Cross is "the Night of non-profit, of subtle, invisible expenditure: *estoy a oscuras:* I am here, sitting simply and calmly in the dark interior of love." This kind of night envelops and overcomes another kind of night, which is the night or rather the fog and shadows of being "blinded by attachment to things and the disorder which emanates from that condition" (171–72). The night of the dark interior of love makes "the darkness . . . transluminous" (171).

51. See Sontag, *Regarding the Pain of Others,* 101–103, 125–26.

52. Campo, *What the Body Told,* 3; hereafter cited in parentheses in the text.

53. Benítez-Rojo, *The Repeating Island: The Caribbean and the Postmodern Perspective,* 10.

54. Kutzinski, *Sugar's Secrets: Race and the Erotics of Cuban Nationalism,* 1–42; hereafter cited in parentheses in the text.

55. Butler, *The Psychic Life of Power,* 182.

56. See the poem "Center Street, Jamaica Plain," *Diva,* 51, in connection with such a reading.

57. Campo, *The Enemy,* 14 and the back cover; hereafter cited in parentheses in the text.

58. Arroyo, *Pale Ramón*, 34; hereafter cited in parentheses in the text.

59. Arroyo, *The Portable Famine*, 40; hereafter cited in parentheses in the text.

60. See Arroyo, "The Mask Museum" in *Home Movies of Narcissus*, 19–38; hereafter cited in parentheses in the text.

61. Arroyo, *The Singing Shark*, 79; hereafter cited in parentheses in the text.

62. Arroyo, *The Buried Sea: New and Selected Poems*, 2; hereafter cited in parentheses in the text.

63. Arroyo mentions Percy Bysshe Shelley, Pablo Neruda, John Ashbery, Emily Dickinson, Hart Crane, Carl Sandburg (the major figure in his dissertation), Vachel Lindsay, Edgar Lee Masters, William Carlos Williams, Rene Char, George Seferis, Reinaldo Arenas, Boris Pasternak, and James Baldwin (*The Buried Sea*, 1–6).

64. References to writers include Edgar Allan Poe, Nathaniel Hawthorne, Ralph Waldo Emerson, Emily Dickinson, Henry James, Wallace Stevens, F. Scott Fitzgerald, Ernest Hemingway, John Dos Passos, Sherwood Anderson, Margaret Anderson, Frank O'Hara, James Wright, and James Galvin. Arroyo also mentions the Bible, William Blake, Thomas Hardy, Aleksandr Pushkin, Federico García Lorca (a favorite with Rafael Campo), Octavio Paz, Sor Juana de la Cruz, Proust, Sartre, Auden, Jean Genet, and Cavafy.

65. Those African American and Latina/o musicians, singers, and/or performers include James Earl Jones, Aretha Franklin, James Brown, Tina Turner, RuPaul, The Supremes, Diana Ross, Desi Arnez, Selena, Ricky Martin, Julio Iglesias, Enrique Iglesias, Shakira, Gloria Estefan, José Feliciano, and Jennifer López. Other performers who appear in Arroyo's poems are Elvis, the Beatles, Madonna, Cat Stevens, Morrissey, Bruce Springsteen, Annie Lennox, and Björk.

66. I. Thessalonians 5:2 in *The Holy Bible*, King James version.

67. See Lawrence, *Love Saves the Day: A History of American Dance Music Culture*.

68. Arroyo, "UFOs over America," in *The Roswell Poems*, 20.

69. See Joseph M. Acaba's biographical data at NASA's website: http://www.jsc.nasa.gov/Bios/htmlbios/acaba-jm.html. Last consulted 2 January 2011.

70. Arroyo, "Prelude: The Hospital," in *The Sky's Weight*, 57; hereafter cited in parentheses in the text.

71. There are poems about and from the simulated perspective of Plato, Aristotle, Ptolemy, Hipparchus (with the first star map), Copernicus (of the sixteenth century), Johannes Kepler (late sixteenth to early seventeenth century), Galileo Galilei (mid sixteenth century to mid seventeenth century), Isaac Newton and Edmond Halley (mid seventeenth to early eighteenth century), Johann Daniel Titus (eighteenth century), Pierre-Jules-César Janssen (mid nineteenth to early twentieth century), W. C. Bond and George P. Light (nineteenth century and American), Heinrich Schwabe (nineteenth century), George Ellery Hale (late nineteenth to mid twentieth century and American, Chicago-born), Edwin P. Hubble (first half of the twentieth century and a Midwesterner whose research

more or less confirmed that the universe is expanding), and Albert Einstein (first half of the twentieth century).

72. Alvarez Borland, *Cuban-American Literature of Exile: From Person to Persona*, 59–60.

73. Weiss, *On the Margins*, 123.

3. Postcolonial Pre-Columbian Cosmologies of Night in Contemporary U.S.-Based Central American Texts

1. See Román de la Campa, *Latin Americanism*, vii, 63–64, and the book as a whole.

2. Arias, *Taking Their Word: Literature and the Signs of Central America*, xii.

3. Rodríguez, *Dividing the Isthmus*, 129–66; hereafter cited in parentheses in the text.

4. E-mail to me from Sybil Venegas, chair of the Chicana/o Studies Department at East Los Angeles College, 29 December 2010.

5. Saldívar-Hull, "Chicana Feminisms: From Ethnic Identity to Global Solidarity," in *Feminism on the Border*, 27–57.

6. Martínez, *500 Years of Chicana Women's History / 500 Años de la Mujer Chicana*, 143, 202, 215, 263, and 304–306.

7. For further information about the controversy at East Los Angeles College over the proposed course "Central Americans: The New Chicanos," see Roberto Rodríguez's article dated 12 July 1997 at http://diverseeducation.com/article/8398. Last consulted 29 December 2010.

8. Carrasco, *Religions of Mesoamerica*, 18; hereafter cited in parentheses in the text.

9. This volcanic crystal is found only in a few places in eastern Guatemala (El Chayal, for example) and in central Mexico. See Berthold Riese, *Die Maya. Geschichte. Kultur. Religion* (Verlag: 1995); in Spanish: *Los Mayas*, 27–28.

10. Miller and Taube, *An Illustrated Dictionary of the Gods and Symbols of Ancient Mexico and the Maya*, 114; hereafter cited in parentheses in the text.

11. Goetz and Morley, introduction to *Popol Vuh: The Sacred Book of the Ancient Quiché Maya*, 5.

12. *Popol Vuh: The Sacred Book of the Ancient Quiché Maya*, 164; hereafter cited in parentheses in the text.

13. The status of Panama as Central American is much contested given that it was part of Colombia from 1821 until 1903, and given the influence of the Caribbean upon its culture, not to mention U.S. domination "[w]ith the completion of the Panama Canal in 1914 and the enforcement of U.S. rule in the Canal Zone" whereupon Panama "was transformed into a virtual U.S. protectorate" (Rodríguez, *Dividing the Isthmus*, 50).

14. For an extensive discussion of the socioeconomic and cultural repercussions of the building of the Panama Canal and the establishment of banana republics,

see Ana Patricia Rodríguez's "Nations Divided: U.S. Intervention, Banana Enclaves, and the Panama Canal" in her book *Dividing the Isthmus*, 44–75.

15. On the subject of history as enacted story encoding cultural values and beliefs, consult Hayden White's *Metahistory: The Historical Imagination in Nineteenth-Century Europe* (1973), *Tropics of Discourse: Essays in Cultural Criticism* (1978), and *The Content of the Form: Narrative Discourse and Historical Representation* (1987).

16. See Burke, *Language as Symbolic Action: Essays on Life, Literature, and Method*, 49–51.

17. Goldman, *The Art of Political Murder*, 3.

18. See DeGuzmán, *Spain's Long Shadow: The Black Legend, Off-Whiteness, and Anglo-American Empire*.

19. Pérez-Torres, *Movements in Chicano Poetry*, 16.

20. See Rodríguez, "K'atun Turning in Greater Guatemala," in *Dividing the Isthmus*, 103–28.

21. Arias, *After the Bombs*, 33, 34, 40, and 116; hereafter cited in parentheses in the text. The original Spanish edition, *Después de las bombas*, was published in 1979 by Editorial Joaquín Mortiz, S.A., México.

22. Arias, *Rattlesnake: A Novel*, 29, 42, 105, 111, 133, 154, 155, and 243; hereafter cited in parentheses in the text.

23. Tobar, *The Tattooed Soldier*, 13, 39, 51, 123, and 300; hereafter cited in parentheses in the text.

24. Goldman, *The Long Night of White Chickens*, 22, 48, 104, 107, 111, 124, 142, 162, 213, 366, 375, 391, 398, and 400; hereafter cited in parentheses in the text.

25. Goldman, *The Ordinary Seaman*, 3, 29, 93, 203, 248, and 333; hereafter cited in parentheses in the text.

26. Goldman, *The Divine Husband*, 217 and 100; hereafter cited in parentheses in the text.

27. http://sellersgarcia.com/sylvia/conversation. Last consulted 27 December 2010.

28. http://sellersgarcia.com/sylvia/conversation. Last consulted 27 December 2010.

29. Sellers-García, *When the Ground Turns in Its Sleep*, 324; hereafter cited in parentheses in the text.

30. Tedlock, *2000 Years of Mayan Literature*, 1–2.

31. Cristina Henríquez was born in the United States and has lived there most of her life, but she frequently travels to Panama and she has said that she prefers to write about her experiences and those of her parents, extended family, friends, and so forth from a distance. Distance, according to Henríquez, gives clarity and sensuous precision to her observations of and experiences in Panama. Public lecture for the UNC Latina/o Cultures Speakers Series, 13 November 2008 at the University of North Carolina, Chapel Hill.

32. Henríquez, *Come Together, Fall Apart: A Novella and Stories*, 2; hereafter cited in parentheses in the text.

33. Emma Pérez, *The Decolonial Imaginary: Writing Chicanas into History*, 5–7; hereafter cited in parentheses in the text.

34. See Ana Patricia Rodríguez's discussion of the human and cultural genocide implicit in the Guatemalan military's destruction of crops during the Guatemalan civil war (*Dividing the Isthmus*, 106–108).

35. For a full explanation of how "Bernal vanquishes the jaguar god represented by Longoria, and Longoria enters the underworld as the jaguar returning home to Xibalba, the underworld" and "[a] new day rises in Los Angeles in the wake of Longoria's death," see Rodríguez, *Dividing the Isthmus*, 119–28.

36. For those readers interested in the contemporary use of pre-Columbian Mayan cosmologies of night (featuring the Tree of Creation with its roots in the Milky Way / underworld) deployed as a critique of Spanish and European colonial world views, and in the blending of these pre-Columbian Mayan cosmologies with other traditions drawn from Kabbalah (mystical traditions of the Jews that emerged in Spain and southern France in the thirteenth century, including the transmigration of souls) and Buddhism, see director Darren Aronofsky's 2006 film *The Fountain*. The film is concerned with the quest to defeat death, a quest gradually transformed into a hard-won acceptance of death. Its uses are not the same as those of the texts I am discussing in this chapter, but the film provides an important occasion for comparison and contrast to what these U.S.-based Central American Latina/o texts do with pre-Columbian Mayan cosmologies of night for those who wish to pursue this line of inquiry in regard to literature, film, and comparative ethnic studies.

37. See Bourdieu, *Acts of Resistance: Against the Tyranny of the Market* and *Firing Back: Against the Tyranny of the Market 2*. See also Nelly Richard, "Cultural Peripheries: Latin America and Postmodernist De-centering," in *The Postmodernism Debate in Latin America*, 217–22.

4. Transcultural Night Work of U.S.-Based South American Cultural Producers

1. Cortázar, "Background," in *Save Twilight*, 152–53.

2. See http://www.acme.org.uk/residencies.php. Last consulted 20 July 2009.

3. E-mail from Mariana Romo-Carmona to me dated 2 September 2008.

4. DeGuzmán, "Night Becomes 'Latina': Mariana Romo-Carmona's *Living at Night* and the Tactics of Abjection," 91.

5. See Bhabha, *The Location of Culture*.

6. Romo-Carmona, *Speaking Like an Immigrant: A Collection*, 1; hereafter cited in parentheses in the text. This is the second edition of a book published in 1998 in New York City by the Latina Lesbian History Project. According to the preface to the second edition, this latter edition "has been re-edited and expanded, with stories now organized in chronological order" based on when they were written.

7. Though no mention of Santiago exists in "Idilio," there is specific mention of a bus ride along "Avenida Catedral," a major street in Santiago, Chile (135).

8. The tenements of the Lower East Side were the hardship-ridden "homes" of millions of immigrants as documented in, among other works, Danish American journalist and photographer Jacob August Riis's early 1890s compendium *How the Other Half Lives*.

9. See Nelly Richard's chapter "Cultural Peripheries: Latin America and Postmodernist De-centering," 217–22.

10. The story of a relatively ordinary flesh-and-blood woman becoming a rather extraordinary outlaw on account of some kind of encounter with and even inhabitation by the spirit of another woman who has lived before her is remindful of the plot of Nicaraguan novelist Giaconda Belli's 1989 novel first published in Spanish as *La mujer habitada* and five years later translated into English as *The Inhabited Woman*. In Belli's novel, an upper-class Nicaraguan woman named Lavinia is slowly awakened to a revolutionary consciousness by the spirit of a native or indigenous woman who lived during the Spanish conquest of Central America and who, in her day, rebelled against the Spaniards, her oppressors. Unconsciously inspired by the spirit of this native woman who entered her body "like an amber cascade" to "swim in her blood" (57), Lavinia defects from the vested interests of the Nicaraguan upper classes and joins "the clandestine National Liberation Movement" (15) against the dictator whom, given that the time is the early 1970s, readers can interpret to be Anastasio Somoza Debayle, who was assassinated by Sandinistas in 1980.

11. Deleuze, *Pure Immanence: Essays on A Life*, 75; hereafter cited in parentheses.

12. Manrique, *Twilight at the Equator: A Novel*, 3; hereafter cited in parentheses in the text.

13. Manrique, *My Night with / Mi noche con Federico García Lorca*, 27; hereafter cited in parentheses in the text.

14. My analysis of Jorge Manrique's work in relation to part of the self-proclaimed liberationist project of Deleuze as well as Guattari does not constitute the first time that Latina/o cultural production has been examined in light of some of the theories of these two French theorists. Chicana/o studies scholar Rafael Pérez-Torres opens up this kind of critical dialogue in an intriguing section of his 1995 book *Movements in Chicano Poetry* titled "Minority Discourse: Deleuze and Guattari," 216–18.

15. See Kelly, *Frederic Edwin Church and the National Landscape*; Manthorne, *Tropical Renaissance: North American Artists Exploring Latin America, 1839–1879*; and Wilmerding, *American Light: The Luminist Movement, 1850–1875*.

16. Alarcón, *Lost City Radio*, 123; hereafter cited in parentheses.

17. E-mail from Carlos Jiménez Cahua to me dated 25 January 2011.

18. E-mail from Carlos Jiménez Cahua to me dated 23 January 2011.

19. E-mail from Carlos Jiménez Cahua to me dated 25 January 2011.

20. E-mail from Carlos Jiménez Cahua to me dated 25 January 2011.

21. E-mail from Carlos Jiménez Cahua to me dated 25 January 2011.

22. http://blogs.princeton.edu/paw/2010/03. Last consulted 7 February 2011.

23. Maurice Merleau-Ponty, "The Primacy of Perception and Its Philosophical

Consequences," in *The Primacy of Perception*, 12–42; hereafter cited in parentheses in the text.

24. E-mail from Carlos Jiménez Cahua to me dated 23 January 2011.

25. E-mail from Carlos Jiménez Cahua to me dated 23 January 2011.

26. E-mail from Carlos Jiménez Cahua to me dated 23 January 2011.

27. E-mail from Carlos Jiménez Cahua to me dated 23 January 2011.

28. E-mail from Carlos Jiménez Cahua to me dated 23 January 2011.

29. E-mail from Carlos Jiménez Cahua to me dated 7 February 2011.

30. E-mail from Carlos Jiménez Cahua to me dated 7 February 2011.

31. E-mail from Carlos Jiménez Cahua to me dated 7 February 2011.

32. E-mail from Carlos Jiménez Cahua to me dated 23 January 2011.

33. E-mail from Carlos Jiménez Cahua to me dated 25 January 2011.

34. Islas, "Saints, Artists, and Vile Politics (excerpt)," in *Arturo Islas: The Uncollected Works*, 183. I quote from an excerpt from a seventy-page monograph on Chicana/o literature that Islas wrote in 1975.

35. On the "cross-cultural hybridization" of Arturo Islas's own work, see José David Saldívar's chapter "The Hybridity of Culture in Arturo Islas's *The Rain God*" from *The Dialectics of Our America*, 105–20.

36. Heredia, *Transnational Latina Narratives in the Twenty-First Century*, 1–12.

37. See Limón, *En busca de Bernabé*, 13, 63–64, 66–67, 77, 103, and the epilogue.

38. Limón, *Erased Faces*, 84.

39. See Chela Sandoval's treatise titled *Methodology of the Oppressed*.

40. See Limón, *The Day of the Moon*, 16–18 and 207–208.

41. See Santos-Febres, *Sirena Selena Vestida de Pena*, 141–42. The English section from the novel in Spanish is written from the perspective of a Canadian queer sex tourist commenting, in a rather neocolonial, unreflecting fashion, on his experiences in the Dominican Republic. The English translation of the novel by Stephen Lytle is peppered with Spanish words and phrases, making it seem like a more standard U.S. Latina/o text, but the Spanish original should be consulted to appreciate its own linguistic experiments.

42. García, *A Handbook to Luck*, 8; hereafter cited in parentheses in the text.

43. García, *The Lady Matador's Hotel*, 104 and 191–93.

Conclusion

1. Grosfoguel, Maldonado-Torres, and Saldívar, "Latin@s and the 'Euro-American Menace,'" in *Latin@s in the World-System*, 8; hereafter cited in parentheses in the text.

2. Seshadri-Crooks, *Desiring Whiteness: A Lacanian Analysis of Race*, 5.

3. See Suro, *Strangers Among Us: Latino Lives in a Changing America*.

4. Martí, "Dos patrias," in *Poesía completa: José Martí*, 210; hereafter cited in parentheses in the text.

5. To read more about these and other myths and informed, well-researched

rebuttals to these myths, see Aviva Chomsky's book *"They Take Our Jobs!": And 20 Other Myths about Immigration.*

6. See Chela Sandoval, *Methodology of the Oppressed,* 16, 33, 57–63, and 178–83; hereafter cited in parentheses in the text.

7. Schivelbusch, *Disenchanted Night: The Industrialization of Light in the Nineteenth Century,* 81; hereafter cited in parentheses in the text.

8. Kristeva, *The Sense and Non-Sense of Revolt,* 25.

9. Jameson, "Postmodernism, or the Cultural Logic of Late Capitalism," 53–92.

10. Gilroy, "Introduction: On Living with Difference," in *Postcolonial Melancholia,* 1.

11. Acosta, "To Whom It May Concern [A Solicitation]," in *Oscar "Zeta" Acosta: The Uncollected Works,* 193–202.

12. Lippit, *Atomic Light (Shadow Optics),* 4.

BIBLIOGRAPHY

Acosta, Oscar Zeta. "Autobiographical Essay." In *Oscar "Zeta" Acosta: The Collected Works*. Ed. Ilan Stavans. Houston, TX: Arte Público Press, 1996.

———. *The Autobiography of a Brown Buffalo*. San Francisco: Straight Arrow Books, 1972. Reprint, New York: Vintage, 1989.

———. "To Whom It May Concern [A Solicitation]." In *Oscar "Zeta" Acosta: The Collected Works*. Ed. Ilan Stavans. Houston, TX: Arte Público Press, 1996.

Acuña, Rodolfo. *Occupied America: A History of Chicanos*. 4th edition. Reading, MA: Addison-Wesley Longman, 2000.

Adorno, Theodor. *Aesthetic Theory*. Ed. Gretel Adorno and Rolf Tiedemann. Trans. Robert Hullot-Kentor. *Theory and History of Literature*, Vol. 88. Minneapolis: University of Minnesota Press, 1997.

Agrippa, Cornelius. *Agrippa's Occult Philosophy: Natural Magic*. Mineola, NY: Dover Publications, Inc., 2006. Originally published, New York: Ernest Loomis and Co., 1897.

Alarcón, Francisco X. *From the Other Side of Night / Del otro lado de la noche*. Tucson, AZ: University of Arizona Press, 2002.

Alcoff, Linda. *Visible Identities: Race, Gender, and the Self*. New York: Oxford University Press, 2006.

Aldama, Arturo, and Naomi H. Quiñonez, eds. *Decolonial Voices: Chicana and Chicano Cultural Studies in the 21st Century*. Bloomington: Indiana University Press, 2002.

Algarín, Miguel. *Love is Hard Work: Memories de Loisaida*. New York: Simon and Schuster, 1997.

Algarín, Miguel, and Bob Holman, eds. *Aloud: Voices from the Nuyorican Poets Café*. New York: Henry Holt and Company, 1994.

Allison, Dorothy. *Bastard Out of Carolina*. New York: A. Dutton, 1992.

Alvarez, Julia. "Freeing La Musa." Introductory essays to Luz María Umpierre-Herrera's *The Margarita Poems*. Bloomington, IN: Third Woman Press, 1987.

Anzaldúa, Gloria. *Borderlands / La Frontera: The New Mestiza*. 1987. Reprint, San Francisco: Spinster / Aunt Lute Books, 1999.

———. *Interviews/Entrevistas*. Ed. AnaLouise Keating. New York: Routledge, 2000.

———, ed. *Making Face, Making Soul Haciendo Caras: Creative and Critical Perspectives by Women of Color*. San Francisco: Aunt Lute Foundation Books, 1990.

———. "now let us shift . . . the path of conocimiento . . . inner work, public acts." In *this bridge we call home: radical visions for transformation*. Ed. Gloria E. Anzaldúa and AnaLouise Keating. New York: Routledge, 2002.

Aparicio, Frances R., and Susana Chávez-Silverman, eds. *Tropicalizations: Transcultural Representations of Latinidad*. Hanover, NH: University Press of New England, 1997.

Arau, Sergio. *A Day Without a Mexican*. Color film. Xenon Pictures, Inc., 2004.

Arenas, Reinaldo. *Antes que anochezca: autobiografía*. Barcelona: Tusquets, 1992.

Arias, Arturo. *After the Bombs*. Trans. Asa Zatz. Willimantic, CT: Curbstone Press, 1990.

———. *Rattlesnake: A Novel*. Trans. Seán Higgins and Jill Robbins. Willimantic, CT: Curbstone Press, 2003. Originally published in Spanish as *Después de las bombas*. México: Editorial Joaquín Mortiz, S.A., 1979.

———. *Taking Their Word: Literature and the Signs of Central America*. Minneapolis: University of Minnesota Press, 2007.

Aronofsky, Darren. *The Fountain*. Color film. Protozoa Pictures / New Regency, 2006.

Arriaga, Guillermo. *The Night Buffalo*. Trans. Alan Page. New York: Atria Books, 2006.

Arroyo, Rane Ramón. *The Buried Sea: New and Selected Poems*. Tucson, AZ: University of Arizona Press, 2008.

———. *Home Movies of Narcissus*. Tucson, AZ: University of Arizona Press, 2002.

———. *Pale Ramón: Poems*. Cambridge, MA: Zoland Books, 1998.

———. *The Portable Famine*. Kansas City, MO: BkMk Press, 2005.

———. *The Roswell Poems*. La Porte, IN: WordFarm, 2008.

———. *The Singing Shark*. Tempe, AZ: Bilingual Press / Editorial Bilingüe, 1996.

———. *The Sky's Weight*. Cincinnati, OH: Turning Point, 2009.

Auster, Paul. *Man in the Dark*. New York: Henry Holt and Co., 2008.

———. *Oracle Night*. New York: Picador, 2003.

Ávila, Rubén Ríos. "Caribbean Dislocations: Arenas and Ramos Otero in New York." In *Hispanisms and Homosexualities*. Ed. Sylvia Molloy and Robert McKee Irwin. Durham, NC: Duke University Press, 1998.

Baca, Jimmy Santiago. *Working in the Dark: Reflections of a Poet of the Barrio*. Santa Fe, NM: Red Crane Books, 1992.

Barnes, Djuna. *Nightwood*. 1936. Reprint, New York: New Directions, 1961.

Barthes, Roland. *A Lover's Discourse: Fragments*. Trans. Richard Howard. New York: Hill and Wang, 1979.

———. *Camera Lucida*. Trans. Richard Howard. New York: Hill and Wang, 1981.

Bausch, Richard. *Good Evening Mr. and Mrs. America, and All the Ships at Sea.* New York: Harper Perennial, 1996.

————. *In the Night Season.* New York: Harper Perennial, 1998.

Bell, Kevin. *Ashes Taken for Fire: Aesthetic Modernism and the Critique of Identity.* Minneapolis: University of Minnesota Press, 2007.

Belli, Giaconda. *The Inhabited Woman.* Trans. Kathleen March. Madison: University of Wisconsin Press, 2004. Originally published in Spanish as *La mujer habitada.* Managua, Nicaragua: Editorial Vanguardia, 1989.

Benítez, Sandra. *Night of the Radishes.* New York: Hyperion, 2003.

Benítez-Rojo, Antonio. *The Repeating Island: The Caribbean and the Postmodern Perspective.* Trans. James E. Maraniss. 1992. Reprint, Durham, NC: Duke University Press, 1996.

Berg, Charles Ramírez. *Latino Images in Film: Stereotypes, Subversion, Resistance.* Austin, TX: University of Texas Press, 2002.

Bhabha, Homi. *The Location of Culture.* London: Routledge, 1994.

Blum, Deborah. *Ghost Hunters: William James and the Search for Scientific Proof of Life After Death.* New York: The Penguin Press, 2006.

Bolaño, Roberto. *By Night in Chile.* Trans. Chris Andrews. New York: New Directions, 2003. Originally published as *Nocturno de Chile.* Barcelona: Editorial Anagrama, 2000.

————. *Distant Star.* Trans. Chris Andrews. New York: New Directions, 2004.

————. *Amulet.* Trans. Chris Andrews. New York: New Directions, 2008.

Borde, Raymond, and Etienne Chaumeton. *A Panorama of American Film Noir: 1941–1953.* Trans. Paul Hammond. San Francisco, CA: City Lights Books, 2002.

Borges, Jorge Luis. *Obra poética, 1923–1977.* Madrid, Spain: Alianza Editorial, 1983.

Borland, Isabel Alvarez. *Cuban-American Literature of Exile: From Person to Persona.* Charlottesville, VA: University Press of Virginia, 1998.

Bourdieu, Pierre. *Acts of Resistance: Against the Tyranny of the Market.* Trans. Richard Nice. New York: The New Press, 1998.

————. *Firing Back: Against the Tyranny of the Market 2.* Trans. Loïc Wacquant. New York: The New Press, 2003.

Bronze Screen, The: 100 Years of the Latino Image in Hollywood. Documentary film. Produced and directed by Susan Racho, Nancy de los Santos, and Alberto Dominguez. Bronze Screen Productions, 2002.

Bruce-Novoa, Juan. "Rechy and Rodriguez: Double Crossing the Public/Private Line." In *Double Crossings.* Ed. Mario Martín Flores and Carlos von Son. Fair Haven, NJ: Ediciones Nuevo Espacio, Academia, 2001.

Burke, Kenneth. *Language as Symbolic Action: Essays on Life, Literature, and Method.* Berkeley: University of California Press, 1966.

Burroughs, William. *Cities of the Red Night.* New York: Henry Holt and Company, 1981.

Butler, Judith. *The Psychic Life of Power.* Stanford, CA: Stanford University Press, 1997.

Cadava, Eduardo. *Words of Light: Theses on the Photography of History.* Princeton, NJ: Princeton University Press, 1997.

Camacho, Julián Segura. *The Chicano Treatise.* New York: University Press of America, 2005.

Caminero-Santangelo, Marta. *On Latinidad: U.S. Latino Literature and the Construction of Ethnicity.* Gainesville: University Press of Florida, 2007.

Campa, Román de la. *Latin Americanism.* Minneapolis: University of Minnesota Press, 1999.

Campo, Rafael. *The Desire to Heal: A Doctor's Education in Empathy, Identity, and Poetry.* New York: W. W. Norton and Company, 1997.

————. *Diva.* Durham, NC: Duke University Press, 1999.

————. *The Enemy.* Durham, NC: Duke University Press, 2007.

————. *Landscape with a Human Figure.* Durham, NC: Duke University Press, 2002.

————. *The Other Man Was Me.* Houston, TX: Arte Público Press, 1994.

————. *What the Other Body Told.* Durham, NC: Duke University Press, 1996.

Camus, Albert. *The Plague, The Fall, Exile and the Kingdom, and Selected Essays.* Intro. by David Bellos. New York: Alfred A. Knopf, 2004.

Cantú, Norma E., and Olga Nájera-Ramírez, eds. *Chicana Traditions: Continuity and Change.* Chicago: University of Illinois Press, 2002.

Carrasco, Davíd. *Religions of Mesoamerica: Cosmovision and Ceremonial Centers.* Long Grove, IL: Waveland Press, 1990.

Casares, Adolfo Bioy. *La invención de Morel.* 1940. Reprint, Madrid: Alianza Editorial, 1981.

Case, Sue-Ellen. "Tracking the Vampire." *Differences* 3, no. 2 (Summer 1991): 1–20.

Castillo, Ana. "Loverboys." In *Loverboys.* New York: Plume, 1997.

————. *Massacre of the Dreamers: Essays on Xicanisma.* 1994. New York: Plume Printing, 1995.

————. *Peel My Love Like an Onion.* New York: Anchor Books, 1999.

————. *So Far from God.* New York: Plume, 1994.

————. *Sapogonia.* New York: Anchor Books Doubleday, 1990.

————. "Un Tapiz: The Poetics of Conscientización." In *Massacre of the Dreamers: Essays on Xicanisma.* 1994. Reprint, New York: Plume, 1995.

Castillo, Mary, Berta Platas, Caridad Pineiro, and Sofía Quintero. *Friday Night Chicas: Sexy Stories from La Noche.* New York: St. Martin's Griffin, 2005.

Céline, Louis-Ferdinand. *Voyage au Bout de la Nuit.* 1934. Trans. Ralph Manheim as *Journey to the End of the Night.* New York: New Directions Publishing Corporation, 1983.

Cernuda, Luis. *Written in Water: The Prose Poems of Luis Cernuda.* Trans. Stephen Kessler. San Francisco, CA: City Lights Books, 2004.

Cherniavsky, Eva. *Incorporations: Race, Nation, and the Body Politics of Capital.* Minneapolis: University of Minnesota Press, 2006.

Chomsky, Aviva. *"They Take Our Jobs!": And 20 Other Myths about Immigration.* Boston: Beacon Press, 2007.

Christian, Barbara. "The Race for Theory." *Cultural Critique: The Nature and Context of Minority Discourse* 6 (Spring 1987): 51–64.

Clark, Tom. *Jack Kerouac: A Biography.* New York: Thunder's Mouth Press, 1984.

Colter, Cyrus. *City of Light.* Evanston, IL: Northwestern University Press, 1993.

———. *Night Studies.* Evanston, IL: Northwestern University Press, 1997. Originally published, Chicago, IL: The Swallow Press, 1979.

Connelly, Frances S. *The Sleep of Reason: Primitivism in Modern European Art and Aesthetics, 1725–1907.* University Park: Pennsylvania State University Press, 1995.

Corpi, Lucha. *Eulogy for a Brown Angel.* Houston, TX: Arte Público Press, 1992.

———. *Cactus Blood.* Houston, TX: Arte Público Press, 1995.

———. *Black Widow's Wardrobe.* Houston, TX: Arte Público Press, 1999.

———. *Crimson Moon: A Brown Angel Mystery.* Houston, TX: Arte Público Press, 2004.

———. *Death at Solstice.* Houston, TX: Arte Público Press, 2009.

Cortázar, Julio. *Final del juego.* 1956. Reprint, Madrid: Aguilar, 1995.

———. *Save Twilight: Selected Poems of Julio Cortázar.* Trans. Stephen Kessler. Pocket Poets Series Number 53. San Francisco, CA: City Lights Books, 1997. Originally published as *Salvo el crepúsculo.* Mexico City: Editorial Nueva Imagen, S.A., 1984.

Costales, Amy. *Hello Night / Hola Noche.* Bel Air, CA: Rising Moon, 2007.

Cota-Cardenas, Margarita. *Puppet: A Chicano Novella.* 1985. Trans. Barbara D. Riess and Trino Sandoval with the author. Albuquerque, NM: University of New Mexico Press, 2000.

Crane, Hart. *The Bridge.* 1930. Reprint, New York: Liveright, 1970.

Cross, St. John of the. *The Poems.* Trans. Roy Campbell. 1951. London: The Harvill Press, 2000.

Crowe, Catherine. *The Night Side of Nature, or, Ghosts and Ghost-Seers.* 1848. Reprint, Boston: B. B. Mussey and Co., 1850.

Cruz-Malavé, Arnaldo. "Toward an Art of Transvestism: Colonialism and Homosexuality in Puerto Rican Literature." In *¿Entiendes? Queer Readings, Hispanic Writings.* Ed. Emilie L. Bergmann and Paul Julian Smith. Durham, NC: Duke University Press, 1995.

Cruz-Malavé, Arnaldo, and Martin F. Manalansan IV, eds. *Queer Globalizations: Citizenship and the Afterlife of Colonialism.* New York: New York University Press, 2002.

Dalton, Roque. *Small Hours of the Night: Selected Poems of Roque Dalton.* Trans. James Graham, Paul Pines, and David Unger. 1st edition. Willimantic, CT: Curbstone Press, 1996.

DeGuzmán, María. "Night Becomes 'Latina': Mariana Romo-Carmona's *Living at Night* and the Tactics of Abjection." *Centro: Journal of the Center for Puerto Rican Studies,* xix, no. 1 (Spring 2007): 91–115.

———. *Spain's Long Shadow: The Black Legend, Off-Whiteness, and Anglo-American Empire.* Minneapolis: University of Minnesota Press, 2005.

———. "Turning Tricks: Trafficking in the Figure of the Latino." In *Trickster Lives: Culture and Myth in American Fiction*. Ed. Jeanne Campbell Reesman. Athens: University of Georgia Press, 2001.

Delaney, Samuel R. *The Mad Man*. New York: Masquerade Books, 1994. Reprint, Canada: Voyant Publishing, 2002.

Delgadillo, Theresa. "Singing 'Angelitos Negros': African Diaspora Meets *Mestizaje* in the Americas." *American Quarterly*, 58, no. 2 (June 2006): 407–30.

DeLillo, Don. *White Noise*. New York: Viking, 1985.

Deleuze, Gilles. *Pure Immanence: Essays on a Life*. New York: Zone Books, 2001.

Deleuze, Gilles and Félix Guattari. *Anti-Oedipus: Capitalism and Schizophrenia*. Trans. Robert Hurley, Mark Seem, and Helen R. Lane. Preface by Michel Foucault. Minneapolis: University of Minnesota Press, 1983.

Derrida, Jacques. *Archive Fever: A Freudian Impression*. Trans. Eric Prenowitz. Chicago: The University of Chicago Press, 1996.

———. *Specters of Marx: The State of the Debt, the Work of Mourning*. New York: Routledge, 1994.

Dimenberg, Edward. *Film Noir and the Spaces of Modernity*. Cambridge, MA: Harvard University Press, 2004.

Dyer, Richard. *White*. New York: Routledge, 1997.

Dzidzienyo, Anani, and Suzanne Oboler. *Neither Enemies nor Friends: Latinos, Blacks, Afro-Latinos*. New York: Palgrave Macmillan, 2005.

Eng, David L., and David Kazanjian, eds. *Loss*. Berkeley: University of California Press, 2003.

Espada, Martín. *Imagine the Angels of Bread: Poems*. New York: W. W. Norton, 1996.

Farrow, John. *Where Danger Lives*. Black-and-white film noir. RKO Radio Pictures, 1950.

Faulkner, William. *Light in August*. Norfolk, CT: New Directions, 1932.

———. *The Sound and the Fury*. New York: Jonathan Cape and Harrison Smith, 1929.

Fernández Retamar, Robert. *Caliban and Other Essays*. Trans. Edward Baker. Minneapolis: University of Minnesota Press, 1989.

Fitzgerald, F. Scott. *Tender is the Night*. 1934. Reprint, New York: Penguin Books, 1975.

Flores, Juan. *From Bomba to Hip-Hop: Puerto Rican Culture and Latino Identity*. New York: Columbia Press, 2000.

Freud, Sigmund. "Mourning and Melancholia." Trans. and ed. James Strachey. In *The Standard Edition of the Complete Psychological Works of Sigmund Freud*, Vol. 14. London: Hogarth Press, 1957.

García, Cristina. *Dreaming in Cuban: A Novel*. New York: Ballatine Books, 1992.

———. *A Handbook to Luck*. New York: Alfred A. Knopf, 2007.

———. *The Lady Matador's Hotel*. New York: Scribner, 2010.

George, Demetra. *Mysteries of the Dark Moon: The Healing Power of the Dark Goddess*. New York: HarperOne, 1992.

Gilroy, Paul. *Postcolonial Melancholia*. New York: Columbia University Press, 2005.

Ginsberg, Allen. *Collected Poems: 1947–1980*. New York: Harper and Row, 1988.

Goethe, Johann Wolfgang von. *Faust, Parts I and II*. Trans. Walter Arndt. London: Nick Hern Books, 1995.

Goldman, Francisco. *The Art of Political Murder: Who Killed the Bishop?* New York: Grove Press, 2007.

———. *The Divine Husband*. New York: Grove Press, 2004.

———. *The Long Night of White Chickens*. New York: The Atlantic Monthly Press, 1992.

———. *The Ordinary Seaman*. New York: Grove Press, 1997.

Gómez, Alma, Mariana Romo-Carmona, and Cherríe Moraga, eds. *Cuentos: Stories by Latinas*. New York: Kitchen Table-Women of Color Press, 1983.

Gómez, Cecil. *A Mexican Twilight*. Bloomington, IN: iUniverse, Inc., 2006.

Gonzalez, J. F. *When Darkness Falls*. Fountain Valley, CA: Midnight Library, 2006.

Gonzalez, Ray. *Cool Auditor*. Rochester, NY: BOA Editions, Ltd., 2009.

———. *Turtle Pictures*. Tucson, AZ: University of Arizona Press, 2000.

Gordon, Avery F.. *Ghostly Matters: Haunting and the Sociological Imagination*. Minneapolis: University of Minnesota Press, 1997.

Gracia, Jorge J. E. *Hispanic/Latino Identity: A Philosophical Perspective*. Malden, MA: Blackwell Publishers, 2000.

Gracia, Jorge J. E., Lynette M. F. Bosch, and Isabel Alvarez Borland, eds. *Identity, Memory, and Diaspora: Voices of Cuban-American Artists, Writers, and Philosophers*. Albany: State University of New York Press, 2008.

Grosfoguel, Ramón, Nelson Maldonado-Torres, and José David Saldívar. "Latin@s and the 'Euro-American Menace': The Decolonization of the U.S. Empire in the Twenty-First Century." In *Latin@s in the World-System: Decolonization Struggles in the 21st Century U.S. Empire*. Boulder, CO: Paradigm Publishers, 2005.

Guzmán, Manuel. "'Pa' La Escuelita con Mucho Cuida'o y por la Orillita': A Journey Through the Contested Terrains of the Nation and Sexual Orientation." In *Puerto Rican Jam: Essays on Culture and Politics*. Ed. Frances Negrón-Muntaner and Ramón Grosfoguel. Minneapolis: University of Minnesota Press, 1997.

Hanson, Curtis. *L.A. Confidential*. Color film. Warner Brothers, 1997.

Henríquez, Cristina. *Come Together, Fall Apart: A Novella and Stories*. New York: Riverhead Books, 2006.

Henry, Paget. *Caliban's Reason: Introducing Afro-Caribbean Philosophy*. New York: Routledge, 2000.

Heredia, Juanita. *Transnational Latina Narratives in the Twenty-First Century: The Politics of Gender, Race, and Migrations*. New York: Palgrave Macmillan, 2009.

Herrera, Juan Felipe. *Night Train to Tuxtla*. Tucson, AZ: University of Arizona Press, 1994.

Herrera-Sobek, María, ed. *Reconstructing a Chicano/a Literary History: Hispanic Colonial Literature of the Southwest*. Tucson: University of Arizona Press, 1993.

Hijuelos, Oscar. *The Mambo Kings Play Songs of Love.* New York: Harper Collins Trade Division, 1990.

Hinojosa, Rolando. Introduction to Américo Paredes's *George Washington Gómez: A Mexicotexan Novel.* Houston, TX: Arte Público Press, 1990.

Hippolyte, Kendel. *Night Vision: Poems.* Evanston, IL: Northwestern University Press, 2005.

Hitchcock, Alfred. *Vertigo.* Color film. Alfred Hitchcock Productions, and Paramount Pictures Corporation, 1958.

Hölderlin, Friedrich. *Odes and Elegies.* Middletown, CT: Wesleyan University Press, 2008.

Holy Bible, The. King James Version. Oxford: Oxford University Press, n.d.

Horkheimer, Max, and Theodor Adorno. *Dialectic of Enlightenment.* Trans. John Cumming. New York: Herder and Herder, 1972.

Hughes, Langston. *The Collected Poems of Langston Hughes.* Ed. Arnold Rampersad and David Roessel. New York: Alfred A. Knopf, 2007.

Hurston, Zora Neale. *Their Eyes Were Watching God.* 1937. Reprint, New York: Harper Perennial Modern Classics, 2006.

Islas, Arturo. "Saints, Artists, and Vile Politics (excerpt)." In *Arturo Islas: The Uncollected Works.* Ed. Frederick Luis Aldama. Houston, TX: Arte Público Press, 2003.

Iyer, Pico. *Cuba and the Night: A Novel.* New York: Vintage, 1995.

Jaime-Becerra, Michael. *Every Night is Ladies' Night.* New York: Harper Perennial, 2005.

Jameson, Fredric. "Postmodernism, or the Logic of Late Capitalism." *New Left Review* 146 (July–August 1984): 53–92.

Julien, Isaac. *Looking for Langston.* Black-and-white / color film. British Film Institute, 1989.

Jung, Carl G., Gerhard Adler, and R. F. C. Hull. *The Archetypes and the Collective Unconscious.* Princeton, NJ: Princeton University Press, 1981.

Kafka, Franz. *A Hunger Artist.* Prague, Czech Republic: Twisted Spoon Press, 1996.

Kant, Immanuel. *Basic Writings of Kant.* Ed. Allen W. Wood. New York: The Modern Library, 2001.

Karlson, Phil. *Kansas City Confidential.* Black-and-white low-budget film noir. MGM, 1952.

Kazan, Elia. *Panic in the Streets.* Black-and-white film. Twentieth Century Fox Film Corporation, 1950.

Keating, AnaLouise, ed. *EntreMundos / AmongWorlds: New Perspectives on Gloria Anzaldúa.* New York: Palgrave Macmillan, 2005.

Kelly, Franklin. *Frederic Edwin Church and the National Landscape.* Washington, DC: Smithsonian Institution Press, 1988.

Kelly, Richard. *Donnie Darko.* Color film. NewMarket Films LLC, 2004.

Kerouac, Jack. *Mexico City Blues.* New York: Grove Press, 1959.

———. *On the Road.* 1957. Reprint, New York: Penguin Books, 2003.

————. *Old Angel Midnight.* Ed. Donald Allen. 1959. Reprint, San Francisco, CA: Grey Fox Press, 1993.

Knight, Brenda. *Women of the Beat Generation: The Writers, Artists, and Muses at the Heart of a Revolution.* Berkeley, CA: Conari Press, 1996.

Kristeva, Julia. *Black Sun: Depression and Melancholia.* Trans. Leon S. Roudiez. New York: Columbia University Press, 1989. Originally published as *Soleil Noir: Dépression et mélancolie* by Editions Gallimard, 1987.

————. *New Maladies of the Soul.* New York: Columbia University Press, 1995.

————. "Place Names." In *Desire in Language: A Semiotic Approach to Literature and Art.* Ed. Léon Roudiez. Trans. Thomas Gora, Alice Jardine, and Léon Roudiez. New York: Columbia University Press, 1980.

————. *Powers of Horror: An Essay on Abjection.* New York: Columbia University Press, 1982. Originally published as *Pouvoirs de l'horreur* by Éditions du Seuil, 1980.

————. *The Sense and Now-Sense of Revolt: The Powers and Limits of Psychoanalysis.* Trans. Jeanine Herman. New York: Columbia University Press, 2000. Originally published as *Sens en non-sense de la révolte* by Artheme Fayard, 1996.

Kushner, Tony. *Angels in America: A Gay Fantasia on National Themes.* New York: Theatre Communications Group, 1993.

Kutzinski, Vera M. *Sugar's Secrets: Race and the Erotics of Cuban Nationalism.* Charlottesville: University of Virginia Press, 1993.

Kuzmeskus, Elaine M. *Séance 101 Physical Mediumship: Table Tipping, Psychic Photography, Trumpet Séances, and Other Important Phenomena.* Atglen, PA: Schiffer Publishing Ltd., 2007.

Lacan, Jacques. *The Four Fundamental Concepts of Psycho-Analysis.* Ed. Jacques-Alain Miller. Trans. Alan Sheridan. New York: Norton, 1978.

La Fountain-Stokes, Lawrence. *Queer Ricans: Cultures and Sexualities in the Diaspora.* Minneapolis: University of Minnesota Press, 2009.

Lang, Fritz. *The Secret Beyond the Door.* Black-and-white noir film. 1948.

Laó-Montes, Agustín, and Arlene Dávila. *Mambo Montage: The Latinization of New York.* New York: Columbia University Press, 2001.

Lawrence, Tim. *Love Saves the Day: A History of American Dance Music Culture, 1970–1979.* Durham, NC: Duke University Press, 2003.

Lima, Lázaro. *The Latino Body: Crisis Identities in American Literary and Cultural Memory.* New York: New York University Press, 2007.

Limón, Graciela. *The Day of the Moon.* Houston, TX: Arte Público Press, 1999.

————. *En busca de Bernabé.* Trans. Miguel Ángel Aparicio. Houston, TX: Arte Público Press, 1997.

————. *Erased Faces.* Houston, TX: Arte Público Press, 2001.

Lippit, Akira Mizuta. *Atomic Light (Shadow Optics).* Minneapolis: University of Minnesota Press, 2005.

Lipsitz, George. *Footsteps in the Dark: The Hidden Histories of Popular Music.* Minneapolis: University of Minnesota Press, 2007.

———. "The Possessive Investment in Whiteness." In *White Privilege: Essential Readings on the Other Side of Racism.* Ed. Paula S. Rothenberg. New York: Worth Publisher, 2002.

Lorca, Federico García. *Sonetos del amor oscuro; Poemas de amor y erotismo; Inéditos de madurez.* Barcelona: Ediciones Altera, 1995.

Lott, Eric. "The Whiteness of Film Noir." In *Whiteness: A Critical Reader.* Ed. Mike Hill. New York: New York University Press, 1997.

Lynch, David. *Mulholland Drive.* Color film. Universal Studios, 2001.

Mailer, Norman. *The Armies of the Night: History as a Novel, the Novel as History.* New York: Signet, 1968.

Major, Clarence. *All-Night Visitors.* New York: Olympia Press, 1969.

Manrique, Jaime. *Eminent Maricones: Arenas, Lorca, Puig, and Me.* Madison: University of Wisconsin Press, 1999.

———. *Latin Moon in Manhattan.* New York: St. Martin's Press, 1992.

———. *My Night with / Mi noche con Federico García Lorca.* Trans. Edith Grossman and Eugene Richie. New York: Painted Leaf Press, 1997. Expanded edition of the original 1995 publication by The Groundwater Press.

———. *Twilight at the Equator: A Novel.* Madison: University of Wisconsin Press, 2003.

Manthorne, Katherine E. *Tropical Renaissance: North American Artists Exploring Latin America, 1839–1879.* Washington, DC: Smithsonian Institution Press, 1989.

Marin, Edwin L. *Nocturne.* Black-and-white film. RKO Studios, 1946.

Martí, José. "Dos patrias." In *Poesía completa / José Martí.* Ed. Carlos Javier Morales. 1995. Reprint, Madrid: Alianza Editorial, 2005.

Martínez, Demetria. *Breathing Between the Lines: Poems.* Tucson: University of Arizona Press, 1997.

Martínez, Elizabeth "Betita." *500 Years of Chicana Women's History / 500 Años de la Mujer Chicana.* Trans. Suzanne Dod Thomas. New Brunswick, NJ: Rutgers University Press, 2009.

May, Gerald G. *The Dark Night of the Soul: A Psychiatrist Explores the Connection Between Darkness and Spiritual Growth.* New York: HarperOne, 2004.

Merleau-Ponty, Maurice. *The Primacy of Perception and Other Essays on Phenomenological Psychology, the Philosophy of Art, History and Politics.* Ed. James M. Edie. Evanston, IL: Northwestern University Press, 1964.

Metz, Christian. "Photography and Fetish." In *The Photography Reader.* Ed. Liz Wells. New York: Routledge, 2003.

Mignolo, Walter. "Capitalism and Geopolitics of Knowledge: Latin American Social Thought and Latino/a American Studies." In *Critical Latin American and Latino Studies.* Ed. Juan Poblete. Minneapolis: University of Minnesota Press, 2003.

Miller, Mary, and Karl Taube. *An Illustrated Dictionary of the Gods and Symbols of Ancient Mexico and the Maya.* London: Thames and Hudson Ltd., 1993.

Montoya, Andrés. *the iceworker sings and other poems.* Tempe, AZ: Bilingual Review Press, 1999.

Moraga, Cherríe. "A Long Line of Vendidas." In *Loving in the War Years: lo que nunca pasó por sus labios*. Cambridge, MA: South End Press, 1983.

Morales, Yuyi. *Little Night*. New York: Roaring Brook Press, 2007.

Morrison, Jim. *The American Night: The Writings of Jim Morrison*, Vol. II. New York: Vintage, 1991.

Morrison, Toni. *Jazz*. New York: Knopf, 1992.

———. *Playing in the Dark: Whiteness and the Literary Imagination*. Cambridge, MA: Harvard University Press, 1992.

Muñoz, José Esteban. *Disidentifications: Queers of Color and the Performance of Politics*. Minneapolis: University of Minnesota Press, 1999.

———. "Feeling Brown: Ethnicity and Affect in Ricardo Bracho's *The Sweetest Hangover (and Other STDs)*." *Theatre Journal* 52, no. 1 (2000): 67–79.

Muñoz, Manuel. *What You See in the Dark*. Chapel Hill, NC: Algonquin Books, 2011.

Myers, Walter Dean. *Somewhere in the Darkness*. New York: Scholastic Inc., 1992.

Negrón-Muntaner, Frances. "When I Was a Puerto Rican Lesbian: Meditations on *Brincando el charco*: Portrait of a Puerto Rican." In *GLQ: A Journal of Lesbian and Gay Studies* 5, no. 4 (1999): 511–26.

Neruda, Pablo. *The Poetry of Pablo Neruda*. Ed. Ilan Stavans. New York: Farrar, Straus, and Giroux, 2003.

Nocturnum, Corvis. *Embracing the Darkness: Understanding Dark Subcultures*. Fort Wayne, IN: Dark Moon Press, 2005.

Novalis. *Hymns to the Night*. Kingston, NY: McPherson, 1988.

Oboler, Suzanne. *Ethnic Labels, Latino Lives: Identity and the Politics of (Re)Presentation in the United States*. Minneapolis: University of Minnesota Press, 1995.

Oliver, Kelly, and Benigno Trigo. *Noir Anxiety*. Minneapolis: University of Minnesota Press, 2003.

Ortíz, Fernando. *Cuban Counterpoint, Tobacco and Sugar*. Durham, NC: Duke University Press, 1995.

Ortíz, Ricardo L. *Cultural Erotics in Cuban America*. Minneapolis: University of Minnesota Press, 2007.

Palmer, Bryan D. *The Cultures of Darkness: Night Travels in the Histories of Transgression*. New York: Monthly Review Press, 2000.

Palmer, Robert. *Deep Blues*. New York: Penguin Books, 1981.

Paltrow, Jake. *The Good Night*. Color film. MHF Zweite Academy, 2007.

Paredes, Américo. *George Washington Gómez*. 2nd edition. Houston, TX: Arte Público Press, 1993.

———. "The Hammon and the Beans." In *The Latino Reader: From 1542 to the Present*. Ed. Harold Augenbraum and Margarite Fernández Olmos. Boston: Houghton Mifflin Company, 1997.

———. *The Shadow*. Houston, TX: Arte Público Press, 1998.

Paredes, Raymund A. "Mexican American Authors and the American Dream." *MELUS* 8, no. 4, *The Ethnic American Dream* (Winter 1981).

Paz, Octavio. *El laberinto de la soledad*. Mexico: Fondo de Cultura Económica, 1959.

Pérez, Emma. *The Decolonial Imaginary: Writing Chicanas into History.* Bloomington: Indiana University Press, 1999.

———. *Gulf Dreams.* Berkeley, CA: Third Woman Press, 1996.

Pérez-Firmat, Gustavo. *Life on the Hyphen: The Cuban-American Way.* Austin: University of Texas Press, 1994.

Pérez-Torres, Rafael. *Movements in Chicano Poetry: Against Myths, Against Margins.* New York: Cambridge University Press, 1995.

Pineda, Cecile. *Face.* 1985. Reprint, San Antonio, TX: Wings Press, 2003.

Platizky, Roger. "From Dialectic to Deliverance: *The Margarita Poems.*" Introductory essays to Luz María Umpierre-Herrera's *The Margarita Poems.* Bloomington, IN: Third Woman Press, 1987.

Poblete, Juan, ed. *Critical Latin American and Latino Studies. Cultural Studies of the Americas,* Vol. 12. Minneapolis: University of Minnesota Press, 2003.

Popol Vuh: The Sacred Book of the Ancient Quiché Maya. English version by Delia Goetz and Sylvanus G. Morley from the translation by Adrián Recinos. Norman: University of Oklahoma Press, 1950.

Portillo, Lourdes. *The Devil Never Sleeps / El diablo nunca duerme.* Documentary film. Spanish and English. 1994.

———. *Señorita extraviada / Missing Young Woman.* Documentary film. Spanish and English. 2001.

Pratt, Mary Louise. *Imperial Eyes: Travel Writing and Transculturation.* New York: Routledge, 1992.

Princeton Encyclopedia of Poetry and Poetics. Ed. Alex Preminger. Princeton, NJ: Princeton University Press, 1974.

Prosser, Jay. *Light in the Dark Room: Photography and Loss.* Minneapolis: University of Minnesota Press, 2005.

Puig, Manuel. *El beso de la mujer araña.* Barcelona: Seix Barral, 1976.

———. *Cae la noche tropical.* Barcelona: Seix Barral, 1988.

———. *La traición de Rita Hayworth.* 1968. Reprint, Barcelona: Seix Barral, 1971.

Purcell, Kerry William. *Weegee.* New York: Phaidon Press, 2004.

Quijano, Aníbal. "Coloniality of Power, Eurocentrism, and Latin America." *Nepantla* 1, no. 3 (2000): 533–80.

Quintana, Alvina E. *Home Girls: Chicana Literary Voices.* Philadelphia, PA: Temple University Press, 1996.

Quiroga, José. *Tropics of Desire: Interventions from Queer Latino America.* New York: New York University Press, 2000.

Ramos, Juanita, ed. *Compañeras: Latina Lesbians.* New York: Latina Lesbian History Project, 1987.

Ramos-García, Luis A. *The State of Latino Theatre in the United States: Hybridity, Transculturation, and Identity.* New York: Routledge, 2002.

Rancière, Jacques. *The Politics of Aesthetics: The Distribution of the Sensible.* Trans. Gabriel Rockhill. New York: Continuum, 2004.

Rechy, John. *City of Night.* New York: Grove Press, 1963.

———. *The Coming of the Night*. New York: Grove Press, 1999.

Richard, Nelly. "Cultural Peripheries: Latin America and Postmodernist Decentering." In *The Postmodernism Debate in Latin America*. Ed. John Beverley, José Oviedo, and Michael Aronna. Durham, NC: Duke University Press, 1995.

Rivera, Carmen S. *Kissing the Mango Tree: Puerto Rican Women Rewriting American Literature*. Houston, TX: Arte Público Press, 2002.

Riese, Berthold. *Die Maya. Geschichte. Kultur. Religion*. Munich: Verlag C. H. Beck, 1995. Published in Spanish as *Los Mayas*. Trans. Juan Fernández-Mayorales. Madrid: Acento Editorial, 2002.

Rodó, José Enrique. *Ariel*. 1900. Reprint, Madrid: Anaya and M. Muchnik, 1995.

Rodríguez, Ana Patricia. *Dividing the Isthmus: Central American Transnational Histories, Literatures and Cultures*. Austin: University of Texas Press, 2009.

Rodriguez, Ralph E. *Brown Gumshoes: Detective Fiction and the Search for Chicana/o Identity*. Austin: University of Texas Press, 2005.

Rodriguez, Richard. *Hunger of Memory: The Education of Richard Rodriguez: An Autobiography*. Boston, MA: D. R. Godine, 1982.

Romero, George A. *Night of the Living Dead*. Black-and-white film. Image Ten, 1968.

Romero, Leo. *Rita and Los Angeles*. Tempe, AZ: Bilingual Press / Editorial Bilingüe, 1995.

Romo-Carmona, Mariana, ed. *Conversaciones: relatos por padres y madres de hijas lesbianas y hijos gay*. San Francisco, CA: Cleis Press, 2001.

———. *Living at Night*. Duluth, MN: Spinsters Ink, 1997.

———. *Speaking Like an Immigrant: A Collection*. Campbell, CA: FastPencil, Inc., 2010.

Rosaldo, Renato. *Culture and Truth: The Remaking of Social Analysis*. Boston: Beacon Press, 1993.

Ross, Christine. *The Aesthetics of Disengagement: Contemporary Art and Depression*. Minneapolis: University of Minnesota Press, 2006.

Ruby, Jay. *Secure the Shadow: Death and Photography in America*. Cambridge, MA: MIT Press, 1995.

Runaway Universe. Color documentary film. Produced by WGBH Boston for NOVA public television program, 2000.

Saenz, Jaime. *The Night*. Trans. Forrest Gander and Kent Johnson. Princeton, NJ: Princeton University Press, 2007.

Sala-Molins, Louis. *Dark Side of the Light: Slavery and the French Enlightenment*. Trans. John Conteh-Morgan. Minneapolis: University of Minnesota Press, 2006. Originally published as *Les Misères des Lumières: Sous la raison, l'outrage* by Éditions Robert Laffont, S.A., Paris, 1992.

Saldívar, José David. *Border Matters: Remapping American Cultural Studies*. Berkeley: University of California Press, 1997.

———. *The Dialectics of Our America: Genealogy, Cultural Critique, and Literary History*. Durham, NC: Duke University Press, 1991.

Saldívar, Ramón. *The Borderlands of Culture: Américo Paredes and the Transnational Imaginary*. Durham, NC: Duke University Press, 2006.

———. *Chicano Narrative: The Dialectics of Difference*. Madison: University of Wisconsin Press, 1990.

Saldívar-Hull, Sonia. *Feminism on the Border: Chicana Gender Politics and Literature*. Berkeley: University of California Press, 2000.

Sánchez-González, Lisa. *Boricua Literature: A Literary History of the Puerto Rican Diaspora*. New York: New York University Press, 2001.

Sandlin, Betsy A. "'Poetry always Demands All My Ghosts': The Haunted and Haunting Poetry of Rane Arroyo." *Centro: Journal of the Center for Puerto Rican Studies* xix, no. 1 (Spring 2007): 163–77.

Sandoval, Chela. *Methodology of the Oppressed*. Theory out of Bounds, Vol. 18. Minneapolis: University of Minnesota Press, 2000.

Sandoval-Sánchez, Alberto. *José, Can You See? Latinos On and Off Broadway*. Madison: University of Wisconsin Press, 1999.

Sandoval-Sánchez, Alberto, and Frances R. Aparicio. "Hibridismos culturales: la literatura y cultura de los latinos en los Estados Unidos." In *Revista Iberoamericana*, LXXI, Num. 212 (Julio–Septiembre 2005): 665–97.

Santiago, Esmeralda. *When I Was a Puerto Rican*. New York: Vintage, 1994.

Santos, John Phillip. *Places Left Unfinished at the Time of Creation: A Memoir*. New York: Viking, 1999.

Santos-Febres, Mayra. *Nuestra Señora de la Noche*. Mexico: Espasa Calpe Mexicana, S.A., 2006.

———. *Sirena Selena Vestida de Pena*. Doral, FL: Stockcero, Inc., 2008.

———. *Sirena Selena*. Trans. Stephen Lytle. New York: Picador, 2000.

Schiesari, Juliana. *The Gendering of Melancholia: Feminism, Psychoanalysis, and the Symbolics of Loss in Renaissance Literature*. Ithaca, NY: Cornell University Press, 1992.

Schivelbusch, Wolfgang. *Disenchanted Night: The Industrialization of Light in the Nineteenth Century*. Trans. Angela Davies. 1988. Reprint, Berkeley: University of California Press, 1995.

Scott, Ridley. *Blade Runner*. Color film. Ladd Company, 1982.

Sellers-García, Sylvia. *When the Ground Turns in Its Sleep*. New York: Riverhead Books, 2007.

Seshadri-Crooks, Kalpana. *Desiring Whiteness: A Lacanian Analysis of Race*. New York: Routledge, 2000.

Sheridan, Michael J. *James Dean Forever Young*. Black-and-white documentary film. Screen Icons, Inc., 2005.

Sommer, Doris. *Foundational Fictions: The National Romances of Latin America*. Berkeley: University of California Press, 1991.

Sontag, Susan. *On Photography*. 1973. Reprint, New York: Picador, 1977.

———. *Regarding the Pain of Others*. 1st edition. New York: Farrar, Straus and Giroux, 2003.

————. *Under the Sign of Saturn.* New York: Picador USA, 2002.

Sotelo, Susan Baker. *Chicano Detective Fiction: A Critical Study of Five Novelists.* Jefferson, NC: McFarland and Company, 2005.

Stettner, Patrick. *The Night Listener.* Color film. Hart Sharp Entertainment and IFC Productions, 2006.

Stevens, Wallace. *The Collected Poems.* 1954. Reprint, New York: Vintage, 1982.

————. *The Palm at the End of the Mind: Selected Poems and a Play.* New York: Knopf, 1971.

Stoichita, Victor I. *A Short History of the Shadow.* London: Reaktion Books, 1997.

Styron, William. *Darkness Visible: A Memoir of Madness.* 1990. Reprint, New York: Vintage, 1992.

————. *Lie Down in Darkness.* 1951. New York: Vintage, 1992.

Suro, Roberto. *Strangers Among Us: Latino Lives in a Changing America.* New York: Vintage, 1999.

Tedlock, Dennis. *2000 Years of Mayan Literature.* Berkeley: University of California Press, 2010.

Tobar, Héctor. *The Tattooed Soldier.* New York: Penguin Books, 1998.

————. *Translation Nation: Defining a New American Identity in the Spanish-Speaking United States.* New York: Riverhead Books, 2005.

Todorov, Tzvetan. *The Fantastic: A Structural Approach to a Literary Genre.* Trans. Richard Howard. Cleveland, OH: Press of Case Western University, 1973.

Torres-Saillant, Silvio. *An Intellectual History of the Caribbean.* New York: Palgrave Macmillan, 2006.

Trujillo Carla, ed. *Chicana Lesbians: The Girls Our Mothers Warned Us About.* Berkeley, CA: Third Woman Press, 1991.

————, ed. *Living Chicana Theory.* Berkeley, CA: Third Woman Press, 1998.

————. *What Night Brings.* Willimantic, CT: Curbstone Press, 2003.

Umpierre, Luz María. "Lesbian Tantalizing in Carmen Lugo Filippi's 'Milagros, Calle Mercurio.'" In *¿Entiendes? Queer Readings, Hispanic Writings.* Ed. Emilie L. Bergmann and Paul Julian Smith. Durham, NC: Duke University Press, 1995.

Umpierre-Herrera, Luz María. *The Margarita Poems.* Bloomington, IN: Third Woman Press, 1987.

Uslar Pietri, Arturo. "The Other America." Trans. Andrée Conrad. *Review* 14 (Spring 1975): 42–47.

Vallejo, César. *Los heraldos negros.* Lima, 1919.

Vásquez, Eva C. *Pregones Theatre: A Theatre for Social Change in the South Bronx.* New York: Routledge, 2003.

Ventura, Gabriela Baeza, ed. *Latino Literature Today.* New York: Pearson Longman, 2005.

Viego, Antonio. *Dead Subjects: Toward a Politics of Loss in Latino Studies.* Durham, NC: Duke University Press, 2007.

Villaurrutia, Xavier. "Nostalgia for Death." In *Nostalgia for Death: Poetry by Xavier Villaurrutia* and *Hieroglyphs of Desire. A Critical Study of Villaurrutia by*

Octavio Paz. Ed. Eliot Weinberger. Trans. Esther Allen and Eliot Weinberger. Port Townsend, WA: Copper Canyon Press, 1993.

Vonnegut, Kurt. *Deadeye Dick.* New York: Delacort Press / Seymour Lawrence, 1982.

Weiss, Timothy F. *On the Margins: The Art of Exile in V. S. Naipaul.* Amherst: University of Massachusetts Press, 1992.

Wells, H. G. *The Island of Dr. Moreau.* 1896. Reprint, New York: Modern Library, 2002.

———. *The New World Order.* 1940. Reprint, Hesperides Press, 2006.

Welles, Orson. *Touch of Evil.* Black-and-white film. Universal Pictures Corporation, 1958.

White, Hayden. *The Content of the Form: Narrative Discourse and Historical Representation.* Baltimore, MD: Johns Hopkins University Press, 1987.

———. *Metahistory: The Historical Imagination in Nineteenth-Century Europe.* Baltimore, MD: Johns Hopkins University Press, 1973.

———. *Tropics of Discourse: Essays in Cultural Criticism.* Baltimore, MD: Johns Hopkins University Press, 1978.

Wiesel, Elie. *La Nuit.* Paris: Les Éditions de Minuit, 1958. Trans. by Marion Wiesel under the title *Night.* New York: Hill and Wang, 2006.

Williams, William Carlos. *In the American Grain.* New York: A. and C. Boni, 1925.

Wilmerding, John. *American Light: The Luminist Movement, 1850–1875.* Princeton, NJ: Princeton University Press, 1989.

Wilson, Eric G. *Secret Cinema: Gnostic Vision in Film.* New York: The Continuum International Publishing Group, 2006.

Wolfe, Thomas. *Look Homeward, Angel: A Story of a Buried Life.* New York: Charles Scribner's Sons, 1929. Reprint, New York: Scribner Paperback Fiction, Simon and Schuster, 1995.

Xavier, Emanuel. *Americano.* San Francisco, CA: Suspect Thoughts Press, 2002.

Young, Robert J. C. *Colonial Desire: Hybridity in Theory, Culture and Race.* New York: Routledge, 1995.

Yúdice, George. "Rethinking Area Studies and Ethnic Studies in the Context of Economic and Political Restructuring." In *Critical Latin American and Latino Studies.* Ed. Juan Poblete. Minneapolis: University of Minnesota Press, 2003.

Zinn, Howard. *A People's History of the United States.* New York: Harper Perennial Modern Classics, 2010.

INDEX

Cuban Americans: as Latina/os, 106, 198, 211, 219, 222, 223; in United States, 109–110, 115, 224

cubanía and *cubanidad*, 116, 117

cultural producers and production, 7, 73, 74, 244; African American, 3–4, 14, 15, 73, 124, 265n65; Caribbean, 73–82, 123–124; Central American, 135–139; Chicana/o, 4, 15, 18, 21–23, 44, 61, 241, 242; Colombian American, 5, 206–225; Jewish American, 14; Latin American, 4, 204, 241; Latina/o, 3–5, 7, 15–16, 124, 203–204, 224, 240–244, 246–254, 265n65, 269n14; Mayan, 155, 178; Mexican American, 18, 124; Panamanian-American, 155–163; South American, 185–188, 198, 203–204, 216–217, 222, 225; U.S.-based, 40, 144–163, 226. *See also* art and artists; dominant Anglo culture; literature; novels; poetry and poets

cultural workers, 23, 35, 43–44, 48

culture(s), 10, 37, 43, 84, 189, 222, 249; acquisition of, 175–176; African American, 115, 126; Chicana/o, 23, 57, 242; Cuban, 118; Guatemalan, 178, 179; Hispanic, 22, 210; hybridized, 21–22, 38, 181, 184, 211; Latin American, 210, 241; Latina/o, 2, 126, 211, 254; marginalized, 30, 199; Mayan, 142, 178; Mesoamerican, 22, 23, 178; Mexican American, 22, 23, 55, 59, 60; Panamanian, 181; of the people, 115, 122, 254, 261n65; phantasmagoria-prone, 142–143, 178; preservation of, 23, 27; Spanish, 142, 161, 178; syncretism of, 176, 183. *See also* counterculture; critiques, cultural; dominant Anglo culture; identity, cultural

Curbstone Press, Inc., 61

Dalton, Roque, 187

dancing, 126, 132–133, 210, 211

Dante, 210

dark gift, 58

dark night, 1, 75, 170, 229. *See also* Cross, St. John of the, "The Dark Night of the Soul"

dark Romantics, 11

dark-light binary, 31–33, 38

darkness, 1, 31–32, 34, 61, 94–95, 101, 103–104, 119; in Campo's work, 110–111; in Chicana/o culture, 23–30; Latina/o tropes, 241, 251, 252, 253; in Limón's work, 241–242; Mesoamerican pre-Columbian conceptions, 141, 143; Mexican Americans / Mexicans associated with, 54, 57, 59; night-related, 10, 100, 107, 201–205; in Romo-Carmona's work, 190–191, 193. *See also* delirium, of oncoming night; midnight; night; twilight

darkskinned people, 31–33, 97–101, 261n60. *See also* brownskinned people; color, people of

Day Without a Mexican (film, Arau), 18–21, 60, 67–68

Dean, James, 45, 46, 47, 48–49, 50, 214

death, 47, 50, 54, 103, 140; acceptance of, 126, 268n36; confrontation with, 114, 132; living-dead binary, 131, 173, 250; loss through, 130, 244. *See also* mortality

decolonial, the, 11, 90, 143–144; consciousness, 9, 207, 210; desire, 165, 181; imaginary, 165; use of term, 164–165. *See also* coloniality

decolonization, 9, 11, 33, 89–90, 245, 254. *See also* colonization

deconstructionism, 74, 80, 215

DeGuzmán, María: "Night Becomes 'Latina,'" 268n4; *Spain's Long Shadow*, 267n18; "Tactics of Abjection," 188

dehumanization, 18, 202

deictics, 205

Deleuze, Gilles, 209, 213, 220, 269n14; *Anti-Oedipus*, 206; *L'Immanence*, 213

Delgadillo, Theresa, 98

MARÍA DEGUZMÁN is Professor of English & Comparative Literature and Director of Latina/o Studies at the University of North Carolina at Chapel Hill. She is the author of *Spain's Long Shadow: The Black Legend, Off-Whiteness, and Anglo-American Empire*. She has published numerous articles on Latina/o cultural production. Furthermore, she researches, writes about, and offers courses on the relationship between literature and various kinds of photographic practice. In addition to being a professor, she is a conceptual photographer who produces photos and photo-text work, both solo and in collaboration with colleagues and friends. She has published essays and photo-stories involving her photography in journals such as *Art Journal* (of the College Art Association), *Centro: Journal of the Center for Puerto Rican Studies, Word & Image Interactions,* and *Mandorla: Nueva Escritura de las Américas / New Writing from the Americas,* to cite a few. Her images have been chosen as the cover art for books by Cuban American writer Cristina García and the poet Glenn Sheldon and for books by scholars in various fields. As both Camera Query and previously as part of SPIR: Conceptual Photography, she has shown in the Golden Belt Art Studios in Durham, North Carolina, the Institute of Contemporary Art in Boston, the Watershed Media Centre in Bristol, England, Pulse Art Gallery in New York City, the Center for Exploratory and Perceptual Art (CEPA Gallery) in Buffalo, New York, and El Progreso Gallery in Madrid, Spain.